TIME FRAMES

A CENTURY OF PROSCENIUM PLAYWRIGHTS

'Dominic Dromgoole's *Time Frames* is a unique theatre book. Part history, part synthesis, part celebration – all scintillating – the book is a savvy tour of seventy-two playwrights who made memorable theatre within the fourth wall. An encyclopedia of sorts, *Time Frames* is written with pep and personality. Dromgoole, himself a seasoned director and a smart cookie, wears his deep knowledge lightly. On the page he is by turns jaunty, witty, authoritative. He brings both news and sprightly argument, which makes *Time Frames* at once a great resource and great fun. The book is a keeper' **John Lahr**

'What a roaring, full-throttle adventure through a century of theatre history this is. A fantastic page-turner; Dromgoole brings his rambunctious wit and ability to weave a great story to every chapter, lacing this journey through the arts with beautiful anecdotes and moments of comic gold. But mostly it's his deep affection for theatre that comes through on every page; this book is not only a compelling read and a wild dive into a fascinating history, it's also a heartfelt love letter to the stage and its essential place at the heart of our culture. I recommend it wholeheartedly to anyone who's ever set foot in a theatre – and even more to those who haven't yet. It will leave you utterly inspired and aching to book your next ticket' **Jessica Swale**

'Dominic Dromgoole has an uncanny gift for plunging the reader headlong into the past, making moments of radical cultural transformation feel as perhaps they once did – urgent, human and unexpected. In *Time Frames*, he thrillingly illuminates a century of such moments, revealing the almost Darwinian evolution of modern European theatre – a dance of adaptation between risk-taking playwrights, the buildings they wrote for and the audiences who paid to watch them. I loved this book – it made me see the familiar entirely afresh' **Mark Rosenblatt**

'One of the best books I've read about the art of theatre and its transformative role in our lives. Dominic writes about the theatre with such deep knowledge, clarity and humour that as you read each page you feel as if you were at the performance yourself' **Giles Terera**

'Dominic Dromgoole's magisterial *Time Frames* is an invaluable addition to our collective understanding of what it is to write for theatre. Like the author, the perspicacious prose is lucid, discerning, and funny; it's a real treat, so if you love play-going and plays, stop what you're doing and read this now' **David Eldridge**

'A radical reconsideration of the theatre century from Eugène Scribe to Samuel Beckett, Dromgoole's dazzling new book offers an entirely new perspective on pretty well everything you ever thought about plays, players and playhouses. If you care about any of these things, you simply have to read it' **Simon Callow**

---

by the same author

THE FULL ROOM: AN A-Z OF CONTEMPORARY PLAYWRITING

WILL AND ME: HOW SHAKESPEARE TOOK OVER MY LIFE

HAMLET: GLOBE TO GLOBE

ASTONISH ME!: FIRST NIGHTS THAT CHANGED THE WORLD

TIME FRAMES

A Century of Proscenium Playwrights

DOMINIC DROMGOOLE

faber

First published in 2026
by Faber & Faber Limited
The Bindery, 51 Hatton Garden
London EC1N 8HN

Typeset by Faber & Faber Limited
Printed and bound by CPI Group (UK) Ltd, Croydon, CR0 4YY

A CIP record for this book
is available from the British Library

ISBN 978-0-571-37411-3

MIX
Paper | Supporting responsible forestry
FSC® C013604

Printed and bound in the UK on FSC® certified paper in line with our continuing commitment to ethical business practices, sustainability and the environment.
For further information see faber.co.uk/environmental-policy

Our authorised representative in the EU for product safety is
Easy Access System Europe, Mustamäe tee 50, 10621 Tallinn, Estonia
gpsr.requests@easproject.com

2 4 6 8 10 9 7 5 3 1

For Siofra, Grainne and Cara,
the three sisters

Contents

Introduction

History and the theatre dance a waltz, lightly gripping each other, distance and connection held in balance with a delicate tension. On consecutive nights in the spring of 1865, two playhouses saw events which changed both history and the theatre.

On 14 April 1865, at Ford's Theatre in Washington DC, an actor with a fixation on Shakespeare in general and Julius Caesar in particular – John Wilkes Booth – erupted into the presidential box positioned above the thrust stage where a company were playing the comedy *Our American Cousin*. Before entering, he waited for the guffaw he knew would follow the infallible laugh line, 'Well, I guess I know enough to turn you inside out, old gal – you sock-dologising old man-trap!' He placed his revolver behind the head of Abraham Lincoln, who was chuckling merrily in a rocking chair, and fired a bullet into his brain. After a brief melee with the other occupants of the box, Booth leaped the twelve feet down to the thrust stage, shouted 'Sic semper tyrannis!' ('Thus always to tyrants!') and stumbled off into the night.

The following evening, 15 April, 3,700 miles away in Tottenham Street, London, the Prince of Wales Royal Theatre opened. Carriages crowded the entrance and the surrounding streets as society's finest bustled and hustled to squeeze their way in. News of the death of an American president would take another ten days to cross the Atlantic, so there was little to dampen the merriment as royalty mingled with literati and the thespian elite. A brilliant entrepreneur – Marie Bancroft – was opening a new auditorium with an architectural adjustment that would change theatre for the next century. Had Booth tried the same leap from a box in the Prince of Wales Theatre, he would have fallen a lot further and never got up again – for here the thrust had been removed. The separation between the stage and the audience had been completed. On that night the full proscenium theatre was born.

Few events housed in these spaces over the next hundred years were as incendiary or as seismic as the assassination of Lincoln, though several came close. Riots erupted to greet the plays of Alfred Jarry, Sean O'Casey, and Edward Bond. 'Strike! Strike! Strike!' the audience shouted at the end of Clifford Odets's *Waiting for Lefty*. 'Fight! Fight! Fight!' they chanted following Langston Hughes's *Don't You Want to Be Free?* Quieter murmurs were heard after plays that mirrored their moment with colours from a gentler palette. But the waltz carried on its stiff-backed whirl throughout, theatre and history reflecting and influencing each other, pulling and pushing across the dance floor.

From its first baby steps, the proscenium was a form ill at ease with itself.

The space Marie Bancroft created, and the many others that followed, catered for a newly wealthy and socially concerned audience. Auditoria were remodelled to attract the well-to-do, who were now more available for evenings out thanks to rail networks, which could deliver them swiftly home for a bedtime whisky or cocoa. Stalls seats were refitted and ticket prices raised to exclude the rowdy and welcome the couth. And the initial plays to greet these patrons? Penned by the first writer to perfect the form, Tom Robertson, they were stories about the injustice of class and the iniquities of wealth and power. A theatre born from class-cleansing presented stories about that very process. A paradox began here that endured.

The audience – thoughtful and literate – wanted to see their lives mirrored. An uneasy bunch, the urban population of the late nineteenth century lived in an era caught between the stifling proprieties of the bourgeois home and a libidinal marketplace kept busy by an unending migration to overflowing cities. Victorians and Edwardians lived with the benefits of an education system and structure of cultural supply which created a new caste, less explicit than the old one of land and money but more insidious. They wanted to know of social injustices but were scared to shake off their privileges.

The picture dramatists reflected back to them was far from harmonious. The pain of jaundiced relationships and the difficulties and shame of divorce were staple topics. The question of suffrage and full independence for women reared its head early and never capitulated. Industrial relations, slum housing, the insensitivities and ineptitude of the justice system, civil rights, and anti-colonial independence movements all agitated in this supposedly staid arena. As the century progressed, militarism and the horrors of war invaded the space. And, as it drew to a close, the confusions of existentialism and the absurd were accommodated. Still the audience came, witnessed turmoil and despair, and rode the trains back to the suburbs.

Far from a hindrance, this tension helped to make the proscenium vital and magnetic. The air crackled from the friction between the elegant casing and the stories within, content often shaking its fist at its own frame. The audience wanted to see themselves portrayed, but how much they wanted revealed, how far they wanted the striptease to go, was a permanent matter of unseen negotiation. Every great theatre epoch needs that resistance to come fully alive. By the end of this era the chasms between content and decorative surround were too great for the form to sustain itself. Yet the area of ground it managed to cover, and the stories it managed to tell, proved something of a marvel.

The original intention of these theatres was as palaces of pleasure. Cherubs, frilly curtains, and rococo excess were meant to house charming comedies, flimsy romances, and affirming tales of good triumphant. There was no shortage of that, with much wild laughter and sentimental sobbing along the way. But if you convene a group into a social space, they will always end up thinking about more than just trivia. And dramatists were ever ready and eager to touch on the concerns riffling the waves of their own moment.

What a liberatingly restrictive form it was while it lasted! Like the fourteen-line sonnet or the twelve-bar blues, there was freedom in the captivity. Stories had to be told, human stories, with the focus and intensity the proscenium demanded. It is a discipline which survives, and when well executed – as recently in Lucy Kirkwood's *The Children*, Jez Butterworth's *Jerusalem*, or David Adjmi's *Stereophonic* among others – it still provides a unique thrill. Human stories unfurling within a picture frame in a single location, in some simulacrum of real time, requires a high level of concentrated skill, and when successfully realised delivers indelible rewards. Subsequent to the end of the proscenium hegemony, there have been many polemics against the well-made play, and many demonstrations of how to deconstruct it, while rarely affording the same pleasure.

Every artist locked into a structure wants to escape from it – the desire to bust out is a mark of the creative spirit. The works of Caravaggio and Manet make a point of trying to crash through the safety barrier of the frame. But how much muscularity and vitality they gain by the battle to push out and make a connection – strength which can evanesce when they work without resistance.

Time Frames roams between 1865 and 1965, and it is a loose century, to be honest. Hopefully in the course of reading, it will become clear why the book is shaped around these dates, an era when the proscenium was in the ascendant. But the well-made-play structure that governed these stages was finding its shape in various experiments long before 1865, and lasted well after 1965. In many ways, writers such as David Storey, Neil Simon, and Caryl Churchill further perfected how to use it. But they worked in an age when it was no longer the dominant or single form. The theatres which once bulged with these plays are now filled with musicals, event theatre, and directorial caprices.

Geographically, the gaze of the book roves across a range of different cultures. In the interests of consistency, it remains tethered to cities that housed the proscenium design and shared a language about making this sort of theatre. From Vancouver to Vladivostok, this architecture achieved its supremacy during this period, with plays moving freely in translation between them. Within a year of *Journey's End* opening in London in December 1928, it was being played simultaneously by fourteen companies in English, and across the globe in seventeen languages in cities including Paris, Stockholm, Berlin, Rome, Madrid, and Moscow. One example from many of how news about contemporary living was shared at speed. It was a form of communication which, broadly speaking, spoke most loudly and clearly to the West, though a host of plays broke out and sang to a wider gathering. For different reasons, *The Cherry Orchard*, *Ubu Roi*, *Blood Wedding*, and *Waiting for Godot* all entered the bloodstream of cultures with no similar tradition of theatre-making. At the end of this proscenium century, Wole Soyinka wrote plays dealing with his own Nigerian concerns, yet housed in the traditional frame. This was an isolated achievement, and a mark of the moment when the sway of the form was diminishing in its potency as international writers and theatre-makers aimed to tell stories their own way for different architecture.

I have attempted to broaden the welcome for this sort of anthology to a wider crowd, to draw some of those previously excluded into the fold, without distorting how each era assessed its own major dramatists in a period which did, undeniably, favour the pale and male. To draw up an exhaustive list of proscenium writers would require an encyclopaedia. Any reduced list will always reveal the biases of the selector. Here, I have tried to achieve a balance of those who have had the weightiest commercial impact – Agatha Christie – with those whose voices cried out in lonelier notes from the wilderness – such as Alice Childress – but left behind a powerful legacy.

Omitted are many journeymen and women who filled theatres throughout this century with entertainment skilled in execution but less remarkable in its commentary. Many a boulevardier, farceur, thriller writer, and purveyor of romantic comedy have been passed over, possibly unjustly. Hopefully the book will awaken an interest in looking further into the plays of the period and others will be championed before long.

This volume is intended as a series of provocations rather than a definitive compendium.

Since this is in large part a tale of influence, of one dramatist sparking another's inspiration, this has dictated the ordering of where each author is placed in relation to others. Rather than following their biographical dates, we have placed them in response to the moments where their work achieved its greatest impact. In addition, there is some shuffling to emphasise counterpoint and the depth of variety. There is quite a distance to travel between Federico García Lorca, Ayn Rand, Clifford Odets and Clare Boothe Luce – adjacent to each other in this selection. Zigging and zagging down a slope reveals more of a landscape than plunging straight ahead. The one glaring exception to the chronology according to each writer's apotheosis is D. H. Lawrence, whose work didn't arrive in the public eye until after the century under discussion. Lawrence remained (true to himself) an artist on the margins, howling at the injustice of exclusion.

The knowledge here is drawn from a fair amount of working experience and from much watching of shows, but the vast majority is from one of my favourite pleasures – reading plays. There is nothing quite like a printed text, a kind of map, suggesting a potential destination, though not yet achieved. Words scattered across the page like confetti, notating the chitter-chatter of new acquaintances talking away at each other free and easy. The most enhanced form of overhearing imaginable. A trigger for the inner director, while reading one is soon watching the ideal production in the mind's eye – perfectly cast and staged. These experiences of the imagination can sometimes be better than the staged play, and I can only recommend that, as well as heading to the theatre, you go to the library and seek out the pleasure of the stage on the page.

Among the glories of the work discussed here is the creation of a whole new myth system, if we understand by that the forging of stories and heroes which help us to read our world. If not comparable to Zeus and Hera and Apollo, then we have unfurled before us in the proscenium pantheon an appropriate Olympus for a more domestic age. Hedda Gabler, Eliza Doolittle, Lady Bracknell, Madame Arkadina, Juno, Six Characters, James Tyrone, Elyot and Amanda, Inspector Goole, Stanley Kowalski, Didi and Gogo, Jimmy Porter, Beatie Bryant, and Mr Sloane – all have acquired legendary status and served as templates for people to understand themselves and each other. Once intimate with them, it is hard not to take them to our hearts and carry them with us as, if not exactly friends, then close acquaintances.

Greater than their exemplary status, or their capacity to inform and instruct, is their fierce independence. Not archetypes or stereotypes or any old types; not part of any argument or intellectual abstraction, nor any style or form; it is their simple aliveness we cherish. We watch them alone up there, within the frame, sometimes fearful within the vastness, but resolutely remaining true to themselves.

Theatre's value is measurable by the way it speaks to each new community. It has to make the air hum between the stage and the audience, and does so by touching on shared concerns. The heart of theatre's strength lies in its importance as a human news service. Uncovering more than facts, it brings into the light the social and individual patterns swirling beneath the surface, giving a voice to the unspoken. Newspapers can deliver bombshell reportage, and television can alarm with the immediacy of its images. But a figure, standing on a stage, stating a truth clear and unmediated, can deliver an impact no other media approaches.

Facts, occurrences, and events are a fraction of the beat that theatre covers. What is yet more acute are the revelations of how society is evolving, and how individuals are being shaped within that collective. Ibsen uncovered a new human genus, Homo Ibseniens, educated into disconnection and disdainful of those left behind. Chekhov showed a culture lost within its own culture, and feeble before the onslaught of modernism.

Coward brought a dizzying disorientation to the dance floor, peopled with uncertain, lost souls, all pre-war certainty gone. Miller showed how intimidated individuals tried to retain a dignity as history bulldozed the landscape around them. These writers endure because they brought something blurry into focus: the refashioned human.

When we watch Nora striding out of her home and slamming the door; the patriarch witnessing his business crumble in Githa Sowerby's *Rutherford and Son*; Blanche DuBois receding into her inner self; Hester Collyer's naked and suicidal despair in *The Deep Blue Sea*; the two co-dependent tramps mumbling their way around the barren heath in *Waiting for Godot*; or the smart and sharp generation of the Younger family in *A Raisin in the Sun* – at all these moments we are watching new formulations of how to be conscious and alive. These lives on the brink of their own modernity, releasing arrows into their future, repeatedly give proof of theatre's live newswire.

The theatre has always been uniquely placed – intensely private and a public forum – to reveal new paths of thinking and uncover newborn patterns of feeling. *Time Frames* attempts to capture some of the excitement of how that information was – and still is – delivered.

History of the Proscenium

The history of the proscenium theatre is replete with paradoxes, not the least being that its creation involved the gradual elimination of the proscenium itself. Classically, the proscenium referred to the thrust space that stuck out beyond the arch which separated backstage from the public. A platform on which actors could strut and share the play in a democratic arena. Slowly it dwindled and shrank away from the audience, until the distinction between stage and spectator became complete. Actor and audience no longer enjoying a shared light, now that the action was observed in its own unique illumination, an imagined membrane between the two.

The first theatres evolved out of festival and ritual, broad open spaces under a common sun. The Greeks and Romans took a little of the temple, the forum, and the sports arena, together with a desire for visual focus and acoustic clarity and confected the amphitheatre. Different forms swept the Western world, and further afield, for a millennium. The religious dramas of the late medieval period, the Mysteries, took ritual stories and scattered them across public spaces, with small cities enlivened by immersive promenade carnivals. One group told a story here by the church, another there by the market cross, and another over yonder on the bridge. Every corner of a city would be filled with chaotic storytelling. Spectators joined the dots at their own pace and with their own imagination.

Touring companies emerged from these religious festivals and, though prepared to perform anywhere, they found their happiest homes in the courtyards of inns. Makeshift stages raised the actors above a standing crowd, and above the actors' heads more people squeezed into the courtyard galleries circling the upper floors. When the opportunity came for companies to build dedicated theatres, they were modelled on these makeshift spaces – a raised stage, audiences standing below, and galleries of spectators around and above. This shaping brought us the *corral* theatres of Spain – several of which still exist – and the Elizabethan theatres of London, including the Globe. The *frons scenae*, an ornately decorated screen at the back of the stage, was modelled after Greek and Roman theatres. There was no need for scenery here, all was left to words and fancy.

Much thrust.
The Swan Theatre, copied by Aernout van Buchel, after a sketch by Johannes de Witt, 1596

Even as the Elizabethan open-air structures with thrust stages were being created in London, experiments were beginning in Italy. The framing arch began its life in their court theatres. Its task was to hide the elaborate machinery that moved painted scenery on and off as if gliding on God's hand. The result, arranged with the genius for perspective of that age, was stage pictures of a beauty and sophistication never before considered possible. England's greatest architect and designer, Inigo Jones, saw these Italian innovations and their capabilities, and was determined to import them to England. With this technology he created dazzling court masques for James I and Charles I. Shakespeare and his company saw these phantasmagorias and resolved to learn and exploit their magical properties in the indoor theatre they were opening, the Blackfriars. Indoors meant candlelight, and scenery, and greater control of theatrical effects; it also meant reduced spectator numbers. Smaller audiences necessitated higher prices, and thus the inculcating of a new clientele. The old public theatre, open to all levels of society, was beginning its unholy transformation into a new specialism and exclusivity.

Theatres, whether inclusive or exclusive, were unwelcome to the Puritans and all were shut down during the Commonwealth. While England indulged its sulky-pants faction, Charles II and his court were in Continental France developing a taste for the latest theatrical wizardry, where the fashion was for expanded use of painted perspective scenery. On Charles II's return to power in 1660, he and his courtiers encouraged such fashions in British theatre, together with the advent of actresses. Two courtiers received royal patents permitting them to produce plays: Sir Thomas Killigrew, who opened the first Drury Lane Theatre, and Sir William Davenant, who converted a former tennis court in Lincoln's Inn Fields. Both realised the public wanted fancy scenery as much as heaving cleavage, and encouraged those with a design instinct to unleash their imaginations. At this time, the proscenium still meant the thrust space where actors performed surrounded by the audience. Here they could maintain eye contact with – and talk to rather than at – their auditors as they occupied a shared space. Collaboration was key, even if the imagination was being slowly usurped by scenery.

An entrepreneurial spirit was flourishing in the theatre, and entrepreneurs are greedy. The thrust space was taking up territory which could be filled with paying customers. In the 1690s, the manager of the Drury Lane cut four feet off the thrust stage to accommodate a couple of rows of seats. Imitating another Continental fashion, he surrounded the remaining stage with boxes. To be fully seen by the swells within these boxes, the actors retreated further back towards the scenery. And if the actors were back there anyway, why not take a little more off the forestage? In 1776, David Garrick brought in the architect Robert Adam to take another ten feet off the thrust of Drury Lane. There is an ineluctable connection between the profit motive and the slow retreat of the play from the audience.

Less thrust.
Interior of Theatre Royal, Drury Lane, *c.*1808

A later architect, Benjamin Dean Wyatt, carried out another transformation of Drury Lane in 1812. He justified his choices in an essay, which includes one of the first definitions of the proscenium arch as a point of division between audience and show: 'the Proscenium is a line of separation between the two, and is to the Scene what the frame of a Picture is to the Picture itself; namely, a boundary line to confine the eye to the Subject within that line, and prevent it from wandering to other objects.' The imaginary and the real world were now becoming separate. A short forestage survived his design, but the actors were under strict instruction not to cross the line drawn by the arch. One actor, a William Dowton, complained, 'If I can't be heard by the audience in the frame, I'll walk out of it!' But the desire of the owners to maximise gains was against him, and soon that small area of forestage would disappear.

Historically, an auditorium was split into three areas: the gallery, with its cheap seats; the boxes, the priciest tickets and the reserve of the posh; and the pit. The pit was below the stage, often with benches and, as with the yard in Shakespeare's theatre where the groundlings stood, it was the heart of the house. Here the educated and the enthusiasts sat at a medium price – students, clerks, and young lawyers. The connoisseurs were here, and it was their approval or lack of it which determined the success of a show. It didn't take long for this area to fall under the purview of the profit-makers, who realised – surprisingly late – that the front of the pit was the best place to watch. Such premium space was clearly wasted on intellectuals and the like. Benches were upended and replaced with rows of plush armchairs, the space rechristened the 'orchestra stalls', since it now butted up against the orchestra pit. The Haymarket announced to its audience in 1843, 'By curtailment of the useless portion of the Stage in front of the Curtain . . . the lessee has been enabled to appropriate the portion so obtained, to form a certain number of orchestra Stalls.'

The movement towards separation wasn't driven by profit alone. For many, there was an artistic impetus to create a theatre where the director could dictate the nature of an evening rather than influence it. The old public theatres offered joy and communication and a sense of the collective, but little or no focus. No one was more avid for focus than Richard Wagner. To that end, he built a temple to himself and his work at Bayreuth, the Festspielhaus. Not satisfied with the single proscenium,

Wagner went for the grandstanding 'double', which, through a trick of *trompe l'oeil*, gave the audience the feeling they were even further separated. He reconceived the orchestra pit, burying it under the stage and covering it with a hood to render the musicians invisible. Nothing – not least the whirling dervish conductors – should distract. For him, this unity would create 'a mystic gulf' between performer and spectator. He wanted to induce an uninterrupted, dreamlike state where mythic archetypes would be free to transport the minds of those watching. Control was everything, and the theatre had travelled a great distance from the public stages of old.

The all-powerful theatre-artist never caught on in England, for good or ill. Something in the local tradition, dating back to the Mystery plays, had too much inbuilt irreverence and human breadth fully to accommodate the tyrant artist. Edward Gordon Craig, a self-proclaimed designer of genius who only ever managed a couple of produced shows, had a stab at creating total theatre in London and ended up in self-imposed exile. Yet what was missing in British vision was made up for in appetite for guineas. Although a few theatres retained a short forestage through to the 1870s, in 1880 the Bancrofts, of whom more elsewhere, took over the Haymarket. They refashioned the auditorium in a way that meant the end of the forestage. Their gilded arch became the admiration and envy of Europe.

Where the Bancrofts would have concurred with Wagner was in the pleasure taken in the new electric lighting. This was first seen at the Savoy Theatre in 1881, following from the pioneering electrification of the Savoy Hotel. Incandescent bulbs provided a regular white light. It may have lacked the beguiling warmth of the old sputtering gaslights, but it transformed what could be done by grading the extent of light across a stage. It allowed scene painters to put away their garish primary colours and adopt a more tempered, naturalistic style. For Wagner, electric light helped forge stimulating phantasms and spooked the audience with manipulative effects; for the Bancrofts and many others, it helped create the realism they sought.

The desire for illusion, whether in service of a realistic drawing room or a world of trolls and Valkyries, was further enhanced by the greater primacy of the curtain. Earlier theatres either had no curtain or used it sparingly at the play's beginning and end, while scene changes were done within view of the audience and considered part of the evening's pleasure – what an old colleague called, 'Lots of burglars in black coming on and stealing the furniture.' This would no longer satisfy theatregoers: curtains now descended at the end of each act and rose at the start of the next to astonish the audience with new settings. This had a great effect on plays, with writers now fashioning narratives towards a climax, furnishing dramatic moments, frozen tableaux, and strong 'curtain lines' for the instant just before it fell. This is the end of the third act of Oscar Wilde's *A Woman of No Importance*:

GERALD Don't hold me, mother. Don't hold me – I'll kill him.
MRS A Gerald!
GERALD Let me go, I say!
MRS A Stop, Gerald, stop! He is your own father!

For obvious reasons, the curtain has to come down fast. This freeze is strenuous to maintain, but nothing to the curtain line of the melodrama *East Lynne*: 'Dead, dead! And never called me mother!'

The rise to hegemony of the proscenium is a long, slow journey towards separation. The old public theatres held actors, audience, and collective imagination together in a generative embrace. Sharing in a democratic light, where everyone could see each other's eyes, the collective forged what Shakespeare called a 'rough magic'. As the thrust stage slowly retreated from the audience, as scenery grew in primacy over imagination, as the audience shrank in number but grew in wealth, as focus and definition increased and the old happy anarchy declined, it is hard not to sense a loss.

Yet history was irresistible and the proscenium arch evolved. The stage was set for a century of drama exploring the concerns of the modern age within its gilded boundaries. Serving as a picture frame for a series of confrontations, the theatre could examine the ethical and social questions of contemporary life. It circuited a mirror that challenged an audience to scrutinise itself and consider its values. Here the audience met itself, and the drama found a new and radical form of significance. As the actors looked out beyond the frame, they asked the audience to join them in imagining the world anew. Each new play and each new voice gave a fresh shading to what seemed familiar, and brought fresh information about how we behave and who we are. Each new story not just a reflection of its audience, but an invitation for them to step forward. And sometimes to jump.

No thrust.
Englert Theatre interior showing box seating, 1918

Eugène Scribe
1791–1861

The well-made play, a maligned beast, was first cooked up across the Channel in France and known as la pièce bien faite. The British have traditionally believed in making and doing, splurging material out any old how, whereas the French have always placed greater faith in arranging to a thesis. We grew our cities from agglomerating villages with all their idiosyncrasies, while the French went up in balloons and urbanised in straight lines and grids. Similarly with drama, where the sprawling mess of Shakespeare was countered by the ordered simplicities of Corneille and Racine. In nineteenth-century France, this ambition to schematise evolved into la pièce bien faite, and was enclosed in the proscenium. No proponent was more important than the preternaturally prolific Augustin Eugène Scribe.

Writing outside the chronological parameters of this book, with most of his work turned out between 1815 and his death in 1861, and his plays now largely unknown, he nevertheless influenced all who came after. Estimates as to the totality of his dramatic output vary, coming in between a staggering three and five hundred plays, burlesques, librettos, and ballet stories. His well-made play became the supposed norm of the new theatre. Like many a norm, it is a trawler's net with a wide mesh to contain a lot of contrary energies. Some of those sit snugly within the catch, some bulge out, while many escape entirely to swim in the sea of life.

There are many reasons to love Eugène Scribe. Primary is his artistic modesty. A staunch believer in entertainment and populism, he had no illusions about his abilities, though hard-headed about his justified rewards. During an argument over royalties with the Paris Opéra in 1841, he said he wanted returns for his work, 'according to what they bring in, that is to say, a great deal', not 'according to what they are worth, that is to say, very little'. Alongside this modesty was an ability to bounce back.

On one occasion, as the curtain descended on a play of his which had failed, he announced cheerfully, 'No matter; I will do it again next year!' His judgement on commercial matters was swift. When one of his many collaborators, Ernest Legouvé, brought him a new idea for a drama, he swiftly wrapped him in a hug, crying out, 'A hundred performances at six thousand francs!' Legouvé defends this not as evidence of mercenary cynicism, but the excitement of an experienced playwright who knew box office receipts were a record that rarely flatters or lies.

Most amazing is his attitude to colleagues, collaborators, and anyone who helped him. In a theatre tradition within which many authors have thieved from and exploited unwitting co-contributors – step forward Bertolt Brecht – Scribe was saintly in sharing credit and rewards. Few people could write as much as him without sharing the load. At the latest count, he is thought to have worked with more than sixty co-authors. Known as the Scribe factory, one myth maintained that he hired one person to plot the story, another for the dialogue, and a third for the jokes. The workings of this attracted scorn. When Scribe was hosted at the French Academy, one sourpuss member grouched, 'It is not a chair we should give him, but a bench to seat all his co-workers.'

Scribe rejected such haughtiness and took pleasure in co-operation. Friends would bring him an idea, or mention in passing a true story, or delight him with a few couplets; whatever their contribution he would happily share the gold and glory. Scrupulously honest, even writers he didn't know received cheques from him as, 'Payment for copyright in ideas', when they were unaware there had been any infringement. Whoever or however many, they were acknowledged on the bill and on the title page and received a fair share. Seemingly all remained friends and it was to them he dedicated his collected works. His generosity extended beyond colleagues. Among his many acts of philanthropy was a foundation for theatre folk on their uppers, into which he paid 13,000 francs (roughly €140,000 in current value) a year.

Scribe wrote his first plays for the Théâtre du Vaudeville, and his form emerged from that tradition. Vaudeville began as essentially a parody of a classic play or opera running at another theatre, or as hasty and jocular representations of scenes from everyday life. It consisted of sung or spoken doggerel and frequent musical interludes. By the beginning of the nineteenth century, it was starting to flirt with more dramatic consistency, and Scribe nurtured this relationship. He often extended a single act to two, and at times three; he replaced stock *commedia* characters with ones drawn from contemporary society and eliminated the musical interludes. The line of attack was sharpened by aiming a light satirical arrow at the fashions and follies of the day. After a while – voila! – scenes of versified anecdote, dramatic only by way of courtesy, had somehow morphed into plays with, however fragile the connective tissue, that old trinity – a beginning, a middle, and an end. The journey to la pièce bien faite was far from smooth, with Scribe notching up a full fourteen flops (what a generous culture to allow that much calamity!) before his first success.

The essence of a well-made play has been incorrectly described as a type of classical, symmetrical perfection, as if they were temples to proportion and balance. This gives an impression of aridity, which is far from just. The essence is action and event. Characterisation, atmosphere, and wit are stripped away so nothing gets in the way of incident. Scribe was writing at the time of romantic drama, which relied heavily on charismatic heroes, crashing and violent poetic language, spectacular tableaux and scenic effects, and windy philosophical musing – a messy and outsized form for star actors. The Scribe method was tidier, more strictly controlled and far cheaper, yet sought similar excitement. Within the fastidious engineering, the compulsion was to space out dramatic effects in order to manufacture constant titillation from start to finish. Not a million miles from the formulaic construction of television drama today.

Rather than classical order, this was about making exciting connections. Each piece of the master-watch was calibrated to serve the whole, all achieved with perfect economy, every character essential to the action, every speech increasing the momentum. No reams of Restoration banter, no *Sturm und Drang* romantic blathering, just action and event. The skill came in the deft arrangement of the incidents, the fertility of the invention, and the concise plotting. A feat of carpentry as much as play-making, the art is in the neatness with which successive links of the ever-shifting narrative are dovetailed together. The efficiency of the piece of work delivers the pleasure. Nature is as antithetical to this creation as the rambling hedge would be to those French gardeners who contorted the yew and the boxwood into the elegant topiary of Versailles.

Within the story well told, there is little concern for credibility. The contents are an amalgam of heightened situations – lovers' confusions, false reports of death, daring escapes from prison, bouquets impregnated with poison, young gentlemen who have got themselves into unpleasant scrapes, and women fighting for the love of said young gentlemen. Shocking reversals occur just before the curtain falls; letters arrive and long-dead relatives come back to life at five minutes to midnight; and surprising twists trump the expected outcome. 'Nothing but bonfires' – the terse summary of the denouement of *The Winter's Tale* – is the most accurate precis. There was some attempt to address social questions, and a little poking of fun at contemporary mores, but never so much as to distract from the chain of continuous incident. Or to distract from the primary purpose to entertain.

Characterisation is as little trusted in Scribe as credibility. No more vitality was invested in the characters than was needed to get them through each ingenious intrigue. As one nineteenth-century critic put it, 'The people who pass through these plays are merely profiles; they are like the plane of the geometricians – without thickness and impalpable.' Scribe birthed his situations with immense care and yet cared not to breathe life into the characters. In his dialogue, they speak with a self-conscious deference to the fashionable language of the day. This determination to catch the changing hues of the hour is the surest way to ensure your palette will look faded and wan within weeks, let alone years. What is contemporary is usually four parts temporary.

No matter the limitations, Scribe ploughed on, waking at five in the summer and six in the winter, and writing until midday, then a busy afternoon in meetings or rehearsals, before watching his own and other shows in the evening. Legouvé tells us he sometimes forgot he was witnessing his own work, and freely criticised it, before being reminded he may bear a certain responsibility. Scribe's career bloomed, from the Vaudeville to the Théâtre du Gymnase, for which he wrote more than a hundred plays, before graduating to the Comédie-Française, the epicentre of French theatrical life. Towards the end, Scribe sensed with the dread of the soon-to-be-out-of-vogue that the audience was starting to look for more. His plays and their meticulous construction had stayed constant, but the public was hungry for work charged with import rather than mere workmanship. Fortunately for him – a luck his consistent and exuberant generosity deserved – he died before the plunge from fashion.

Throughout his life he suffered from the sneers of the *de haut en bas*. One said he was 'the ultimate in bourgeois art and philistinism, pleasing the masses and writing théâtre vide' – empty plays. Another wrote that his work was 'devoid of poetry, lyricism, style, philosophy, truth and naturalness', which is quite the absence for a play. Scribe's response was disarmingly guileless: 'The theatre-goer loves me because I take care always to win his trust; he is in on the secrets of the comedy; he has in his hands the threads that pull my characters along; he knows the surprises that I am going to spring, and he thinks he is managing them himself; in short, I take him for a collaborator; he feels he created the play with me, and naturally he applauds.' Charming and consistent that his generosity to collaborators extended to the audience.

Posthumously, there was praise. The plays of Tom Robertson in London accepted the inheritance of Scribe's populism and non-literal approach and adapted his ebullient narrative invention to the commonplace elements of contemporary middle-class life. Ibsen, who in many ways would seem Scribe's antithesis, borrows heavily on his narrative tricks and surprises, and acknowledged the debt. He took the innovations and curbed their wildness, domesticating them in claustrophobic settings. Shaw also drew on it, particularly in *Arms and the Man*. By the time the late-Victorian critic and advocate William Archer was describing the nature of the well-made play as an artefact of neat and balanced overall construction, with the appearance of verisimilitude, it had travelled a long way from Scribe.

Sneering at the well-made play abides. Craftsmanship is distrusted as something suspicious. In the depths of the Covid-19 madness, I saw two gurus of performativity opining online that anything which showed craft was inherently right wing! We have lost the popular boulevard tradition in our playwriting, which is one of the reasons so many playhouses built for drama are now filled with musical theatre, a discipline that has never forgotten its responsibility to an audience. Wilde, Maugham, and Coward all kept an astute eye on the gallery. Tutored by Scribe and his successors, they had an instinct for the sensational incident, the dramatic curtain, and the cheap joke. Sadly, we have had better taste forced on us. So now we can all be miserable together.

Vive Le Scribe!

Never a dull moment.
Eugène Scribe: *documents iconographiques*

Marie Bancroft
1839–1921

Theatre history of the last two hundred years is studded with tales of mould-breaking led by women entrepreneurs. Elizabeth Robins gave us Ibsen and the riches of European drama; Lilian Baylis gave us Sadler's Wells and a methodology for popular high drama; Joan Littlewood turned theatre upside down, and downside up again; Jude Kelly taught producers how to fully commit to their local community; and now Sonia Friedman is leading the way in internationalising British stage success. All have had a massive effect, yet none greater than a Doncaster woman who midwifed the modern proscenium – Marie Bancroft.

Born Marie Effie Wilton in 1839, she was the daughter of travelling players hoofing their way around roughhouse Northern theatres. On the boards from the age of five, variously got up as a jockey or whirling a hornpipe in a sailor suit, one of her earliest named roles is Fleance in *Macbeth*. As with Banquo's son, her legacy proved significant. Like many a child actor, she was born into both fun and disgrace. Her parents had both been disowned by their families for joining the rogue and vagabond tribe. The young Marie once entranced an audience of the well-to-do at a charity fundraiser with songs and recitations. Purses were opened and coins spilled, until someone enquired who the young bobby-dazzler was: on discovering she was the daughter of actors, smiling lips soured and purses shut with a genteel snap. The child was stung with shame. Much of what she achieved professionally was a revenge on such hauteur.

Marie had no desire to be a tragedienne; she wanted to sparkle. After an apprenticeship in Bristol, she stormed into London in 1856 in pantomime and burlesque, playing breeches roles. These drag transgressions were all the rage in the spinning top of early Victorian theatre. Their aim was entertainment and a not-so-discreet eroticism. Breeches roles gave Victorians the chance to see a lot more of a lady's leg than would otherwise be deemed proper. Though Marie didn't have a lot of leg to show, coming in at under five feet, what she did have she flourished with ebullience. Charles Dickens wrote: 'Miss Wilton is so stupendously like a boy, and unlike a woman, that it is perfectly free from offence . . . I call her the cleverest girl I have ever seen on the stage.' However much she dazzled, life on the margins was never easy. Marie had two illegitimate children, one who died in infancy. Various potential fathers have been speculated on, including the future King Edward VII. A woman of acuity, she knew she needed stability and respectability. As did her profession. She set out to make both happen.

In 1865, at the age of just twenty-five, she realised that male managers were never going to see beyond her burlesque persona or her legs and it was time to manage her own destiny. Going against the grain, she became her own manager and took a lease on the Queens Theatre in Charlotte Street, off Tottenham Court Road. A small and scruffy dive, the Queens played to its local community. Nicknamed 'the Dusthole', it was surrounded by pubs and fried fish shops in what was then an unsavoury part of London. Marie wrote of her first visit, 'oh the audience! My heart sank! Some of the occupants of the stalls (the price of admission was, I think, a shilling) were engaged between the acts in devouring oranges (their faces being buried in them) and drinking ginger-beer. Babies were being rocked to sleep, or smacked to be quiet, which proceeding, in many cases, had an opposite effect! A woman looked up at our box, and seeing us staring aghast, with, I suppose, an expression of horror upon my face, first of all took a sight at us, and then shouted, "Now then, you three stuck up ones, come out o' that, or I'll send this 'ere orange at your 'eds."'

Marie loved nothing if not a challenge, and even after this introduction was determined to make the Queens London's most fashionable spot. Following refurbishment, she reopened it as the Prince of Wales Royal Theatre. The name may offer a clue as to how she found a £1,000 loan for the lease. Her ambition was to make a contemporary playhouse with modern working practices and a fresh aesthetic. The reputation of the stage could only be cleaned up if the auditorium was spruced first.

Her care with interior design lured the middle classes by inviting them to feel at home in a space that felt like their own drawing rooms.

New theatre needs a new styling of home. Konstantin Stanislavsky and Vladimir Nemirovich-Danchenko refashioned the Heritage Theatre in Moscow thirty years later to house the Moscow Art Theatre and the plays of Chekhov. Marie pre-empted them, redecorating her space entirely. Boxes were transformed with elegant curtains, lights were brightened, colours were vivified, and the floor acquired a carpet, a rarity in that age. Armchairs in the stalls were freshly upholstered in blue leather with white enamelled studs. White antimacassars were draped over the tops of the chairs to protect the fabric from gentlemen's copious hair oil. Such front-of-house elegance was there to create a novel sensation of comfort, and to let everyone know that care was taken with every detail.

The same principle operated backstage. A company of talented actors was gathered, chosen for their ability to mimic human behaviour rather than their lovely legs. The emphasis was on ensemble rather than star ego, all combining to make homogenous theatre. Marie treated her actors with dignity, increasing their pay steadily. Equally important, she delivered their wages individually, rather than asking them to join a humiliating queue. Small acts of respect make big differences, and Marie's ensured a company that stayed loyal. Costumes were provided, and frequently they bore some relation to the play. This was something of a novelty since actors were usually asked to don their own moth-eaten dresses and jackets, which they had been wearing out in show after show, sometimes for decades. Time was allocated for thoughtful rehearsal rather than crazed panic, the presiding methodology of the era.

Such innovations were noted by the public. Together with Marie's address book, stuffed with the names of the glamorous and the well-to-do, they ensured that on opening night Charlotte Street was packed with carriages bearing the fashionable set. An achievement in itself, but the greater challenge was for her to grow it into a steady trade. The Prince of Wales was spectacularly successful. This was down to not only pretty curtains and antimacassars but the quality of the work. Realism is a slippery term, yet it was the most literal kind which governed the Prince of Wales. Marie took the box set and perfected it. Three-walled rooms furnished with carpets, curtains, chairs and sofas sat square on the stage floor, impressive in their solidity. What may seem drearily prosaic in the present day was at the time thrilling. Dubbed 'drawing room comedy' or 'cup-and-saucer drama', this was an untrodden path. Actors stopped trying to be bold, or interesting, or strange, and performed the mundane with liturgical simplicity. They came on, poured tea, and then drank it. Or opened a book and read it. The audience glowed with excitement. Patrons in armchairs in the stalls looked through the frame at the re-creation of their own lives, its variegated textures and tones, its dullness and its deceptions. They didn't only recognise what was presented, they lived in it.

Two years after opening, and having managed the theatre alone, Marie Wilton became Marie Bancroft, taking one of her most gifted and handsome actors for a husband and partner – the dashingly named Squire Bancroft. They proved a durable partnership, onstage and in management, with Squire regularly crediting his wife for their success. They soon became properly rich. 'Mrs Bancroft's theatre has become what we call an institution,' the *Illustrated London News* told its readers.

A rapidly improving public transport system from the suburbs promised a potential new audience. The innovations of Bancroft, and her imitators, helped to change the theatre from a turbulent and populist imbroglio into a form of entertainment the respectable middle classes felt they could embrace. A spark of happy derangement was lost, the joyously vulgar was expunged, but the pursuit of profit was too powerful a motivator to be neglected. And there is something seductive and mystical in the group fascination of an audience watching themselves reflected, even if only sipping tea from a china cup.

Credit for making theatre respectable is often attributed to Henry Irving, the actor-manager who parked himself at the Lyceum for several decades in the late nineteenth century and demanded respect loud and long. His version involved continuous courting of the press, flattering of the monarchy, and steamrolling of the public with his grandiose affectations. He organised tours of North America akin to the visitation of a small nation, hiring entire trains to move companies from state to state. His act of will succeeded, securing Irving the first actor knighthood and the kind of awestruck adulation usually reserved for a conquering general or a domineering politician. Such grandstanding is easy to scoff at when we forget the vast distance travelled to gain dignity for the profession. Outlawed at many moments in history, denigrated at others, and often patronised (even to the present day) by those who suspect theatre people are having too much fun, it took monumental will to change the narrative. Irving achieved that and deserved plaudits. But alongside him, and more stealthily, Marie Bancroft was setting in place systems and structures that achieved the same.

The Bancrofts knew how to turn a success into a smash. To run a play on its own, rather than in repertory, was a new practice. Prices rose fast and steep. At the Queens, a seat in the stalls had cost one shilling. At the Prince of Wales, it was six. By 1875, they had gone up to ten shillings, the equivalent of £55 in today's money, and were the most expensive stalls seats in London. When *Man and Wife* – Wilkie Collins's adaptation of his own novel – was presented, speculators sold tickets for the first night for up to five guineas, an astronomical sum. Then and now, there are always punters willing to pay a premium, prizing value as highly as substance. Marie Bancroft had cannily reduced the capacity of the theatre, while radically increasing its cash return. An exclusive pleasure at a high price was far more profitable than populist pleasures at low prices. These were the early murmurs of late capitalism.

Such success enabled the Bancrofts to move on to vaster fields. Finishing with a flourish after precisely four thousand performances, the Bancrofts quit the Prince of Wales in 1879. They had acquired the lease on the Haymarket, then as now the grand old duchess of the West End. Marie, the queen of the makeover, went to work with the same loathing of dirt and detritus and the same determination to upscale as when she had swept clean the Queens. The rundown interior was refreshed with liberal splashes of gilt. The splendid new proscenium was painted entirely in gold. Marie had learned the needs of her audience, and knew they treasured the embrace of comfortable respectability, with a hint of regal plush.

The plays toyed with the same naturalism as at the Prince of Wales, but with extra grandeur. The venue they created housed two of Oscar Wilde's plays, the ideal hand for this glove. There was the same hunger for technical innovation – with a special delight taken in the advent of electric lighting – used to create vivid storm scenes and the illusion of moving clouds. The old pit with its two-shilling bench seats was replaced by ten-shilling stalls seats. This provoked a muted riot on their opening night with a small section of rowdies shouting, 'Where's the pit?' But the glitterati were delighted.

Marie and Squire Bancroft cleaned up at the Haymarket and felt sufficiently flush to retire in 1885 after only five years. Unlike most theatre-makers, they quit the scene at a height, rather than after a crash. And also unlike most, they never seemed to look back, rarely appearing onstage again. The *New York Times* wrote about the occasion of their retirement: 'A brilliant and memorable event. The Prince and Princess of Wales and their daughters were present and the auditorium was crowded with persons prominent . . . Mr and Mrs Bancroft were repeatedly recalled and showered with bouquets. The curtain was raised again, displaying a stage fairly converted into a garden with bouquets, wreaths and other floral offerings. Mr Bancroft appeared, struggling with emotion, and made a long speech. At the conclusion of his remarks there were loud calls for Mrs Bancroft and when she appeared, the whole audience arose and waved their handkerchiefs, while the stage was again showered with bouquets.'

Taken all in all, that amounts to quite the revenge for the little Doncaster girl for whom smiles soured and purses shut.

No one messes with Marie.
Ms Bancroft as Nan in *Good for Nothing*, 1879

Tom Robertson
1829–1871

Curious how often the world leaps forward with light comedy, and how often it gets stuck in inertia with tragedy. We are reared on an excess of respect for tragedy – a specific course at some universities, and the largest and most sombre element of English A level. From the cradle it is drummed into us that suffering brings wisdom. I have always suspected this to be a myth constructed as scant compensation for those who have to endure most of the pain – the poor. The single show I was involved with which had the greatest social effect – *Beautiful Thing* by Jonathan Harvey – wrapped its two revolutionary messages in the glittery paper of benevolent comedy. A simple story set in a Thamesmead housing estate in 1993, it pronounced two truths at the time unpalatable in the dominant culture – that being gay was not a tragedy but a joy, and that working-class cultures were not mired in prejudice but capable of greater tolerance and generosity than most. These simple propositions went off like a rainbow-coloured firework in an age of excess seriousness. Minds stuck in neutral were liberated by joyous elucidation.

The quiet revolution that initiated the proscenium century began with a light touch and a spritz of laughter. Heavy gates can be knocked down with sweat and tears, or they can be bounced over with a little trampolining delight. Thomas Robertson, who kicked off the revolution, wrote with a freewheeling inanity and marvellous sense of silliness. Here was someone seeing the detail of his own day, overhearing its dialogue with its jagged, lively rhythms, and presenting it – marvel of marvels – on the stage. His plays were radically different, with a focus on everyday objects and modern tones bringing fresh concerns. This was not done with gnashing teeth and phoney tears, but with a kick-step.

Such energy was stirring in London thirty years before the glory years of Tom Robertson and Marie Bancroft. In 1830, Lucia Elizabeth Vestris took over the Royal Olympic Theatre, becoming the first female actor-manager in London theatre. Another veteran of breeches roles in opera, Vestris had earned enough to take a lease on the prized theatre. Her ambition was to transform the burlesque into a more integrated form. Whatever was coarse or overblown she reined in or rendered delicate, all in the name of coherence and harmony. A box set was put onstage – with a ceiling! Possibly the first on a British stage. Furniture was functional rather than painted on backdrops, and of high quality. Real blinds, practical windows which opened and closed, lush carpets, and elegant draperies garnished the scene. And more – fireplaces, mirrors, clocks, and doorknobs. (The early history of stage design pivots quite frequently on the quality of the doorknobs.) An easy and natural acting style was needed to steer an unaffected path through all the clutter. Careful casting and lengthy rehearsals were instituted to move on from the artificial style which had preceded. Vestris's partner, the actor Charles Mathews, characterised this as a 'lighter phase of comedy, representing the more natural and less laboured school of modern life'.

Tom Robertson's thespian pedigree was impeccable, emerging from the old stock companies that trundled round provincial touring circuits. Based in larger cities, they would venture to small towns to play in halls of all shapes and sizes, on unelaborated stages with scant facilities. The term hand-to-mouth would dignify the working conditions. Sometimes a London pro would join the company and drop into a part with little or no rehearsal: mostly it was the same peripatetic players, trained for type-cast roles which barely changed attributes from play to play. Though flat broke and threadbare, this was a sterling school within which a young actor could learn their craft. And not just acting. Robertson's parents ran the company which toured from Lincoln, their son serving as factotum – stage-managing, prompting, painting the scenery, and managing the business. There were fledgling writing efforts for young Tom, adapting plays to suit the troupe's requirements and writing additional comic songs. Hard to imagine a better education than such a hands-on apprenticeship.

The Robertsons' company was one of the more admired, and Tom's mother considered a fine actress. London actors who joined them with condescension often found the commitment and skill in these companies required them to raise their game. But history was against them: by the 1840s such enterprises were in precipitate and terminal decline. The system of patronage by the local squirearchy was falling away at the same pace as the local squirearchy itself; the audience's appetite had shifted towards spectacle, and the new railways criss-crossing the landscape enabled them to travel further for their thrills. By 1849, the Lincoln company had gone the way of all flesh, along with many others. With them went a chain of human connection that held the UK together.

Young Tom was nothing if not a worker, and for fifteen years he hacked and drudged his way through various forms of employment to keep his head above water. He briefly worked as an assistant teacher in the Netherlands, a journalist on Grub Street, an occasional turn onstage, and a prompter wherever he could earn a crust, sometimes at the Lyceum for a company run by Madame Vestris. Occasionally he translated and adapted drama from the French. Once settled in London, he became a fixture in ne'er-do-well gangs of artists, journalists, and performers who hung around clubs like the Savage or the Arundel – a bohemian milieu he depicted in his play *Society.* Never an intellectual, he had no plan for a career, just as he had none for the plays that made his fortune.

All this activity fostered no manifesto to overturn the theatre; he was more of a craftsman than a rebel, driven by his own taste and a curiosity as to what was possible. 'What if we tried this?' feels like a question that drove him, more than the statement 'We must do this!' In *Trelawny of the Wells*, Pinero portrays his predecessor as the character Tom Wrench, with his driving fetish to see 'locks on the doors, real locks, to work', and who passionately declares his characters must 'talk and behave like live people', fashioning supermen out of 'actual, dull, everyday men'. He makes a revolutionary Robertson: in reality it was more a matter of instinct than a plan to storm the palace. He simply looked for a good recipe for a stew.

Society, his first major play, was rejected by every London management, with one curtly describing it as 'rubbish'. It was deemed too casual, too low-key, with loose slangy dialogue and a lack of proper pretension. The preceding age set a high value on ambition, whether the loftiness of romantic drama with ripe monologues delivered in hysterical vein by tortured poets or lovelorn empresses, or the clashing colours of melodrama. Robertson's play was too everyday to satisfy a craving for spices or dualities. The play had its faults – there is no shortage of absurd misunderstandings and sudden volte-faces – but the rejections were a response to its virtues. He was saved by a bold company from outside London, the Prince of Wales in Liverpool, and after *Society*'s success there it was picked up by its namesake in London, under the management of Marie Bancroft. Here Robertson found a young company that wanted to pursue the same high standards, and here he also found his luck.

The Prince of Wales was successful but hadn't yet found the plays to define it. Their relaxed, natural, underplaying style was looking for the right words to complement a company committed to truth. The small size of the theatre lent significance and strength to most stories, but it required subtle and delicate inflections to pitch them at the right volume. Dialogue needed to convey rather than declaim. In a space where a shout would deafen, conversation had authority. In Robertson, they found someone who could write intimate scenes in which actors could develop characters of complexity and substance. He relished quiet moments onstage, instances of privacy, much like the camera's close-up in cinema when characters reveal themselves in repose.

When *Society* was taken up by the Prince of Wales, Robertson told his father he would need real onstage coat hooks. His sceptical reply was, 'You'd better try something more romantic than hats and coats on pegs in which to interest the public'; but his son's instincts were sharper. The audience were looking for the minutiae of everyday life to be reflected, and Robertson's 'cup-and-saucer' plays fitted the bill. There are serious themes in *Society* – that money is no replacement for a good heart; that snobbery and hypocrisy are malodorous in any class; and that confederacy and loyalty count for more than social prestige. But they are swathed in colourful comedy – two characters are named Lord and Lady Ptarmigant – and the issues matter less than the details.

The best scenes are pure naturalism, where the denizens of the Owl's Roost – a club for dissolute boho hacks and intellectuals – banter and sing and gossip and call for more drink, scribblers in a smoke-infused blear working through their drunk or hungover biorhythms. This was the modern world onstage, presented for no other purpose than its loose and wayward honesty to itself. Not since Shakespeare's Boar's Head scenes in the two parts of *Henry IV* had a reprobate milieu been so loosely alive. *Society* was praised in the *Telegraph* as 'a clever, sketchy, picture of modern men and manners, dashed off in a spirited style, and giving perhaps a new view of some of the gradations in the social scale'.

His next and most renowned play, *Caste*, went the whole hog on gradations. In *Caste*, a quiet rage about class runs through every beat. The refrain, 'True hearts are more than coronets/And simple faith than Norman blood' is frequently sung, and every encounter bears the stain of prejudice. A marquise, the mother of one of the blue-blooded young chaps, is the ultimate villain, a character as devotedly unsympathetic as Lady Catherine de Bourgh in Austen's *Pride and Prejudice*, and similarly devoted to securing the right match for her progeny. Within the hierarchy, theatre itself is seen as an agent of change, since the two aspirant young women, rising out of their own class and attracting the attention of two young swells, are both ballerinas.

But class rage, even in a turbulent world, was not what marked the play out: the achievement was more the styling. In part this found its form in one character, a comic creation of advanced awfulness called Eccles, a drunken father of dedicated disreputability. He steals from his daughters, drinking and betting away their short-term financial gains, and whenever he stumbles onto the stage chaos and collapse are never far away. In one terrifying scene, he is left alone with a baby. Showing not an iota of sentiment, he blows smoke in its face, shouts abuse in jealousy at the attention the infant receives, and attempts to steal the necklace from around its neck. A far more chilling creation than the stock stage drunk, Eccles is a lethally executed riposte to the benevolent onstage grandparents of the preceding century. At the end, the only solution for this demonic comic creation is to send him to Jersey with two pounds a week to drink himself to death. His unrepentant response, 'I think I could – I'm sure I'll try.'

The other achievement is in the temper of the dialogue, a semi-colloquial, telegraphic, loose conversational mode – the antithesis of the highfalutin strain of sentimental rhetoric that preceded it. Eddying, shifting, and sliding with the uncertain tempo of life, it is matched by small details of daily existence. Meals are consumed, pipes smoked, shillings borrowed, and peas shelled, not in service of a larger narrative but for no purpose beyond their own. Appreciating the excitement it was greeted with at the time is hard without knowing the context. Writing later, George Bernard Shaw said, 'the eagerness with which it was swallowed long ago was the eagerness with which an ocean castaway, sucking his bootlaces in an agony of thirst in a sublime desert of salt water, would pounce on a spoonful of flat salutari and think it nectar. After years of sham heroics and superhuman balderdash, *Caste* delighted everyone by its freshness, its nature, its humanity.'

The idea that all Robertson could handle was interior domesticity was blown apart in his next big success, *Ours*. The third act of this play travels to a ramshackle hut, jerry-built in the middle of the Crimean War. Robertson's brother had served there, and the same attention to detail holds even in far-flung war zones. Here is the setting in its obsessive detail:

> Interior of a hut, built of boulders and mud, the roof built out, showing the snow and sky outside. The walls bare and rude, pistols, swords, guns, maps, newspapers etc., suspended on them. Door right. Window in flat right centre, showing snow-covered country beyond; rude fireplace left; wood fire burning; overhanging chimney and shelf; small stove right, very rude with chimney going through roof, which is covered with snow and icicles; straw and rags stuffed in crevices and littered about floor; a rope stretched across back of

hut, with fur-rugs and horse-cloths hanging up to divide the beds off; camp and rough makeshift furniture; camp cooking utensils etc.; arm-chair made of tub, etc. Cupboards round left containing properties; hanging lamp, a rude piece of planking before fireplace, stool, tubs, pail etc. Portmanteau left of table, rough chair, broken gun-barrel near fireplace, for poker and stack of wood. Stage half-dark, music "Chanson", distant bugle and answer as curtain rises. ANGUS discovered, very shabby, high, muddy boots, beard etc., seated at table, reading by light of candle letters which are lying on an open travelling-desk.

Most delicious here is the occasional 'etc.', as if this description is only a flavour of what is needed. Though excessive, it is part and parcel of the form itself, and in its own way glorious. Robertson knew he couldn't skimp – there should be no suspicion of tourism in depicting a war zone – and serves up meticulous representation.

However tragic the backdrop, the scene is comic delight. Three love-lorn women who had been left at home have travelled near the battle-field to find their loved ones. (Historically this was accurate.) Soldiers march by outside the window, guns are heard far off, and sergeants come and go, reporting on the action. All the while upper lips remain commendably stiff. Within this environment love scenes are played out as a meal is prepared for and by the newly arrived women. Painstaking detail is shown in the cooking, with a leg of lamb turning over a fire. The most beguiling scene is when Mary Netley improvises with the few ingredients available to make a roly-poly pudding, with Hugh Chalcot as her sous-chef. In the process, which takes a fair chunk of stage time, they get over their initial antipathy and fall in love. Marie Bancroft demanded this scene, since she didn't feel there was enough flesh on Mary's bones. Robertson provided her with gold. After mixing, laying out, then rolling the sponge, then applying what will serve for jam, they put the pudding – a compacting of all most British and Victorian – on to boil. Personality is revealed and story progressed through everyday action performed in extremis. This must have been a revelation to watch. At the conclusion, the table is laid for supper as singing troops march by outside. Closely reminiscent of the end of *Three Sisters*, it has none of the melancholy sorrow of the later Russian play, but a mad English poetry of its own.

Several magic moments punctuate Robertson's work. In *Society*, in a West End square to which a leading male character is trying to gain access to its gardens, he tricks a nursemaid with a child into unlocking the gate. Then in silence, we see, '*NURSEMAID and CHILD go out at gate; LIFE GUARDSMAN enters, speaks to NURSEMAID; they exeunt*'. That is all; we have not seen the characters before and we do not see them again, we don't know what they say to each other, or if they know each other, or anything at all. A small moment of life drifting past, and a chimerical sort of poetry, such relaxed inconsequentiality rarely having been seen onstage before. Closer to the drifting eye of the film camera than the usual focused orchestration of a play. Robertson's gift was for observing (more than hearing); he saw the world, allowing its currents to shift within the arch. In a later play, *School*, a young lord and his belle converse in a garden in the moonlight. They look on shadows cast by the powerful moon, comment on them fancifully and shadowplay with them. An exquisite scene, and, without preciousness, enlivened by a splash of Watteau. Within these moments, the characters emerging are not psychologically complex – nothing so deliberate – but full of the inconsistencies and accidence of life.

It would be unjust to describe his writing as 'ultra real', as some have, since he happily strayed this way and that. The writing slips and dips in and out of different modes; there are sentimental strands, lyric passages, and comic monologues to go alongside the stretches of loose naturalism. Acts often end with speechless montages, where characters pursue intentions as if in dumbshow, climaxing in static tableaux, establishing lattices of relationships before the curtain falls. One can see the genesis of silent-movie acting in these sections, storytelling of gesture and attitude. In bizarre ways this inconsistency of form makes it feel more like life, with all its surprising contingencies. There are many solecisms – an excess of coincidence, trite speechifying, arbitrary endings, and sudden influxes of providential goodwill. But the same criticism could be aimed at much Victorian writing. The 'bread and butter' gibes expressed at his plays have stuck, but they are richer and stranger than that.

This was too much for many. Henry James derided the focus on 'little things, a great many charts and tables, carpets, curtains and knickknacks', and said the plays seemed created for 'the comprehension of infants'. Later, Robertson came under attack from both sides: from the radicals for his lack of consistency and from conservatives for his lurches into sentimental homilies. Shaw, though critical, was a steady defender, declaring that Nature was to be found in 'the kettle, the fireplace, in the ham, in the tea, in the bread and butter, in the bassinet, in the hays and sticks and clothes, in the familiar phrases, the quiet unpumped, everyday utterance'.

Like Chekhov, Robertson's career involved a long wait, late success, and then work crammed in before an early death. After *Society*'s great success in 1865, he had only five years, before dying of heart disease. Yet in that short time, along with his collaborators in Bancroft's company, he took the English theatre a long way, far from the hysterical verse of Renaissance cardinals and Russian czars, far from the goodies and baddies of melodrama, and closer to bewildering real life as expressed in doorknobs, roly-poly puddings, and lost galoshes. He relished the mingled yarn of good and ill, and the audience happily joined him.

The theatre had freed itself from the shackles of its previous mannerisms, with the mould-breaking buoyancy of laughter.

Eccles passes the nose-touch sobriety test.
Sir John Hare as Old Eccles
in *Caste*, 1887

Emile Zola
1840–1902

Naturalism and realism as words and concepts are used rather interchangeably throughout this book, and may be used too often in this chapter. The principal reason is that it is long decades since anyone was able to tell them apart. Both are an indication of a movement in the same direction, towards truth, though they shelter under their broad umbrellas a host of diverging aesthetics. Long ago in France – the hothouse of dramatic theory – they were clearly distinguishable and separated by epochs.

First came realism, commencing fully in the 1840s and 1850s, equipped with its own journal to espouse its cause, *Réalisme*. As a movement, this was a reaction against the high-flown poetic rhetoric, grand gestures, and overblown intensity of romantic drama, and the sensationalism and moral preaching of melodrama. Its high priest was the young Dumas *fils*, son of the elder Alexandre who had given the world ripping yarns such as *The Three Musketeers* and *The Count of Monte Cristo*. The son wanted none of that: he wanted stories from an observable reality, truthful characters and even, horror of horrors, grammatically incorrect dialogue. In his new age, 'Invention does not exist for us. We have nothing to invent. We have only to look and remember, to feel, to co-ordinate and give back . . . under a special form.' That last phrase 'under a special form' turned out to be an effective get-out clause, since it lent Dumas *fils* the latitude to do an awful lot of invention and tear-jerking – if his signature work *La Dame aux camélias* is anything to go by. This archetypal template for the whore-with-the-heart-of-gold-who-pays-with-her-own-life tale stretches credulity way beyond breaking point. Which is why it is better served in Verdi's recreation *La Traviata*, which few would mistake for verismo.

The reaction to realism was naturalism, determined to be . . . well . . . a whole lot realer. The prime mover of this movement was Emile Zola, already a successful novelist with a genius for authenticity when he took up the cause in the 1870s. He went on the attack directly against Dumas *fils*, and Victorien Sardou, then king of the well-made play. Both were denounced as fake realists: 'I am waiting for the time to come when they will tell no more incredible stories . . . I am waiting for them to abandon the cut and dried rules, the worked out formulas, the tears and cheap laughs.' Zola loved a scrap. Alongside writing the enormous Rougon-Macquart series of twenty outsized novels, he picked the great fight of the *fin de siècle* when he took on the corruption and prejudice of the French Establishment over the Dreyfus affair. This scandal went on to define a schism in French and European intellectual life for much of the twentieth century. According to conspiracy theories – claiming that anti-Dreyfusard assassins killed the polemicist by blocking his chimney thereby causing carbon monoxide poisoning – it also took his life. So when Zola picked a fight, he went all in, and his place in theatre history is more for his capacity to take a stand than for the quality of his drama.

In prefaces to plays, in an essay titled 'Naturalism on the Stage' from 1881, in his promotion of the work of international peers including Strindberg and Ibsen, and in his own work, Zola pushed the argument. He called for a science of naturalism. He had been bowled over by the discoveries of Darwin in *On the Origin of Species*, and its contention that heredity and environment came together to create character. He believed the stage was the ideal arena in which to explore this hypothesis, making use of two sciences not yet fully conceived: psychology and sociology. The former to explore the interior life of characters, the latter to reveal the effect of their exterior context. Bringing together these studies – in a world before Freud and Durkheim had codified such practices – would create the new science. Plays would be driven not by the meticulous plotting of la pièce bien faite but by the dynamics of their characters. The theatre would be the laboratory in which to carry out such investigations.

His ambition ran: 'Heredity has its own laws, just like gravity. I will attempt to find and to follow, by resolving the double question of temperaments and environments, the thread that leads mathematically from one man to another.' He rightly attested that the novel, and in particular the French novel, with nods to Flaubert and Balzac, had achieved breakthroughs in the portrayal of private behaviour and public environments thus far eluding the theatre. No matter, electrified by Zola's enthusiasm, the stage would catch up. The polemic is bullish and vehement, contagious in its nineteenth-century galvanic self-belief.

Zola's practice did not match his theory. He never had the same skill at creating characters with the ebullient independence of a Dickens or a Balzac creation. His stage adaptation of his first great success, *Thérèse Raquin*, opened in 1873, six years after the book's publication. Although it brought a grubby and lowlife intensity to the stage, its plot of murder and adultery, embellished with additional incident, takes it on a long walk away from verisimilitude. Relishing a *Crime and Punishment* febrility in the way his lead characters, two lovers, unravel after killing her husband, the adaptation packs a toxic punch but falls swiftly into overheated psycho-melodrama. Zola's special capacity in his prose is to meander, garnering detail along the way, bringing characters slowly towards a crescendo. It takes at least a week to read a book of his, with a lot of breathing space. To squeeze the same freight into a two-hour evening is to bust credibility. *Thérèse Raquin* has been described as the first proletarian stage tragedy, which again doesn't stack up. The dramatis personae – shopkeepers and artists – are lower middle class, and though it certainly plunges headlong towards disaster, it is more car crash than tragedy.

The lure of the stage for nineteenth-century novelists was similar to the quickened heartbeat of the call from Hollywood today. Zola was intoxicated by similar fantasies of fame and fortune, as well as the fun of destroying falsity in the art form when he presented *Thérèse Raquin* at the Théâtre de la Renaissance on 11 July 1873. However, picking fights lines up a queue of enemies, and his contemporaries had already dubbed him 'A fat, pot-bellied whiner'. Various claques, including a vociferous faction for Victor Hugo, came along to boo. Many of the radicals considered the material too dirty for the stage and joined in. It closed after nine performances. A year later, Flaubert had his play *Le Candidat* booed off the stage. He set up a series of Dinners for Hissed Authors: Zola was an honoured guest. Yet the play was revived before long and it travelled, though maybe not as far as the argument. Whatever people thought of the play (and Ibsen thought Zola a 'gutter-wallower'), contemporaries across Europe, and those who came after, appreciated the early salvoes he was firing in the battle for truth.

Since this early rift between realism and naturalism, the two terms have become almost interchangeable, and have been taken up in so many ways and for so many diverging purposes as to be rendered almost meaningless. They can describe the use of vernacular language (Brendan Behan and Shelagh Delaney); the use of language fresh to the theatre (David Mamet); acting that is not rhetorical (many from Gerald du Maurier to Peggy Ashcroft); putting content on the stage that hasn't been seen before (from Ibsen to Edward Bond); the rhythms of life playing out without affectation (Chekhov); the anti-heroic comedy of life (Noël Coward); and a hundred other things. Some schools thought to be realistic turn out to be anything but. The Method school, originally intended to counterbalance the superficial charm of actors such as Cary Grant, quickly turned with its rhetoric of emotional intensity into a style considerably less truthful than Cary Grant's. There are as many forms of real as there are writers and actors heading towards truth.

The concern for honesty remains a vitalising cause. The quest still provides food for the soul fresher and less packaged than the theatre of mannerism and artificiality, which so frequently wants to dominate. A battle often renewed, it was the luck of the theatre that Zola was there in early proscenium days to lead the charge.

Feel the real.
Italian actress Giacinta Pezzana in *Teresa Raquin* at the Teatro dei Fiorentini, 1879

Henrik Ibsen
1828–1906

Twenty years ago, on 7 July 2005, four young men travelled down to London early in the morning, their studenty backpacks bearing an unquantifiable freight of pain. They hugged briefly at King's Cross station before separating in four directions, knowing within the hour they would be shredding their own and others' flesh and spirit. After every such event, one lurches around yearning for understanding. One can frame the history and the dispossession and the rage, but still not see the action clearly. I asked friends in dumb despair how anyone could do such things. I read history books, journal essays, and testimonies. Understanding is often resistant to applied effort: insight prefers to sneak in by a side door. The coincidence of two Ibsen plays on in London around the same time – *Hedda Gabler* and *The Wild Duck* – helped understanding down the road a little.

What was it about these two stories that seemed to match a moment of horror over a hundred years later? In both, an unfamiliar brand of hero expressed grave dissatisfaction with the reality surrounding them. Hedda is, among other things, trapped in a loveless and unfulfilling marriage, and in a society that cannot contain her energy or her desires. Gregers Werle in *The Wild Duck* is an evangelist with a dangerous addiction to honesty, who re-enters a world he has left behind determined to speak uncomfortable truths. Both destroy themselves and those around them. Hedda causes emotional mayhem before scattering her own brains with a gun – a 'beautiful death' in her pathological terminology – while Gregers shatters the happiness of a family and inadvertently causes the death of a young girl. Both consider themselves to be above the people around them, believing they perceive and articulate higher truths. In these two productions at that particular juncture, without being stage villains, Hedda and Gregers became unsympathetic to a degree hard to quantify. You wanted to storm the stage, grab and shake them, crying out, 'You! You're the problem! Not the rest of the world – you!'

Ibsen seemed to have diagnosed an ultramodern human type. Not the tragic heroes of Aristotle's construction, these were not figures of impressive charisma with a capacity for good who have taken a wrong turning and attracted the punishing finger of fate. Ibsen's protagonists had a minimal capacity for kindness, and expressed a dissatisfaction with life bordering on hatred. Their only purpose seemed to be the slow or rapid dismemberment of the happiness of others. Hedda operates in the austere surroundings of a Norwegian front room, and Gregers alters family dynamics in a small, nestlike attic, yet at that moment their governing impulse didn't seem a million miles from terrorists capable of inflicting blind and irreparable damage in a crowded train carriage. They seemed like ancestors.

We wouldn't look to Ibsen if we were wanting a flavour of mid-nineteenth-century Europe and its highways and byways. But to understand a new sense of human possibility, and to record the appearance of a new classification of the species, he is vital. Homo Ibseniens arrived, a lonely soul (male and, in a revolutionary stroke, also female), their persona forged in pain and frustration, who believe in a better world and their isolated capacity to perceive a path towards it. Whether Hedda or Gregers, the eponymous Brand or Borkman, Thomas Stockmann in *An Enemy of the People*, Rebecca West in *Rosmersholm*, Halvard Solness in *The Master Builder*, or Arnold Rubek in *When We Dead Awaken*, all these titans tower angry and desperate, like gods from a drawing room Valhalla. A distinct and tragic setting for the human.

Henrik Ibsen was born in a minuscule town, Skien, lost in the far south of an overlooked country which had been ruled by foreigners for a thousand years, and whose language was spoken only by its inhabitants. Norway had been handed over from Denmark to Sweden fifteen years before he was born in 1828, and didn't achieve full independence until a year before his death in 1906. The country had a rich folk culture, spoken and musical, but no formal culture to speak of. Ibsen transcended these beginnings to become the most important literary figure of his age. No writer included in these pages receives more doffs of the cap from peers. Shaw was an apostle in his fervour; Wilde not far behind; even smooth Pinero was a fan. Chekhov was a little frosty, but that may be explained by how much of the Moscow Art's repertory was taken up with works by the Norwegian. Ibsen revolutionised the theatre and its possibilities and scored the triple bullseye of raging scandal, regard from the academy, and cult success. In 1900, the young James Joyce, still a student, wrote of him: 'It must be questioned whether any man has held so firm an empire over the thinking world in modern times . . . his genius as an artist faces all, shirks nothing . . . the long roll of drama, ancient or modern, has few better things to show.'

His family, like that of Shakespeare, Dickens, Chekhov, Miller, and Williams, was comfortably off until a catastrophic fall left them poor as poor. The disaster galvanised Ibsen – as it did the others – and he resolved to rebound in triumph. His chosen mode of attack may have been influenced by playing with a puppet theatre with his mother as a child. One contemporary said he was a boy 'creative in solitude, who provoked peers with his superiority and arrogance' – the child clearly father to the man. By good fortune, having written two young efforts, he was given the directorship of the new state theatre in Bergen at the age of twenty-three. In control of a house which produced forty-four plays a year, he received a crash course in all things theatrical. His nerves must have been frayed, and the amount of information he absorbed about playmaking prodigious. He served up five plays of his own for this space – verse dramas on epic subjects – but the staple diet was translations of boulevard French classics, many by Eugène Scribe.

After five years, he moved on to the Norwegian Theatre in Christiania (now Oslo). Here the rate of output was just as hectic, and the pressure even higher with the national press on his case and the more exquisite and oppressive politics which accompany a higher profile messing with his head. Running a theatre is no walk in the park, and at any age that rate of turnover is spirit-sapping. Pile on the perceptions and vulnerabilities of a playwright, and it is surprising he survived. He almost didn't, hitting the bottle hard. Realising he had to get out before he lost the narrative, a group of friends raised enough money to augment a small government grant. This enabled him to travel and work in Italy. He didn't return for twenty-six years.

A crabby émigré, he remained the exemplar expat, upholding his Norwegian identity, wearing as many medals as would fit on his coat, and asserting his national hero status. He insisted his critics had sent him into prolonged exile, while eliding the fact he had found success abroad and chose not to return home. A true European, with Italy as his base, wherever he roamed his subject was always Norwegian life. His greatest plays were written in exile, and it was in the south that he found a way to remember and reimagine his north.

Ibsen's status as a presiding deity is assured, a mountain as grand as those which loom behind the settings of his work. The number of productions, together with a history of emotional effect on individuals and cultural effect on societies, ensures a monumental stature. But what sort of shadow does he cast? What influence has he exerted?

Ibsen said he had 'no time for flowers, children or music'. Beyond wondering how any artist, or any human, could say that, it is worth enquiring what sort of narratives are born, and what sort of purposes pursued, when anyone forgoes those joys.

His play *An Enemy of the People* is the first great work about institutional corruption and the individual conscience, serving as a template for stories including *Jaws* and *Erin Brockovich*. Revolving around the seepage of industrial toxins into a spa town's water supply, we watch the frantic attempts by the townsfolk to cover up the catastrophe. One man, Dr Stockmann, stands up for the truth and garners our fervent admiration. Slowly his integrity spills over into a zealous individualism, which shades into something akin to proto-fascism. The story just about holds together the damage caused by a collision between messianic integrity and the need to perceive the wants of others. Yet it provokes questions. As one graduates from admiration for Stockmann's integrity to wariness about his spiritual zeal, it is hard not to feel something similar about the author.

Ibsen's greatest attachment was always to truth, but his truth is a narrow and fierce one, and negligent of the perspectives of others. The metaphor from *Enemy of the People* that sticks, inadvertently, is the poisoning of the water. In examining the content he chose, and the disquiet he bequeathed to the world, it is sometimes difficult not to perceive a steady flow of toxins poured into the cultural river. Like his character Stockmann, one applauds Ibsen's adherence to integrity, and his outrage at corruption and dishonesty, while worrying that his imagined worlds leave little room for a democracy of points of view. Ibsen's attachment to his protagonists is fierce.

With major artists there can be a spacetime gap between their reflecting the reality of their age, and their birthing of a new one. Among the greats (and impossible not to include Ibsen) there is a capacity to rearrange the fabric. Shakespeare's perceptions of what it was to be human afforded us all a more complex way of being. Chekhov, with his grasp of life's impermanence and of the much ado which whirs above an abyss, birthed a tragicomic sensibility. Pinter created a landscape of brooding menace and inexplicable violence and waited for history to catch up. All conceived a universe and watched the world shift towards it. Hedda Gabler herself craves the influence of the artist, to 'change the destinies of others'. Ibsen's legacy is the lofty individual, the spiritual warrior at war with their herd.

Brand was his first major success at home and internationally. The author's statement that the eponymous main character represented 'himself in his best moments' is a worry. A young and passionate idealist forging a new religion based on terrifying fundamentalism, he sacrifices his mother – at slow and painful length – then his sick child, and finally his ultra-loving wife. All so he may live clean and clear. His enemy is compromise, and a small-town moral shabbiness portrayed in satiric brushstrokes. For some his spiritual absolutism is admirable; for others it is detestable and sad, the cruel posturing of someone with no capacity to see or hear other people. In *Hedda Gabler*, Eilert Lovborg is idealised by Hedda as someone who has never lived by petty man-made rules, who follows higher principles, a practice she tries to imitate. As with the person Stockmann becomes, these are tragic monuments to monomania.

We witness here an unmooring of the educated class, a moment when esoteric philosophies and lofty perceptions started to create a form of cultural apartheid. Power here is less about wealth or force than the mind. The narrative action of *Hedda Gabler* pivots around a manuscript; the agent of change in *Brand* is an unusual theology; other works revolve around sculptures, bold architecture, ideologies. Ibsen was writing for a new, well-educated audience endowed with intellectual excitement and a dangerous sense of superiority. Their presence in the theatre was now dominant, with the unruly gallery almost extinct for Ibsen. The mere act of attending a 'difficult' drama established entitlement. To further feed that, Ibsen furnished parables reinforcing their separation.

Thus sprach a new drama with a worrying dynamic. Characters reach out for invisible higher realms, a transcendental ambition funded by their contempt for the mess swirling beneath, and overwhelmingly fuelled by a pain writ large. Throughout Ibsen an uneasy equation of suffering with authenticity takes precedence. Only the truly anguished have access to truths, whether stifled wives in *A Doll's House* and *Hedda Gabler*; striving artists in *The Master Builder* and *When We Dead Awaken*; the bereaved parents in *Little Eyolf*; the failed businessman in *John Gabriel Borkman*; or any of the satellites of these titans who suffer from misplaced love. They seem to be running some marathon of agony, turbocharged by accidents and mishaps, refusing any trace of happiness, hoping to set new records for willed masochism. Cult status accretes around the tortured figures at the centre of Ibsen's dramas, their despair an end in itself, a means to heroic purity. This is the *homme* or *femme sérieux* writ large, suffused with self-congratulating Kierkegaardian woe.

Ibsen recognised and nailed this new manifestation of human despair, the desperate soul seeking authenticity. With prophetic powers he diagnosed an archetype that had a baleful effect on the twentieth century. A disturbing thread runs from the artist/man/woman of purity in Ibsen's plays through to the deluded extremist of the present day. He gave us Nietzsche's *Übermensch* figure in domestic dramatic form. He understood before anyone the danger in ideologues of all brands, their adamantine certainty, and their attachment to loneliness. At the same time, there is a queasy suspicion he was seduced by them himself and served to glamourise them further. Where we see only a fleeting connection between Sophocles and Oedipus, or between Shakespeare and Othello, Lear or Hamlet, there is a troubling degree of self-identification between Ibsen and his statuary of heroes.

Crucially, Ibsen fails to test any of his spiritual legislators in perspectives that would help others see their failings. At the very least, a sense of humour would mitigate the suspicion that, detestable as they are, he wants us to admire them. Comedy, a physical context, the importance of others, any of these qualities would provide a friction which seems absent. All that matters is a commitment to an idea of 'truth'.

One can suffer from veil-tearing fatigue. At a recent, rather brilliant production of *Rosmersholm*, I lost count of the number of times the characters tore off their own and each other's masks. Every time the play seemed to settle in an accepted truth, a voice would cannon, 'But noooooo . . .', and we would be off again, digging for a deeper stratum. In *Peer Gynt,* our hero famously peels an onion, contemplating with each layer his many selves – fraud, liar, survivor, gold digger, cheat:

> There's an alarming number of layers!
> Will we get through to the kernel?
> There is no kernel! In its deepest heart
> It remains just layers, ever smaller.

Yep, but it's still an onion. And no two onions, nor any two layers, are the same.

Just as there is an absence of sunshine in the landscape, or tenderness in the relationships, there is a fatal lack of jokes. Having trawled afresh through a substantial number of his plays, I am at pains to find a single worthwhile joke in the canon. (For a man who showed so little humour in life, he came up with a brilliant gag on his deathbed in 1906. When his nurse assured a visitor he was a little better, Ibsen spluttered, 'On the contrary.' And died.) There are a few funny stock characters – the prattling old lady, the drunken buffer, the uppity servant – but they provoke little more than cringe. One work – *An Enemy of the People* – has the temerity to describe itself as a comedy. This wouldn't be a fallacy in itself – Ibsen could claim good company with the Greeks, Racine, Corneille, Goethe, and Schiller at the low end of the laughometer – if he didn't claim to be a naturalist. He saw much of his mission as returning reality to the stage, but what a woeful, artificially bleak reality.

The bleakness might be more palatable, if not so deliberately chosen. Much of the pain appears to be at the deluxe end of the market. These are often people leading comfortable lives, awash in luxury provided by an army of staff (whose more immediate agonies are ignored). Even the bankrupts or failures like John Gabriel Borkman seem to have no trouble working up lunch. Yet what the world has to offer is shunned in favour of the glamour of spiritual agony. In the absence of flowers, children, or music, only the martyrdom mattered. As much as we admire obsession in an artist, if they take no food from the world, the work is undernourished. 'Ibsen the fanatical sceptic,' wrote Strindberg. 'So repellent, so attractive.' (Though Ibsen reciprocated this animosity to Strindberg in public, his final study was dominated by a large painting of his Swedish contemporary.)

The lack of contact with external reality in these characters is matched by the prime failing in the writing: a lack of textural context. Everything in their progress towards conclusions feels shaped, arranged. Not for nothing did Ibsen admire Scribe and his mechanical perfection. There is no aimlessness here, no love for the nurdles and noodles of existence. While living in Munich, Ibsen saw the socially realistic prose plays of fellow Norwegian playwright Bjørnstjerne Bjørnson. They inspired him to start the process of what would become *The Pillars of Society*. While writing it, Ibsen watched a production of his own play *The Pretenders* by the troupe of the Duke of Saxe-Meiningen, famous for their fastidious verismo. He thought and studied hard to write in this new style. The hard work shows in the effort he made to escape his old poetic rhetoric, and in the fact it is highly effortful. We never see those meandering digressions, those daft non sequiturs and cul-de-sacs which convince us writers are observing a world outside their heads.

The lack of naturalistic detail impoverishes. In *Ghosts*, we get a first, a second, and a third act all in the same drawing room. Between each act we jump from morning to afternoon to night. Any attempt at following the shifting light of the day is dismissed by declaring there is a persistent thin drizzle outside. Characters come and go, but offer little sense of why they are there, how they are negotiating the furniture, what they are thirsty or hungry for. Between Acts I and II they have a big lunch. We might imagine this could induce indigestion or lassitude or at least a comment, but there's nothing. They yadda-yadda at the end of Act I, and the moment they reappear in Act II they yadda-yadda on the same theme. For Act III, the orphanage down the hill is on fire, and any number of opportunities for watching the blaze, feeling the cold, feeling exhausted, feeling hungry, anything is available, but no, after a couple of cursory comments, they pick up the yadda-yaddaing where they left it. Detail is eschewed so the logic of Ibsen's admittedly brilliant schematic about sexual hypocrisy can be worked out. Purity and intensity yes, but at what cost?

Some plastic sense is vital to the theatre. At its worst during the twentieth century, it degenerated into fussy fiddling with cocktail sticks around drinks cabinets. But a well-placed prop, a forceful symbol, any surprising object can have a potent effect. A great writer can draw the class violence out of a pepper pot. Even Strindberg, nearly as abstracted a soul as Ibsen, was able to shape fictions around iconic objects – the canary in *Miss Julie*, the flowers in *Easter* – all encased within settings where one senses the grimy hems of the curtains, the dirt under the character's fingernails. In *The Wild Duck*, Ibsen creates in the attic of the family a *mise en scène* full of shade and resonance, and writes a continuous dining scene both real and swirling with tensions. The achievement of texture in that play only makes the absence of it elsewhere all the odder. Too often it feels like the mirror is held up to thought not phenomena, a quality perhaps accentuated by long absence from his homeland. The lack leaves us feeling confined within a mental claustrophobia.

Ibsen was not forever stuck in the drawing room, nor did he begin his career bearing a flag for neurosis. The early plays were epics of poetry and action traversing historic landscapes. His favourite work, *Emperor and Galilean*, was an overambitious two-play, ten-act spectacular charting the battles of the Emperor Julian against the rise of the Christian faith. Sadly, these big-lunged, capacious uber-dramas failed. His attempts to revive the narrative freedom Elizabethan writers enjoyed were unfeasible within the theatre of his day. Chariots and togas rarely look anything but awkward framed in the baroque decor of a proscenium. Paradoxically, it was after he left Norway and gave up on the plays he wanted to write that his reputation flowered. Only once he took the ambition of his attempted epics and concentrated it into crucibles of contemporary hysteria did his audiences go wild.

One aspiring masterpiece did survive the restrictions of the proscenium – *Peer Gynt*, his rumbustious picaresque about the carefree and driven sprite who goes on an odyssey through a smorgasbord of realities. Beginning in a contemporary working-class world, Gynt hikes off into the mountains, has an escapade with trolls, makes a fortune in America, disappears into the desert, gets locked in an asylum in Egypt, before making his weary and weather-beaten way home to the woman who loves him. Each world is not only different in itself but observed through a fresh lens. At one moment, Ibsen is writing with realist precision about peasant life; at another he is writing like an early Beckett in a chamber of echoing voices; at another it is a panto with lots of perky trolls; and later there is Brechtian satire among international financiers. Each time the story moves the framing shifts. There is no rigid consistency, or stylistic uniformity, and the play is much the better for it.

The sense of adventure, heady as it is, is not what sets it apart. Tenderness distinguishes it. The first section displaying Gynt's brutality, his sexual wantonness, and his desire to exclude himself from the throng is resistible. Here is another egregious Homo Ibseniens, busy separating himself from the herd, rising above and looking down, like the others. Then suddenly, as he sits with his dying mother, there is an excursion into a different vein. Silence and gentleness descend. He tells his mother a story, tucks her in, allows quiet to enter a noisy play, and her spirit passes in peace. No matter that he is a pig and she was a wayward influence, the access of love startles. The sensibility spins into original territory and makes all that comes after rich and complex in a manner that feels unique. Human need asserts itself, the need for touch that sits within the squalling independence of all those self-made warriors of the spirit. The friction between the two, the clutch for others, and the drive to be alone, fills the play with emotional tension.

A zanily contrary episode occurs late in the play after Gynt has gone down on a sinking ship. He floats in the sea, clinging to a section of keel. He is soon joined by the ship's cook, who clutches the keel with equal force. They realise at speed it cannot take the weight of both, and with a farcical relish start beating each other around the head. The cook loses and is washed away. Promptly Gynt risks his life to save him. A graphic and *plastic* demonstration of the tension that holds the whole play taut. His soul is caught between the need to survive and the need to belong. Oscillation between separation and attachment keeps Peer Gynt mysterious and breathing.

Elsewhere the heroes separate so wholly there is no chance of them returning. Suspense goes AWOL. With Gynt, after the episode with his mother, we never know which way he will pitch. He wants to devour the world – to be an emperor, an existential hero, a dreamer, an artist – but he is always being called back to his home, to his long-lost love Solveig and to ultimate connection. The path of the self leads to a madhouse in Egypt. There he finally realises we only discover our true identity in the hall of mirrors that is the eyes of others.

Ibsen did not think of himself as the creator of modernism in the theatre, though many ascribed that to him later. But his ambition was allied to the modernist cause. He believed he was leading us up the mountain to a better place, a clear-skied and cold plateau with a better view of human folly. 'In every play, I have aimed at my own spiritual emancipation and purification,' he wrote, stating that his calling was 'to wake the people and make them think big'. Modernism, with its continual revolution against its immediate predecessors, its desire to purify and clarify, is based on an assumption of continual progress. How one wishes Ibsen could have stilled his ambition, relaxed, had an ice cream, talked to some people, and enjoyed the sun on his face. 'An author who wants to achieve anything,' he wrote, 'must isolate himself and live alone in his thoughts and for his work.' Hmm . . . If he wanted society to be his subject, it might not have hurt to give time to it.

The relentless yearning for tomorrow which itches through his work often seems to block out the joys of the past and the charisma of the present. We are now understanding afresh that at many times the past may have been more organic, more holistic, more merry, more light, and more democratic than today. If we do not respect that past and bear some of its benefits into our present we are impoverished. The relentless desire to move forward restricts. Time as progress was an aggrandising European conceit in the industrial and colonial eras, and a terrifying technological one now. Ultimately, a blind drive forward becomes an obstacle to full insight, because eternity is only ever with us when we allow time to curl back on itself, when we allow past, present and future to meet in the here and now.

In *Peer Gynt* this sense is made manifest, as it is glimpsed whenever his heroes realise briefly what they have missed through all their striving. In those rare moments, they understand the value of one another. Yet more often than not, they and their creator, Ibsen, push forward, troubled but determined, climbing, improving, trying to shape a future out of an ideal picture in their heads, desperate to teach the world a beautiful lesson. Whatever the destruction that may tumble in their wake.

Young Peer, old Peer.
Henrik Klausen as Peer Gynt, Christiania Theater, Oslo, 1876

Georges Feydeau
1862–1921

What is that thing the French can do that no one else can? And why are the English, their close neighbours, so damned poor at what those neighbours excel at? The French series *Call My Agent!* delighted the world, tickled up laughter and demonstrated, like a perfectly baked soufflé, that imperceptibly immaculate combination of weight and lightness. The English version, *Ten Percent*, followed the same scripts, cast awesome actors, aimed in the same direction, and came out like a series of meat pies. Where was the elan? The éclat? And what do those words mean? A certain deft lightness of touch, a speed of thought, an invisibility of effort, sudden flicks of the lightest violence? The dictionary provides us with 'vigorous spirit of enthusiasm' for elan, which is too hearty by half, and with 'ostentatious display' for éclat, which sounds too greedy for something best achieved with modesty. When we invited a French company to bring a version of *Much Ado About Nothing* to a festival at the Globe, the play was transformed into the dextrous sophisticated comedy it always wants to be. We sat, laughing and gawping, and wondered how they did it. While we tend to play light comedy like heavy-legged middle-distance runners dragging themselves around the last lap, the spry and lean French come bouncing past, floating on their own insouciance – boing boing! (There's a joke about farce there.)

In our age of globalism, it is a treat that so much culture is still specific to place. The Bangla drum is best played and heard in Bangladesh; Noh theatre looks daft when imitated elsewhere; Yoruban culture makes most sense when emerging from Yoruban people. I have worked in Spain on Lope de Vega plays, and there are things Spanish actors can do that no one else can – an electrifying speed of incantatory delivery, an openness of passion, and an Olympian capacity to sustain a heavy-lidded smoulder over long arcs of verse. I have worked with actors in Italy and delighted at the irreverence and joy and wit with which they clown, drawing on the centuries-old tradition of *commedia*. All these qualities evanesce when imitated by awkward boys from Oxbridge unearthing their inner clowns. Cheese tastes better in France, beer in Germany, and dumplings in Beijing – in an era that likes to homogenise we should be grateful for such differences.

The farces of Georges Feydeau, largely written between 1886 and 1914, are the quintessence of this elusive what-is-it-called. *Fin de siècle* masterpieces, they largely revolve around hanky-panky and deceptions involving the urban middle class. Their world is sometimes invaded by a duc or comtesse from a class or two above, or by a bellboy or police officer from the one below, and there is often a light sprinkling of volatile Russians, or passionate Spaniards, or blundering English to tickle Parisian prejudice, but it is dominantly a bourgeois universe. Characters are identifiable without ever becoming so vivid as to usurp the primacy of plot. What is crucial and often overlooked is that at the beginning they must seem nonchalant and unflappable in the loftiest Parisian manner, all laissez-faire and Gallic shrugs, so their descent into screaming mania is the more remarkable. They also usually have a strong fund of antipathy among themselves. As Feydeau said, 'When I sit down to write a play I identify those characters who have every reason to avoid each other; and I make it my business to bring them together as soon, and as often, as I can.' Together they interact to confect a world of prosaic solidity, which we watch as it fractures into frenzy. The engine for the escalating mayhem is usually adultery, attempted or achieved, or a suspicion of it, blended with misunderstandings, deceptions, and mistaken identity. The matrix of disempowering confusion leaves the characters trapped within patterns of chance and behaviour, which grow a terrifying logic of their own.

Almost always in three acts, the first will imperil something of weight, habitually a marriage, and will establish the desperate need for secrecy. In the second, we move to a separate locale, often an insalubrious hotel, where our leading characters are forced into stratagems of subterfuge or duplicity to uncover or further conceal the secret. The third act attempts to restore the normality and order of the status quo, though the happiness of the ending is usually precarious, given the chaos that has erupted. Throughout, possibilities of hope or disaster pivot on split-second choices as couples criss and cross the stage in ever more bewildering mazes, doors flung open as others slam shut to reveal ever more baroque potential combinations. At a magical moment, the characters' initial objectives are suspended as the game takes on an inexplicable momentum of its own. In these moments of divine chaos, when solid folk find themselves tested in dissipating whirlpools of madness, the plays reach dimensions far beyond their everyday springboards and enter a plane of pure existence, as in the most elemental tragedy. An early French critic trying to analyse how these plays spin so airily from concrete beginnings said simply, 'It doesn't look like anything and it looks like everything. It's made of everything, and it's made of nothing.' Such words could apply to Samuel Beckett or *King Lear*.

Essential to the execution of all this is speed and precision. The action starts at a canter, is galloping by the beginning of the second act, hits breakneck speed by the middle, before accelerating to a pace bearing no relation to reality. As the third act winds down, it eases its way back to a canter. It rarely trots. And never walks. The prestissimo of the action is crucial to the suspension of disbelief. If the audience has time to think, or catch their breath, the house of cards will tumble. Dizziness and giddiness are the desired effects. It is here that Feydeau's most original mirroring of the world is captured. France was the centre of the West in the 1890s. Britain may have had the power but France had the culture, the innovation, and excitement. Paris was the draw. A city where trams and trains were shifting crowds at new speeds, cinemas were showing humans in new lights and telegrams were spreading the word at new velocities. Life was accelerating. A rumour that might have crawled around Paris in a previous century, moving at the rate of an arrondissement a month, now flew across the city in an afternoon. Drama had to quicken to match. Feydeau dramatises both the speed and the loss of control that went with it. We see here the beginnings of Futurism, with its vision of mankind marching to the frenzied beat of a whirring electric machine. Just as today, we shiver at the prospect of descending into a world run by AI, our forebears were beginning to fear entrapment in the technology of their age.

Precision is expressed in the arrangement of incidents. Economy and elegance in the plotting is at the heart of Feydeau's achievement, as with Eugène Scribe. Jokes are absent, verbal wit is secondary, characterisation is cursory: all are subjugated to pattern. Working with a hypnotic exactitude, the storytelling is so well arranged, symmetrical, and mechanical that technique blooms into art, a victory of pure form.

Clockwork is the word most frequently used in relation to Feydeau's craft. He wrote his first play at the age of six, and when he showed it to an experienced playwright, the man said, 'My boy, your play is stupid, but it is theatrical. You will be a man of the theatre.' Feydeau served an apprenticeship with one-act plays and wrote with the measurement and precision of an engineer. Previous farceurs, such as Eugène Labiche, wrote with a discursive looseness: Feydeau tightened the screws. For critics this can lead to a rigid regularity, but there is something maniacal within it, a cruel pleasure in entrapping characters, actors, and audience within claustrophobic mechanisms. The gathering hysteria is flecked with a terror that the game will never end. Jonathan Lynn, the farceur behind *Yes, Prime Minister*, described the form succinctly as 'the worst day of your life'. We laugh uproariously but there is inflection in the laughter. We fear our own attempts to impose order will fail similarly, leaving us trapped in a vortex, a prison of our own making.

With bitter irony, such was the fate of the clockmaker. Feydeau, who created such elegant and controlled patterns onstage, led a life surrounded by mess. An inveterate gambler and a bad one, his marriage a calamity, and ever afflicted by depression, his mind deteriorated to such an extent late in life that his family called in the doctors. Their judgement was dementia, the result of tertiary syphilis. He was committed to a sanatorium near Paris, where he lived out his last two years under the impression he was Napoleon III organising his government and stage-managing his coronation. Released from this mental jail two years later, he died aged fifty-eight.

So what is that thing the French – and thus Feydeau – can do, their special capacity to reduce us to a laughter close to abandonment, a sort of narcotics-free delirium? A dash of craziness, a sprinkling of mischief, and without wishing to further stereotype, a soupçon of sexiness? (When we entertained the French company, we did notice several of them disappearing into the night with just-met companions.) So several crucial ingredients in the bouillabaisse, but as with any stew there will be myriad other components. And some secret ingredient – as there should be – known only to the chefs.

Je ne sais quoi.

Whole-hearted ensemble work.
La puce à l'oreille (*A Flea in Her Ear*),
Théâtre des Nouveautés, Paris, 1906

Arthur Wing Pinero
1855–1934

For much of an exceptionally long writing career, Arthur Wing Pinero was – for many – the high-water mark of British theatre. The longevity is mind-boggling; his first piece written for the Globe in 1877 and his last for the Duchess in 1932, a continued commercial productivity of fifty-five years. Within that time, he wrote a profusion of farces, a gaggle of comedies, librettos and burlesques, and a handful of problem 'social' dramas. Within a wide community he was revered as the maestro. An affectionate/amorous introduction to his works by an acolyte called Clayton Hamilton from the 1930s is embarrassing in its fulsomeness, posing Pinero as the saviour of British theatre, awoken after a long sleep since the time of Shakespeare.

For Hamilton, the British theatre had been cast into a prolonged doze by the Puritans, and then sedated by the degeneracy of the Restoration. Recovery was hindered by the swamping influence of the Stratford Bard, and by the preponderance of great acting as the motor of British theatre rather than great plays. These are sound, if sweeping, points. More astute is noting the lack of any effective international copyright legislation, which made it convenient and *cheaper* for a commercial management to steal a French play and pay for a quickie translation than to commission original work. Whatever the spell that induced the coma, for Hamilton it took Prince Pinero to hack his way through the undergrowth and plant his kiss on the sleeping princess for her to flutter her eyelids and awaken to life.

In later years, Pinero was the ultimate clubbable elder, pottering in and out of the Garrick, immaculately turned out, his face and fashion overshadowed by his preternaturally bushy eyebrows. Sir Arthur was the first playwright to be knighted (taking W. S. Gilbert to be a lyricist), his honour coming in 1909 after much canvassing by George Bernard Shaw, who felt the movement for a national theatre needed a titled figurehead.

Pinero had travelled a long way to achieve his apotheosis as the quintessential Edwardian gent. From Portuguese Jewish ancestry, he was born in 1855 into a family of solicitors. Serving his apprenticeship as a proper 'rogue and vagabond' player, he eked out a hard living for ten years as a jobbing actor in shows touring the provinces. He despaired at the shabby standards of production and chaotic rehearsals. Small wonder he later became a tyrannically precise director of his own plays.

Soon he found himself alongside quality craftsmen, falling in briefly with the Bancrofts before they acquired the Haymarket, and spending five years at the Lyceum with Henry Irving. It is hard to overestimate the influence of this latter company and its megalomaniacal master, also known as the Guvnor. Irving was determined to make the theatre respectable and banish its outlaw reputation. He transformed the Lyceum into a hybrid of high temple of the performing arts, hot celebrity circus, and green room for politicians and royals. This cause consumed all his energies and eventually killed him, dying on tour halfway up the staircase of the Midland Hotel in Bradford, allegedly in the arms of his amanuensis and slave, Bram Stoker. But not before he had manifested his dream and become the first knighted actor. In retrospect, the hankering after honours looks lickspittle, but for Irving, who had spent his early years shivering in midwinter on carts shunting from venue to venue across the Pennines, the honour had weight.

Pinero was a 'utility man' for the Lyceum company, a Victorian euphemism for spear carrier and dogsbody. He pushed his opportunity hard, and among a host of other juvenile dramas wrote three curtain-raisers. He pushed sufficiently hard that he was asked to leave, since, as he put it, 'Irving did not want to have a dramatist around.' The apprenticeship served him in good stead, as did dozens of failed plays. In the antique allegory of Clayton Hamilton, 'A dramatic author must have many plays "killed under him" before he can be promoted to a position of command.' Before long, Pinero discovered his genius as a farceur, approaching his work as an exercise in technical craft, while also giving licence to an ebullient sense of humour and a taste for ripe and fruity characters who hovered midpoint between caricature and the grotesque. Like Feydeau, he knew the comic value of seeing the staid and solid liquified by panic and hysteria. This ability he maximised in some of the funniest plays in the English language, including *The Magistrate* and *The Cabinet Minister*, both revived recently in London and still evergreen.

Pinero understood it was a time of change and pivoted with it. Ibsen's *Ghosts* had erupted onto the London stage and he saw it was a game changer. He was critical of Ibsen, disliking the thesis part of thesis-drama, and preferring concrete portraiture to abstractions. But he knew that benevolent comedy would no longer satisfy an audience who appreciated a serious approach to human misconduct and social problems. Though critics fulminated against this 'gutter filth', and polite society dismissed the original Scandi noir as needlessly avant-garde, Pinero knew that what was reviled today would be the fashion of tomorrow. He read the lush drawing room tragedies of Dumas *fils*, and more Ibsen. His first attempt at the *drame moderne* or problem play, *The Profligate* of 1889, was chosen to open the new Garrick Theatre. The ending – the suicide of a man whose past misdeeds have returned to claim his soul – was deemed too edgy by the management. They insisted it be softened by the saintliness of a forgiving wife; Pinero reluctantly acceded. For his next foray into seriousness, there would be no compromise.

The Second Mrs Tanqueray shifted the central role to 'a woman with a past'. In the course of it, Paula, a society survivor and an intriguingly inchoate presence, lost between a liberated modernity she can't enact and an idea of purity she can't recall, walks dazed and drunk towards suicide. The Garrick turned it down immediately. When Pinero offered it to actor-manager George Alexander at the St James, he responded bluntly, 'Sorry, I daren't do it.' Thankfully for the play, Alexander grew a backbone and changed his mind. This is no Ibsen, but it displays Pinero's usual storytelling chops, and a surprising spring of human empathy. A heartfelt need for tolerance and mercy shines through in an age that judged fast and crushingly hard. Both playwright and manager worried it was too strong a flavour for the Victorian stomach, but it proved a hit, running for almost a year and making an astronomical profit of £10,000 (approximately £1.7 million in today's money). A critic declared that 'nothing in the history of the modern stage has been more remarkable than the success gained by Pinero's latest, boldest and most brilliant play.'

High praise continued for his *drame moderne* throughout the Edwardian period, yet has not reverberated down through time. This may be because the initial gushing was excessive; or perhaps it was an excess of meretricious facility in the plotting. The odd inertness of the titles can't have helped. *The Second Mrs Tanqueray* doesn't sing but it sounds like a cooing dove beside the title for Pinero's favourite work – *The Notorious Mrs Ebbsmith*. Hard for any play to recover from that title. It could be he suffered from bad literary timing, being sandwiched between Ibsen and Wilde, Shaw and Maugham. Possibly the problem plays simply lack the vitality of the comic. Something in his farces allowed him to cut loose into the realms of invention the social plays struggled to match.

Above all, he was a character writer. As he described it, he envisioned a group of people who invited him to investigate them. He would retire to the country for a month or so to get intimate with these imaginary acquaintances, receiving them as guests: 'When they talk, I listen to them. When they act, I watch them. When they wait, I wait for them. Of course, if they disturb themselves at dinner time, I have no dinner.' Such vigorous beings were given more licence to express themselves riotously in farce than in the artificially restrained dramas. (It remains an irresistible pleasure to hear characters erupt into 'Pish! Pash! and Pah!' There's little of this in the serious plays and a lot in the silly plays.)

Most treasurable is the work that lands in a drifting place, moving freely in and out of comedy and documentary and sentiment and homage – his love letter to his own profession, *Trelawny of the Wells*. The onward and cruel march of fashion scars this play, as does the perennial problem of class. Here as elsewhere it is almost impossible to overstate the distance between the classes. This era-defining chasm is revealed in *Trelawny*, alongside the miraculous power of the theatre to help people ladder up and snake down. A star of the Barridge Wells Theatre, Rose

Trelawny marries into the aristocracy, where she soon atrophies, before returning to the theatre to rediscover her lost mojo.

Happily, within the company is one Tom Wrench, an affectionate and astute tribute to Tom Robertson, the writer whose light-touch theatrical realism had inaugurated the form in which Pinero now thrived. When praised as a pioneer, Arthur was quick to correct: 'If it hadn't been for Robertson, I should never have been able to do what I have done.' Tom Wrench writes in a less rhetorical, gentler and more natural tone, and the melody is one with which Rose, changed by her brief immersion in the outside world, is able to harmonise. Pinero doesn't only give us Robertson, he gives us the adventure of Marie Bancroft's first theatre, a company to which he casts back an adoring eye – he described *Trelawny of the Wells* as his sole experiment in autobiography. As Imogen, a young actress (clearly an homage to Marie), rushes in with the offer of a new theatre and some early investment, she lists her ad hoc budget – five hundred pounds for a theatre, two hundred pounds for refurbishment, three hundred pounds for the first production – and one feels the excitement of the first stirrings of the Prince of Wales.

'Let's put on a show' is one of the most ineluctably charming rallying cries of any play within a play, and travels down from Bottom and Quince in *A Midsummer Night's Dream* to any number of musicals. In *Trelawny*, it supplies the usual quickening heartbeat of madcap optimism, along with the sense of genuine change.

Bold facial hair choice.
The Magistrate poster, printed by Clement-Smith & Co, Lithographer, London, 1885

August Strindberg
1849–1912

On a surreal and funny American website there are five animated short films within which August Strindberg, the definitive Swedish gloomy-boots, addresses a wife, his children, nature, and the elements in tones of sepulchral despair. To his intense annoyance, a small bright pink balloon named Helium bounces around, imitating his words in a high-pitched voice and spraying cascades of joy. Strindberg scowls. He has been rumbled. Check it out on www.strindbergandhelium.com.

Something about the Swede invites a risible response. When you read his biography and stumble across his seventy-third suicide threat to lovers and friends, you wonder whether they weren't tempted to have a whip-round and buy a rope. He sometimes seems in on the joke, aware how comical his extremity is. When Ibsen looks out from his photos, you are confronted by a flattening stare, a man marbled into a monument. Strindberg glares wildly and, in the excess effort, there is something fragile. 'Look at me, I'm glaring,' it proclaims. Behind it glimmers a twinkle of humour.

Strindberg took being cranky to new heights. He acted as the back end of a horse not once but three times, and a fourth with his second wife. Once while out walking in violent rain sharing an umbrella, he stopped, shut his brolly, and banged it against a tree, destroying both shaft and fabric. 'Damnation!' he cried. 'If our Lord allows it to rain, he must mean it to fall on us mortals too!' He halted his first child's baptismal service in a fury because his best friend had forgotten to wear his medals. 'Where are your medals?' he screamed. 'When I invite people to a baptismal party they must wear everything!' The service was delayed for two hours until his friend returned fully bedecked. In his most committed act of insensitivity, when his first wife was in labour, he tenderly leaned over and told her she was not to scream, since everyone knew childbirth was a naturally pleasurable experience for a woman. To have done this once would have been audacious but, Strindberg being Strindberg, he repeated the advice for wife number 2. To cap the parade of eccentricities, three centuries after most people had given up the ghost on alchemy, Strindberg still experimented, his hands stained and bleeding as he tried to convert iron into gold.

One of my favourite instances of quintessential Strindbergism came early in his life. In 1873, a new insurance company was founded. In order to turn a fast buck, Strindberg wrote a naive and sentimental story in which a young girl is persuaded of the benefits of life insurance. The company was so pleased they asked him to edit their new insurance periodical. All started well, but after a few issues boredom set in, so he wrote a strident article about overloaded and overinsured 'coffin-ships', which took the periodical and the parent company down with it. Strindberg never bit the hand that fed him, he wolfed the whole arm.

Many labels have been thrown at him, and the bad ones stick. Misogynist was loudest at the time, and since. It's hard to square entirely with the man who wrote complex and sensitive roles for women and campaigned throughout his life for universal suffrage. He searched Europe for the fiercest and most independent women to love. His three wives – Siri von Essen, Frida Uhl, and Harriet Bosse – were sophisticated, tough, gifted, and liberated. Each was consumed with passion for Strindberg, then having figured him out, resolved to put a considerable distance between them. They also each, in separate memoirs, declared they would love him till their dying day.

Throughout the work, he places strong female characters onstage and shows his own, and his characters', terror of them. The titular Miss Julie battles her inheritance and her below stairs staff with flagrant independence; Tekla dances through the triangle of *Creditors* with the strength of the unknowable; and Alice digs her trench with relish for the war of attrition with her husband in *The Dance of Death*. Tough women, and Strindberg wants his men (and to a degree himself) to wrestle with them. There is something more honest and respectful about that bellicosity than the ubiquitous penchant for the perfect 'strong woman' of contemporary television drama. It is a war, but conducted, as far as Strindberg was able, on a level playing field.

Most of his major working relationships with publishers and theatres were carried out in comradeship with Jewish colleagues, remarking of his first publisher, 'Seligmann is the most enlightened person I know.' This was probably one of only three recorded compliments to pass his lips. Yet the gibe of antisemitism is impossible to shrug off, since he also wrote sordidly foul comments. Self-control was never a feature. In a long career, filling volumes with castles of gold thread and dungeons of dross, he contradicted himself on every subject known to man. An absence of intellectual organisation disorients his output. He let his rage burn wherever wind and time and circumstance took it. 'I am the biggest fire in Sweden,' he proclaimed. Such energy is its own meaning.

A friend praised a recent production of *The Dance of Death* as 'unhinged'. He celebrated this as a relief since everything modern seemed tediously 'hinged'. The play isolates a married couple locked in mutual loathing on a remote island. The antagonism of Edgar and Alice, sustained over two plays, instigated a series of feuding lovers who carried on warring through the proscenium century, climaxing in Edward Albee's George and Martha in *Who's Afraid of Virginia Woolf?* For Strindberg, to make a play entirely filled by marital strife – and nothing else – was a transformative leap of endeavour into new content. The unhingedness incorporates a carnival of psychoses – the monomania of the central pair, the eruptive physical jerkings of the colonel, the paranoia of their interplay with a third character, Kurt, and nasty whispers of vampirism and cannibalism. Beside the smooth transformational arcs of modern writing, such broil proves an emancipating wilderness. This is what Strindberg brought to the party: the courage to embrace derangements. His was not a theatre to occlude the strangeness of reality, he turned perversity into a firework display.

Strindberg has proven a perennial on the back of only a few iconic works. His surrealist extravagances – *A Dream Play*, *To Damascus*, *The Great Highway* – appear all too rarely. A theatre starved of the imaginatively free can always benefit from their nonsensical exuberance. However, his staple works – *Miss Julie*, *The Father*, *Creditors*, and *The Dance of Death* – are never far away from the world's stages. In 2005, I had the good fortune to direct *Easter*, his vernal miniature of light and redemption. The direct encounter with Strindberg's work was as vivifying and nourishing as anyone could wish for.

The works have flourished without being epic of scale or, in truth, locked in the public memory. While their flavour may be known – we expect hyperrealism, mythic oppositions, and men and women locked in claustrophobic antipathy – we are less familiar with any given play. He often seems to stand more for a weather system than a particular work. 'Ah, yes, Strindberg . . .' people mutter with an air of meaning, and then move on before getting into any detail.

In a formal sense he was a restless innovator. Whatever the medium, he was happy to fall on his face in uncovering fresh ways to deliver old truths. In the early days of photography, he eschewed stiff bourgeois tableaux – families surrounded by the accoutrements of wealth – for what he called 'psychological portraits'. In shots of himself, loved ones, and friends, he attempted to capture the essence of each person. In his painting, he absorbed lessons from the Impressionists and adapted them into a distinctive personal style. He innovated in technique, daubing paint with a thick sculptural impasto, which prefigured some of the roughness of later experiment. His favourite content he described as 'the sea, with the coast in the foreground: gnarled pines, a few naked rocks in the distance, a white beacon, a sea-mark, a buoy. The sky was usually overcast, with a faint or a strong light on the horizon; sunsets or moonlight; never clear day.'

Never clear day serves as an effective summary of his dramatic work. His stage directions have great specificity about the power of light. *Easter* charts in three acts the progress from a glimmer of sunshine blotted by clouds in Act I, through a murky lamplit darkness disturbed by shadows in Act II, to a grey day ambushed by spring sunshine in Act III. His opus is as susceptible to the shifts of light as an early summer day when clouds pass swiftly. He wrote overweening historical epics, allegorical spiritual journeys, surreal fantasias such as *A Dream Play*, and in the best-known works compressed this eruptive and imaginative energy into hermetic spaces – *Miss Julie*, *The Father*, *The Dance of Death*, and *Easter*.

The purpose of artistic innovation for Strindberg was not an end in itself, nor a way of demonstrating how interestingly different he could be. He raged and hungered to find ways of living life anew – socially, morally, and sexually. His era was a prodigious one for reimagining the rules. While the English may associate the nineteenth century with the adjective Victorian, and the repressive morality that walked alongside it, much of the Continent was having a ball, déjeuner-ing sur l'herbe merrily and enjoying all sorts of postprandial refreshment. The sexual mores of Sweden at the time made the 1960s in Britain look like a Tuesday lunchtime in Tunbridge Wells.

Stockholm, Strindberg's birthplace, was reinventing itself at speed, accelerating from a small almost medieval town to a flourishing European metropolis in the space of fifty years. Great dramatists are often magicked into existence by the bursting entrepreneurial energy of certain epochs; the rapaciously expanding consciousness of Athens produced Aeschylus, Sophocles, Euripides, and Aristophanes; the greedy human bustle of Elizabethan London gave birth to Shakespeare and his contemporaries; and the technological revolutions and monumental urban growth of nineteenth-century northern Europe gave us Ibsen, Chekhov, and Strindberg. In several decades, we may be heralding the millennial renaissance of Beijing and Shanghai.

The search for the new was a search for freedom. Genuine, comprehensive freedom, from all forms of coercion, and all received thinking. The hunger for that stares out of Strindberg's cold-as-ice eyes. He got into a thousand messes because of that need; it led to disasters in his professional, social, and emotional life, but he could not let the ambition go. He could never organise this desire for liberty into a clear intellectual programme. Whenever he got close to one, he would throw everything up in the air, fearing that anything coherent would become repressive. Such self-subversion manifested over and over.

Such an attitude led to shattered marriages, recurring dismissal by the critical academies of Europe, a social loneliness, and a life of almost complete penury. Yet, on Strindberg's last birthday, his sixty-third, when he climbed out of bed in his small flat in Drottninggatan, a district in Stockholm, and walked to his fourth-floor balcony, he was greeted by a crowd of ten thousand Swedes holding torches and chanting his name. Largely made up of working people, they had raised an enormous sum by subscription to secure his future. Almost on his deathbed, it came too late to bring good health, but in time to ensure a gentle last sleep.

His was an idealised freedom inflected by absinthe and sexual jealousy and noxious chemicals, a freedom muddied by human impulses. But at its best, in his art and plays, it gave him a particular insight into the fragility of the human figure, lost in the great broil. His best paintings show small emblems, buoys or distant towns, maintaining a frail existence between turbulent skies and seething seas. His plays too, most exquisitely *Easter*, portray their characters' lonely dazzle under the stars.

One of his most touching experiments was also one of his most passive. He called them his 'celestographs'. He simply laid photographic plates on the ground on clear nights and let the stars slowly burn impressions into the film. The results are blurred, smudgy, and from a riotously noisy artist, strangely peaceful.

All too much.
Strindberg asleep at his desk

Gerhart Hauptmann
1862–1946

How best to put a revolution onstage in 1891? With fastidious realism, of course, thereby turbocharging the politics with aesthetic rebellion. What Zola preached and Ibsen flirted with, Gerhart Hauptmann brought to life with incendiary zeal within a Berlin theatre, Die Freie Bühne (The Free Stage).

Passionate adherents of naturalism, Die Freie Bühne was one of a trinity of European theatre clubs formed to promote unhindered expression. Each funded their shows through subscription, charging nothing on the door, and thus eluding the clutches of the censor. Paris began with André Antoine's Théâtre Libre in 1887, formed to stage Zola's *Thérèse Raquin*, and soon after presenting Ibsen's *Ghosts*. The Berlin outfit followed in 1889, with the Norwegian play opening proceedings, and London's Independent Theatre Society came third in 1891, with first the Ibsen and then the Zola. Each organisation favoured careful rehearsal, ensemble playing, and an unswerving commitment to truth. None of the three lasted longer than six or seven years, since soon the commercial theatre was copying them and their existence was no longer necessary. They serve as shining examples of successful artistic activism, and together with *Ghosts* and *Thérèse Raquin* prove punchy rejoinders to any blowhard claiming no theatre or play ever changed the world.

Gerhart Hauptmann was born in Silesia in 1862, the son of an innkeeper and the grandson of a weaver. This may have something to do with his first play being about alcoholism, and his second about a weaver rebellion. His family had a radical streak; his father, present on the barricades in Paris in 1848, was known to his neighbours as 'the red Hauptmann'. Studying at the University of Berlin, Gerhart became enamoured with Ibsen's plays, and by Zola's new theories of heredity and environment.

His first play, *Before Sunrise*, shocked and alarmed its first audiences with an unsparing and sexually frank vision of two lovers in a working-class milieu scarred by sudden wealth and addiction. One lover deserts the other, believing (rather incredibly) that she is irredeemably stained by an inherited dependence on alcohol. The new dawn this character is heading towards is perhaps less about the end of a relationship and more about a world cleansed of alcoholics, and those with bad genes. The audiences were not shocked by the dodgy science or the suspicious eugenics but by the coarse language and the openness about sexual desire. Hauptmann was soon crowned the father of a new German theatre.

A batch of plays followed, the masterpiece of which is *The Weavers*, an epic telling of a rebellion from 1844, in which Hauptmann's family had participated. A play for an enormous cast spread across five acts, one of its chief features is the lack of a single protagonist. In the swirl of political turmoil, characters come and go, with each new act introducing a fresh grouping. The intention is clear – to make the weavers as a class into the principal character – and the execution is successful. For the first time in dramatic history the collective is the hero, with everyone mattering equally. In testament to Hauptmann's skills of draughtsmanship, every individual who briefly emerges from the rank and file is etched with such deft strokes that they are both vivid and recognisable. This is no gathering of stereotypes or mouthpieces. In brilliant thumbnail sketches, we see and hear and smell them as if they had walked in from Silesia in 1844. Each is twisted and torqued into cramped physical postures by their unceasing work on the looms. All suffer the same hardships – hunger, enfeebled eyesight, no medical care – yet somehow, through microscopic attention to detail, the author keeps them independent and unique. We have here that rare combination of commitment to the communal and a respect for the dignity of the individual.

With true Marxist rigour, we see in the opening two acts how humans are measured only by their labour and their productivity. For the weavers, work is everything. Their homes, rented from their employers, are crammed with looms, shuttles, and lathes, and domestic life is given over to production. They receive thread from their employer and sell cloth back to him. The employer can set what price he pleases, and in the first act the workers stand in line begging for higher prices, for advances, for charity, for anything to alleviate their destitution. They are frightened by market forces, by the arrival of new machinery, and by the ease with which capital can take work elsewhere. The depths of degradation are not skirted. In the first act, someone carries a bag containing a dog butchered for roasting; in the second, it is consumed, and in the third there is the nausea that ensues from such rarely rich food.

By the time we get to the third act, set in an inn, the cumulative effect of the enforced misery has created a powder keg. Different trades face off, and agitators and a brute policeman snarl at one another. The arrival of a soldier fired up by his own rage, and everyone's liberal consumption of booze, causes an explosion into violence. A communal protest song ignites a need for vengeance. In a thrilling fourth act, delicately calibrated in its gradations of violence, we see their employer's house being surrounded, invaded, and ransacked. The growing terror of the onstage bourgeois at this invasion of their inner sanctum is vividly charted, a fear that must have echoed through the auditorium. This was the ultimate subversion of proscenium manners. The audience's imaginary safe space – their inner panic room – was being breached and violated by excluded outsiders. There is an exquisitely observed moment when a mob of young and skeletal weavers pauses before entering a drawing room, acknowledging the Rubicon they are about to cross. This is a transgression rarely if ever repeated in the proscenium century. In some ways it is surprising it happened even once. In the final act, we get a sense of the breadth of the weaver revolution as it rages across the landscape. The forces of the state, in the form of a militia, are brought in to put it down. At the conclusion of the play the rebels are still in the ascendant, though stray bullets have begun to kill the innocent.

Hauptmann followed an innovative methodology, akin to our more recent verbatim theatre or journalism. Relying not only on family stories, he travelled to Silesia and interviewed the revolution's survivors. Following the new scientific discipline of naturalism (similar to a nascent sociology), he brought his recollected family lore together with first-hand observation of social conditions, declaring, 'What was revealed in these huts of the weavers was . . . misery in its classical form.' The drama grows in epic style by an accumulation of scenes presented with an objective detachment rather than swelling and subsiding with the symphonic movement of an organised narrative. The formulaic continuities of prior dramatic structures are overturned by a strategy of dislocation. The great trick of *The Weavers* is that, while maintaining a documentary realism, it remains fully charged with feeling, the expanse and the ambition of the romantic stage combined with forensic attachment to detail. Büchner, the leading light of the romantic era, was an influence here with his melding of naturalism and a wild poetry.

The Weavers was greeted with an unsurprising uproar in Berlin, sparking notorious political censorship trials, and by a feverish excitement across the world. It has had a rackety journey through time and space since. Lenin's sister translated the play into Russian, and it became an influential force in their revolution. It was a favourite of the Yiddish stage, until Hauptmann's later relationship with the Nazi regime became a little too close. The Third Reich embraced some of his works and banned others, celebrating the playwright as a public intellectual while also holding him at arm's length. After the Second World War, the Americans banned his work from the theatres in their zone because of that relationship, whereupon the Russians invited him to East Berlin and staged a mini-Hauptmann festival shortly before his death. Hauptmann – perhaps suitably – finished his days stranded in a dislocated community, a German-speaking enclave of Poland.

Both for its great impact and by virtue of its bold and brilliant execution, one would have expected *The Weavers* to be as regular a visitor to our stages as *The Crucible*. Yet it is seen once in a blue moon. After its incendiary first appearance, its subversive energies were buried away in the bottom drawer. Some works – *A Clockwork Orange* comes to mind as a comparator – go too far. The degree of their transgression was always going to fray too many nerve endings to be easily accommodated.

As sweatshops and McJobs recreate the conditions Hauptmann depicted so long ago, *The Weavers* should perhaps be celebrated again.

Storming the barricades.
Poster for *Die Weber* (*The Weavers*), 1897

Oscar Wilde
1854–1900

Wilde was both the zenith of the proscenium era and its most admonitory catastrophe. No one epitomised more fully society's capacity for glamour and dazzle, and no one saw more clearly the violence necessary and the damage done to keep a shine on privilege. Contained within his finessed epigrams shimmered the paradox at the heart of the proscenium. Somehow the frame became an arena of empathy and identification serving up moral parables to people whose sanity depended on neglecting those same qualities beyond their brief blooming while watching a play. Wilde's poised irony exposed the yawning chasm between enjoying tales about goodness over class and kindness over profit, before leaving the theatre to walk briskly and blithely past beggars outside on the street. Living with that corrosive doublethink, pointing it out remorselessly and delighting in its absurdity, was a dervish dance he performed with elegant abandon. Until its continuing impossibility spun him off his axis.

The Oscar Wilde Season opened in October 2017, the first offering from Classic Spring, a company I founded after leaving Shakespeare's Globe. Within the plain but elegant walls of the Vaudeville Theatre on London's Strand – without being flash, one of the most functional playhouses in London – we resolved to present the four social comedies (*Lady Windermere's Fan*, *An Ideal Husband*, *The Importance of Being Earnest*, and *A Woman of No Importance*) beside his prolonged howl from prison, *De Profundis*, as well as a musical rendition of one of his magical short stories, and a children's show compounding several fairy tales. The reasons were manifold, beyond the most obvious 'Why not?'

After my tenure at the Globe, a theatre founded on a fascination with the relationship between plays and the architecture for which they were written, it seemed fitting to pursue that experiment with a different epoch. As Shakespeare and his contemporaries wrote for the epic scale, the imaginative commitment, and the 360-degree embrace of the Globe, so, three hundred years later, generations of playwrights wrote for the velvety darkness, the enclosed acoustic, and the picture framing of the proscenium. Just as the Globe offers a cascade of insights into what Shakespeare was up to, the same might be true of the framed theatre and Oscar Wilde. The playhouses were built for the plays and the plays written for the houses. Something in the dance between drama and architecture reveals and releases the energies of each.

We also wanted to effect the same happy trick we managed at the Globe – to occupy the radical mainstream. British theatre spends a peculiar amount of time defining itself against an orthodoxy that doesn't exist. Shakespeare is barely ever done traditionally, and proscenium plays in our post-Covid world are rarely produced, let alone produced straight. Yet directors deconstruct, critics preach, and academics plot in reaction to a predominant culture that isn't actually there. At some strange inflection point during the last thirty years, the word 'unorthodox' stopped meaning 'being different' and started meaning 'being the same as everyone else trying to be unorthodox'. At that moment, it became unconventional to do what no one else was doing: sit in the empty centre ground and present plays as the complex and alive documents they are.

Beyond its perfect sightlines and modest plainness, the Vaudeville seemed apposite for other reasons. When Oscar Wilde first came to live in London in the 1870s, he moved into Salisbury Street with the artist Frank Miles. With Wilde's vivid talent for arriving in places, declaring 'Here I am!' and drawing stunned attention, Salisbury Street was soon a magnet for the glitterati – Lillie Langtry, Henry Irving, the Prince of Wales, and many others paid homage. Sarah Bernhardt left a footmark on the wall to prove just how high she could kick. If you stand outside the Vaudeville Theatre and look directly across the road and a little to the right, you see a small alleyway obscured by a forbidding grille.

That is, or was, Salisbury Street. Squint a little and indulge your imagination, changing red buses to omnibuses, taxis to carriages, horsepower to horses, and a different Strand emerges, bustling with an equal energy but differently clothed. Into that Strand, Oscar would arise from Salisbury Street each day, look across the jostle and see the Vaudeville in the prime of its youth. Such connections may be tenuous, but there is something stubbornly actual in them, a thread of connection that, no matter how thin-beaten, links us now to them then.

Before undertaking the season, proper research was necessary to understand a man whose fame can mislead into a presumption of intimacy. Throughout my life I've loved the plays, quoted the quotes, and enjoyed the biopics. Together with others under the spell, there were stronger personal reasons for gratitude. The incantatory rhythms of *The Ballad of Reading Gaol* had imprinted themselves early as a nursery rhyme that could awaken depths of pity; *De Profundis* had proven invaluable as an analgesic against depression; and only William Morris's *News from Nowhere* had more influence on my politics than Wilde's 'The Soul of Man Under Socialism'. Yet there was much to learn. Revisionary biographies appear on an almost yearly basis, reframing and reconfiguring. I kept pace as far as possible but work on the ground was needed.

First stop was Dublin, and a tour around Trinity College. I found myself at the top of a twisted staircase in a Victorian townhouse, now annexed into the walled estate of Trinity. The house seemed to shrink with each floor ascended, like *Alice in Wonderland* – on the ground floor we were dwarfed by high walls, then we were looming giants boxed into a cramped landing. On a drab locked door hung a prosaic sign advertising a student course.

'What happened in there?' I asked.

'Oscar Wilde was born,' the guide informed me.

The whole story, all that blood spilled in the long civil war between gays and straights, had sprung from behind this nondescript door. No plaques, no fuss, no garlands – the uneasy quadrille of noise and silence around him continues.

As we descended the stairs, the ghosts of his family – the formidable totem pole of a mother, Speranza; the intellectual fireball and inveterate philanderer of a father, Jack; the dissolute and wayward genius of a brother, Willie; and the much-adored and doomed younger sister, Isola – all flit from drawing room to nursery to parlour in self-dramatising Wildean agitation. Only a little digging dislodges his legend – both the excessively polished Oscar in his ascendancy, and the doomed Oscar in his precipitate fall. Standing in the house where he stumbled his first steps, and no doubt muttered his first infant joke, it is hard not to sense the clumsy humanity behind the myth. Minutes later, across several Trinity courtyards, I am in one of his student rooms, hearing how his first engagement to Dublin beauty Florence Balcombe was broken off when she ran into the arms of the eager Bram Stoker. From Dorian Gray to Dracula. Poor Florence.

Flesh and blood connections further chip at Wilde's smooth, lacquered persona. We walk to Merrion Square, to stand before the Georgian house where the family lived throughout his childhood. His younger sister Isola, whose blamelessness shone within a family of dissolution, perished here at the age of eight. When he died in Paris, wrecked by the hard labour and anguish of his awful imprisonment, bloated by a decade's bad living, and with a cocktail of Europe's most desolating diseases coursing through his body, one of the few objects found on him was a lock of his sister's hair enclosed in an envelope he kept with him for thirty years. A more emotional Wilde emerges from the shadow of history's bright dandy.

Next was a trip to Reading Gaol for an exhibition put together by Artangel commemorating Wilde's two long years in prison. Together with hundreds of visitors, I was given a brief snapshot of what life was like in the dehumanising panopticon of the Victorian gaol – Jeremy Bentham's 'mill for grinding rogues honest'. The governor's central inspection house squatted in the centre, sternly surveying long spokes of multistorey cell blocks emanating from its all-seeing gaze. The art on display was intriguing, but none as affecting as the geometric precision of the gaol. Even as a tourist, shuffling from floor to floor engendered an instant deadness of spirit. Gloom was relieved by a meditative interval spent in Oscar's cell, C-3-3. A blue sky lit by bright winter sun filled the window, painting a clean block of light on the wall. The curators had the discretion to put nothing inside the cell, though earlier visitors had left one modest candle and a wilted rose on a table. There was a lull in the cortège, and I spent twenty minutes alone in the room that gave birth to *De Profundis* as the low sun circled and lengthened its splash of light.

Further revelations in the two cells beyond. Each contained the books Wilde requested from the governor once he was permitted distractions. In the first cell was a line-up of pious tales – lives of cardinals and religious commentaries – possibly to satisfy a spiritual appetite, perhaps to appease the authorities. In the next was a racier array, including two volumes that might have raised eyebrows – the *Collected Plays* of Strindberg and Ibsen's *Little Eyolf*. These plays would have been hot off the press in 1895; for them to stand among the few books he hungered for showed that Wilde, heralded for so long as the founder of an Atlantic, frivolous drawing room drama, was in fact a fan of the new European theatre.

Weeks later, I talked to the Wilde scholar Peter Raby, who amplified this insight. Wilde attended the first London production of *Hedda Gabler* three times, presented in club performances by the radical producer Elizabeth Robins. Where? At the Vaudeville on the Strand. He is said to have watched the play 'with great intentness'. Raby offers a fresh nugget: when *A Woman of No Importance* was first produced, it played in repertory with Ibsen's *An Enemy of the People*. Its star, Herbert Beerbohm Tree, doubled as Lord Illingworth and Stockmann; Wilde's glittering wit was set alongside Ibsen's savage fable. How could the two plays not bleed into each other? Our inherited impression of his plays' brittle shallowness was giving way to a more muscular sensibility. 'I regard the theatre as the greatest of all art forms,' said Wilde, 'the most immediate way in which a human being can share with another the sense of what it is to be a human being.'

Recent biographies have studied Wilde by looking at the women around him and the fortunes of his family. Oblique insights reveal through relationships how he invested in others, how much he learned from them, and how the egotist of report misrepresents. As Gyles Brandreth told me over tea in a London hotel (the Langham, one of Oscar's haunts), what marked out his conversation, as many noted, was his brilliance as a listener. His wit was great, but not as great as his capacity to hear. Every dramatist must have an ear, and Oscar Wilde heard more than most.

Wilde-world is broad and expansive, proving it perfectly possible to drift from tea with Gyles Brandreth, to a drink with Howard Brenton to discuss Wilde's politics, and then on to meet Neil Bartlett, the theatre-maker and queer historian. Neil wrote a book called *Who Was That Man?* more than thirty years ago, comparing the queer London of the 1870s and 1880s with that of a hundred years later. He unpacked an enormous amount of research into the burgeoning scene in *fin de siècle* London, a time when an underground movement was daring to outrage, and delighted in doing so. Drag acts onstage, cross-dressing off, and a growing knowledge that 'the love that dared not speak its name' had every right to shout its merry head off, were changing the public arena at a pace that scared the wits out of conservative England. The Prime Minister Lord Rosebery was engaged in a romance with the older brother of Alfred Douglas, Oscar's lover. Wilde's disproportionate punishment was not just the breaking of a butterfly. It was an act of deliberate state terror aimed at a community, pushing it firmly back into the shadows. He took for the whole team one of the most vicious retributions ever inflicted.

There is as little chance of imagining a definitive Wilde as of conceiving a definitive Shakespeare. But looking further revealed confusions and clumsiness, bringing him briefly closer.

Wilde's career spent a long time threatening to go nowhere, beyond a brilliant exhibitionism. For over a decade he dazzled with lecturing, journalism, essays, and short stories, a whirling energy in search of a form. That form eluded his early attempts at drama. He wrote one work with as unprepossessing a title as any author has managed – *Vera; or, The Nihilists*. Even the punctuation is a disaster. There was a second catastrophe, this one in verse – *The Duchess of Padua*. Frustrated by their failures, he ventured forth into French for his next tyro effort, *Salome*, a maddening demonstration of his own passion for the purple (though still admired by many).

An actor-manager of taste and distinction, George Alexander, who ran the St James's Theatre, had read and enjoyed Wilde's novel, *The Picture of Dorian Gray*. He suggested that the playwright turn his dramatic gaze away from Grand Guignol or biblical epics and towards the society of his day. The most brilliant of prompts. In retrospect it seems obvious that Wilde should have dazzled the world by relishing and lampooning high society, but it took an actor to suggest it. When *Lady Windermere's Fan* opened in 1892, public and critics were amazed by what seemed to be mastery of form at his first attempt. William Archer, a champion of Shaw and Ibsen, wrote, 'how comes it that, for the past twelve years or so, we have been entertaining a dramatist unawares, when he ought, on the contrary, to have been entertaining us?'

In his essay 'The Decay of Lying', one of Wilde's mouthpieces says, 'the two things that every artist should avoid are modernity of form and modernity of subject matter . . . we have mistaken the common livery of the age for the vesture of the Muses, and spend our days in the sordid streets and hideous suburbs of our vile cities.' Well, his plays eschewed the streets and suburbs, but they were nothing if not modern. *Lady Windermere's Fan* and the three other social comedies which followed in rapid succession, each of which wowed London audiences, were all determinedly set in a contemporary Britain and stuffed with characters and locations immediately recognisable.

The narrative situations these characters found themselves in would have been equally familiar from earlier writers' works. Wilde was contemptuous about the crudity of melodrama, while being perfectly happy to steal its plots and mannerisms. The mainsprings for his stories are happily antique: a single mother abandoned by the father of her child; the public figure with a dark secret; the woman who returns to her homeland she left in disgrace. This is not Samuel Beckett. In his final play, *The Importance of Being Earnest*, Wilde took all the tropes of melodrama – characters leading double lives, mistaken identities, confusion over parentage resolved by stunning revelations – and backflipped them into delirious farce. 'In families of high position strange coincidences are not supposed to occur,' proclaims Lady Bracknell. 'They are hardly considered the thing.' Yet they are the foundation stones of the old drama. During our season at the Vaudeville, it was a mysterious gratification sitting in the theatre and sensing the audience hold their breath and sit forward with a welcomed tension as the mechanics of plot took hold. You could almost hear a soft purr of submissive pleasure as everyone gave in to the grip of a well-engineered narrative.

Wilde was acutely sensitive to visual styling. A keen critic and connoisseur of art, he saw fully the potential of the proscenium for aesthetic display, declaring that 'Theatrical audiences are far more impressed by what they look at than by what they listen to.' The scene painter, he resolved, should be 'restored to his proper position as an artist and not hammered to death by the carpenter', insisting that the visual dimension of his plays should never compromise on 'beautiful dresses' or 'a sense of the luxury of modern life'. This was no realism, it was a passionate and moral belief in beauty, whether expressed in the retroussé nose of the leading lady, the shimmering silk of the curtains, or the lambent tulle of the dresses. To us, this can seem decadent and otiose, a spiritually redundant obsession with the material. To Wilde and his era, the realm of aesthetics was a religion: they seemed, in their rejection of the ugly and everyday, revolutionary. He described the stage as 'not merely the meeting place of all the arts, but . . . also the return of art to life', somewhere art and costume and movement came together, and gave vitality back.

The capstone of this arch of pleasure was the language – the generous giveaway of epigrams, gags, bon mots, mots justes, paradoxes, puns, and much else. Wilde loved dialogue and encouraged the audience to share his passion. In the British Library, I read through several of his notebooks. Scattered across the pages were phrases, thoughts, ripostes, and screeds of to and fro, all set down before he knew where they might find a home. Long stretches of dialogue were written down without character names. He simply relished the music. Stories were a secondary consideration, a temporary home for shining words. 'Plots are tedious,' he said. 'Anyone can invent them. Life is full of them. Indeed one has to elbow one's way through them as they crowd across one's path.' Putting all four plays together, it became apparent what an arrant self-plagiarist he was. If he liked an epigram in one play, with unabashed self-indulgence he reproduced it in another.

In the first act of *A Woman of No Importance*, Wilde attempts something truly bold. Thirty minutes of chitter and chatter, as tea is served outside a large country house and the sun sinks slowly into the South Downs, all with the barest smidgen of plot. A little flirting, some game-playing, some discreet planting of information for later, but fundamentally fourteen characters come and go, with nothing to tether them beyond their existence in that moment. A quintessential aimless sunny English afternoon, the only music the delicious sound of people talking. Not Chekhovian – the language is too ostentatious and artificial – but during our shows, when we got it right and the words spilled into the auditorium with relaxed ease, it was magical. Though the rest of the play cranks up into hysterical melodrama, the first act is somehow fluently exquisite without being precious. Wilde's instructions to his star, Beerbohm Tree, were 'forget that you ever played Hamlet, forget that you ever played a duke in a melodrama by Henry Arthur Jones, forget that you ever acted at all.'

All the paradoxical thinking is not merely a display of cleverness; it is there to subvert. Most crucially there is no end to it. It is a mode of thinking, a process which is being showcased – silly, sophisticated, and Socratic – not a destination. The goal is the refinement of a technique, a journey of enquiry whose essence is the desire to keep looking. No absolute truth – the very idea would be anathema! If not worse, ugly! We are not being invited into the enclosure of a moral definition, we are being set free to think ethically across an ever-shifting landscape where conclusions are temporary. Without settled thinking there can be no prejudice, and an absence of prejudice was something that Wilde – a Protestant born in Catholic Ireland, an Irish student in England, and a gay adult within straight society – fervently prayed for.

What was most surprising about that season was how persistently it touched on the modern world. We presented our plays in the middle of a prolonged period of austerity – an attitude towards social inequity reminiscent of the Victorian. The year was full of glimpses of past and present meta-versing over each other. Scutty alleyways spear off the Strand on either side of the Vaudeville up to Maiden Lane, dusty reminders of a London of shady encounters and intimate muggings. When our audiences spilled out, they walked up these narrow passages past aproned waiters sneaking cigarette breaks, sleeping beggars, and small-scale criminals doing small-time deals. The Victorian era seemed a trick of the light away. One night I walked past two junkies lying huddled together in a sleeping bag, looking up with stoned fascination at the stars. Wilde excoriated the gulf between rich and poor in his political essays; the evidence of our lack of progress was chilling.

The social parallels could have been predictable, less so was how this season touched modern nerves. Its initial intention was archaeological. For more than four hundred years, the English theatre has been the home of the new and the old, the premiere and the revival, the groundbreaking and the classic, always dynamically locked in a restless conversation. Each age has brought forth great plays, and each following age has folded those plays into the repertory to carry on the bustling chatter between present and past. The new is the ultimate aim, but the new would be thin gruel without full knowledge of the past. The season was intended as a corrective to our current monolithic presentism, so its ability in the course of the year to speak to a lively present was an eye-opener.

We opened with Wilde's second society play, *A Woman of No Importance*, since it is his least known and least popular, and an early risk seemed advisable. A difficult second album of a work, it feels like too conscious an imitation of Ibsen, full of bugbears and obsessions, swollen and lurching in its structure, yet full of magical surprises. Always having had a weakness for the inelegant, it is my favourite. Just as it was opening, revelations about Harvey Weinstein started sprouting in the press, and a couple of weeks later the full MeToo movement went viral. Suddenly a whole host of lines about sexual behaviour, predation, and irresponsibility, which had been provocative in rehearsal, became too hot to touch. The conversations in the theatre and backstage went from intrigued to exasperated, from provoked to indignant.

In *A Woman of No Importance*, Lord Illingworth makes a heavy move on the young American Hester Worsley. In rehearsals this seemed a clumsy pass. By the time we got to performances, the air outside the theatre had changed and it was the action of a serial predator. In *An Ideal Husband*, Sir Robert Chiltern has won his fortune by shabby financial opportunism, and he fears the social disgrace his nemesis Mrs Cheveley wants to effect through public exposure. The idea of a life spent walking beside a precipice came into sharper focus in an age given over to mass public morality. Society's glare was now everywhere and startlingly intolerant. However righteous that judgement was, the adamantine casting of its certainties evoked a strong concurrence between Victorian public morality and that of our new present. Wilde seemed to have caught the spirit of his own age and ours.

He was able to demonstrate something beyond the age-old war between the puritans and those they loathe, beyond the chill of the definite. For Wilde, theatre was the place for adventure, for questioning and imagination. Throughout the season, we witnessed audiences relishing his ability to balance manifold points of view in one paradoxical sentence. Not for him the hammer-headed tweet with its nauseatingly narrow point of view. Theatre, as he knew, is in a constant search for more complex moral judgements; it uses interrogation and empathy to reveal the multifaceted nature of human transaction. At a moment when everyone was searching for absolutes, one could feel the audience relishing a holiday in nuance.

Wilde also knew from his own experience that charity is more likely to be found among sinners than the pious, and kindness in the free of mind than the closed. He had lived with wolves, and had lived out his own wolfishness – there is a retrospective movement to damn him for that – but as Virginia Woolf said of Tolstoy, 'It is not the priest who shatters our desires most effectively; it is the man who has known them, and loved them himself.' Each of his puritans – Hester Worsley, Lady Chiltern, and Lady Windermere – discover that those they thought of as entirely bad have reserves of kindness, and those they idolised as perfect have meanness in their souls.

Towards the end of our year-long residency, I stood outside the Vaudeville on a sunny Saturday afternoon and saw two tribes gather in exuberant harmony on London's Strand. The rainbow-coloured members of the Pride march commingled in noisy elation with the St George's flag clad men and women who had just watched the England football team triumph over Sweden. LBGT slogans shared the air with anthemic chants, and each amplified the other's decibels of joy. They even managed to include some despondent Swedes in the party. A vision of England offered itself up – raucous, festive, happily cosmopolitan – and cheered the heart. Here on the Strand, where Oscar Wilde first made his London mark in the 1890s on a jostling highway newly electrified, a street jolted with a sense of the modern. Now here were gay and straight singing together, class distinctions dissolved in celebration, a scene the playwright would have hoped to witness, and the exiled man would have despaired of ever seeing. And which – an argument could be made – few people did as much to usher along as Wilde himself.

Underneath a lifetime of flippancy and display and generous silliness, he was always on a personal ethics quest, and one at odds with the hypocritical public ethics of his day. He was born out of time and is coming ever more into focus as a necessary figure in this one. Partly for his combination of socialism with imagination and kindness, partly as one who had the courage to live life in his own truth, and partly as someone whose life and work put a premium on forgiveness and mercy. Primarily because his first principle was the oldest one – a value we have lately lost sight of and need more urgently than ever – that morality starts with judging oneself and not others.

Jack specifies the size of the notorious handbag.
George Alexander and Rose Leclercq in
The Importance of Being Earnest, 1895

Edmond Rostand
1868–1918

A genuine throwback, not least in his extravagant moustache, Edmond Rostand is a vivid reminder of what the proscenium arch theatre might have become, had it not developed a social conscience. In fact, his work is an excellent showcase of what it was originally intended to be. An architecture built for glamour, overripe sentiments, dash and panache, somehow got diverted, becoming a gilded frame for content constantly angry at the grandeur which enveloped it. There are no such problems with Rostand's masterpiece, *Cyrano de Bergerac,* which was made to measure.

Cyrano is the lost and lonely great-grandchild of the romantic drama movement that flourished in the late eighteenth and early nineteenth centuries, before withering on the vine. Grand emotions and their grandiloquent expression were then the order of the day. Passionate love stories in oversized harems; despairing men looking out over chasms from craggy escarpments; and doomed heroic sailors disappearing into fathomless seas were all de rigueur. Perilously close to melodrama, the work was elevated into romanticism by its dark and fatalistic imagining. There is a wonderful stage adaptation of Mary Shelley's *Frankenstein* called *Presumption*, written in 1823, just five years after the book was published, which concluded with Doctor and Monster chasing each other up an Alpine mountain, locked in a mutually dependent path to destruction. As an avalanche of ice falls to freeze them for eternity, all the essential romantic criteria were fulfilled.

These works were the inspiration for Rostand, a determined neo-romantic from a school that repudiated the aridity and paucity of naturalism. They still sought the tumultuous passions and grand gestures which wrapped up the universe into a single ball, rather than splitting it into a bewildering collection of fragments. The hero and self-appointed leader of neo-romanticism was Richard Wagner, a one-man advert for the dangers of grand gestures. Rostand wrote several plays for the great Sarah Bernhardt, not averse to a gesture herself. These included a tale of a twelfth-century troubadour and his hidden love for a Jerusalem princess; a biblical epic about the Good Samaritan; and a spy drama set in the age of Napoleon, with Bernhardt taking the trouser role. All a long way from Ibsen.

Such technicolour vivacity could have been the natural progression of theatre had others not shaken it about. *Cyrano* is a determined outlier. First performed in 1897, it tells the story of a real character from the early seventeenth century. Bearing no relation to its own time, it has no responsibility to be relevant, nor any social duty. It has little correspondence to the speech of its own day, written in bouncing rhyming couplets of twelve syllables per line, close to the Alexandrine form. The rhymes are joyous, Byronic in their wit and self-glorification. Occupying its own fabular island outside history, it is heroic, uproariously funny, dashingly glamorous, nonsensical, and enormously moving. The purpose is to entertain, delighting in its excess and its defiance of the depleting movement of cultural history around it.

Cyrano also created a paradigm of a story, the inhibited lover silenced by self-loathing (in this case by the size of his nose), who discovers a voice to speak to his love through composing letters from someone else. This model has been turned into film after TV series after radio play after novel after ballet after film after film after film. The technique, using a proxy to ventriloquise one's love for another, has also impacted considerably on the methodologies of love.

Rostand was an eager historian and the real-life Cyrano (1619–1655) – a celebrated playwright, epistolarian, and duellist – was a boyhood hero of his. We know the original had plentiful vigour and swagger but little about the size of his schnozz. An engraving from the period features a nose which is impressive, hawkish even, without being embarrassingly long. Something of Rostand's childhood passion transformed this work from his earnest efforts elsewhere into the empyrean. A unique mix of flamboyance and earthiness in every daft moment helps: its gestures are extravagant, but the characters have dirty boots; its rhetoric of love is purpler than purple, yet a subversive sense of humour threads through every syllable, keeping it self-aware and true. When it confronts death, it does so with the insouciant styling of the truly brave and breaks every heart in the house.

Forget the real, feel the poetry. Le Bret, Roxane and Cyrano smiling at the moon, *Cyrano de Bergerac*, 1898

The play opened on the 28 December 1897, at the Théâtre de la Porte Saint-Martin in Paris. It triumphed, the audience still applauding over an hour after the curtain fell (or so they said). It ran a further four hundred nights, showing a degree of enthusiasm for verse drama that no one had thought would ever return. Soon the show was packing up its trunks, its two hundred and fifty costumes, and sending its forty actors on a tour across Europe and beyond. Its staggering itinerary included Belgium, Switzerland, Austria, Hungary, Serbia, Romania, Bulgaria, Turkey, Egypt, Greece, Italy, Spain, Algeria, and Tunisia.

Rostand is a determined non-fit in the various movements that flourished around him. That may explain no little of the success.

Alfred Jarry
1873–1907

On 10 December 1896 at the Théâtre de l'Oeuvre in Paris, an actor named Firmin Gémier strode down to the front of the stage, looked out over the fastidiously refined Parisian crowd, and shouted at the top of his voice, 'Shit!' (Or 'Merdre!' to be precise, the extra 'r' there to bamboozle the censors.) Some would have us believe theatre was never the same again.

He was playing the lead in a new play, *Ubu Roi*, by a peculiar young malcontent from the west of Normandy, Alfred Jarry. The play enjoyed a weird genesis. Eight years before, Jarry had sat in a classroom in a Rennes lycée, under the tutelage of a Monsieur Hébert. It is hard to think of another physics teacher who had such a prolonged cultural effect. Jarry and his friend Henri Morin delighted in inventing and writing down episodes in which this teacher, redubbed 'le Père Ebe', suffered protracted agonies and embarrassments as king of a make-believe Poland. It's a standard schoolboy tactic – take a loathed authority figure, make him behave in the most degrading manner possible, and drench him in shame and poop. *Ubu* is one of the first examples of a student prank being translated into something considered a major work of art.

Jarry incubated the project over a number of years, adding further episodes and imposing on it a pseudo-Shakespearean structure. He begged theatres to put it on and, once he succeeded, got the reaction he desired. The audience jeered and screamed at *Ubu*, and each other. Fist fights broke out, later transcribed into print as critics fought over whether the play was an ordered work of art or a work of arty ordure. Jarry had the sort of *succès de scandale* he had dreamed of, and spent the rest of his short life as a *fin de siècle* Johnny Rotten, until absinthe rotted his internal organs.

Turning the tables and shouting 'Merdre' back at Jarry's play now would be a temptation. You could call him a one-trick pony, but that might exaggerate his versatility. He wrote two further plays, *Ubu Cocu* and *Ubu Enchaîné*, which, as their titles suggest, didn't extend his range. He had a remarkable lack of ability as a playwright – no ear for speech, no complex psychology, no sense of texture, no narrative purpose. His ability to spin his one gift – for wilful outrage – into a passable imitation of genius is the reason he is the patron saint of those who love gestures more than application.

Simultaneously, Ibsen, Chekhov, Strindberg, Shaw, and Wilde were producing work on surer foundations. They shared Jarry's critical eye for the present moment but wanted to achieve more than shouting abuse. Jarry was pure punk, all takedown, a snarling, sniggering voice screeching from the margins. As the play continues, Ubu achieves his ambition of becoming the king of Poland, before bleeding it dry of finances and slaughtering nobles. He is then deposed by the advancing Russian army. As he murders and pillages and connives, you keep hoping for one brief instant of complexity or contrapuntal energy. It never comes. The consistency is admirable, but consistency is not itself a mark of genius.

The legacy of Ubu is pervasive. Throughout the twentieth century he became an iconic allegorical figure. His singularity of purpose rendered him a one-size-fits-all metaphorical leader. He stood in variously for Stalin, Hitler, and Mao in socially telling productions, becoming one of the great dictator lookie-likies. This seems an odd distortion, since Ubu is actually not that interested in power for power's sake, more akin to the old English figure the Lord of Misrule. Ubu is a compulsive anarch, a vandal, with little desire for control, simply a grotesque appetite for more and bigger cakes right now. A closer parallel is with today's rampant consumerism; Jarry's analogous figures are not dictators as such, more the supersized monsters of conspicuous consumption, self-delusion, and narcissism. Their current epitome, Donald Trump, is probably reality's best attempt at emulating Ubu.

The legacy Jarry left behind is disproportionate to his output. His debunking of naturalism proved an iconic encouragement for anyone else who couldn't write dialogue or shape a scene. The Dadaists and surrealists of the early twentieth century acknowledged a debt to him, as did the German expressionists of the 1920s and 1930s. Beyond them, Jarry could accept a portion of responsibility for the cul-de-sac that was the Theatre of the Absurd. Eugène Ionesco, Boris Vian, and N. F. Simpson all viewed him as a dramaturgical grandaddy.

The sad and unloved great-grandchildren of the *Ubu* plays are now scattered all over Europe. Whenever you see a cast list that includes the Philosopher, the Policeman, the Poet, the Prostitute, and the Politician, and when the curtain goes up on a heavily allegorical setting, you know you are in the presence of those who worship at the Ubu shrine. I once saw a play in Romania called *Toilet* – an unpromising title – which featured all of the above. When the curtain rose, there was a double gasp. Not only were we in a toilet for the whole evening, but the toilet was the shape of Romania! Though the intention behind such works was and is justifiable – how else to make sense of much of history – the plays often amount to little more than gibberish screamed in a wood. To some, that is the sum of human nature, to others it is just a man screaming in a wood.

For all their malingering influence, there remains something wild and riotous about the *Ubu* plays. Appropriately, many later productions were in marionette theatres, since it has the vicious energy of a Punch and Judy show. Relations between Père and Mère Ubu follow in that tradition of love expressed as savage and undying enmity. Remorseless insults rebound with the exuberant invention of deep loathing, the brooding distrust never flagging. The sheer lack of sentimentality carries its own exhilaration. Ubu himself is a cartoon of pathological violence. At one moment a timorous coward, shrinking from a raised voice, at the next a Viking berserker, hurling himself into danger and smashing to a pulp everything in his path.

Iconoclasm at a certain courageous pitch – or produced by folk so steeped in absinthe they don't know what courage is any more – brings its own benefits. Forcing the door open and into the modern, being the first to walk in new rooms, creates an energy. Ubu is crammed with that freedom. The punk desire to howl the house down shouldn't create anything enduring, but it does. Will *Never Mind the Bollocks* stand up in five thousand years' time if there are enough cockroaches left to pogo to it? Undoubtedly yes. And will they enact Ubu with puppets on their blasted wastelands? Probably. A good thing too.

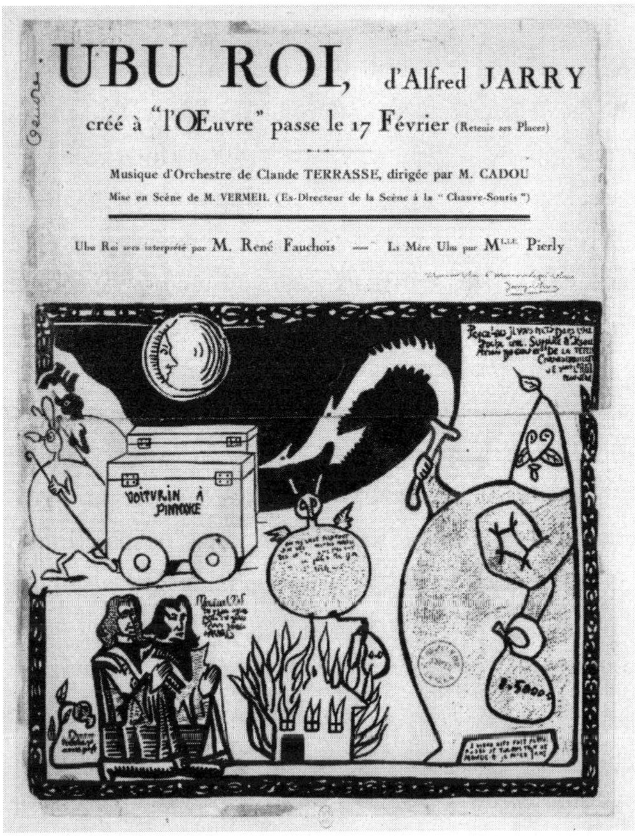

Brace yourselves.
Programme for the premiere of *Ubu Roi*, 1896

Lady Gregory
1852–1932

No theatre exemplified the potential or influence of the proscenium stage as combustibly as the first Abbey in Dublin. Many stages introduced writers, and started movements, and changed perspectives. The Abbey did all that and changed the course of a nation to boot.

In Ireland, since the 1650s, theatre had proved the arena where politics got thrashed out. Often with laughter, regularly with tears, rarely without rage, and not infrequently with flailing fists. Rioting at the theatre did not start with the Abbey and J. M. Synge. It began long before at Smock Alley in 1663 for a performance of *Pompey*, and resurfaced regularly thereafter, with notable unrest during *Mahomet* in 1754, and an attack on the Lord Lieutenant Marquess of Wellesley by the Orange Order at a showing of *She Stoops to Conquer* in 1822. In the absence of a representative body anyone could trust, with no parliament of their own and no authorised public forum, the theatre was the place where the public could decide what it was to be Irish. This was not a passive process of being lectured to; the audience were voluble and pushed back. If you could not express dissent in a parliament, you could in a theatre. The Lord Lieutenant might sit in his box (and find himself on the wrong end of jeering and hurled fruit while there), but he was an observer and could not control the feelings in the room. Cardinals and prelates might attend, but this was one zone where they could not monitor the political temperature. In addition, the Lord Chamberlain's writ did not operate in Dublin, so there was greater freedom of expression, which only stoked the fires further. Theatre was inflammatory in Ireland, and it was waiting for a crucible to harness that energy and tell stories of moment.

From the colossal effect of the Abbey, you might imagine it was a unified, streamlined operation. Modern management speak would wish it to be on-message. Nothing could be further from the truth. The Abbey was riven by the political, class, and religious divides that kept Dublin ever on the verge of violence. Its management – W. B. Yeats and the formidable Lady Augusta Gregory – were from the Anglo-Irish Protestant Ascendancy; its acting company, led by the two Fay brothers, William and Frank, were working-class Catholics. The trustees were from the landowning class, the workers from the professional world. Such profound splits could have been irreparable, yet somehow they proved beneficial. They found a way to coexist, though rarely without tension. The Irish Literary Theatre of the landowning class, dedicated to Irish folklore, ancient idealism, and the new European theatre, was conjugated with the Irish National Dramatic Company of the workers, who were passionate about truthful acting and Irish stories. In aesthetics they were worlds apart, Yeats's mystical symbolism clashing with the Fays' desire to represent reality and craft. Their public statements about what they were doing often collided, but within those tensions, they were able to make work more interesting than anything on-brand.

The attitudes of Yeats and Lady Gregory certainly required no little tolerance from colleagues. At the opening ceremony W. B. quoted at length from *The Faerie Queene*. This interminable poem was by the Elizabethan English poet Edmund Spenser, who participated in massacres of the Irish, and argued for their 'pacification' by violent extinction of their culture and language. An odd choice for the founding ceremony of an Irish National Theatre. Both poet and Lady were the definition of *de haut en bas*: Yeats dismissed one skirmish saying, 'The people who were protesting didn't have books in their houses'; Gregory defined a clash between the theatre and Catholic nationalists as, 'the old battle between those who use a toothbrush and those who don't'.

To their credit, they didn't only punch down, in financial terms at least. In its early years, the theatre survived through the generosity of a benefactor called Annie Horniman, who had inherited significant tea profits. Gregory said of her, 'I think it is a mistake treating tradespeople as if they had one's own table of values.' After Yeats had asked Horniman to design costumes for a show, he dismissed her efforts by saying that everyone looked like 'fire extinguishers got up as Father Xmas'. Gregory's regular gift to the company of a gargantuan barmbrack – a cartwheel of a fruitcake, two feet in diameter and eight inches in depth – is undeniably generous and festive, but has a touch of the Marie Antoinette about it. And Yeats's semi-permanent bow tie can't have helped.

Yet both had willpower, bravery, and endurance. History has no shortage of instances of the posh deciding to colonise a cultural zone, and not a lot coming of it. These two made it happen. Surviving traumatic failures and scandals, and even more dangerous successes, they kept pushing forward for over thirty years. With the courage of their convictions, they launched new play after new play, leaving few safe spaces for classics or revivals. With new plays, no one knows whether the parachute works before you jump. Taking that risk over and again has its cost. Of course, their class would have oiled the wheel. Not only so they could forge connections, and schmooze and fundraise, but also to stare down the many obstacles they faced – whether the Church, the Lord Lieutenant, the patriotic rebels, or the Free State when it came – and continue making original art with original politics. The entitled self-confidence of the Anglo-Irish, however infuriating, enabled them to walk through barriers that might have cowed others.

Several important decisions impelled the whole company to rub along together. Greatest was a fidelity to the playwright's vision, a duty superseding all else. The singular glory of working on new plays is that the process leaves little room for creative ego. Actor, director, or designer, all have to park as much identity and ideology as possible, working in service of the play and entering an artistic landscape imagined by another. Above all, however different their backgrounds or political beliefs, the Abbey company was there to create an Irish theatre, specific to the pleasures and needs of their own community, and united by a common enemy: the Brits. In settling their differences, and in bridging the gap between the mystical and everyday realism, they created stories of compulsive gravity that magnetised audiences and artists.

Another slice of luck for the company was the venue they found after peripatetic early years. The Mechanics' Hall in Lower Abbey Street had nothing grand about it. The City Morgue was next door, which provoked no shortage of witticisms. Having been the site for a circus, for variety shows, for classical music, and for improving lectures, it had a loose, improvised feel rather than being drowned in plush decor. Horniman and William Fay resolved to buy the Mechanics' Hall and an adjacent building to fashion their new theatre, when both were on the market at low cost. Modesty was key to its success, with 592 crammed into a space with a fierce focus. The back wall of the auditorium was close and hard, and rebounded voices sharp and clear. A clattering little room, like acting inside a taut drum, it proved the sort of space where revolutions happen. This was no palace of cherubs and rococo like the new theatres designed by English architect Frank Matcham, nor a big, energy-absorbent sofa like many modern designs; it had a rickety energy where language became active and feisty. In this compacted space full of wooden surfaces, words, actions, and energies hurtled around the room like balls pinging around a pinball table.

The stage was never intended for theatre and was better suited for lectures or front-cloth music acts and comedians. With little width and almost no depth, the stage carpenter did what he could to improve the dimensions, but to little avail. There was no crossover at the back of the stage, so if an actor left a scene on one side, they had to exit the building, walk down a short alleyway, and return through another door. In the exceptionally tight space, actors had to form a line across the front looking out, with instructions from director Yeats: 'No windmilling' (arms) and 'don't hurl yourself around' (as if they could). The company described it as acting in a barrel. The stage was high, so the actors' eye level went straight into the balcony, making audience connection hard, with older performers complaining they 'were up on the first floor'. Five footlights across the front added a Grand Guignol aspect. And the sightlines weren't great from the gallery. The restrictions made life hard, but the virtues were manifold and alchemical. Big stories full of soul and heart were reinforced by additional galvanism from the tightly packed audience. Acting had to be focused, with no room for fidgets. As in a Manet painting, where there is little space for perspective or soft distances, and where the initial white undercoat thrusts all the details forward, there is a sense of life pushing out of the frame towards the observer. A modest theatre, with a small box stage, this was the right platform to change history.

The first of many plays that benefited from this alchemy, and one which made their reputation, was *Cathleen Ni Houlihan*. Initially and steadfastly claimed by Yeats, it turns out (in not the only instance of credit larceny in the proscenium century) to have been largely written by Lady Gregory. A notable Irish folklorist, as with many from the Protestant Ascendancy, including Oscar Wilde's parents, she loved to collect and anthologise fables and poems from neighbours in the West of Ireland. In her words, 'It was not to the corners of newspapers I looked: it was to stonebreakers and potato diggers and paupers in the workhouse, and beggars at my own door.' The surprise in this sentence is not only the content, but also the rhythm and syntax. Though Gregory was from the landowning class, connected to literary London (there was an adulterous affair with Wilfrid Scawen Blunt) and Westminster potentates, in her middle age she became an Irish nationalist and her writing voice came over all Irish rural.

At her estate at Coole in 1903, Yeats told her of a dream 'almost as distinct as a vision, of a cottage where there was well-being and firelight and talk of a marriage, and into the midst of that cottage came an old woman in a long cloak . . . Ireland herself, that Cathleen Ni Houlihan for whom so many songs have been sung and about whom so many stories have been told and for whose sake so many have gone to their death.' This powerful and ancient siren would inspire the young man of the house to drop all bonds of family and love to follow Cathleen and fight for his country. Both had adapted such folk stories before, and they set to.

Though the incantatory verse at the end belongs to Yeats, the story depends on the creation of a believable world into which strangeness can intrude. Believable was not the poet's forte. Yeats himself once said his defect as a dramatist was that 'normal men did not interest' him, which pretty much disqualified him at the get-go. The naturalistic setting, the easy dialogue about marriage and money, the rhythms of family chatter, were all down to Lady Gregory. In some ways their partnership marked the essence of what the Abbey was up to in its first years, Yeats's symbolism summoning spirits from the ether, while Gregory's realism and humour kept mud on the characters' boots. In later years, Yeats was open about the amount his friend had contributed, writing to her that 'it was always you who gave the right turn to the phrase and gave it the ring of daily life.' When her family pressed her as to why she didn't stake more of a claim, she said, with a tiny note of acid condescension, she did not want to take from the poet any part of 'what had proved, after all, his one real popular success'.

Short plays and one-acts were the staple of the early Abbey diet, and *Cathleen Ni Houlihan* opened in a double bill with *Deirdre* by George Russell in April 1902 in St Theresa's Hall on Clarendon Street. The play became the powerhouse of the repertoire and opened the Abbey when the company moved in two years later. Set in 1798, with Wolfe Tone's rebellion hovering in the background, the largest chunk of the play revolves around a happy family preparing to celebrate the nuptials of its young son. Into this sublunary set-up walks Cathleen Ni Houlihan, the mythical symbol of Irish nationalism, old and young and old, and embodied in the first shows by the legendary beauty and muse of Yeats, Maud Gonne. Her entrance proved a showstopper that changed a nation. Filling the doorway of a spartan cottage, dressed in a heavy cape and long dress, Gonne, with her carefully inculcated otherness, electrified the audience. Talking in easily readable symbols, she describes her four 'beautiful green fields', representing the four provinces of Ireland, robbed from her by force. She says they must be taken back, that a blood sacrifice must be given, and that 'many a child will be born and there will be no father at the christening'. After her departure, with the family taxed by the visitation, the father asks his son if he saw an old woman leaving, and the son replies he saw a young girl who had 'the walk of a queen'. Gonne had a mesmeric capacity given to few. Her message was clear: the time had come to leave material things and to give up happiness, hope, and health for the good of Ireland.

Maud Gonne fills a doorframe and a nation's destiny moves forward.
Scene from *Cathleen ni Houlihan*

The effect was electric, and neither Yeats nor Gregory had seen it coming. A critic, Stephen Gwynn, wrote, 'I went home asking myself if such plays should be produced, unless one was prepared for people to go out to shoot and be shot . . . Miss Gonne's impersonation had stirred the audience as I have never seen another audience stirred.' George Bernard Shaw later described it as a play that might lead a man to do something foolish. Another critic wrote that *Cathleen Ni Houlihan*, and another work of Gregory's, *The Rising of the Moon*, 'made more rebels in Ireland than a thousand political speeches or a hundred reasoned books'. Though Yeats later disclaimed the work was any form of political propaganda, he wasn't fooling anyone. The effect of the play clearly troubled him, as he wrote later:

I lie awake night after night
And never get the answers right.
Did that play of mine send out
Certain men the English shot?

Cathleen Ni Houlihan was the beginning of a journey, a roller coaster ride through blood and flag-waving and history, and it began on a cramped proscenium stage in a rackety theatre. An adventure that drew J. M. Synge and Sean O'Casey into its adrenalised quest started here. The stated aim of Gregory and Yeats was 'to create a theatre that would add dignity to Ireland'. They, and the Abbey, achieved that and much more.

Anton Chekhov
1860–1904

Beyond.

(Or as the Abbey Theatre actors would say of nights when they touched the quietest heights . . .)

Beyond beyond.

Inimitable.
A scene from the Moscow Art Theatre production of Chekhov's *Three Sisters*

George Bernard Shaw
1856–1950

Bertrand Russell told this personal story of his one-time friend and ally George Bernard Shaw. A female friend of Russell's had fallen in love with a Russian colleague at London University. She married him and returned with him to live in the Soviet Union in the 1930s. Before long, her husband had fallen foul of the authorities and disappeared into the gulag. In despair, she returned to England, and lobbied friends with influence to help uncover what had happened, and maybe save her husband. Russell knew GBS was *persona grata* in the Soviet state, and had connected friends there, so took her to meet him. Hardly giving this devastated woman the time of day, he wrote to her brusquely afterwards, 'My dear lady, you have no idea how comfortable Russian penal settlements are. I'm quite sure your husband is much happier there than he would be being nagged by you.' Russell never spoke to him again.

Few people have striven as energetically to make themselves insufferable as George Bernard Shaw. His life's ambition often seemed to be to live, if the expression can be excused for an Irishman, beyond the pale. Having left the country of his birth and education to make his way in London, his career began as a critic, which can be a sure-fire path to alienating sections of the thespian community. Thankfully, as a critic he generously championed the work of others (including Robertson, Ibsen, and Pinero); he acknowledged his own partiality and wrote from a passionate desire for the theatre to make itself worthy of greater respect. In his definition: 'Only the ablest critics believe that the theatre is really important. A theatre to me is a place "where two or three are gathered together". The apostolic succession from Aeschylus to myself is as serious and as continuously inspired as that younger institution, the apostolic succession of the Christian church.'

His published works are enveloped by this sense of what theatre should be. The prefaces for each play are remorseless sermons on the context behind his work, the ideas within it, the purpose of theatre, and proscriptions for the improvement of society. You feel obliged to read them when addressing a work. After a couple of pages you find life, joy, and purpose draining slowly out of your body into the earth. If you skip the next thirty pages of the preface to start the play, you discover a further impediment: three or four pages of stage directions, which describe in microscopic detail the cluttered setting. With other playwrights, like Robertson, Galsworthy, and Lawrence, these can prove revelatory in their detail, but somehow with Shaw they deaden. The denial of one of the primary pleasures of play-reading – the freedom to imagine one's own landscape – is a sign of neurotic control it is hard to bypass. Having waded through this clotting detail, you keenly await the arrival of the characters, only to discover their first words are preceded by lengthy and thorough descriptions outlining exactly who they are and how they should be played. Imagination is again headed off at the first pass. Thereafter, almost every line is preceded by a controlling nudge as to how it should be delivered. This puppet-master instinct sucks every molecule of oxygen out of the room. The greater part of an atom is space: the corresponding thrill of the theatre is that it leaves almost as large a proportion of its matter open, the words serving as provocations for possibilities.

Many of the plays themselves reach for heights of resistibility. *The Apple Cart* seems to defy an audience's attempts to remain engaged; his retellings of the doings of historical celebrities, with Napoleon in *The Man of Destiny* and the eponymous in *Caesar and Cleopatra*, don't lift off the page (neither for me does *Saint Joan*, though many love it); and a lot of the supposed flat-out comedies are flat-out unfunny. The epitome of his commitment to defying playability was no doubt *Back to Methuselah*, five linked plays almost as eternal as their subject matter, whose narrative stretches from Adam and Eve in 4004 BC to imaginary beings of wisdom in AD 31,920. Shaw was a great fan of Wagner, and no doubt wanted to produce something as proudly excessive as *The Ring*, about which he wrote an adoring philosophical exegesis. He proclaimed *Methuselah* his 'supreme work in dramatic literature', though acceded that it was written more for the page than the stage, which makes it hard to see how it is dramatic. (Though within the ten hours of spewed verbiage there are diamonds, including the inspirational line Robert Kennedy later nabbed: 'You see things; and you say, "Why?" But I dream things that never were; and I say, "Why not?"') All of these works survive most effectively as narcotic sleep inducers, to be played softly on smartphones as a way to cope with broken nights.

Shaw wrote brilliantly about the ego and its dangers in plays and pamphlets, yet seemed to forget such acuity when he looked in the mirror. He drove his celebrity status as far as it could take him, and it took him all the way to the unique (in his lifetime) double of a Nobel Prize and an Oscar. A legend in his own day, liberally photographed and filmed and never averse to a bit of speech-giving, he was ever keen to confound new publics with his taste for controversy and for tweaking the noses of the *bien-pensants*. His relentless hunger for attention has lasted way beyond his death, with revivals and biographies and documentaries churned out on a regular basis.

And yet, and yet . . . Within this tsunami of know-it-allness, relentless authorial presence, and sermonising, there are lines which gleam, scenes which soar, and sometimes, on good nights, whole plays which tell us something intangible about ourselves. A devotee of what he praised as the 'theatre of ideas', it is only when he lets go of that unhealthy proscription that the strange and exciting occur. A similar rule applies to theatre as to conversation: anyone talking, acting, or writing from an elevation of moral or intellectual superiority soon becomes insufferable. Though that was Shaw's default position, sometimes blessedly his own verbosity, a topic of turbulence, or some personal trigger could trip him out of his certainty and into a more vulnerable realm. Sometimes he wrote out of the confusion of his psyche, from an ethical stance bewildered by the strangeness of human behaviour, and a philosophical one dazzled by the unknowability of the universe.

What should be the most irritating play of all, *Man and Superman*, a not-so-well disguised self-portrait in which a verbose drawing room sage

John 'Jack' Tanner (first played by Harley Granville-Barker with clothes and facial hair very like GBS's) bangs on at extravagant length, drawing a host of people (including attractive women) towards him, somehow backflips out of its potential ghastliness to be as enlivening and intoxicating as a glass of vintage bubbly. Tanner's fame comes from his booklet *The Revolutionist's Handbook and Pocket Companion*, an imaginary work (unsurprisingly published with the play as a 58-page appendix). I studied the play at A level (managing to read almost two-fifths of the preface), and even that didn't kill it.

As part of our studies, we coached up to the National Theatre to see the play in the Olivier, one of those water-cooler theatrical events we don't see any more. The mythic substructure for the play is that of Don Juan. In the full version of the play, there is a two-hour-long dream section – Don Juan in Hell – where the Jack Tanner character argues at length with the Devil, Doña Ana, and the statue of her father, Don Gonzalo. The National presented this whole. Somehow what should have been unendurable became thrilling, a firework display of idea and argument and speculation. Its presence in the here and now was sharpened by one of the most epic dries I've ever witnessed, when Daniel Massey, the actor playing Tanner, seemed to lose sense of which century he was in, let alone what line came next, before making a brilliant recovery. In the exhilaration of its dialectics and discourses, it genuinely felt like breathing a higher air. Theatre at its best can stimulate a communal intelligence sharper than any individual within that community could manage alone. We all take in more oxygen together. This was one of those nights. The sheer excess of rhetoric transported Shaw to a place where he wasn't on sure ground, where he could write from giddiness rather than certainty. On an unsteady precipice he was sounder and more generous-hearted than when stood four-square in the pulpit.

A year later, another production, directed by my father and starring Peter O'Toole, stormed the West End. This one didn't aim for the same philosophical expanse, dumping the dream section, but served up bravura thrills and more laughter within a well-constructed tale of a woman slowly tracking down her man. O'Toole had the old-school singing style of the Edwardian theatre, together with all the charisma of that era, and a lot of the same mischief. On two occasions he fell asleep onstage when his co-star had a long speech, and she had to shake him awake. On another, in front of a flat audience, whenever one of his jokes failed to raise a titter, he turned to the stalls and said 'Thud'. His performance was maybe compromised by his fuelling regime, whereby he would enter each act at a hundred miles an hour with braggadocio, then as each scene continued he would slow to lethargy, his light diminishing as he edged his way towards the back, before disappearing and then returning for the next act with the wind in his sails again. Somehow the play, which subsumes a witch's brew of subject matter into itself – anarchism, Darwinism, Nietzschean ideas of human aspiration, and the old battles for supremacy between the yin and the yang – sang with a fresh voice and spoke fully to a very different moment from its original one.

A similar aura of mystery hangs over *Heartbreak House*, subtitled (so no one is in any doubt) *A Fantasia in the Russian Manner on English Themes*. This play gathers an unlikely collection of influences – the Chekhovian house party setting, the wild coincidences of French farce, some Ibsenian symbolism, and Shaw's usual tennis rallies of sprightly debate – to create something happily misshapen and unlike anything else. Captain Shotover, an ancient inventor (again not unlike the author), wanders through, scattering gnomic utterances and transporting the play to a realm rich and strange. The play is set in a house designed like a ship, while far away the guns of the First World War are heard wreaking destruction. The metaphor of a broken ship taking on water acquires an awesome heftiness of effect, just as the civilisation preceding the Great War was dealt blows too tough for its survival.

A more personal mystery pervades *Candida*, a perverse love story where a dazzling and supremely irritating young poet – Eugene Marchbanks – tests the love of a charitable but stolid churchman and his wife, Candida. In tighter focus than most of Shaw's work, the play is almost a Strindbergian three-hander, though the tension in the centre ripples out to other characters. Shaw's love life was an unholy mess of platonic obsessions, relentless skirmishing, epistolary feuds, long pursuits, and failed campaigns. At the Oxford Stage Company, we produced *Candida* on tour, exquisitely directed by Chris Luscombe, and rooted in a set that looked like it weighed a hundred tons and embodied all the heft and tradition of the Church. A play without a kiss or even a touch, it purrs and hums with an almost overpowering sexuality. Options are opened up, considered, and explored, and the fact it all remains in the head – the place where it would seem Shaw was keenest to keep his sexuality – made its effect the more fierce.

As Shaw frequently reminded everyone, there was no greater engineer of social change working in the theatre in the nineteenth or twentieth centuries than GBS. The fact he boasts of his own achievement doesn't dissolve it. In a series of plays, he brought us information about a range of issues which needed light thrown within the open and democratic domain of the theatre. He went at this with a firebrand enthusiasm in his early years in the 1890s in what he later termed his 'Plays Unpleasant'. One, *Widowers' Houses*, exposes the slum-housing industry, another, *Mrs Warren's Profession*, exposes the sex industry and the cloud of hypocrisy wreathed around it. Within both, capitalism is seen as a pervasive poison which taints all who engage with it. These were plays written for a campaigning purpose, not solely for entertainment, though to be fair they do have stirring plots and are not ungarlanded with gags. Their principal role was to raise awareness and expose the webs of corruption and exploitation which the rich, the intended audience, were inescapably trapped within. Shaw soon moved away from explicit reportage, without ever losing his desire to raise the shutters on businesses that involved the whole of society. The arms industry comes under the microscope in *Major Barbara*, and the practice and ethics of modern medicine in *The Doctor's Dilemma*.

All needed an airing. Shaw brought ethics into an arena less compromised by money and influence than Parliament. For this he deserves praise. More importantly, when we watch these plays, and several of the others, even those on abstruse historical subjects, we see much of the early formation of the socialist consciousness. Shaw, through his proselytising, his associations, and his role within the Fabian Society was close to the heart of how modern socialism in Britain was formed. He invested a one-fifth share – £1,000 – to help launch a new publishing venture known as the *New Statesman*. He wrote the first manifesto for the Society, named 'Fabian Tracts, No. 2', and a further 'Tract, No. 13', with the unambitious title 'What Socialism Is'. He was a proponent of gradualism rather than Marxist revolution, of permeation rather than overthrow, and steered society away from anarchism towards change effected through institutions. He pushed for change and at the same time pulled for slowing it down. Too much of a control freak and a crank to last long in any movement, he squabbled with fellow Fabians, remaining disaffiliated from and suspicious of the Labour Party, yet the energy and profusion of his ideas helped propel these movements forward. Though his socialism may be tainted with a host of sins, it remains preferable to its opponents or its absence.

Perhaps my greatest surprise with the plays of GBS was when I directed *John Bull's Other Island* for the Tricycle Theatre (now the Kiln) in 2003. The crux of Shaw's play is the effect of capitalism on Ireland, and on the Irish character. A central question in Ireland now, when Irishness has become one of the world's most commodified national identities, and as we see the legendary sharp craic of the Dublin pub being branded and exported across the globe. Though the play was a hit on its first outing in 1904 and holds a significant place in the history of English and Irish theatre, it has been rarely produced since then. This obscurity was confounding, since it rapidly became clear that, if not Shaw's finest play, it was certainly in the top five. Indeed, given its wildness, naturalism, and truth, it often seemed to be a play by another writer – Shaw Redux.

The problem with its reputation may have been the title. What's in a name? Well, quite a lot if you're a playwright. A good title will encapsulate some of the energy of the story, stick in the minds of its potential audience, and draw them towards it. A bad title will miss the mark, confuse, and leave people cold. To take Noël Coward's titles: *Private Lives* – great, sharp, mysterious, and slightly dirty; *Hay Fever* – even better, delightful, summery, yet with a hint of sneeze; *The Vortex* – exciting, a bit Gothic, and scary. GBS rarely rose to the same heights of title-work as Coward or many others. *Major Barbara* hardly oozes sex; you can't exactly hear the champagne bubbling in *Arms and the Man*; and *Man and Superman* smacks of a heavyweight philosophical lecture at the Royal Geographical Society (rather like the play). Yet of all Shaw's titles, few scale the same depths of awfulness as *John Bull's Other Island*. The poverty of the joke, the aggression of 'John Bull', the nothingness of 'Other'.

The play's genesis was an invitation by his friend/rival/alter ego Yeats to write a play for the Abbey. Shaw was a giant of the commercial theatre at the time, and there could be no greater way to help inaugurate an Irish national theatre than with a play from the world's most popular playwright. But if they were expecting a commercial Rolls-Royce of a play, they were due a surprise. Commissions have a powerful effect on writers, shaping what they believe their obligations to be, and this was a resonant one for Shaw. He had never written of Ireland before, had never dealt with his own childhood, and never discussed the twisted romance between his native and adopted countries, rarely allowing his imagination to delve into the murk of his identity. He was going home, so he had to tell the truth, and the truth would be queasy.

John Bull's Other Island is not a Synge nor an O'Casey play, but Shaw felt a commitment to honouring the motherland he had left behind. His scenes of Irish rural life are more easily, relaxedly naturalistic than almost anything else he wrote. They are infected with his wild comic spirit but have the rough charm of the true. The commission from Yeats also spurred the poetry in his pen. He was ever jealous of the Apollonian acclaim given to the versifiers, and felt unfairly left out. In some passages about Ireland, both of adoration and of deep loathing, Shaw reached heights of lyricism he rarely approached elsewhere.

In addition to the truth and the poetry, GBS knew he could not get away with boulevardier's charm. It had to come from his heart. So in place of a well-oiled narrative, he came up with three iconic figures: Broadbent the bumptious Englishman of hard Fabian facts, Doyle the Irish expat who has made his way in the world and learned nothing but self-loathing, and Keegan the lapsed priest and king of the saintly paradox. These are sharply realised individuals yet also exemplify different aspects of Shaw's divided soul. Instead of a story of suspense and surprise, and instead of a lecture from a triangle of known positions, GBS splits himself into a trinity and sees what comedy, what heartbreak, and what insight ensues. All is in flux. Deeply personal and, in its lack of conventional dramatic structure, surprisingly modern.

Yeats and his committee hardly knew what to do with it. They liked the play, and could feel a freshness, originality, and importance. Yet they were cautious, worrying its political and moral equivalence was not what they had in mind for the Gaelic theatre. Eventually they let it go with a flurry of excuses about lacking the hydraulic equipment necessary for staging it. Their loss was the Royal Court's gain. *John Bull's Other Island* was the first new play performed by Granville-Barker's Stage Society. Though only presented for matinees, it was a raging success. The prime minister came four times, on one occasion bringing the leader of the opposition as his guest (can you imagine that now?). The future King George V came and laughed so hard he broke his chair.

Then the play disappeared. Possibly because of its lumpen title, and possibly because of its treatment of Ireland. The play discusses Home Rule but does not turn on it. For eighty odd years of the last century, English culture suffered from a peculiar myopia in relation to Ireland. If anything was Irish, then it had to be about the Irish question. Nothing else mattered. Now we gaze with envy on a resurgent economy, we have come to understand that Ireland is and always has been about a lot more than weeping women and murderous men. In that context, *John Bull's Other Island* looks more pertinent. Not for the only time, Shaw was ahead of the game. The play still needed cutting, but drew people to the scruffy truth of its naturalism. The romance (underscored in our production by a lot of Wagner) acquired a mythic edge, the love story was sincere and affecting, and it enjoyed no shortage of wild and inane laughter.

A complicated image. Harley Granville Barker (right) in a scene from *John Bull's Other Island*, *c.*1905

The laughter, when it works, is a great part of the Shaw effect, because it has a benevolence not always present in the arguments. As he said of the theatre, it is a 'church where the oftener you laugh the better, because by laughter only can you destroy evil without malice, and affirm good fellowship without mawkishness'. In its final long trialogue between the protagonists on a heathery hill, Niall Buggy, the Irish actor playing Keegan, raised it with paradox and passion and pathos to the strange mystic realm it aspired to.

Floating there with a packed and attentive house, one couldn't help but be grateful to Shaw – for all his many sins – for constructing the balloon to lift us up.

Arthur Schnitzler & Frank Wedekind
1862–1931; 1864–1918

Sex forms a staple of the diet that fuelled the proscenium story factory. The derangement of lust is what sets the carousel of farce spinning, before deception and accidence send it further out of control. There is no Feydeau without the mania of le désir. The black dog of infatuation spins characters off their axis in Chekhov and Strindberg and Synge. Mae West found fame and ten days in jail for her 'immoral' Broadway hit *SEX* – the three big capital letters banishing subtlety and pulling the punters in. Federico Lorca and Tennessee Williams showed in a variety of guises the dangers of trying to control unruly eros. And adultery, imagined or achieved, is probably the prime plot spring across the whole century. Sexual desire furnished punchlines, undergirded narratives, and provided the chemistry for many a crackling moment. It also shifted more tickets than any other selling point in the century.

Yet few playwrights dealt *directly* with sex. There was an awkwardness and a *pudor* around it, which made it not a subject for proper conversation. We spend much time watching the ramifications and hearing the echoes of sex without looking directly at it. This is hardly surprising for an age that saw a boom in the sex worker industry, while insisting it remain shameful and clandestine. That is until two writers, often colleagues and close correspondents, stepped forward and covered the subject of sex with a blunt intensity. Where else could they have emerged from than *fin de siècle* Berlin and Vienna? Benjamin Franklin Wedekind and Arthur Schnitzler brought desire to the stage with an honesty and a cool detachment that startles over a century later.

Both men were, to choose a polite term, adventurers. Wedekind, a sometime circus performer, actor, and cabaret singer, was a prodigy of polyamory, with an enthusiasm for experiment, contracting syphilis from sleeping with prostitutes. One of Strindberg's wives – Frida Uhl – bore

Wedekind a child. Schnitzler wrote a diary for over fifty years, which amounts to almost eight thousand pages. Juggling a variety of lovers at any one time, he recorded everything with analytical candour, at one time keeping a written record of every orgasm. This is the sort of studied promiscuity that chills.

The age was driven by a desire to dig into the roots of human behaviour and to apply science to what was uncovered. Schnitzler and Wedekind were part of a social circle – including Hauptmann among the playwrights, and Nietzsche, Freud, and Rilke among friends and lovers – that orbited around a Russian-German writer, Lou Andreas-Salomé. Renowned as 'the mother of psychoanalysis', she had a brief affair with Wedekind, which she turned into a novel. Schnitzler was close to Freud, and after witnessing the long-delayed first performance of *Reigen*, the psychoanalyst wrote, 'You have learned through intuition – though actually as a result of sensitive introspection – everything that I have had to unearth by laborious work on other persons.' When Schnitzler was later quizzed as to his central theme, he replied, 'I write of love and death. What other subjects are there?' – which more or less sums up Freud's opus. This was the birth of the psychology age, and both playwrights were close to its cradle.

Wedekind achieved his greatest renown for his two-play 'Lulu' cycle – *Earth Spirit* in 1895 and *Pandora's Box* in 1904 – a hollow picaresque which charts the rise and fall of a temptress dancer through late-nineteenth-century Europe. Propelled by the allure of sexual modernity, these dark expressionist works migrated from Berlin to Hollywood. The film they inspired immortalised their heroine, her first interpreter (Louise Brooks), and a haircut (the sculpted bob). At one moment Lulu is a gilded courtesan, at another a poor prostitute. Various taboo subjects are aired, including lesbianism, and Jack the Ripper makes an appearance – played, disturbingly in the premiere, by Wedekind himself. The vacancy at the heart is Lulu herself, revealed more through the variety of male gazes than her own agency. Her name remains a mystery to the end, Lulu being one of a series of monikers applied by those she encounters.

Some emptiness around sex itself, some lack of texture or tangent in its carnal essence, makes it exacting to translate with interest to the stage (and notoriously difficult to write about in the novel). The storytelling and empathy of each rely, in some way, on clothing.

Though Wedekind's *Spring Awakening* also lacks a centre, our sympathies and hearts are engaged by the callow ensemble, all in their teenage years. Written with a unique blend of naturalism and early expressionist gestures, the play is a series of strange, tender, lyrical snapshots, as if derived directly from life in all its strangeness. The heart-rending fumbles of these kids in an arena where they have had no education inspires profound compassion. Here we have the full smorgasbord of pubescent experiment, including sadomasochism, group male masturbation, and homoeroticism. The disjunction between the passions of these youths and their lack of a language to understand their feelings leads to bleak outcomes: a rape and a suicide. In a world that leans on shame, where dresses must be worn long and babies are delivered by storks, the silence and moral repression open a door to tragedy. In its time, Wedekind's play was a revolution of openness and knowledge. On a subject parents couldn't address with their own children, the theatre brought a storm cloud of knowledge that had previously been sequestered.

Schnitzler's most celebrated play *Reigen* is now better known by the title of Max Ophüls's film adaptation, the masterpiece *La Ronde*. Written in 1897, printed privately in 1900, and published to enormous success in 1903, the play did not come to the stage until 1920, so controversial were its themes and their presentation. When it did finally appear, its author was branded a pornographer. The play follows a series of successive encounters between pairs of characters either preceding or following sex. Different attitudes to class and sexual morality are revealed as a whore meets a soldier, and then the soldier seduces a maid, and then the maid encounters a young married gentleman, and on the roundelay dances from person to person as class boundaries are transgressed and fleeting moments of human contact shared. The rhythm of each encounter is repeated – want, satisfaction, and then emptiness. The play has been adapted in myriad reworkings on film, television, and in the theatre. Something in the neatness of the concept draws artists. Yet it often leaves behind a flattening chill. People are drawn to it expecting sensation and flavour, and are served up the cold porridge of human indifference.

When it first appeared onstage there was an unsurprising scandal, and the virulent reactions shaded into a bitter and vicious antisemitism. This is a theme Schnitzler explored further in *Professor Bernhardi*, a canary-in-the-mine revelation of how that toxic prejudice can metastasise into collective psychosis. A minor incident – a doctor blocking a doorway in a hospital to prevent a priest from giving last rites to a dying patient – escalates into a social crisis. This was one of three plays, alongside *Musik* by Wedekind and *Rose Bernd* by Hauptmann, we co-produced at the Oxford Stage Company at the Arcola Theatre in 2003.

We chose not to concentrate on the racy side of their work but to celebrate plays showcasing other virtues. These three playwrights – acutely aware of one another as friends and inspirations – presented theatre of exquisite humanity. A world of care and precious attention is expended on each human action, however insignificant. Within Hauptmann's social analysis, and Schnitzler and Wedekind's precise medical diagnoses, lies the suggestion, however faint, that things are getting better, and that their work is part of that process. Living in the same milieu as Einstein, who was busy evaporating Newton's certainties and turning the world inside out, and Freud, whose case histories and essays were sending millions diving into the wells of their psyches, this was a time of searching for new understandings, a time when there was a glimmer of hope for the human condition. The playwrights were realists and shared in a despair at much of what they looked on. But they also shared in a moment when a certain dream was alive – of understanding the self, of recording the dance of the atom, of watching light bend as it slipped past a planet, of making the world a better place. And the aim of our season was to commemorate and perhaps once again inspire that hope.

It was a worthy cause but it didn't ignite at the box office. Maybe we should have leaned more heavily on the sex.

Everybody loves Lulu.
Poster for the film *Pandora's Box*, 1929

J. M. Barrie
1860–1937

Drugs don't seem to have been a large part of the diet of J. M. Barrie, but few writers came up with a story more hallucinogenic than *Peter Pan*. A child psychopath kidnaps a gaggle of siblings from their bedroom and transports them to an imaginary world where lost children, Native American tribes and pirates fight bloodthirsty battles, a mutilated old man sits on a mushroom which turns out to be the chimney of an underground hovel, and a crocodile prowls around emitting the sound of the ticking clock he has swallowed. Barrie had no need of LSD, he just dipped his bucket down into the well of his subconscious and dragged up some crazy.

When *Peter Pan, or The Boy Who Wouldn't Grow Up* had its first stage performance on 27 December 1904 at London's Duke of York's, Barrie was already an experienced playwright. His first success, bizarrely, was a parody of Ibsen – *Ibsen's Ghost* – in which Thea Elvsted has married Torvald Helmer and suffers from an obsessive compulsion to kiss everyone. How they laughed! Following that success, Barrie wrote a succession of social comedies. Knowing the theatre well, he would have understood the sheer spatial thrill of seeing a boy lifted up to fly (quite literally) away from domestic normality. For an audience accustomed to the static dimensions of the frame, this undermining of the rules of gravity was transporting.

Peter Pan became a mythic figure, one of many in this, the great British age for forging legends. Something within the exploratory imagination of empire builders, and the pathology of Edwardian repression, created a soil fertile for myths to sprout up like mushrooms. Contact with new cultures and the loosening of Victorian stays must have provided nurturing weather too. Barrie founded a cricket team with the unfortunate name of the Allahakbarries, believing that 'Allahu Akbar' meant 'heaven help us' rather than 'God is the Greatest.' The team sheet is an extraordinary list of myth-makers: A. A. Milne, who gave us Winnie the Pooh; Arthur Conan Doyle, Sherlock Holmes; P. G. Wodehouse, Jeeves and Wooster; G. K. Chesterton, Father Brown; Rudyard Kipling, *The Jungle Book*; Jerome K. Jerome, *Three Men in a Boat*; and H. G. Wells, who gave us a gallimaufry of invented icons – alien invasions in *The War of the Worlds*, time travel in *The Time Machine*, and *The Invisible Man*.

Barrie was not short of pathologies. At the age of six he went out skating with his much-loved elder brother David, who slipped and fell, cracking his head open on the ice, an injury which proved fatal. This was followed by a catastrophic withdrawal of love by their mother, who had lost her favourite son. In a desperate move, the young James tried to compensate for the loss by wearing David's clothes, and wandering the house imitating his whistle. To no effect, as his parents sent him away to a boarding school at the age of eight, one of a series of educational institutions that distanced him from parental love. Lost boys and a child who never grows old (*Peter Pan*), a girl who gets stuck at a single age (*Mary Rose*), a childless couple who discover a fantasy daughter in a midsummer wood (*Dear Brutus*), all of these plays seem to have grown from emotional injury. Each features open-hearted yearning for a mother.

As the child psychologist John Bowlby later diagnosed, the Edwardian age was a time of devastatingly distant parenting among the upper middle class. Children, as Bowlby argued, need a careful balance of attachment and separation, maturing gently from the first to the second to grow with balanced psyches. The late-Victorian and Edwardian habit of banishing offspring to the nursery and the care of nannies, before exiling them to remote and often abusive institutions didn't make for balance. In many, it stunted and cauterised a capacity for love. Not least Barrie, who suffered a loveless, unconsummated marriage, and whose fascination with the Llewellyn Davies boys – the inspiration for *Peter Pan* – has raised eyebrows. Whatever his proclivities, he certainly cannot write romance with anything but an arch stiffness. Yet when he writes of loss and the need for family devotion the floodgates open and he is at his most theatrically articulate.

His awkwardness with love comes to the fore in *Dear Brutus*, which attempts to write human passion and comes a cropper. Whether it is jealousy, 'Freddie Finch-Fellow is a rotter, Alice!' or desire, 'There's just one cup I want to drink – and its name is Mabel!' this is far from Barrie's comfort zone. But digging for coal in the emotional substratum with the richest seam – abandoned children and a father's mourning of missed opportunities – he hits a plangent note. Even more with *Mary Rose*, an effective ghost chiller about a young woman who disappears into the mists of an island, only to reappear years later at exactly the same age. Her parents, husband, and child yearn for the love they have lost. The play makes spooky use of ghost story tropes, both out on the lake and in a West Sussex house disturbed by angry spirits. None of it feels gratuitous, the strangeness manifesting naturally as an extension of Barrie's divided soul, torn between the London boulevardier and the Lowlands mystic.

Angst meets innocence.
J. M. Barrie (as Hook) and Michael (as Peter Pan) on the lawn at Rustington, 1906

For Mary Rose as for Barrie, something stops in childhood in Scotland, and can never mature. The drama plays games with time, much as J. B. Priestley did later in a variety of works, but here it expresses human truth rather than being philosophically playful. When trauma occurs, as it did for the six-year-old James Michael out on the sheet ice, time stops for a brief aperture and emotional gravity makes its mark. A scar is left on a place and an instant, which cannot be rubbed clean. Something of ourselves is left behind, some stock of the soul deposited, and it will call us back. In events as cataclysmic as the accident for Barrie, and the subsequent withdrawal of his mother's love, the trauma inhibited him from ever moving forward.

In a beautiful and poignant scene at the end of *Mary Rose*, the searching spirit finds what she has lost and is allowed to find rest. One can feel J. M. Barrie's pent-up need pulsing through. In the audience's thrill at that moment, and in their tears, one can sense their need to transcend childhoods marred by evanescences of connection. Barrie remains the laureate of lonely children, and the lonely child still shivering with playground anxiety in every adult.

John Galsworthy
1867–1933

A character in *The Skin Game* is described as having a 'stubborn look of veiled choler'. An apt description for the character and his rival, it serves well for the sensibility of John Galsworthy. One wonders if it is not a precise way of describing much of the Edwardian male temperament. Stubborn veiled choler.

With Galsworthy, the generic proscenium unease – an audience who come for comfort, and artists who want to needle them – reaches a sharp point. Screeching social tensions are encased within whip-smart narratives, full of hoary old tricks of suspense and whodunnit and who-will-win. The combination led to further exemplars of the classic proscenium paradox – entertainment encasing dysfunction. War stories of social discontent, demonstrating an era's sickness to itself, playing to packed and appreciative theatres.

Galsworthy served up a series of documentary reports on the world as it was. His early training as a lawyer brought a fastidious eye for detail, alongside an inherent balance and understanding of all points of view. In one instance, the news he brought via the stage led to swift legislative reform. His play *Justice* shows, with the unbiased reportage for which he was renowned, a weak and vacillating young clerk committing a petty felony for the best of intentions – to protect a young mother regularly battered by her husband. A minor misdemeanour, it precipitates a headlong fall into the machine of Justice, whose seeming care veils structures built to grind will and crush spirit. The focus tightens step by step from a fully realised courtroom to a prison corridor and finally to a prison cell, where we watch the young man's fragile self break into pieces. The scenes of disintegration were so powerful they harrowed their audience. One spectator, Home Secretary Winston Churchill, was prompted to hurry through legislation ensuring inmates could no longer be held in solitary confinement for their first month.

Elsewhere, Galsworthy brought information about the red-raw conflict between labour and capital. *Strife* takes us into the homes of striking workers at the Trenartha Tin Plate Works, alongside granting us access to the directors' discussions over lavish lunches. No polarities are simple: the strikers are at war with each other – socialist radicals espouse principles in one corner, while placating moderates want to end the strike in another. Among the company directors, the humane faction wants to concede, while the worshippers of capital are happy to let women and children go to the wall rather than be seen to lose. In *Loyalties*, we see the prejudices of race play out in London's high society as another case works its way through the courts, and society's chosen beautiful turn their backs on a Jewish member of their cohort. As screws tighten within these narratives, it is never possible to know which way judgements will settle, nor to doubt the procedural truth.

The premieres of these explosive documents generated a galvanic energy which can still be imagined a century later. Galsworthy kept his own and the audience's hands close to the fire. Communal breath was held when they first witnessed Roberts the firebrand striker preaching the downfall of capitalism, or a prison governor walking down a long corridor interviewing inmates in disrepair, or the unmasking of virulent antisemitism in a London club. The characters may have been familiar – that familiarity was the audience's passport into these stories – but the depths to which they travel, as a consequence of their actions, less so. The unsentimental and blunt reportage would have exhilarated.

The chief antagonism through all the work is the fundamental one of class. Not the easy and assured sense of class from *Downton Abbey*, where all know their place and live happily within prescribed grooves. This is a turbulent understanding, where superiority is no natural state but one that needs regular enforcement by violence and vigilance. Galsworthy was no Marxist, but he had witnessed the brutality of class exclusion. At an early age he fell in love with his cousin's wife, Ada, trapped in a dysfunctional marriage. Unable to suppress their love, they chose to cohabit and were swiftly shut out from drawing rooms which had previously extended a welcome. The harshness of the exclusion reset his understanding of the society he was born into.

The bare bones of such antagonism are laid out in *The Skin Game*, where the Hornblowers, newly wealthy manufacturers, are buying up the land around a country house belonging to the aristocratic Hillcrists, to build potteries exploiting local clay. What starts out as nimbyism descends into open warfare, where no trick is too low to achieve victory. The eternal battle between the upward and the static is stripped to its essence here. The distinction between the two families is made transparent in an exchange between the Hillcrist daughter and father:

JILL But, Dodo, why all this – this attitude to
the Hornblowers?

She purses her lips and makes a gesture as of pushing people away.

HILLCRIST Because they're pushing.
JILL That's only because we *are*, as mother would say,
and they're *not* – yet.
But why not let them be?
HILLCRIST You can't.

However innocently and charmingly questioned, the blanket othering of claiming that 'we *are* . . . and they're *not*' contains within its pithy sharpness centuries of dehumanisation. In a modern world which appropriates the language of othering for distinctions of race, gender, and sexuality, it is easy to forget how much those attitudes were originated by the great othering of class. And equally easy to ignore how prevalent it remains.

Galsworthy knew the battle he was joining, and its theatrical antecedents – in *The Eldest Son*, the play the young amateur thespians try to rehearse is *Caste* by Tom Robertson. Sands were shifting in the world beyond the theatre. At the 1906 general election, the Labour Representation Committee had won a groundbreaking twenty-nine seats, and later that year it reconstituted itself as the Labour Party. Galsworthy's first play premiered a year later. Class-consciousness was on the rise, a source of excitement for many, and terror for others. Containing all these energies within the frame created plays with combustible impact.

After 1918, morality, identity, and language were all under strain. In *Loyalties*, one character observes of the moral disintegration of another, a hero of the trenches now lost in gambling, whoring, and theft, 'The war loosened "form" all over the place.' That simple phrase crystallises all sorts of collapse. The challenge for Galsworthy and other dramatists of the age was to contain 'loosening form' in an arena that demanded tight framing. The strain between the two could make some plays seem obsolete, in blithe denial of the world without. It electrified others, including Galsworthy's.

Streamlined Rolls-Royce naturalism was required for his plays to achieve their effect. Though the settings are varied, from a pauper's cottage to a solicitor's office, the voice is assured, and once one has stepped on board, one feels effortlessly carried forward. Oblique, sparing, flinty details summon a world at speed – an accountant numbering his sums, a maid setting out flowers for guests, a prison doctor describing his lunch – all presented with a procedural meticulousness which seduces the audience into engagement.

Character descriptions are sometimes an encumbrance for actors, designers, and directors. They create a perfect picture impossible to live up to. Or an indelible image hard to wipe from an actor's brain as a character develops. Galsworthy's are a pleasure, an aesthetic treat all their own. Detailed, precise, and evocative, they bring ghosts to life, ranging from the functional, '*COKESON – a man of sixty, wearing spectacles; rather short, with a bald head and an honest pug dog face*', to the tantalising, '*She appears in the doorway in under-garment and a wrapper. She is fair, about thirty-five, rather delicious and suggestive of porcelain*', to the mischievous, '*JOHN LATTER, in a clergyman's evening dress, comes sedately downstairs, a tall, rather pale young man, with something in him, as it were, both of heaven and a drawing-room.*'

Here, staggeringly, is the description of a minor character, the Auctioneer, not even afforded a name, from *The Skin Game*. His sole scene lasts eight minutes, his function to carry out an auction, but the scrupulosity of observation is a matter of principle: '*He is a square, short, brown-faced, common-looking man, with clipped grey hair fitting him like a cap, and a clipped great moustache. His lids come down over his quick eyes, till he can see you very sharply, and you can hardly see that he can see you. He can break into a smile at any moment, which has no connection with him, as it were. By a certain look, however, when bidding is slow, he discloses that he is not merely an auctioneer, but has in him elements of the human being. He can wink with anyone, and is dressed in a snuff-brown suit, with a perfectly unbuttoned waistcoat, a low, turned-down collar, and small black and white sailor-knot tie*.'

That level of particularity raises everyone's game. Often when rehearsing a show, an excessive level of attention to a minor detail can create a numinous truth in one area, which spreads like a benevolent infection to the rest. Galsworthy is a master of this – in such descriptions, in use of props, in snatches of overheard dialogue from an attached room, he sets a standard of rigour which it ill suits collaborators not to match.

The narratives serve up the main pleasure, but also the fault lines. These are plots with a capital P, big boys' plots. We have policemen investigating crimes, trials with speeches for prosecution and defence, investigations of crime scenes, people spying on others from behind curtains, as well as revelations, cliffhangers, and denouements. All the tools of melodrama are on well-buffed display, and to be relished. All mitigate against the quieter virtues – observation and modest truth. Squaring the circle between rapacious storytelling and commitment to the whirligig of life is never fully within the author's grasp.

Antagonisms pulse throughout Galsworthy in a state at war with itself: between strikers and trustees, between the nouveau riche and old money, between the clubbable not-so-inclusive and those they exclude, between those who would use justice gently and those who relish punishment. There are no happy resolutions. His two most monumental pairings of bull-in-a-field antagonists – the workers' leader and the chairman in *Strife*, and Hillcrist and Hornblower in *The Skin Game* – lay waste to each other. None can claim a final victory. The victim of the machine of the law in *Justice* finally hurls himself down a flight of stairs to his death; the veteran of the First World War in *Loyalties* shoots himself; all end loveless in *The Eldest Son*. The spirit is far from comic: no one dances off to a wedding at the close. Galsworthy reported from a world whose oppositions were bound to wound, with no wish to plaster over the resulting hurts.

Not so veiled choler. *The Skin Game*, 1920

He believed battles worked their way towards resolution: 'My view of the universe is that of a perpetual conflict between opposing principles, dark and light, life and death, ebb and flow. Between these conflicting principles in nature there is a mysterious and by us not to be appreciated point of reconciliation. In moral and spiritual spheres there is just this same perpetual state of conflict through which the human mind and spirit travels towards the mysterious harmony, which stills and reconciles.' The 'mysterious harmony' often proves hard to discern. An open wound, with blood flowing, seems more apposite. It is to Galsworthy's credit, and that of his theatre, that the battles were allowed to rage freely, ferocity undimmed.

Characters in his plays often accuse each other of a lack of 'imagination' when dealing with other people. Their inability to imagine their way into the minds and souls of others condemns them. Not an argument that could be levelled at the author. 'All human problems,' Galsworthy said, 'certainly all those I raise will turn out to be more soluble by an increase of sympathy and understanding.' He hoped to effect in his audience 'a sort of mental and moral ferment, whereby vision may be enlarged, imagination livened and understanding promoted'. In this cause he steered his audience into the homes and hearts of the wives of strikers on the point of starvation, of the administrative staff of a barely functioning prison, of rich children careering around a country house in search of a room to rehearse in. Whoever and whatever their circumstances, he allows them the same panoptic sympathy and largesse. All in the hope the audience would step outside themselves.

Art, Galsworthy stated, is 'the continual unconscious replacement, however fleeting, of oneself by another'.

J. M. Synge
1871–1909

'I'll fight any one of you!' Rarely has an anonymous figure cut such a dash at a seismic cultural event as the unknown Galwayman. It was Tuesday 29 January 1907, the third night of J. M. Synge's *Playboy of the Western World* at the Abbey. With tensions broiling in the theatre, and in Dublin at large since Saturday's first night – tensions happily stoked by Yeats with inflammatory comments to the press – everyone was waiting for something to kick off. Dressed in a heavy coat (he was later dubbed Napoleon in satires), the Galwayman decided to waste no time. He was one of a cadre of Trinity students whom Lady Gregory had invited – 'a few fellow athletes' of her nephew, 'that we might be sure of some able-bodied helpers in case of an attack on the stage'. This qualifies as history's worst bit of house management. Trinity College students (then almost exclusively Protestant and unionist) had a long tradition of drunken uproar in Dublin theatres. The play had already caused grievous upset in the nationalist community, who catcalled and barracked the first two shows. Inviting the students to perform a bodyguard role was the equivalent of putting out fires with gasoline. Giving them alcohol to boot was insanity.

Already blotto before the show began, the Galwayman resolved that if there was any fighting to do, they might as well get on with it. He issued his challenge from the stalls to the pit. Sensing no takers, he climbed on a chair and made an incoherent speech, concluding with the touching admission, 'I am a little bit drunk and don't know what I am saying.' Pleased with the attention, he zigzagged his way with the help of upright objects to the front of the pit and played a wobbly waltz on the theatre's piano. Ushers steered him back to his seat, as he protested 'they won't allow me to speak, though I am a Labour member', which raised a big laugh. Sitting down quietened him, and thankfully the rest of the house. The sombre curtain-raiser, Synge's one-act requiem *Riders to the Sea*, passed in respectful quiet.

All might have carried on with some decorum had not Yeats – the provocateur of provocateurs – come onstage in his bow tie before the main show. Talking down from his lofty social and spiritual height, he made a few comments about 'the freedom of the theatre', and how 'no man has the right to interfere with another man who wants to hear the play.' Fingers itched and fists clenched. Yeats knew what he was doing: he was a connoisseur of theatre riots. He attended the first night of *Ubu Roi* in Paris and wrote about the chaos that ensued. He tracked down a more obscure symbolist opening in Paris, *Axël*, on the off chance of some mayhem and was satisfied. His own play *The Countess Cathleen* was greeted with outrage, especially by the Church. He knew the value of scandal to drive ticket sales and, like his near contemporary Sergei Diaghilev, knew that the life of a performance was not just its run in the theatre. The noise it made in the wider world was part of the effect. A play was not a play unless there was a rumpus. He was not to be disappointed.

When the character Christy Mahon appeared, the audience began a counterpoint between outraged nationalists, who stomped their feet and hissed, and those who wanted to watch the show (aka hired thugs), who cheered and clapped. The actors' voices disappeared quickly under the ballyhoo, and the house lights were brought up. Brightness penetrated the brain of the Galwayman, who took this as a cue to start some punch-ups. Yeats – not a renowned pugilist – tried to stop him, before retreating to the stage to make more inflammatory comments. This time he gave a brief lecture about the Irish renown for 'courtesy and intelligence', which was met with a burst from a bugle. The Galwayman harmonised with cries of 'Woa, woa, you chap there. Woa, be a sportsman', as he tried to escape the clutches of friends holding him down. Chairs went flying. Finally, the author himself, Synge, and the sturdy actor playing Old Mahon, grappled the Galwayman out of the theatre. Yeats bounced back onstage, and with no shortage of understatement, said, 'we have persuaded one man who was, I regret to say, intoxicated, to leave the meeting. I appeal to all of you who are sober to listen.'

The play having stopped, the police were brought in, and half the audience turned snitch on the other half, pointing out those who should be chucked out. As rabble-rousers were ejected, the orchestra pounded out some jaunty tunes to give the arrests some swing. Once the play started again, the cry 'That's not the West' rang out often, a mark of how the nationalists felt their idealised image of the Western Islands was being traduced. There was a loud suggestion that the police, still ejecting troublemakers, should arrest Christy Mahon, the main character. As the volume of noise rose and fell the curtain shuttered down and flew up like a yo-yo. Somehow the actors soldiered on, trying to make a fiction real. As the evening staggered to its conclusion, lo and behold the Galwayman reappeared! Substantially refuelled! He reiterated his kind offer to fight anyone in the pit, but was drowned out by his Trinity chums who launched into a chorus of 'God Save the King', soon swamped by a counter-chorus of 'God Save Ireland'. Finally, the curtain brought an end to it. The audience spilled out into the city, and after a ramshackle wander through night streets, faction shouting abuse at faction, fell into the almost inevitable brawl. Yeats had his event. The next day, and days after, the world was talking about the Abbey.

Several years earlier, Lady Gregory, in her folklorist guise, had been wandering Inishmore, the northernmost of the Aran Islands, fishing as usual for myth and legend among the people, when she noticed to her consternation someone else doing the same. John Millington Synge was twenty-seven, a writer of talent, but one who had not yet found a voice. He was still looking for the material to unlock the heap of images and mess churning within. Like Yeats and Gregory, he was also an upper-middle-class Protestant, though he worked harder to screen his hauteur than the other two. Yeats had already met Synge in Paris, and soon he was invited to the Gregory estate at Coole, a sort of refuge for semi-permanent awaydays from the Abbey. In her flattening estimation, 'he had done no good work until he came back to his own country. It was there that he found all he wanted, fable, emotion, style . . . Bringing a cultured mind to a mass of primitive material, putting clearer and lasting form to the clumsy expressed emotion of a whole countryside.' Amazing how many people can be insulted within one generous comment.

Gregory was right that something in Synge was unlocked by the landscape and the people of the West. A wildness and a tenderness; a raucous honesty and a vulnerable dignity; a violent capacity to slag people off and a commensurate ability to fall in love with a pair of shy eyes. He had the same anthropologist's ear as Gregory herself, but more – a capacity to arrange heard speech into complex and symphonic music. Synge himself was a reserved and almost unknowable man. Yeats said he told him once that 'when he lived in some peasant's house, he tried to make those about him forget that he was there, and it is certain that he was silent in any crowded room. It is possible that low vitality helped him to be observant and contemplative.' Yet just as he could disappear in company, becoming all eyes and ears and notation, he could occasionally erupt and come blazingly alive playing his fiddle. That exuberance is more of a constant in his plays. They teem with noise and life.

Synge was sophisticated about drama and opinionated. He found a richness of flavour in poetry and prose poems, which he failed to see on the European stage, where he only saw 'Ibsen and Zola dealing with the reality of life in joyless and pallid words. On the stage one must have reality and one must have joy; and that is why the modern intellectual drama has failed, and people have grown sick of the false joy of the musical comedy, that has been given them in place of the rich joy found only in what is superb and wild in reality.' Something in that quote is close to the essence of the Abbey achievement, rolling down from Gregory's plays into Synge and on to O'Casey. Truth is the aim, always, but truth does not have to mean deadening earnestness. Just as much a part of truth is laughter, and poetry, and joy and life in all its inestimable variety. Yeats himself said of Synge and others, 'I notice that when anybody here writes a play it always works out, whatever the ideas of the writer, into a cry for a more abundant and intense life.'

There was unease among the three writers, and among them as senior figures within the institution. Synge was resentful that his plays didn't get the same exposure as those of Yeats; Gregory felt that Synge was ungracious and never expressed enthusiasm for anything but his own work. But there was also generosity. Yeats was big enough to recognise he had been struggling to find a theatrical language, and that his mystic-poetic plays were not setting the audience alight. When Synge appeared and somehow managed to do exactly what the poet had been attempting, to write something rooted in the earth and the actual, yet which also evolved imperceptibly into myth, it must have been a bitter pill to swallow. In public, Yeats remained a steadfast defender.

The focus of the Abbey stage, and the passionate political and social expectations revolving around it, magnified everything birthed on it, turning a one-act play into a full meal. Synge understood this intuitively and maximised its potential with two early one-acts, *In the Shadow of the Glen* and *Riders to the Sea*. Knowing how much food to serve is sometimes as important a skill as cooking. Even his full-length plays are short and divided into acts. Synge understood he was offering rich tucker, and the audience needed a moment to adjust their belts between acts. *Riders to the Sea* is a tense and then moving threnody as a small group of women await news of their men at sea, and see their worst fears realised. *In the Shadow of the Glen* tells a short story of how a woman is tricked by her husband into thinking he is dead, and then chooses to run off with a passing tramp. Her name is Nora, and as she closes the door on her possessive spouse, the intentional chime with Ibsen is heard. Yet how much fuller is this world than the parched Scandinavian drawing room. These people may be destitute but their language is abundant.

In the Shadow of the Glen opened up a schism between the Abbey management and the nationalists and their party, Sinn Fein. Their leader Arthur Griffith sensed a corrupting classical influence in the writing, and Maud Gonne, while pleading for a free theatre, qualified it disastrously by saying, 'I would ask for freedom for it from one thing more deadly than all else – freedom from the insidious and destructive tyranny of foreign influence.' Righteous nationalism carries strange sentiments as bedfellows. Nora leaving her husband for a stranger was bad, the characters' language and its casual desecration was worse, but worst of all for this community was the sense that Synge and Dublin were laughing at the West, implying it was full of a risible primitivism. For the nationalists, the West held on to a purity of what it was to be Irish. It was a holy place, and lampooning it was blasphemy.

Rumour travels fast in Dublin, and at the end of 1906, everyone knew that a new play by Synge, then in rehearsal, would double down on the offence caused by *In the Shadow of the Glen*. Members of the Abbey board got hold of the script and were nervous. Yeats and Gregory were told that they had lost the support of the Church with the poet's *Countess Cathleen*, and they had lost the Fenians with *In the Shadow*. To lose both at the same time, as the new play risked, might mean no coming back. One of the Fay brothers in the company said in rehearsals that all the bad temper in the play 'would inevitably infect the audience and make them bad-tempered too'. Synge came up with new lines in rehearsals, though his word on what stayed in and what went was final. 'We might as well have tried to move the Hill of Howth as move Synge,' as William Fay said.

'My next play will make them hop,' Synge told a friend of *The Playboy*, fully aware of its potential. The stakes were raised by casting a five-foot-three-inch comic actor as the father-slaying anti-hero Christy Mahon. The echoes of the Irish mythic figure Cuchulain were being mocked even by the casting, as well as underlining Synge's comical point that in County Mayo anyone can be turned into a hero. Christy, a supposed parricide at the beginning of the play, is the embodiment of the disjunction in any small community between the swagger and the hard truth. Since for centuries the reality for the Irish was one of poverty and oppression, a strain of self-mythification was a way of keeping dignity intact. An acute scenario within Irish culture, the chasm between boast and fact is also universal, and one of the many reasons the play has translated far and wide.

The provocation that tipped the balance on the first night was the mention of petticoats. Across the whole of the proscenium century, it is sadly regular how often audiences will put up with a multiplicity of challenges but fall to pieces when it comes to defending what they consider women's inviolable modesty. After Christy has made a second attempt to kill his recently resurrected father, he returns to announce that he would marry only Pegeen Mike, even if he was offered 'a drift of chosen females, standing in their shifts itself' (the actor flubbed the line, saying 'Mayo girls'). Pandemonium ensued. On that first night, it was only Lady Gregory present, since Yeats was in Aberdeen and Synge had tactical flu. Her two telegrams to Yeats have gone down in theatre history: after the first act, 'Play a great success', and at the end, 'Audience broke up in disorder at the word "shift"'. It is the mark of many a state excessively influenced by the Church that men go bananas at the thought that wives and daughters are being traduced. Too much was at stake on that first night, and on the more notorious third, for all the energies to be contained.

A faction in Ireland in 1907 had a desire to project an image of sober and steady decorum to the rest of the world. *The Playboy* blew that up with its tale of a scamp who cracks his father's head open with a spade then runs away, only to be talked up as a hero by a community starved of myths. Staging such a play in a new national theatre, and flirting with what some viewed as buffoonery, many saw as a dereliction of duty. The critic of the *Irish Times* wrote, 'It is as if a mirror were held up to our faces and we found ourselves hideous. We fear to face the thing. We scream.' Patrick Pearse, later the hero of the 1916 rebellion went further, 'It is not against a nation that he blasphemes, so much as against the moral order of the universe.' Pearse later recanted, recognising Synge as a patriot sending out messages people were not yet ready to receive.

Another faction at the time, and a growing one since, would have seen the production of such a play as an act of devil-may-care courage by a pivotal institution at the heart of a nascent state. The Abbey was forging a new identity out of blood and rhetoric and argument: here and later with O'Casey, they were able to see an honest picture in the mirror and to laugh heartily. Staging the play was not a million miles away from a theatre in Kabul programming satires about the extremism of fundamentalism after the Taliban regained power. It took courage alongside brazen effrontery. Many were the naysayers lined up against Yeats, Gregory, and Synge, but they held their nerve.

The play grew and prospered, a strange fable for the twentieth century from which everyone cherry-picked their own meanings. The parricide element was catnip for the Freudians; Sartre took Simone de Beauvoir over and over to the play, so she might understand the authenticity of a protagonist who has cut ties with his past, and 'who wished to derive only from himself'; and Brecht and others idolised Christy Mahon as un underclass rebel against an oppressive culture. He is the exemplar of the Brechtian maxim: 'Unhappy the land that has no hero. No; unhappy the land that needs a hero.'

Ever sickly, Synge died only two years after *The Playboy of the Western World* premiered. John Masefield, a friend, though held at distance as almost everyone was, wrote, 'His relish of the savagery made me feel that he was a dying man clutching at life, and clutching most wildly at violent life, as the sick man does.'

As Yeats said, 'Whenever a country produces a man of genius, that man is never like the country's idea of itself.'

The world he knew.
Pat Mac Donagh's cottage on Inis Meáin. Photo taken by J. M. Synge

Harley Granville-Barker
1877–1946

Harley Granville-Barker has been dubbed the 'father of modern British theatre', with some justice. A prodigy as a youth, he soon became a quintuple threat – actor, writer, director, entrepreneur, and activist. He burned a fiery comet trail through Edwardian theatre, quickly exhausting most of his spirit fuel, retiring as an actor in his twenties, as a director in his thirties, and altogether soon after. Born, without the hyphen, in 1877, to a mother famous for bird impressions and a father from the leisured classes who dabbled in architecture, young Harley was dreamily handsome. Leaving school to exploit his looks and talents as an actor at the age of fourteen, he launched his career from the stage school at the Theatre Royal, Margate. Before long he was originating a series of iconic roles for his friend George Bernard Shaw – Marchbanks in *Candida*, Cusins in *Major Barbara*, Dubedat in *The Doctor's Dilemma*, and Tanner in *Man and Superman* – with Shaw writing for his particular talents.

Such energy clears its own path, and Granville-Barker's was allied to a reformer's zeal. He wanted a more serious theatre, more engaged with the problems and pressures of the present day, and achieving respectability from its moral zeal, rather than from the hieratic grandeur Henry Irving sought. As Richard Eyre put it, he did not want the theatre to be 'a respectable art, he wanted it to be an art to be respected'. Together with a business partner, J. E. Vedrenne (another impressive moustache), they took the Royal Court Theatre from 1904 to 1907. The years after 1956 have been dubbed the golden age of the Court, yet there is a strong argument to be made for the luminous period of three years when these two ran the shop. They mounted almost a thousand performances of thirty-seven new plays by seventeen authors, eleven of them major works by Shaw, which is some rate of productivity. Granville-Barker acted in many, directed more, and wrote a few to boot. In addition, he proselytised for women playwrights, inspired much of what became the regional repertory movement, and with the critic William Archer drew up a blueprint called 'Scheme and Estimates for a National Theatre', a plan covering all the bases from choice of plays to staff and wages, pension funds, and royalties.

The Court is in many ways the perfect playhouse. Small enough for the human figure to commune with the room, actions can be observed in miniature detail, and words can be heard without boom or bombast. There are few spaces in the world that give the same invisible lift to a new play. And it is not too small; the capacity is large enough to matter, and for word to spread. In the Vedrenne-Barker days it packed in six hundred, who must have sat in tormenting discomfort; it now squeezes in about four hundred. For that reason it has attracted the interest of those who try to balance the competing claims of art and commerce.

The drawback of the Court has always been its top-table hauteur. Positioned in the heart of British wealth and snobbery (Sloane Square in Chelsea), it has suffered from its osmotic capacity to imitate the casual arrogance of those who walk past its front door. A top-table contempt paradoxically amplified by the distaste the theatre-makers often feel for the Sloanes from whom they learn their stylings. In the Edwardian era, as with the Lyceum – Irving's temple in the West End – it was at pains to court the royal family and the government. Granville-Barker himself boasted of personally knowing three prime ministers. In the post-1956 era, even when performing Marxist plays representing the underclass, the manners were still those of the super-elite. Old patrician snobbery mutated into an artistic elitism which looked down its nose at the popular. The shame is that so many great writers – from John Osborne through to Caryl Churchill – have been inculcated in a cradle that rocks on such a high branch.

Granville-Barker was not immune from loftiness. Several of his works deal with the machinations of the powerful and can lapse into a sort of intricate new language – mandarinese. Paradoxes, metaphors drenched in sophistication, sophistic little aphorisms that self-invert, all pile up, leaving the audience belittled and bewildered. Worse is the competition between characters to out-gnostic each other, everyone attempting a bittersweet riddling utterance more mysterious than the one before, each a last-word-merchant in a long game of smoke and mirrors. For a committed crossword puzzler, there is a pleasure in this, but it is enjoyment at the expense of anyone left behind. I am all for intelligence in the theatre – it is the most significant of its virtues that a collective intelligence can facilitate a grasp unavailable to any single individual. Granville-Barker gets to this place often, but he also showcases the intelligence that divides.

The majority of the plays deal with a toxicity in the air of Edwardian England. Far from complacent in their content, they attack society with rigour. *The Voysey Inheritance* throws up a complex lattice of family and financial ties, all sent shivering by the financial chicanery of a previous generation. A young man, Edward, joins the family law firm and discovers its success is based on illegal speculation, a crime whose co-conspirators include many of those he previously admired as solid burghers. He realises that being a 'grown-up' for many means accepting moral shabbiness, not just in his family, but in an England mired in institutional corruption. And that the contorted mandarinese the elders speak is not solely to enshrine the status of a hieratic class, but also to conceal their duplicity. An elegantly told story, with group scenes juggling twelve speaking characters onstage and keeping each alive (a signature skill of Granville-Barker's), *The Voysey Inheritance* portrays a world of mutually dependent greed and self-delusion, without succumbing to preaching or certainties. Characters remain fluid and confused, or rather they become more so, melting under the pressure of what they discover.

Waste is set four-square in the corridors of power and proves one of the best exposés of its intricate machinations (Granville-Barker making good use of his many connections). An idealistic innocent is brought into a coalition Cabinet to help effect the disestablishment of the Church. An irredeemably optimistic man, with considerable reserves of intellect and energy (not unlike the author), he is undone by a sex scandal. The waste of the title refers to two unfulfilled potentials: a bill for Parliament killed off by the scandal and a life aborted. Brutal and worldly truths cram in here, surprising from the pen of someone not yet thirty. Equally surprising is his nuanced understanding of the goings-on behind closed doors in smoke-filled rooms, where power is cut up and shared out in tense negotiations. Some of these scenes descend into the obtuse prolixity which was often his go-to place, some remain thrillingly human where conversation becomes a gut-twisting blend of chess game and arm-wrestling. In 1906, *Waste* was banned by the censor, spurring a fresh campaign of Granville-Barker's to remove the censor, but it has returned in triumph in productions since, its depiction of the clash of political idealism and personal peccadilloes keeping it forever close to the front pages.

During a year working with Peter Hall at the Old Vic in 1997, we presented the play, and I'll never forget his exhilaration at one particular moment during rehearsal. As lunchtime approached, a gaggle of people would gather outside his rehearsal room, rather like courtiers at Versailles, waiting to lobby him as he walked around the corner for lunch. On this day, when I was to be his lunchtime companion, he steamed out of the room like a headlong train, scattering the courtiers and practically running, so great was his joy. 'We've found it!' he cried. 'We've got it! The music, it's there!' He was describing the epiphanic moment in a room when one actor, or a couple in a dialogue, or better, a group, suddenly hear together the particular cadence of a play. Settling like a blessing on the room, once one person has it, the others pick it up more easily, spreading it like a benevolent infection. The music, once in their bodies, rarely leaves. Granville-Barker's cadence is one of the most dense and refined you can encounter, yet exquisite to hear when understood and sung well.

The Madras House suffers more than any from the life-draining effects of mandarinese. Through a fog of elite verbals can be discerned hard truths about the brittleness of civilisation anticipating the wrecking ball of the First World War. Philip Madras, the leader of an haute couture emporium, has determined to sell off his family business and stand for local government. He has matured into a hard, concrete socialism, with a distaste for aesthetics and luxury. Sick of being a trafficker in beauty and extravagance, Madras wants to dive into municipal politics, sorting out the drains and the dentistry in schools. There is no William Morris strain of idyllic romance in his politics, it is all pre-Soviet brutalism. There is a summoning of Brecht in some of his sentiments, such as, 'Give me the art and the artists that'll make most of the life we're content with impossible.' *The Madras House* offers a glimpse into the white-walled utopia of early socialism with its iron-clad logic. The lack of warmth and tenderness in its proponents points the way to a bleak destination. When Philip's father, the presiding genius of the house, returns from a long exile converted to Islam, the scene is set for the mother and father of ideological battles.

The Madras House – a long, really very long, play – also offers an extended inquisition into the question of sexual equality. Judging past works of art by today's common moral standards is a hiding to nothing, and there's more than enough to upset current sensibilities in plays written for the proscenium. That said, even I am a little stumped by a play in which 'the woman question' is interrogated in Act III – at inordinate length – by a group of men, sitting in the showroom of an haute couture house, while a group of women parade silently in front of them in elegant attire. Not one woman speaks. Of course, this is intended as an exposé of blatant sexism – Granville-Barker was an impeccable suffragist and promoter of female playwrights, and he had a subtler and deeper-running mind than my own. But the optics aren't tip-top. It may be a while before we see it staged again.

Granville-Barker's least known play, *The Marrying of Ann Leete*, is his most surprising and by a fair stretch his finest – a matrix not uncommon in the proscenium century. The play begins with a woman's cry in darkness, light slowly rising to reveal a misty dawn in a Georgian garden. Figures solidify softly into characters, say their piece, and melt back into the dewy vapour. As much dream as setting, the play occurs in 1799, a hundred years before it was written. There are power politics here again, as a grandee hovers between different parties and the 'woman question' is addressed as a daughter rebels against her family's expectations in matrimony, but there is also something new stirring in form. There is none of the singularity of argument found in later plays; the dialogue is elliptical and straying, scant and scratchy phrases float on the air; some statements chirrup out of the fog; characters jump from secure to insecure across a beat; poetic symbols abound; and absurd and haphazard choices and incidents keep interrupting the flow of the argument, while revealing a stranger patterning. As close to Chekhov as an English writer gets. Something in the mist allows scattered thought and muddied motivations; some of the mystery of human behaviour, which withers elsewhere in bright drawing rooms, flourishes here.

Shaw, Granville-Barker, and Galsworthy (and to a small degree Pinero before them) saw themselves in part as drawing room legislators, changing the world from well-upholstered stage sets. Theatre spurs change in a variety of ways, of course; it can change the atmosphere in the air, as did the Greek tragedies, and Shakespeare from the Globe; it can change the perception of society at large and of individuals, opening eyes and ears; and it can change the spirit of the times, opening up avenues to new tenderness and tolerance. Those who say theatre, or art, never changes the world are flying in the face of millennia of evidence. The scope of ambition of the Edwardians was narrow and focused – on the justice system, on industrial policy, on class antagonism, on suffrage and more. The progress they helped to spur was a colossal achievement and cannot be gainsaid. The world would be poorer without the work done. The unfortunate side effect of the medicine was the enshrining of our 'better' theatre as an educated-class activity for the concerned liberal, where society is diagnosed and improvements are prescribed. Theatre needs energies that are unruly, sometimes Dionysiac, and sometimes just the singular enclosed anarchy of a human psyche. Occasionally the prescription of the social drama excludes those wildernesses, to everyone's loss.

Granville-Barker was out of the game by the age of forty, exhausted. His first marriage went sour, and an American millionairess stepped in to salve the wound. Harley added a hyphen to his name and started playing the country squire in a manor house in Devon, with liveried servants. His second wife has been rather vilified by posterity, though she was an intellectual and author in her own right, and husband and wife had success translating plays from Spanish. In his quietened exile, Granville-Barker wrote a series of *Prefaces to Shakespeare*, abounding with the insights he had learned from life at the coalface. He argued consistently for the sort of theatre that was the ideal of my youth, one of lucidity, clarity, realism, and grace, with writer and actors front and centre and not masked by juggernauts of theatre-maker hullabaloo. An idea less in fashion now, it will return, and one of its greatest apostles will always be Granville-Barker.

Often castigated in his own lifetime and later for his withdrawal from the scene, taking his leave early may have been a form of courage. The fire in his belly had gone out and he chose not to fake it. The gift and the desire pass for most, whether ABBA or Arthur Miller, and the question is how you negotiate it. Granville-Barker had already left a sizeable quantum of good behind.

Never argue with the playwright.
Shaw rehearsing a scene from *Androcles and the Lion* (1912) with Lillah McCarthy and Granville Barker

Elizabeth Robins
1862–1952

For a palpable sense of the challenges the suffragettes faced, or the old roughhouse style of politics, it would be hard to beat the second act of Elizabeth Robins's *Votes for Women*. The manipulative stylings of contemporary political discourse, all algorithmed and airbrushed for mass media, are a century in the future. Here is old-fashioned, face-to-face, hand-to-hand, mouth-to-ear activism.

At the beginning of this electrifying act, the curtain rises on a crowd 'of several hundred' in uproar in Trafalgar Square. How many bodies you could fit on the Royal Court stage in 1907 is open to question, but the director Harley Granville-Barker was renowned for his marshalling of crowd scenes. An improvised platform is raised before the gathering, on which mill an assemblage of excited and nervous speakers easily recognisable from any protest platform of the present day. In front of them, women supporters are outnumbered by 'weedy youths and wastrel old men', and some 'beery out-o-works'. Chauvinism – whether idle or enraged – confronts hope. The heckling and barracking are continuous and effective, disrupting the train of thought of the speakers, sparking small skirmishes within the mob, and making any consistent rhetoric impossible.

This is not only pre-mass media but pre-amplification, when all a speaker had to rely on was their lung power, their clarity of thought, and a focused anger to lend charisma. Here we see in close-up detail the difficulties of live political persuasion. Two contributors fail calamitously, the crowd proving too bucking a horse for them to keep hold of the saddle; then a prosaic and pragmatic speaker commands the respect of the crowd with her matter-of-fact directness. Finally we witness our heroine tentatively connecting her voice to her moral centre as she articulates her rage. The rawness and raucousness summon up a very distinct democratic process.

The baldness of the play's title and the noisy roistering of the central scene suggest agitprop, but the surrounding acts proceed with more conventional proscenium styling. Atmosphere and character are nurtured with slow deliberacy. There's a mercurial subtlety to the dialogue, with the aristocratic women having two distinct modes of speaking: one in the presence of men, where they are acquiescent and indulgent; and one without, where they are strategic and impatient.

A generous spread of individuals has gathered at a Whiggish house party. They exhibit a wide spectrum of opinions – though almost all in favour of incremental reform above revolution. In the wake of a display of suffragist outrage in the House of Commons, most are still shuddering at the transgression of 'making a scene'. Grandes political dames lament that this noisy scene of rebellion will set back the slow progress made over generations. The chaps exhibit a blithe confidence and, when confronted with awkward truths, skirt around them with jokes. The task of the play is to reveal, through the dawning political enlightenment of a young woman, the necessity of making uncomfortable scenes and adopting positions that the patriarchy cannot smooth over with bluster and bravado.

The conclusion to *Votes for Women* is one of hard-won optimism, where all reveal the best of themselves, transmuting personal loss and pain into a determination that others in the future should not suffer the same. Each sacrifices the joys of personal satisfaction for a belief in the greater health of the community. That might sound sappy, but it is presented with a hard moral clarity which bypasses sentiment. To render this optimism more surprising, the final agent of female empowerment proves to be a Conservative and Unionist grandee (though from our present perspective in the UK where the Conservative Party is now onto its fourth female leader, and the progressives have still not managed one, this shouldn't come as too great a shock). Most surprising is the first publisher of this incendiary text – Mills & Boon.

Elizabeth Robins made her mark first as an accomplished actress. Born in Louisville, Kentucky, when she was nineteen she joined a company containing American thespian royalty. It was run by Edwin Booth, the brother of Lincoln's assassin, and featured the young star James O'Neill, father of Eugene. Robins enjoyed such success that she drove her husband, a jealous journeyman actor playing small parts in the same company, to suicide. He leaped into the Charles River in Boston, leaving a begrudging note: 'I will not stand in your light any longer.' The consequent trauma drove her across the Atlantic to England, ultimately to fulfil her long-held dream of playing on the British stage.

Elizabeth Robins had a transformative effect on British and European theatre. Word of her talent crossed the Atlantic with her, and she soon befriended Henry James, Shaw, and Wilde. She made a close compact with the critic and proselytiser for European drama William Archer, with whom she is said to have had an affair. It is rumoured that Shaw and the publisher William Heinemann each proposed to her, both being warned off by Robins with guns. Common cause for all these allies was Ibsen. Robins led the charge, becoming the 'high priestess' for the Norwegian deity. To produce quality drama, she formed a joint-management company with another American actress, Marion Lea, desiring not only good parts but artistic control of their futures. In Robins's words, 'We arraigned the managers, we raged, dreamed, and then more or less awake, began to consider ways and means.' They wanted to mount productions independent of the commercial actor-manager system, believing it far from conducive to quality.

Hearing of a new Ibsen play with a central female role, Hedda Gabler (a name they at first mispronounced in a variety of ways), they sought out a new translation, and 'fell upon it with unforgettable eagerness. We read with jeers, we rolled with irreverent laughter; then brought up short by a thrust at our vitals from the Ibsen rapier, blinked, stared at each other and ended in a state of demoralised excitement.' To get the play on they had to secure the rights from the publishing patriarchy and despaired of raising the funds. Robins had a small box of fire-assay gold, which she had been left by her father. She 'had never thought to risk that treasure of many memories on anything not a matter of life and death'.

Hedda Gabler seemed worth the potential sacrifice. Together with a jewelled bracelet of Lea's, they pooled together and secured a £300 loan to lease the Vaudeville.

The first matinee on 20 April 1891 was a triumph, and the run was soon extended into a series of matinees and evening shows. Shaw came, Wilde came, Henry James wrote an essay, and Ibsen had landed in Britain with an elegant splash. Hedda became Robins's signature role – in addition to leading roles in *Little Eyolf*, *Rosmersholm*, *The Master Builder*, and *John Gabriel Borkman*. Ibsen's work and the centrality of Robins in interpreting and producing it had a tonic and empowering effect. GBS wrote that 'what is called the Woman Question has begun to agitate the stage.'

Unsurprisingly, Robins grew into a formidable activist and prominent member of the Pankhursts' Women's Social and Political Union. She remained uneasy with their commitment to violent militancy, an unease which finally led to her breaking with them. Such is the tension between reform and rebellion dramatised so beautifully in *Votes for Women*. However, her commitment as an advocate remained steady, and she later transformed her house into a recuperative home for hunger-striker suffragettes after their release from prison.

Robins blew through late-Victorian theatre like a clarifying gale. Her first written play, *Alan's Wife*, was a sensation, with one of the most sinister curtains of the era at the end of the second act as a young mother, downcast with postnatal depression, moves ominously towards the crib of her newborn baby. The ferocity of her acting in this role – a sexually hungry bride in Act I, a widow suffering from puerperal psychosis in Act II, and a convicted murderer awaiting execution in Act III – introduced a whole new grammar of emotional extremes conveyed with truth and understatement. This play, and Robins's performance, shivered the timbers of late-Victorian theatre and set a high-water mark of dignified intensity.

As a producer, an activist, and an actress Robins illuminated the age. There seemed little she was not capable of. She was slowed down only by a bout of typhoid fever, picked up when she went to the gold rush camps of Alaska to find her brother, feared lost in the Yukon. It was that sort of life.

With *Votes for Women*, she read the temper of the age and staged it.

Any great revolution needs hats.
The International Advisory Committee of the National Woman's Party at the American Women's Club, London, 1925. Elizabeth Robins second from left

D. H. Lawrence
1885–1930

By a strange happenstance, the proscenium theatre had a chance to redeem its ills, an opportunity it chose to forgo. At the height of its highest era of gilded importance, it was offered a series of plays which reported with Chekhovian honesty and mystery the lives of those who dwelt beyond its privileged circle. Plays which encapsulated the lives of working-class people in constructions of high artfulness. Each was refused entry by the gatekeepers. The plays remained excluded for forty years after the death of their author, D. H. Lawrence. Like the paintings of Van Gogh, another ginger firebrand whose lust for life and for making was unquenchable, Lawrence's theatrical works were never to prove their worth to their own creator, beyond his inner convictions. Three of the greatest plays of the twentieth century remained on the shelf until the Royal Court took up their cause in 1967 and presented them in definitive productions by Peter Gill. Had they been presented when they were written, the story of twentieth-century theatre, its scope and purpose, could have been entirely different.

As a creator, Lawrence exhibited a hectic profuseness. His novels brought him fame, as well as the notoriety of *Lady Chatterley's Lover*. Beyond them, he painted prodigally and badly, wrote many of our greatest short stories, poured out poetry, manically sent letters winging across continents, and recorded all that passed before him in his journals. He is now celebrated by many for everything in his output that wasn't his novels. His most particular capacity, especially in occasional work, was for instant writing. He had a rare ability to respond with immediacy to what was before him, without filtering or arrangement. And without the constructed literary voice, the overwrought psychobabble, and the focus on loins of darkness (whatever they may be), which can clog up the novels. Many of his poems execute their thinking in front of you, rather like the progress of a mathematical equation where the working is part of the whole. The determination is to capture the quick essence of what is seen – whether a snake on the move, a chrysanthemum freighted with dew, or a Native American ceremony in its mystery – and to recreate its flickering existence afresh.

This, of course, is the heart of drama, the capacity to write life, and enable its recurrent return night after night. To hear speech, see the movements of people, sense the dynamics of relationships, and feel how the space in between is shivered by communal energy. Few had a more acute sense for such events and the space between than Lawrence. Theatre was sacred to him. As a child he loved putting on plays. Throughout his life he was a relentless performer, strutting his comic abilities in skits and sketches, in the homes of the aristocratic and rich he grew to love. His first dramatic experiences came from rural touring groups who visited his hometown of Eastwood, Nottinghamshire. He relished the power of these populist events, the enthralment of the audience, and the energy of the storytelling. His child's eyes widened at the magic, and he wished to recreate the same for others.

The quality of his three landmark plays – *The Daughter-in-Law*, *The Widowing of Mrs Holroyd*, and *A Collier's Friday Night* – is the more extraordinary when set against the ghastliness of his other efforts. Effort being the aptest word for plays that try hard to ape the stylings of others. There is a biblical epic, *David*, written in incantatory pseudo-biblical prose; a dizzyingly confusing sex farce, *The Married Man*; and a tale of love trying to break the boundaries of class with the unpromising title *The Fight for Barbara*. This last is exemplified by the immortal line: 'I would have spilt my blood on every paving stone in Bromley for you.' In such work, Lawrence's eagerness to please those he despises, and to join a club whose values he suspects, lead to a stilted phoniness.

His three plays drawn directly from the world he grew up in have spellbinding authenticity. A relish for physical life breathes through them, for the thinginess of things – coal fires glowing in stoves, cups of tea, miners' metal boxes for their snap, the washing of bodies, bread tins, clothes horses, treasured books, heavy boots, polished plates, buttered bread, mahogany tables set for supper. Everywhere there is coal, coal and more coal, black-facing the miners, sullying the tablecloths, infecting the lungs, killing the innocent, and scarring the souls of men and their families. Relentless details – and the phonetic dialogue is as earthed and substantial as the physical life – create the purest naturalism, a form not there to serve a purpose but an end in itself. As in the arresting suddenness of a Vermeer, or in the concentrated stillness of a Chinese poem, what matters is the life, the happen-ness of it. Our pleasure is not in where it takes us, but in momentarily losing ourselves in what we observe, and through that loss of self we grow. We are not asked to adopt an argument, we are invited to spread our empathy to a whole conceived world. Each play features an act of washing, of both the living and the dead, always achieved with a hyperrealism. Somehow this echoes our response as we are cleansed of preconceptions and predeterminations, and left clean-eyed to gaze on the phenomenon of life and the beauty of the everyday.

The particular rough magic of English theatre, a tradition from the North stretching back to the Miracle plays of the medieval period, has always been the capacity to present working-class life in long stretches of pure inconsequence, during which one falls into the gyroscope of others' lives. The two long scenes from the Boar's Head tavern in Shakespeare's *Henry IV* plays are at the heart of this tradition. One scene in Part 1 lasts twenty-five minutes or so, during which there is barely any narrative or serious argument. There is just play and chat and joking and business – just *life*. There is little to match it in the French or German dramatic tradition. There are pastoral scenes in the Spanish Golden Age plays, but they are fleeting. The same line stretches through many proscenium plays, from Robertson's *Society* onwards, but it reached an apogee with Lawrence.

The anguishes and joys of working-class life are played out, their dilemmas and arguments as vexed as any others. Lawrence offers no solutions, because there are none, the moral ground beneath every decision shifting and unknowable. On a micro scale, small surprises hold us spellbound. A matriarch brings home a paper bag of pine nuts, a taste unknown to most. She and two younger women savour them with an almost sacred excitement. Through them we share in the quotidian magic of a new flavour and an expanding world. Nor is the poetry only in the objects. A young couple in whom love is burgeoning share their pleasure in Baudelaire, and the particular charm of his language: 'That's what they can do in France, it is so heavy and full and voluptuous: like oranges falling and rolling a little way upon a dark-blue carpet; like twilight outside when the lamp's lighted; you get a sense of rich, heavy things, as if you smelt them, and felt them about you in the dusk.'

When Peter Gill produced the plays, he realised that 'the physical life, the accumulation of the everyday actions during the course of the play was essential to its meaning.' He understood that all actions, whether the pouring of tea, the stealing of a kiss, or the striking of a match, had to be actual, to be realised rather than demonstrated. Yet there is art in the arrangement. Each act is carefully sculpted, and there is a sure sense of how to use the stage. Long stage directions verge on the controlling as Lawrence proscriptively details how to create stage pictures. Any director would be foolish to ignore them. Just as the Mystery and Miracle plays knew how to combine realism and ritual, Lawrence knew how to make actions in his plays sacred.

A miner father, blotto with drink, is watched with scorn by his better-educated wife and by an aspirant son who has left for college (a self-portrait for Lawrence). He has just had a blazing row with both. He tries to retain a little dignity before retreating to bed. '*He rises, pulling himself up with the arms of the chair, and, turning round, takes a Waterbury watch with a brass chain from the wall beside the bookcase: and winds it up, swaying on his feet as he does so. Then he puts it back on the nail, and a key swings at the end of the chain. Then he takes a silver watch from his pocket, and, fumbling, missing the keyhole, winds that up also with a key, and, swaying forward, hangs it up over the cupboard. Then he lurches around, and, limping pitiably, goes off upstairs. There is a heavy silence. The Waterbury watch can be heard ticking.*' The image of a man grabbing for props to set his head straight, to show his continued functioning, to restore his patriarchal dignity is delicately observed. The fact that both watches need to be corrected to retain their purpose adds a dimension of time running away uncontrollably. The final flailing lurch and the retreat to a higher realm is exquisite stagecraft. This is life as poetry, wrought to a fineness worthy of Chekhov.

On sending *The Daughter-in-Law* to a potential producer, Lawrence wrote: 'It is neither a comedy nor a tragedy – just ordinary. It is quite objective, as far as that term goes, and though no doubt, like most of my stuff, it wants weeding out a bit, yet I think the whole thing is there.'

Was it bad luck that dogged Lawrence's theatrical career or was it his own character? Always famous for his temper, he seems to have been capable of starting an argument in an empty theatre. This is the man who on first seeing the famous reclining Buddhas in Ceylon – distillations of meditative stillness – was heard to hiss, 'Stand up!'

Potential collaborator after collaborator failed Lawrence, or were driven away. His best and first opportunity, the Vedrenne-Barker-Shaw axis, was approached, at probably the wrong moment since they had a long-running show on. Granville-Barker looked at *The Widowing of Mrs Holroyd* and replied, 'I read it with much interest, but afraid I don't want it.' This sort of cursory rejection is part and parcel of a writer's life. It requires a steely chin to take the blow. Lawrence proclaimed, 'I am sure we are sick of the rather bony, bloodless drama we get nowadays – it is time for a reaction against Shaw and Galsworthy and Barker and Irishy (except Synge) people – the rule and measure mathematical folk.' Galsworthy and he later had an unsuccessful lunch date in 1917, with Lawrence finding the senior writer a 'Sawdust bore', and Galsworthy pronouncing Lawrence 'Obsessed with self. Dead eyes, and a red beard, long narrow pale face. A strange bird.'

He approached Yeats's former manager Ben Iden Payne with his usual initial enthusiasm: 'I believe that, just as an audience was found in

Russia for *Tchekhov*, so an audience might be found in England for some of my stuff, if there were a man to whip 'em in. It's the producer that is lacking, not the audience.' They soon fell out. The Stage Society tracked him down after they had a great success with Stanley Houghton's *Hindle Wakes*, under the impression that tales of Northern hardship were a route to commercial prosperity. But the trajectory of Houghton's play from suffering to celebratory comedy was the opposite of Lawrence, who tunnelled his audiences into a pit of tragedy. His plays proved too bleak for them. The celebrated actor Esmé Percy told him he loved the work, then promptly enlisted to fight in the war. Thoughtlessly, he didn't leave the army until 1926, only a few years before Lawrence's death.

Becoming desperate, he attached himself to a firebrand called Douglas Goldring, who was determined to start a revolutionary People's Theatre Society. This outfit was going to bring undiluted socialism to the masses, performing hierarchy-flipping dramas to miners, transport workers, postmen, and the police, all to establish a properly Labour Theatre. One of Lawrence's lesser-known plays, *Touch and Go*, begins with a turbulent strike meeting addressed by a radical, very like the pivotal scene in Galsworthy's *Strife*. (Lawrence had in fact nakedly stolen the scene, having been electrified by *Strife* when he saw it in Nottingham in 1909.) What Lawrence failed to tell his new comrades was that he didn't agree with any of them. His rather straightforward definition of a people's theatre was not one that preached Marxism and practised mass re-education, it was simply a theatre in which the seats were inexpensive, and which produced plays 'about people'. His estimate of the prospects of revolution was that 'We shall crawl from under one cartwheel straight under another.' As he expressed in letters to Lady Cynthia Asquith, he loathed pacifists and idealists. The People's Theatre rumbled him before long, voted him off their committee, and decided to produce the more ideologically aligned Serbian work, *The Liberators* by Srgjan Tucic, a play which didn't set the box office alight and led to the end of the People's Theatre Society. Lawrence's reaction to these events was not atypical: 'Curse the sly mongrel world.'

Compton Mackenzie's mother, Virginia Bateman, another renowned actor-manager, decided in 1920 to open a repertory theatre in Nottingham and to light a flame of pure art which would blind the eyes of the world. Her son approached Lawrence for a play for the first season. His response was quintessential – mad loathing equalled only by mad desire to harm: 'About the theatre – thrilling but terrifying! You know my horror of the public! Well, it's a phobia of phobias in Nottingham. Nottingham! Cursed, cursed Nottingham, gutless, spineless, brainless Nottingham how I hate thee! But if my two plays could be thrown so hard into thy teeth as to knock thy teeth out, why then, good enough.' Sadly, he never got to knock Nottingham's teeth out. Such passion among the theatre-makers only met indifference from the public, and the theatre had shut down before Lawrence had his chance.

Bizarrely, *The Widowing of Mrs Holroyd* did open in Los Angeles, of all places, in the Little Theatre in 1916. It was a hit attended by Charlie Chaplin and many of the film stars of the day. But from all that can be gleaned from Lawrence's letters and writings, he was oblivious. The play had been published in the US and the rights licensed, but nobody seems to have informed the writer. Another failure of communication in a litany.

Writers know there is frequently a disjunction between the value of a piece of work and the size of its reception, a truth they are bitterly aware of. Claptrap can thrive and masterpieces can sink. Rarely has this been proven more eloquently true than it was for Lawrence, who wrote three plays that stand alongside any from a century of extraordinary achievement. In their own time, and for a full forty years after his death, they sank (almost) without trace. Thankfully, a proscenium theatre that had rejected them fifty years before rode to the rescue.

Déjeuner-ing sur l'herbe.
Bertie Farjeon, Rosalind, Frieda and D. H. Lawrence in the woods behind Spring Cottage, Bucklebury, West Berkshire in 1919

Interval

A good day out at a festival of drama in Athens 2,500 years ago would comprise three tragedies throughout a long afternoon, and then as the light closed in, an uproarious comedy. In the gaps, there would be breaks as long as the shows, with ample time for wine, picnics, politicking, gossip, and for watching the sun arc the sky before sinking into the Aegean. In a Shakespeare play of the early 1600s, we are not certain how many act-breaks were taken, but four is a good guess. During those apertures, packed crowds splurged out towards the Thames to guzzle on food, drink, and all the hurly-burly as greedily as they gorged on language and story. A classic proscenium play would generally comprise three acts, including two lush breaks for elegantly consumed nicotine and gin.

Two-interval evenings are now unusual. Many directors seem loath to have even one. While at the Oxford Stage Company, we toured a series of three-act plays and decided to run counter to fashion by instigating and enjoying two intermissions. The experiment proved fascinating, since during the first break there would always be slight discomfort and unease. Should we stay in our seats or go for a walk? A drink now, and an ice cream later, or an ice cream now and a drink later? How can I be expected to entertain my husband through two of these breaks? It reinforced the suspicion you sometimes have that people go to the theatre not to be with each other.

By the time the second interval swung round, people started to thaw and unwind. They talked about the play, about each other, or sat in happy silence. It was then all began to remember that theatre is a social event, a public get-together, a place where you take a good look at your fellow humans through the prism of the show; somewhere people have gathered for millennia to flirt, to politic, to traduce, to gossip, to fight, to face out social disgrace or to enjoy it. Whether it's Athens, or Jacobean London, or seventeenth-century Paris, or late-nineteenth-century

Moscow, showtime isn't just about what the actors do with the audience, it's also what the audience do with each other. You get the impression that in the past the plays were often an unnecessary distraction.

Chekhov's four-act plays enjoyed three long intervals. Forever absent from his own first nights, he received telegrams in Yalta about each act as if it were a separate event – 'First Act, a triumph', 'Second Act, disaster' etc. The actors took curtain calls at the end of each act, rather capsizing the suspension of disbelief. Then the audience were off for half an hour of beluga caviar and heavy eye contact. Just what theatre is supposed to be, a rowdy, unifying social event, with the play as its focus, not its tyrant.

Part of the problem lies with the hegemony of directors, several of whom enjoy the enforced agony of making people sit in the same place for two hours. An unbroken spell, they call it. This incarceration strikes me as a form of defensive aggression. Not just a terror the audience will leave (although that comes into it), but also a fear that if the audience have a chance to think, if the unrelenting intensity stops for a minute, then the house of cards will collapse. This is the neurotic insecurity of the nervous conversationalist, the one who won't pause for breath to let you speak, because they can't admit another point of view. Theatre should be one group of individuals openly and respectfully inviting another group of individuals to enter into an illusion for the sake of entertainment and thought. Locking the audience in for two hours of imposed intensity lacks the same respect.

There is a limit to what the mind can take. Only so much music, emotion, insight, humour, and colour can be consumed in one gulp. After that you need a cigarette or a breather. If you don't get one, your concentration slips and the evening prolongs. Chekhov wrote for his intervals. He knew that after forty minutes of *Three Sisters*, you need a break. If you string two acts together, you swiftly get slow, boring Chekhov, because it's not what he intended. While you're grinding your way through the second act, Chekhov intended you to be downing a vodka or falling for a pair of sad eyes.

No matter who the writer, theatre is tense. It is intended to be, a high-wire act. Actors can forget their lines, or fall off the stage, or have a heart attack and die. That, to be callous, is the fun. The essence of its liveness is that it is always on the point of collapse, one of the few arts whose thrill lies in its potential for disintegrating before your eyes. A point missed by those who strenuously underline the liveness of theatre. It is already live. The audience knew that when they bought their tickets. They want to see something complex, difficult, beautiful, and wise being brought off with speed, agility, and grace. That particular walk over the tightrope is what makes theatre tingle. Even in a classic drawing room comedy, with French windows and drinks cabinets, calamities can occur. Doorknobs snap off, bottles refuse to release their corks, and third-act pistols fail to go bang. That fragility makes the experience enjoyably tense. Compare a picture of a cinema audience with a theatre audience and the difference is sharp. In the cinema, people slouch, relax, lounge, and reflect; in the theatre, they are alert, febrile. The tension is right and proper – it makes an evening crackle – but there is only so much spectators can take at a time. Before long, for that alertness to be maintained, they need ample opportunities for its contrary: a stiff drink.

Keep calm and carry on. Wartime interval tea, New Theatre, St Martin's Lane, London, 1943

Time is mysteriously elastic, nowhere more so than in a theatre. No one understood that like Chekhov, who saw more clearly than most its potential for heavy length, and for elusive brevity. An excellent production of *The Cherry Orchard* with *no* interval would last three hours and feel like a month; the same production with *three* intervals and good company could last four hours, and make you shiver at the speed with which it passed.

Githa Sowerby
1876–1970

Is it possible to rediscover a play too often? Does the noise of constant revelation against the odds start to wear down a play's value? Githa Sowerby's *Rutherford and Son* may be a case in point. Every seven or eight years for the last forty it seems to have been dug up from seeming obscurity and with trembling excitement revealed to the light. A feminist company called Mrs Worthington's Daughters had a just claim to proper legwork when they moved the play back into public view in 1980; a revival soon after at the New End Theatre pushed its luck when talking of its neglect; subsequent productions at Scarborough, the National, Salisbury, and the Royal Exchange even more so; Northern Stage claiming in 2009 the play 'has vanished from history', but that 'digging around in the archives' had been honourably carried out, was frankly a cheek; and when the National presented their second production and leaned hard on the rhetoric of obscurity, you started to wonder. Partly about the forgetfulness of an ahistorical age, and partly about the debasing notion that every production must be turned into a cause. *Rutherford and Son* is a great play – hopefully at some moment that will suffice.

Sowerby's initial road was a hard one. The play was first presented in 1912 at the Royal Court under the name K. G. Sowerby, the author cautious of revealing her gender to a male-dominated industry. Hailed as an instant classic, she revealed her full name, and an inherent chauvinism made it hard for later work to gain the same success. The comparisons with Ibsen showered on K. G. seem to have been more profuse than those doled out to Katherine Githa. Nevertheless, the tough stock she came from kitted her out for such vicissitudes.

Art and industry came together in Sowerby's early life. Her father was both an accomplished painter and the director of the Ellison Glass Works – the family business and Europe's largest pressed glass producer.

Patenting several technological innovations, John George Sowerby rose through the company to become chairman, before several episodes of artistic overreach, trying to branch the glassworks out into higher-end markets, resulted in losses. Githa's father was dismissed from his own company and bankrupted. Significantly for his daughter's play, this was not just the story of a man driving himself to ruin from malice and territorial aggression, it was a visionary chasing that elusive holy grail – the storied union of profit and art.

A glowering father figure spreads toxic clouds over Sowerby's play. Critical writing has assessed it as a savage denunciation of patriarchy, as well as capitalism. Though fatuous to deny the justness of this – Sowerby originally titled her work *The Master* – it seems reductive. For all old Rutherford's faults, the playwright has the artistic courage to present much from his warped perspective. Like Sowerby's father, his passion is for the ineluctable glories of making. The obsession that inspired such men is what drove the Wedgwoods, the Chippendales, and all the families whose names pop up on stylish vases and bespoke furniture on *Antiques Roadshow*. A passion more consuming than branding, their companies shared a pride in making mass products of elegance and style – an impulse to leave something behind. An aspiration bringing communities together in the comradeship of production. The wages were criminal, the abuse of workers a historical disgrace, and the treatment of women barbarous – the play exposes these appalling conditions and makes a case for correcting them. All the human beings, whether workers or family, are shown to be commodities for exploitation. But Sowerby is a human enough judge and a shrewd enough historian to show that powerful bonds of collective creation tied these people together.

In the play, Rutherford has one son who has dedicated his life to religion, a vocation exposed as soft and idle beside the hard graft of the glass business. Another son has invented a new method of glass-pressing and is prepared to sell it to a rival. His father steals it from him: the bond of company is shown to be mightier than that of family. Rutherford's trusted foreman has fallen in love with his daughter, and yet he sacrifices any future with her for the sake of the business. These people believe in their work with a faith beyond the church. They worship their product, and only achieve a full sense of self through making. The damage caused by this mania is catastrophic – the family is destroyed, the father is denounced – but patriarchy and capitalism seem limiting labels for the root of the sickness.

We are invited into a world of procedural detail, watching from the perspective of the owners. Their lives are a roundelay of broken furnaces and strikes and engineering and bank loans and supply chains and interest on loans. As the business is revealed to be teetering on the brink, the effort to stop it tipping over comes to seem heroic, an act of energy and willpower going back generations: 'We've made it for you, stone by stone, penny by penny, fighting through thick and thin for close on a hundred years.' As the title implies, inheritance is the heart of the drama. No one is allowed to escape the unbreakable prison of duty to fathers and grandfathers. Rutherford has educated his two sons out of their own environment, and his efforts to warp them back into previous moulds leads to tragedy.

The patterns are unquestioned, until resoundingly attacked by a daughter at the end of Act II. Tired of a life of subservience and bondage, she turns on her father with excoriating bluntness: 'Who are you? Who are you?' The other act of usurpation is tougher still. Rutherford having broken his family to pieces, his daughter-in-law drives a hard bargain to ensure her son ends up with the business on his majority. Her voice – sharp, clear, and steady – is a radical change from the preceding testosterone-driven shouting, and a sign of the future.

Rutherford is a broken and deflated figure at the play's end, slumped in an armchair, all love (or any pretence at it) gone. We know his days are numbered, and power is shifting to a new settlement in which bullied sons and angry daughters will find different patterns. The vanquished Rutherford has been little but a brute throughout, humiliating one son, stealing from the other, diminishing his daughter, manipulating and then breaking his most trusted employee, and all with a bluntness and viciousness that would put *Succession*'s Logan Roy to shame. His demise is overdue and just. Sowerby's considerable achievement is to make us feel for him, and for the vanishing world of manufacture to which he dedicated his every breath. In a world now where little is made beyond the virtual, that ensures a continuing resonance.

Githa, Flora and Fauna.
Portrait of Katherine Githa Sowerby from the *Illustrated Sporting and Dramatic News*, 1917

William Somerset Maugham
1874–1965

Shortly after leaving university, I travelled down to see a friend acting in Somerset Maugham's *The Circle* with the Colchester Repertory Company. Stuffed with the messianic zeal of youth, I was fired with belief that drama should upend the hierarchies or transcend the mud or shock the complacent or whatever the passing rage was. And I was pre-programmed to mock. A three-act play in a posh drawing room? What could be more retrograde and stuffy? I was militantly shabby and stood out from the crowd decked in their Friday-night finery. They all seemed to show little knowledge of Artaud and the Theatre of Cruelty. One man, I vividly remember, had managed to combine a cravat with a bow tie, which is quite the feat. When, after ten minutes, my actor chum wandered in through French windows carrying a tennis racquet and said, 'I say, what about this tennis?' I snorted with derision.

What followed was subversive. A group of rep actors, with rock-solid technique, told the story of two love triangles, one revisiting the pain of a runaway romance from thirty years before, the other depicting three young lovers about to be enmeshed in the same chaos. At first intrigued, I was soon beguiled, then enchanted, and finally deeply moved. *The Circle* is funny with an even-handed mix of standalone wit and character observation, and tough as teak about the heart. Few works are better on the pain of love in decline, the cruelty that age inflicts on romance, and the chilling effect of indifference. To cheering surprise, it comes out finally in favour of recklessness and irresponsibility. Play and production purred along like a smoothly upholstered old motor. The Colchester audience enjoyed it hugely, but nothing like as much as the transfixed scruff who had come to scoff but stayed to sob.

Theatre has always been, and will ever be, a balancing act between taking an audience somewhere previously unexplored and giving them what they want. In the madness of youth, one believes only in the former – my delusion as I trained down to Colchester. An evening of consummate professionalism and irresistible storytelling meant I headed back wondering what was wrong with giving an audience what they want. This is a balance we have been getting wrong in the UK for the last forty years, with metropolitan taste dictating what the rest ought to enjoy. Sometimes the greatest music can be heard by listening to the variety of different audiences' desires.

The evening began a love affair with the work. While running a touring company, subsidised by the government on the old-fashioned premise it was to take theatre to places which otherwise wouldn't see it, we decided to produce *The Circle*. The company had been driven (largely by my folly) into something of a financial hole and needed a show that theatres would book and audiences attend. A young director was chosen, Mark Rosenblatt, who had written a dissertation on Galsworthy and Granville-Barker, and understood the particular pleasures of the proscenium. His production was elegant and precise, and replete with intellectual fizz. We opened in Salisbury, which is spiritually not unaligned with Colchester. The average age of the audience was about eighty-three. They laughed with such vigour and abandon we worried whether they would make it through the show. By the end, they looked wrung out with their collective engagement. Great bliss it was to give them what they wanted.

The production was revived twice and rescued the company. The second featured two beautiful character actors, Sheila Reid and Robert Lang, both of whom had been in Olivier's National Theatre company at the Old Vic in the 1960s. Bob played the diplomat Richard in the 1964 production of *Hay Fever* directed by Noël Coward himself, which had revived the Master's reputation for a new generation. During the run of *The Circle*, long evenings were spent in hotel bars quizzing Bob and Sheila about theatre history, old techniques, and truths. Both held esteemed places in the tradition of character acting, a centuries-long continuum of handed-down tricks and insights and survival tactics. Character acting is a mystery, in the antique sense of a craft or trade, with a shading of something stranger clouding around it. Both had a capacity to swathe themselves onstage with a mysterious film, a shimmering extra skin of fizzing humanity, which implied they bore knowledge of mystic truths. It's a trick, of course – they could be thinking of shopping in Tesco – but it worked. Long seasons in empty theatres hanging around upstage while stars grasped at limelight downstage had taught them how to invest the smallest actions with a numinous particularity. Not enough to draw the eye and get themselves sacked, but just enough to add significance to truth. Stars are great, but ensemble truth made proscenium theatres hum, and the character actors brought this jazz with them.

Writing about Maugham is hard, as futile an endeavour as an in-depth analysis of custard. His work is the finest of custards, or as the Francophile and Riviera resident Maugham may have named it, crème anglaise. The French appellation is apt, since the Gallic version is thickened only with egg yolks, and without flour, thus serving up a more silky and pourable sauce. Maugham's plays are the essence of pourable and silky. Admired by many as the apogee of the well-made play, his work seems the perfect content for the proscenium form. And in the fine and fastidious artificiality of its presentation, it defies discussion. Whether sweet or tart, it should simply be enjoyed. As with custard, it shares the quality of having made ingredients disappear. Milk, cream, eggs, vanilla, and sugar all lose their individual identity in a perfect crème anglaise into something wholly synthetic. In a similar way, men, women, and real life often seem to have been subsumed in Maugham into a higher confection.

Several of his characters share his passion for artefacts, most specifically for cosmetics. Lady Champion-Cheney, the elderly bolter from *The Circle*, is as possessive of her make-up kit as she should be of her child; one long scene in *Lady Frederick* involves a detailed demonstration of the arts of dressing and getting made-up. 'Putting on a face' – that character-defining English expression – and the artificiality of human beauty are shown as both fraudulent and a perverse wonder. In these plays, we are invited to critique the shallowness of mere civility and simultaneously admire its unabashed phoniness.

In *The Letter*, set in Malaya, a subtle unpeeling of the attitudes of a group of colonials reveals the constructed masks they use to bolster a bogus superiority. (No one should look here for a sympathetic portrait of the Malayans – they tend to say 'velly' for 'very', and the characterisation doesn't extend a long way beyond that.) In *For Services Rendered*, Maugham's sharpest and sourest piece, normality itself is shown to be a construction, as characters steer past griefs and bitter losses resulting from the Great War. They make a new reality, distractingly busy with tennis and tea and squalid affairs, all in denial of the generational trauma afflicting each. The application of lipstick and the dabbing of powder prove a template in Maugham's work for the national religion of putting on a face and walking stiffly past troublesome emotions. Maugham's own persona was the result of high fashioning. Fastidiously well turned out, hair slicked back, cravat, cigarette holder in hand, his expression was usually rigid with an austere severity, while garnished with a twist of discreet devilry.

Disguise became an urgent matter for Maugham during the Great War, when he was called on to work in intelligence for the British. First in Switzerland, working with agents from across Europe and ferrying information home, later in Samoa, deemed a pivotal spot for the British Empire, and finally in revolutionary Russia, where he arrived too late to do more than witness the convulsions. In each place, his disguise, however thin, was as a playwright searching for material. Maugham fell ill in Russia, a mix of tuberculosis and nervous collapse, and was invalided home, where he recuperated for three months in a sanatorium in Scotland.

As all this painful material swirled inside him, with habitual perversity he took the opportunity to write a farce of advanced silliness and glibness, *Home and Beauty*. It treats the war as a vehicle for an infantile sex farce about a frivolous woman who discovers the accidence of war has led to her being married to two men. Accustomed as we are to solemnity around the 1914–18 war, it is a jolt to see it treated with such determined frivolity. An enormous success, the audience welcomed such froth in reaction to catastrophe. Those close to tragedy are often less precious in their response than those at a distance.

The importance of the carapace was de rigueur in matters of sexual relations. Maugham was a central figure in the long relay race of playwrights who passed the baton of lonesome masquerading from one to the next. Each wrote about heterosexual passion using insight gained from its homosexual counterpart. Maugham picked up the baton from Oscar Wilde, and relayed it to Noël Coward, who passed it on reluctantly to Terence Rattigan. (The international image of the repressed Englishman owes a lot to these gentlemen.) Coward returned the favour by making Maugham the subject for his one play that addresses being queer, a late work called *A Song at Twilight*, which deals with an ageing celebrity author being blackmailed over letters from his past. A fascinating curio, it is a long way from being a *cri de coeur*, glittering with the restraint and repression which shielded these men.

Maugham wrote, and successfully, in every period between the Victorian and modern, and was the most glamorous figure in that in-between moment, the Edwardian, an age that prized styling. He was a boulevardier and knew it, aware of his audience and how to entertain and manipulate them. One is rarely allowed to admit it, but in the right hands it is often a pleasure to be manipulated, to be steered in our sympathies towards a greater understanding of the characters onstage and hence of ourselves, as from act to act we grow less skittish and more humane. There is flattery and low psychology in such manipulation, but it remains seductive. Maugham's jokes play to the gallery often, and his plotting, always consummate, is determinedly sensational. *The Letter* begins its first act with a gunshot, and a figure staggering onstage wounded; its second begins with the consumption of heroin. In times when people treat storytelling in bold strokes as if it were an aberration against good taste, this sort of cinematic coarseness is refreshing.

One envisages Maugham as a lonely man at the end of a jetty looking out to sea, aware of sorrows and carrying their burden, wearing a red scarf perfectly circling the neck, and whose corduroys seem too well creased for someone lost in pain. The worldly sage who glides forward with wisdom, self-deprecation, and a soupçon of self-regard. Maugham looked hard at life with a sour sardonicism, but somehow not broadly enough. He was a painter, like Chekhov, but could not look with the same neutral completeness to see a place beyond his own personality. He never, or rarely, broke through to the garden of generosity or joy, which comes with egoless and devoted contemplation. Trapped within his own style, without ever being overwritten there are always two too many notes of calculated graciousness, the scarf too elegantly draped.

Above all others, Maugham exemplifies the proscenium mannerism of smooth elegance spreading a sheet of ice over a lake filled with murk. He gave and continues to give audiences a pleasure as refined and complete as the finest cuisine, determinedly haute. And in one play, *The Circle*, his masterpiece with a transgressive centre, he sang a joyful hymn to the importance of being true to love at all costs, and to respecting how the heart is its own boss.

They don't act like that any more.
The Circle, Broadway, 1921

Susan Glaspell
1876–1948

The acorn myth is a powerful one in the performing arts. The phenomenon that became *Fleabag* began at an anarchic scratch night for a handful of people in an East London pub. Many artistic oak trees start minuscule, and few smaller than the Provincetown Players. This was the company that went on to launch Eugene O'Neill into the world; premiere work by Wallace Stevens, Edna St. Vincent Millay, and Theodore Dreiser; launch the Little Theatre Movement; stir up racial controversy across the nation; and provide the guiding intellectual and moral light for what would become alternative theatre and off-Broadway.

It began on a verandah.

On 5 July 1915 in Provincetown, Cape Cod, a tiny audience gathered on the verandah of Neith Boyce's cottage, the crashing waves providing sound effects and the salt air the atmosphere. Once children had been put to bed, the assembled company set their chairs looking out to sea for the first play, Boyce's *Constancy*, a thinly veiled depiction of the volcanic affair between Mabel Dodge, the queen of the New York salons, and John Reed, the activist and radical journalist, who later inspired the film *Reds*. Both were present. At the interval, they turned the chairs around and faced the parlour to see *Suppressed Desires*, a comedy by Susan Glaspell and her husband, George 'Jig' Cook. The authors, who also performed, depicted a young couple undergoing Freudian psychoanalysis, and the sexual arousal it provoked. Both pieces flew. The evening on Boyce's porch galvanised a community to make work, and inadvertently started a movement. Rough theatre, good acting, simple but eloquent gestures, plays by women, and new content – the DNA was there already.

Provincetown provided one of the earliest twentieth-century templates for a town transformed by artists. Its ecosystem stripped out by centuries of timbering, and its economy wrecked first by over-whaling and overfishing and more recently by battering storms, by the 1910s it was severely impoverished. Homes could be rented for almost nothing, studios for less. Artists were attracted by the beautiful light, thinkers by the philosophic space of long beaches and crashing Atlantic waves, and everyone by the cheapness, with much cash left over for their greatest god – booze. Its position, nestled in the fist of the long, clenched arm of Cape Cod, lent a sense of freedom from the rest of America, a freedom to imagine new ways of living (which, as throughout history, also meant a freedom to hop in and out of bed with one another). So a community of lefties and anarchists, American dissidents and discontents, with a strong injection of European émigrés, gathered. They had already formed loose coalitions in Greenwich Village, and now decided to extend their empire of bohemia, colonising a section of the seaboard.

At the heart of their theatrical aspirations were Glaspell and Cook. Their dream was to create a new American drama, distinct from the commercial imperatives of Broadway. They wanted to shuck off the influence of classic European theatre and Victorian melodrama and create a fresh idiom to reflect modern times. They admired the plays of Europeans such as Ibsen and Strindberg and Wilde and Shaw – and wanted to make work to encompass socialist politics, the New Woman, and the new psychology, driven by the psychoanalysis of Freud and Jung, then so contemporary as to be hot to touch. They had performed small one-act plays at the Liberal Club in New York and participated with outsized theatrical gestures at a strike pageant in Madison Square Garden. Provincetown offered quiet and seclusion for a community to further pursue a vision inspired by the ancient Athenian one – an amateur group of citizens, without regard to monetary reward, enacting stories for the polity they lived within. With some Dionysiac celebration as a side order.

The success of the verandah evening led the company to seek a larger venue. A benefactor offered them a fish house at the end of Lewis Wharf. The present occupant, an artist, was booted out, and Glaspell and Cook, with manic urgency, led a group of friends in transforming it into a space for one hundred with a candlelit platform stage. Electricity soon followed, together with circus seating – planks laid out on rows of barrels. When a fire damaged two of the walls, the company liked the effect, so a special ash-grey paint was mixed to match the two burned walls, and they were ready to open. The sea's regular plash rose up through the cracks in the floor and the wind whistled through the walls, adding to the rough-hewn aura. In this arena, the Provincetown Players were born. An idea if powerful enough will travel, and it can begin as quiet as chat.

The loudest noise that emerged was O'Neill, but there is a case to be made that Susan Glaspell deserved similar volume. The acknowledged 'mother of American modern theatre', she led the charge in Provincetown, corralling together a community not without ego, and later helped them to establish a base in MacDougal Street in New York. Her capacity as an entrepreneur may have masked her abilities as a playwright. An early one-act, *Trifles* (1916), was a calling card, and soon became a much-anthologised staple of the repertoire. Cunningly, it wraps a message of subversive action in the shiny paper of entertainment. With elements of the police procedural and whodunnit, this early feminist masterpiece begins in a rudimentary cottage where the dead body of a farm labourer has been found. His widow, now jailed, is the prime suspect. As sheriffs and attorneys blunder around, spouting a priori assumptions and missing clues, two local women stumble across evidence and motives. Eventually, having had no such intention, they resolve to conceal everything from the police. A polemic is submerged within a taut plot, and we find ourselves happily egging two women on to commit a crime.

Born in Iowa in 1876 to a hay farmer and a teacher, Glaspell was able to hold in balance the rural and the modern, the pioneer spirit and the cosmopolitan, though the two different Americas tear away at each other. In her Pulitzer Prize-winning play, *Alison's House* (1930), inspired by the life of Emily Dickinson, she leans heavily on the literary side. The play deals in the ethical dilemma faced by a family regarding the last wishes of a poet, Alison, and a posthumously discovered collection of verse. Set in Iowa on the last day of the nineteenth century, the family members represent different aspects of the nascent America. Their arguments are at once familial, generational, and about what their burgeoning country should be. On one side is decorum, reticence, and repression, on the other freedom and candour. Glaspell is wise enough to see virtues in both, and to make the spectator emotionally attached to differing goods. Written long after her Provincetown days for a commercial New York management, *Alison's House* displays deft stagecraft, and has a swelling emotional effect.

Her play *Inheritors* (1921), written for the Provincetown Players, is nearly a titan, marred by some occasional ill-considered prolixity. In the first act, set in 1879, Silas Morton, a doughty pioneer farmer, looks out on the hill beyond his family home, and dreams of using the land they have 'stolen from the Indians' to found a college. With a fervent belief in the power of education, he wants the future to be better for everyone. The next three acts jump forward to a different America in 1920, where any prelapsarian innocence is lost. The college has been built, and the campus, with many a contemporary resonance, is in uproar. The First World War has ended, and now the attorney general is conducting drives against radicals and conscientious objectors. A young woman, the granddaughter of Silas Morton, takes up the cause of a wrongly imprisoned pacifist, and of two Hindus handing out leaflets against British rule in India.

Glaspell paints a broad picture of contemporary iniquity; professors sacrificing principles to the pressures of investment; the labelling of dark-skinned visitors as un-American simply because they are 'foreigners'; the theft from Native Americans of traditional lands; and self-appointed vigilantes who bully any who disagree with them and pursue witch-hunts with the tacit support of the law. Madeline Morton defies her family and risks imprisonment for her radical beliefs. In a powerful series of dialogues, family and friends pile on all forms of pressure to try and force her to understand the virtue in compromise.

Finding a play from 1921 which pits revolutionary progress against the ties that bind is quite the surprise, and a salutary reminder that many of the hardest battles were fought by previous generations, and by finer people. In an inspirational and beautifully realised ending, Madeline discovers moment to moment her own courage. Her father, Ira, has been rendered almost silent by the buffeting of life, having lost a wife who died going to help neighbours sick with diphtheria, and a son who perished in the fields of France fighting for a better future. All he can now commit to is the perfecting of his corn crop, and he is driven to distraction by the winds, which blow the success of his experiments onto the fields of his neighbours, who have made none of the same sacrifices to perfect their crops. At the end, Madeline resolves (and the hints to the actress about how to play it are peerless): 'But father has been telling me about the corn. It gives itself away all the time – the best corn a gift to other corn. What you are – that doesn't stay with you. Then – (*not with assurance, but feeling her way*) be the most you can be, so life will be more because you were, (*freed by the truth she has found*) Oh – do that!' The earlier speechifying crystallises here into overpowering and simple sense.

Glaspell catches America at a crossroads, as the simple pieties of Emerson (oft quoted) are contrasted with the fast new world of a superpower. She knew, from her Iowa childhood, the farmer beginnings of the country, and she watched as it tried to retain some of its old civility within a landscape of rampant growth. Those attached to the past spit out the word 'Aspiration!' as if some sort of curse. Yet the dream of more is unavoidable. Glaspell asks that all should be allowed an equal share, and that no voices be shut down in the name of defending the American way. For that, she and her peers were branded communists, when all she was championing was a goodness defined by standing up for others rather than walking by.

The Provincetown Players, as with many such ventures throughout the century, was undone by its own success. The centre of gravity of the operation migrated from Cape Cod to New York. Its amateur company in the full flush of praise decided they wanted to be professionals. Success on Broadway corroded the equality of the spirit, and before long it was resolved to shut the operation down. Yet their dream found its way into the body of American and world culture, proliferating many more cherished projects from shambolic beginnings. Glaspell's achievement in founding that dream was formidable, and as a playwright no less.

Scruffy beginnings.
Lewis Wharf, home of the Provincetown Players, 1915

Luigi Pirandello
1867–1936

Luigi Pirandello, as he liked to recount, was born in chaos. His family's grand home in Sicily sat on land once belonging to a Greek estate named Kaos. The name fits, since he arrived on earth at a time of Heraclitean flux. Different histories layered themselves around him. Southern Sicily itself, and the nearby town of Agrigento, was sculpted from a layer cake of heritages. A prosperous and cultured Greek colony in the classical era, the landscape is studded with temples and amphitheatres, perching on hills presiding over the landscape. Being on the southernmost coast of Italy, there was historically much traffic with Africa, its merchandise and ideas, with the architecture, food, and street life of Pirandello's youth showing a profound Arab inheritance. These contrasting cultures collided alongside the predominant Italián influence, yet even that was less than stable. Italy, the unified country, was only six years old when he was born in 1867, and its diversity was still more pronounced than its unity. Florentine Italian was the dialect officially adopted as the national language (largely because of Dante, Petrarch, and Boccaccio), but only about 4 per cent of the country spoke it fluently, and to many it was meaningless. Pirandello was far more comfortable writing in his native Sicilian, and always found translating his work into 'proper' Italian arduous.

As he grew up he would have negotiated these diverging influences, as well as a technological advance which illuminated his home in fresh ways every decade or so. He bemoaned the disorientation of living through four generations of light – born by oil lamp, growing up by paraffin, studying by gaslight, and writing by electric. As the new century dawned, as if reality wasn't already wobbly, the cosmos lost its settled fixity. Einstein's theory of relativity, and other associated revelations, brought harvests of confusion to the intelligentsia of Europe, who found them both liberating and terrifying. What had seemed solid was fractured: time, which had seemed an onward march, was looping back on itself. By the end of the Great War, these conjectural disjunctions had been made manifest in every direction. There was no mistaking the change between the physical and emotional landscapes pre-1914 and that of post-1918. By 1919, the idea of a logical, Newtonian universe lay in ruins all over Europe. Chaos *veramente*.

Alongside external disorientations, Pirandello's private life was fragmented. Brought up in prosperity, and having been married off by his father to his business partner's daughter, all went belly-up in 1903. Both families' principal source of income – a sulphur mine – was catastrophically flooded, taking most of their wealth. Sadly, it also took Signora Pirandello's sanity with it. The reality of wealth and the reality of poverty are jarringly distinct, and the chasm proved unbridgeable for Antonietta. After some time in catatonic shock, she became unmoored from her previous self, her mind hemmed in by depression and paranoid suspicions. Chief among these was a belief that Luigi was having an affair with their daughter. After sixteen years of cohabiting within the claustrophobia of his wife's paranoia, Pirandello gave up and committed her to an asylum. There she succumbed to fantasies long waiting to envelop her.

The narrative we have of Antonietta's mental health has largely come down from Pirandello, and may skimp on the degree to which his personality was a contributing factor. After she was committed, there followed a period of extraordinary creativity. The playwright revealed in a series of works his honed and attuned access to the shifting uncertainties, anxieties, and formlessness of modernity. Chief among these were two plays that mark out his reputation and had a profound influence.

Six Characters in Search of an Author begins in a rehearsal room where a theatre company hang around loose and informal, preparing to work on Pirandello's *Rules of the Game*. Into this laid-back and shapeless environment walk six not-fully-embodied entities, a family once imagined by an author who have never found a narrative to call home. They wander in search of a frame for their inchoate existence. The family's need is driven by a well of pain and dysfunction. Long before, the father had engineered a situation in which the mother could leave for another man, with whom she had three children, before returning to her first husband. By a shameful coincidence, the father has visited a brothel and almost/maybe had carnal relations with his stepdaughter. The transgression of this act has created the Munchian Scream-like woe of this wandering tribe. They look not for resolution – nothing is sappy here – but simply for a form to counter the formlessness of their abyss. Once the theatre company have vaulted the weirdness, they try to help these lost souls find a shape. Their tale comes to life before us in incoherent fragments we are invited to assemble into a narrative, thus making us complicit in the authorship. As we watch, story emerges from the flux. Simultaneous to Pirandello, Brecht was asking the audience to question the solidity of the realities presented to them. For him it was a way of encouraging critical thinking about society; for Pirandello it was to make the audience share a horror at human pointlessness.

Henry IV, Pirandello's other signature work, plays similar games with appearance and reality. An Italian nobleman, twenty years before the events we witness, was dressed as Henry IV, the Holy Roman Emperor, at a historical cavalcade when he was thrown from his horse, landing on his head. In the instant, he was mentally shocked into believing he was the real Emperor. Since then, his family have hidden him away in an Umbrian castle, transforming it into an elaborately staged medieval backdrop to maintain him comfortably in his delusion. As the play begins, they arrive as a group, dressed in medieval garb, determined to shock him from his fictional state back into contemporary reality. In Act II, we learn – aha! – that he is in truth no longer mad and is merely playing with them. We are invited to ponder a whole collection of questions about memory and fantasy, solidity and emptiness, and who is mad and who sane. By Act III, all but the professors of philosophy in the audience have lost interest and are working out which train to take home. Just in case we are in any doubt as to the meaning of the play, Henry makes it clear that our existence, the conventional one of bourgeois comfort, is as crazed as any madman's.

The play opened in 1922, the same year as, in another moment of historical theatricality, King Victor Emmanuel III stepped aside and invited Mussolini to take over the Italian state. Henry IV in the play, like the dictator in life, is a domineering character with a taste for theatrical performance, who outmanoeuvres the herbivorous folk around him, twisting the movements of history to his advantage. Soon after the play in 1925, Pirandello was gifted the custodianship of the Teatro D'Arte in Rome by the new elite, and in response wrote a fawning letter to Il Duce. Here is one of several instances of the uneasy alliance between fascism and modernism. There was a strong strain in the latter movement that believed the attempts of artists to renew culture and perception were matched by the fascists' endeavours to renew politics, and that both were singing a similar song of the new. Pirandello was never as strong a cultural ally to fascism as Filippo Marinetti and the Futurists, but it is hard to ignore his evident delight in dressing up in their regalia, and his several pledges to the cause. There is a queasy correspondence in modernism, as in the present day with those saturated in social media, between those who question the solidity of reality and shameless political opportunism.

What redeems Pirandello's plays from the uncomfortable political attachments and the philosophical ponderousness is his honesty about his own pain. One feels in every pulse an involuntary echo from his own lived tragedy. Equally raw and energising is the freewheeling Sicilian improvisation of his writing. The Commedia Dell'Arte tradition is key here, a genre which encourages freedom in creation moment to moment. *Commedia* actors know before they begin a show their situations and the archetypes exemplified by their masks: they do not know which way a story will flow. Content and styling are there, but not a complete narrative. Just as in our daily existence, however hard we may plan, we must improvise a way through. The *commedia* performer's skill at being fully alive is what marks them out, with charisma and dizzying speed the key requirements.

That vivacity crosses over into Pirandello's writing, most notably in *Six Characters*, where we see each realm of the real – the actors and the floating characters – contrive existence moment to moment. Those who visited the playwright when he was composing a new piece told of watching him alone in his room, in animated argument with his characters, urging them to consider another point of view and pausing to hear their replies. To the playwright, his characters were wholly real – joking, arguing, and spinning their way through the void. Once he had committed them to the page, he bore this ever moving and changing jabber to rehearsals and performance, and there he allowed it to hop and fly and screech like a wild aviary, trapped within the immutability of the proscenium.

For a long time, these large existential questions had powerful currency within the theatre – Who am I? How do I know what I know? What is reality? What is fantasy? Is the mad person sane, or the sane person mad? As questions, they have weight and eternal relevance. Particularly for students, where they speak to that jarring dislocation between two different realities: the one where their mother does their laundry, and the one where they discover the laundromat. My last ever bit of acting was in a production of Pirandello's *Rules of the Game* at university. In our production, at regular intervals, we all had to freeze while a euphonium player wandered among us playing tunelessly. My inability to perform without succumbing to hysterical giggles didn't survive this meta-theatrical gesture.

However large those questions, they are a bit tiring. It is always fun at a party to drop in on the earnest teenager in the corner and listen to their cosmic enquiries. Such teenagers seem to be blooming now at an alarming rate, in a world assaulted by social platforms which maniacally proliferate metaverses. For all it is good to listen, it can be pretty fatal to get stuck with that sober-sided questioner. You look out at the rest of the party and see that it is full of stories and jokes and transactions and gaiety. You start to feel that being burdened by one person's sorting out of their intellectual *Weltanschauung* may not be the optimal use of time. You also see people who need genuine comfort to patch up harder bruises. With Pirandello, it is great to know the plays are there exploring their cosmic interstices, but often time spent in his alternate universes feels rather an affectation. We do, in all good reason, live in a single reality, where so much needs care and attention.

Pirandello left a series of doom-laden instructions for how his body should be handled after death. Many seem mutually contradictory – in keeping with his desire to flummox – though all share the same determined bleakness. 'Burn me,' he commanded, 'and throw my ashes to the winds, for I want nothing not even my ashes to remain.' His other instruction looped him back to his beginnings – he wanted to be buried under a pine tree at his old home, Chaos.

Snow White and the Six Characters.
Scene from London production, in Italian, of *Six Characters in Search of an Author*, 1925

María Martínez Sierra / de la O Lejárraga 1874–1974

One woman, and two names; the first a married and professional name, the second an independent and natural one. Debate rages among Spanish theatre-makers and feminist historians over which name María should be known by. She stuck with the first, though no woman in history has been offered more reason to divest herself and return to her birth name.

Born O Lejárraga in 1874, she wedded the distinguished theatre practitioner Gregorio Martínez Sierra in 1900. A director and essayist, before their marriage he had made a few unsuccessful attempts at translating and playwriting. Once married, the two began to collaborate, embarking on a partnership as profuse and various as their Golden Age forebears. Work poured forth, and their outsized opus became a foundation stone of twentieth-century Spanish theatre. They translated Shakespeare, Ibsen, Maeterlinck, Pirandello, and Shaw. They churned out librettos for operas, operettas and musicals, and wrote play after play. First staged in Madrid, they transferred with dazzling success to Dublin, London, and New York. Stars queued up to perform in them and audiences delighted. Bar Lorca, Gregorio and María were the most successful Spanish playwrights of the twentieth century. Their earliest work went out solely under Gregorio's name, the main tranche under both. Before she died in Argentina, having lived to almost a hundred, she released a memoir, *Gregorio and I, Half a Century of Collaboration*.

In her memoir, as in public statements and accreditations, María distorted the truth to an astonishing degree. Gregorio, though he suggested and discussed and inspired and scribbled, hardly wrote a word. Later textual analysis, research into letters and working documents, and the testament of friends and colleagues revealed the truth – María was the prime, and often the sole, author. The husband wrote petulantly to his wife demanding new drafts, actors sat around in rehearsals waiting for

María to send pages, and the work reflects a singular sensibility. Within the profession it was an open secret, but one to which María was fiercely attached, however misplaced her loyalty.

Never has anyone been further provoked to correct a credit. Seven years into their marriage, Gregorio began an affair with an actress named Catalina Bárcena, around whom he formed Spain's foremost troupe. Catalina, ensconced as mistress, paraded her jealousy of María's status as wife: María suffered in silence. The lovers had a child: María churned out plays her husband claimed to have a hand in. Catalina demanded that Gregorio leave his wife: María departed for Nice, where she turned out more work for him to produce and publish as his own. In France, María developed a feminist voice, supporting socialist causes, yet still the manuscripts were mailed to Gregorio. He was now touring internationally, to escape a Spain leaning towards authoritarianism. On his travels, he found himself in Hollywood, where he sold a pile of his wife's scripts, his name proudly up front. To cap a high place in the annals of perfidy, Gregorio even had the audacity to sport a dastardly moustache.

Defying possibility, the humiliation gets worse. Gregorio and Catalina left for Buenos Aires to make a film based on a script of his wife's. When he died in 1947, María only learned of it on a British radio broadcast. Still forgiving, she composed a tribute written 'in love and pain'. When she moved to Argentina herself, she discovered that her ex-husband had told everyone she was dead, to legitimise his affair. To add insult to stupendous injury, Gregorio left all the rights to their plays to Catalina, who was now living off their steady income. Destitute at seventy-four, María had to earn her own way, scraping by on lectures for the radio and pieces for newspapers. She proposed a collected edition of Gregorio's works – solely accredited to him – for which she would write an introduction. Catalina screamed the project down. María's two semi-autobiographies kept the secret closely grasped, dying with it held in her embrace.

Chaucer wrote of his Patient Griselda, who endured unending insult and neglect before finding her true love; Shakespeare wrote of Helena and her transfixing adoration of the feckless and heartless Bertram.

Neither of those two seems to have endured half of what María went through, and both were afforded some measure of salvation. None came to María. The cause of her boundless self-sacrifice remains a mystery. Was it proof of love? Was it the nature of her faith that it should find no reward? Did she achieve her fullest self as an artist in anonymity? Did she become at ease in her own skin only in privacy? If so, it is impossible not to admire her, while screaming with frustration at the cruelty of each hand of cards she was dealt.

Her work may hold the answer. She wrote two startling pieces set within religious communities. In the first, *The Cradle Song,* an enclosed community of nuns is left a baby in a basket on their doorstep. The first act recounts their delight, and confusion over whether to keep her. The second jumps eighteen years to the moment when the girl is set to leave the community to marry. The hearts of the nuns we met when they were young are breaking, though all have grown richer and fuller from their unstinting love. A story told without cynicism or grandstanding morals, it proves a rare demonstration of natural goodness. Virtue fuses through every moment; a sacrifice without sentiment, and a charity robust and practical. In direct contrast to Lorca's *The House of Bernarda Alba*, it shows a natural generosity flowing from an all-female community.

In a second play, *The Kingdom of God*, we leap through time again, now in the company of Sister Gracia, who belongs to the order of St Vincent de Paul. In the first act, she is nineteen, working in an asylum for destitute old men; in the second, at twenty-nine, she cares for unmarried mothers; in the third, aged seventy, she presides over an orphanage. In each environment, the harshness and impoverishment of daily existence is realised unsparingly. Each minor character stumbles through with documentary reality, as if the camera of María's eye is passing over the victims of her country's injustices. And each hellhole is partially redeemed by the kindness and clarity of Sister Gracia. The particular virtues of Christianity are not advertised here – the stories could as easily be in a Muslim, Hindu, or Buddhist setting – this is simply the action of charity at work. Uniquely in this century of drama, they portray what it means to be good, and the benevolence that ripples out from acts of mercy.

Not that O Lejárraga was some passive milksop. Her plays are too full of vitality and sharp wit; each good character is compromised by bouts of spikiness and smallness – their virtue is hard earned. In photos, María has a beguiling, lambent softness. She had a passionate friendship with the composer Manuel de Falla, evidenced in some spicy postcards, seemingly written partly in code. And there are at least two spry comedies, in no way from the hand of an anchorite. Set in large family houses, encasing generations of a single bourgeois family, they sparkle with mischief. Both feature a zany looseness, with haphazard jumps of behaviour and incident keeping the audience unsteady. Passion resides here but, unlike with Lorca, it will not destroy happiness, held as it is in the forgiving embrace of light comedy.

Take Two from One is a gallimaufry starting on the deck of a cruise ship and, through mishap at sea, ending up with a man accidentally married to two women. One of them has been squirrelled away with an African tribe, where she seems to have learned a freedom that confounds the stultified world to which she returns. The two wives fight over their shared husband, something María knew all about, but her agonies are dramatised without anguish. In a prescient touch, his eventual desire is to have them both, in what would now be described as ethical non-monogamy. Society, bourgeois propriety, and the Catholic Church will not allow this, though the author does not seem to disapprove. In a madcap touch of meta-theatrical fun, the bigamous husband's final solution is to leave the stage and climb into a box outside the proscenium. The wives cannot follow, and as the curtain descends they are cruelly separated from him until the following night, when they must perform again. In the first production of this play at the Haymarket Theatre in London in 1931, the two wives were played by Gertrude Lawrence (Noël Coward's muse) and the very young Peggy Ashcroft. Coward would seem to have stolen a large chunk of the narrative for his *Blithe Spirit* ten years later. (In yet another case of male larceny, when María was briefly in Hollywood, she submitted her story *Merlin y Viviana* to Walt Disney; he rejected it, purloining the story for *Lady and the Tramp*.)

Complaint on María's behalf may be churlish or presumptive, when her sensibility is so free of special pleading. Her husband may have been a heel, but who can understand the love of others? Her loyalty mattered to her, and she honoured it. Through encountering her plays – their humanity, fun, and profound charity – it is hard not to conclude she could have claimed, with Shakespeare's Beatrice, 'there was a star danced, and under that was I born'.

Look who's writing.
María Martínez with her husband
Gregorio at home in Madrid, 1907

Noël Coward

1899–1973

Towards the end of the First World War, the poet Siegfried Sassoon, on leave from the front and having just published his collection *Counter-Attack*, spent a day in London. He bumped into Winston Churchill, who complimented him on his verses, dined with Maynard Keynes, said hello to the Sitwells, and chose to end his evening with Robbie Ross, Oscar Wilde's first lover and best and longest friend. Had Siegfried been a name-dropper, there was a lifetime's crop in a single day. As Ross and Sassoon were talking, Charles Scott Moncrieff, the first translator of Proust, turned up, bringing along a baby-faced prodigy called Noël Coward.

Sassoon found Coward annoying; his excessive flattery for the older man's poems and his overattentive manner were such a distraction he called it a day. He departed, leaving Ross, the great, steady keeper of the Wilde flame, in the gossipy company of Coward. Two days later, Robbie Ross died of a heart attack. Sassoon remarked of his brave friend it 'must have been the only occasion when Robbie's heart failed him'. Theatre legend is full of baton-passing moments, one generation directly or indirectly influencing another. This encounter between Ross and Coward, however accidental and trivial, glows in hindsight as one such. The work Wilde began in the 1890s, infiltrating decadence, variety, and joy into English life, was continued by Coward, and democratised in his own era.

In the early 2000s, I travelled to Newcastle to appear on a panel discussion about politics and drama. It turned out my role was the comedy hate figure, a sort of Piers Plonker, the effete New Labour Southerner. My accent dug me into a trench, and my assertion that political theatre was not solely about dense pieces on pensions policy necessitated extra sandbags. Still just about surviving, I mentioned I had recently produced Noël Coward's *Hay Fever* – then the serious shells started landing. Funny how Coward could still arouse rage and contempt among the angry and *sérieux*. Even association with the man can be treated as a sinister collaboration with frivolity.

The Coward effect obscures the Coward opus. The persona he created is such a vivid concoction it can occlude the art. All over the world, from Moscow to Mandalay, when jokers attempt an English accent, they adopt a clipped, sharp tone and over-enunciate with their lips. Little do they know they are imitating the voice and mannerism a boy in dowdy Teddington strained to achieve over a hundred years ago. No dreams of stardom afflicted him at the time, nor of social elevation. He just wanted to make himself clear to his entirely deaf mother. Odd to think how much the received idea of the English is a result of the hearing problem of Violet Coward.

This much-imitated affectation is one of many examples of the Coward cultural diaspora, the clouds that skim over the world shading it a little more British. Who gave further accreditation to the running joke of the British royal family than their most ostentatiously loyal subject? Who helped more to kid the world we could punch above our weight with the New Yorkers as verbal pugilists? What exemplified our fame for sexual repression better than his magnificent refusal to state the obvious? (He insisted, justifiably, to his deathbed that coming out would hurt too many old ladies along the southern seaboard who harboured a dream that one day their prince would come – in a smoking jacket.) Who did more to invent the modern celebrity?

All these masks – the sophisticate, the celeb, the brittle wit – cluster around our image of Coward. What do we miss? The single most important fact – he was a playwright of genius. Maligned as thin concoctions – fragile entertainments tricked up to keep his ego's pantry well stocked with applause – study of his work, and even more producing them, sets that prejudice straight. He was a radical innovator with form, an acute observer of social patterns, and a brilliant cartographer of the human heart. More than that – these are talents, his was a gift – he wrote from a private place, a granary of poisoned dreams and soured romances, that defies full understanding. His work lives beyond dull meaning, somewhere lonely, independent, and sunlit.

Why do we not study him? It's hard to say when so many lesser talents are studied in schools and crack under the weight of university theses. Probably because in his frivolity he nailed our greatest shame, that many of us are frivolous too. The earnest Establishment hates that fact, and it's one of the reasons the conjunction of suffering and art is enforced. Education promotes that the noble cause is to think of oneself as a Hamlet or a Faustus or a Jimmy Porter, but never as a Judith Bliss, even if Judith Bliss is closer to our marrow. Probably also because the British are so petrified of our own instinctive genii. We look fondly on colour, freedom, and imagination from abroad, while preferring to elevate our own stodge. When a home-grown talent cuts free and just invents, they are often treated as if they've let the side down.

Coward was inventive. As with many of the big cheeses of the proscenium century, his first great achievement was formal. He reinvented what an evening in the theatre could be. In dialogue terms, his plays marked a decisive shift from the ostentatious phrasing of Wilde and Maugham towards the recording of direct speech. His voice is light, but also jagged, spontaneous, and fresh, with none of the deliberate stilting that came before and after. In construction he went further. He took the melody of the Victorian well-made play and handed it over to a jazz band. Where previously there were straight lines, he wrote squiggles: tunes were replaced by riffs. *The Vortex* is footloose in its construction, lurching from a conventional opening to a dreamlike middle to a big stichomythic ball of rage at the end. *Fallen Angels* is an ingenious attenuation of a single joke. *Easy Virtue* parachutes a disturbingly modern figure, Larita, a sort of Jimmy Porter in pearls, into the middle of a Victorian melodrama.

The fourth great hit of 1924–25, *Hay Fever*, is structurally the real surprise. On close inspection, this standard-bearer for conventional drama turns out to be a modernist creation. There is no plot. Literally nothing happens. It's as driven as *Godot*. The last act is a nonsensical denial of narrative, suspense, and climax. Opening with three passages from a silent movie as guests descend for breakfast, we watch nothing but behaviour for six or seven minutes. The most perfect example of Peter Brook's '*Empty Space*' theory, but with the pleasing addition of boiled eggs, barometers, and haddock. Having set up the tension between the Bliss family and their guests as the mainspring of the play, Coward decides to forgo conflict and keep them apart. For the whole of the third act they never meet, and the last five minutes is a passionate argument about Parisian geography. As you watch this insane but appropriate nonsense taking place, you start to realise why Virginia Woolf and the Bloomsbury set descended on Coward with such crushes. He was the Damien Hirst of his day, merrily shoving Semtex under aesthetic rules, and making people see the confusion of their lives with an unsynthesised and unexcused directness. Like all true artists, he created a form to suit the subject.

These four plays each opened and flourished within a year when Coward arrived in the West End with the most immense 'Ta-da!' A glittering star, he was quoted, photographed, and caricatured here, there and everywhere. The tools of modern celebrity were used to promote him, and he mastered each. In the full flush of youth and exultation, he sprayed wit and attitude into the air around him, greedily caught by crowds and cameras. At a moment when despair was pervasive, how lucky to encounter a young genius determined to pivot towards joy. *The Waste Land,* a near simultaneous emanation, is of course one response to a meaningless world, but if it were the only one, we would be a poor lot.

Politically, there is no questioning that Coward followed the classic journey of the English playwright from firebrand to crustily clubbable. His later hymns to snobbery, the Church, the royals, and other elements of a Never-Never-England didn't do him many favours. But his ageing mask concealed a turbulent youth. These four plays face head-on the political subject of the day: the schism in the 1920s between two Englands.

On one side there was the England preserved in aspic, stuck in a pre-war Edwardian world, rigid behind a mask of denial. This was the England of duty, conventions, and doing the right thing; the England of tennis and tea; of 'Rather!' and 'Ripping!'; of minutely detailed codes of etiquette; all underpinned by a corrosive moral hypocrisy. This was the England that had followed orders, gritted teeth, starched its upper lip, and marched silently into a catastrophically venal waste of human life. The England that had taken away so many of Coward's friends, and his first great love, Philip Streatfeild.

Set against this was the decidedly other England that arose during the 1920s, the one starring Coward. The new Albion of much alcohol and more cocaine; of nightclubs, jazz, stylish little catchphrases, and much rumpy-pumpy; of wild, regular, and merry experimentation. A place peopled by bobbed flappers in satin and long gloves, their beaux clouded in cigarette smoke. They danced the improvised mazurka of those who had seen with horror the result of too much custom and practice, and decided to pursue gilded lives in semi-permanent revolt, their moral wildness afforded a little moral weight by their capacity for emotional generosity.

Coward summons the two Englands of history, changing costume and ideology as the centuries roll by: the Celts and the Normans, the Roundheads and the Cavaliers, the Tories and the Whigs, the hip and the straight, the flower children and the rat-racers. Each were combatants in unending civil wars over the English character. As we look for some moral direction, Coward's dancing ladies, Parisian Pierrots, and poor rich girls, lost in their whirl, still speak to us. He is too discreet an artist to come down heavily in favour of either side, shading both with good and bad and highlighting their curious co-dependence. No one has delineated the English schism between the wild and the locked-down more truly.

Social observation was not all Coward took from the First World War. He also inherited a heart marinated in grief. He often disclaimed any great involvement with the war, but it would be impossible to imagine his sensibility untouched by the deaths of so many. Nor by the sight of his Peter Pan-ish idyll of a childhood, performing in fey theatrical spectaculars dressed as a mushroom or a goldfish, disappearing under a cloud of mustard gas. The strain Coward was ever under is exhibited in the bronze bust in the National Portrait Gallery by his friend Clemence Dane – cast when he was twenty-nine but showing all the mileage of a seventy-year-old. The frequency with which he fractured offers further evidence: three reasonably savage nervous breakdowns by the time he was thirty. Listen to the plangent lilt of 'Mad About the Boy', 'World Weary', or 'Twentieth Century Blues', to the desperate yearning of Elyot and Amanda in *Private Lives*, or the agonised repression of the tea-room tremblers in *Brief Encounter* (drawn from his play *Still Life*) and it's hard not to hear the lapping waves of a tide of loss.

In preparation for working on *Hay Fever*, I spoke to the playwright Neil Bartlett, who said he would find it hard to work on Coward since he couldn't bear to deal with so much scotched love. A just way of putting it. There is love in abundance in Coward's work – it's his principal theme – but it is scorched, frozen love, the suffocated variety that Wilde, Maugham, Coward, and Rattigan all articulated and gave resonance for an audience way beyond their own coterie. During a technical rehearsal for *Hay Fever*, to fill spare moments, I scribbled some period classics into a prop book of poems. I jotted down Auden's 'As I Walked Out One Evening', and was brought up short by his evocation of Time watching from the shadow and coughing 'when you would kiss'.

Precious though it may be, it was a way of unlocking *Hay Fever*. In the play, almost every time a couple is about to kiss, the doorbell goes – the running gag of the first act. Or someone enters, or an offstage noise interrupts a reverie. Throughout the play interruptions pile up – rain stops sex in a punt, a couple are discovered in flagrante in the library, Judith Bliss walks in on her husband on the point of seducing Myra Arundel. *Hay Fever* is a cacophony of unachieved moments, a symphony of stopped love. Coward's genius is to take this theme, of Time's cough from the shadow, and make it light, riding with buoyancy on the airstreams of his comic invention. With a twist and a spin he takes his material, a persistent rueful romance and an ever-recurring heartbreak, and flips something grave into something delightfully silly.

Coward was disarmingly, wildly funny. Two instances spring to mind from when we were on tour with *Hay Fever*. Once in Exeter, in the second act, when performing the 'In the Manner of the Word' section, the show stopped. Chris Luscombe – then an actor and playing Richard Greatham, now a distinguished director and blessed with bones as funny as Coward's – walked across the stage to pluck a rose from a vase, then moved towards Judith Bliss. For two minutes the audience barked, screamed, howled, and roared with laughter. The actors could do nothing against the gale of hilarity sweeping over them. They had to down tools and wait for the hysteria to pass, standing there looking sheepish as the audience quelled its mania. I witnessed something similar once with the Pyramus and Thisbe section in *A Midsummer Night's Dream*, like *Hay Fever* a midsummer frolic, and in the same tradition. Something about the play within a play construction of both, their amateur joy, their suspension of logic, all mainline into a spirit of puckish English mania liberating to behold. The à point brigade find such merriment alarming, but its lack of control is part of the ongoing health of our theatre.

The second instance was touring *Hay Fever* in Cheltenham. Early in the first act, a woman sitting in the back row got the giggles. Soon her giggles became continuous and their volume began to unsettle. An usher asked her to quieten down, and she politely apologised but failed to calm herself. The front-of-house manager told her she had to be quiet. 'I'm trying,' she said, 'but it's so funny.' The resident St John Ambulance guard attended and asked if she was all right. 'Yes,' she said, 'I just can't stop laughing.' That woman kept right on. Eventually, the theatre staff hailed a passing policeman. He came into the theatre, issued a warning, and once that warning failed, marched the poor lady off into the night, still cackling maniacally. To see someone arrested for laughing at a comedy felt appropriately perverse.

Asked to sum up his life's work, Coward said, 'Now comes the terrible decision, as to whether to be corny or not. The real answer is one word: love. Other answers would be jolly good company, filthy stories, anything you like, but the real answer is to know that you're among people whom you love and who love you.' His wisdom about the heart extended into his private life. He was never immune to the sharp grip of possessive love, periodically submitting to what he called 'that old black magic', diving headlong into shallow puddles with pretty faces, dissolving his store of common sense in obsession for a few months or years. He would always emerge from his midday madness, take a shower, and calm down in the evening sun. Somehow he managed never to destroy the assembly of ex-lovers, friends, and colleagues he accumulated over the years. 'Not your conventional Victorian family,' as Coward's devoted companion Graham Payn described it, 'but in many respects something better, more alive, because we chose each other.' Reading the diaries and biographies, it often seems that this large and self-supporting family, generous to outsiders yet loyal to its own, was almost his greatest success. The achievement of a mature spirit who perceived the ephemeral nature of art beside the enduring resonance of a good heart.

While working on *Hay Fever*, we passed around videos of old documentaries during rehearsals, and several colleagues said they felt the same at the end of each telling – they wished he'd never died. Death seemed to puncture some ongoing balloon of fun. No matter, we have the songs, the poems, the diaries, the autobiographies, the performances, and most importantly the plays. At some point soon, we could maybe stop being intellectually sniffy about Coward and start applauding the truth that a genius tripped lightly among us for more than seventy years. Perhaps a Royal Coward Company – something modest, situated in some small, louche boulevard theatre. Or maybe not; maybe that would be the most efficient way of killing him off. He travelled alone.

A masterclass in smouldering.
Gertrude Lawrence and Noël Coward in the Broadway production of *Private Lives*, 1931

Eugene O'Neill
1888–1953

'I'm sorry but this is a ritual I can't follow any more,' declared a director friend after attending a recent production of *Long Day's Journey into Night*. She was talking about the collective act of silent homage to a mind-crushingly long, remorselessly serious piece of work, a sombre rite which weighed down a significant portion of the proscenium century. O'Neill is the prime exemplar of this liturgy. Feeling that any play coming in under three and a half hours was indicative of personal laziness, he created extreme sports of endurance.

Some of the fault here lies with wrong-headed production, and not a little with O'Neill himself. There is a music to his writing, whether the broad Oirishisms of *A Moon for the Misbegotten*, the stevedore muscularity of *The Hairy Ape*, or the educated Connecticut self-analysis of *Long Day's Journey*. While part of his achievement, it can also prove a problem. The endless repetitions create an incantatory spell but also sound endless; the relentless probing at truths, though laudable in forensic rigour, can feel eternal. The music is a fatal attraction for actors: they spend rehearsals searching for it, and once found, discover that rigid adherence kills the play. There is an excess of modulation, a lot of repeated patterns of statement – Ah, de diddledy-dee, followed by riposte, Oh de doddledy da. The speed at which one stops listening to content and starts sinking into nursery rhyme sing-song is swift. The pattern's regularity, and the absence of jaggedness or stops, induces a brain shutdown from which lucidity can be hard to relocate.

Cutting it radically would be a solution, but there is a stubborn magnificence to the overloading, which is part of the point. And the problem is larger than the music. Contained within the testing is a sensation of being squashed by something bigger than boredom, of being told off, of failing in some indefinable way. The ritual my friend balked at is wrapped up in the twentieth-century Church of Earnestness, a religion of which, if bewhiskered Ibsen were the godhead, O'Neill would be a high priest.

Here one is sucked ineluctably back into the quicksand of the 'suffering is wisdom' mindset. Allied to this contentious truism, there grew throughout the century a strand of elitism that believed only the sourly po-faced to be true artists. Fully legitimate priesthood within the cult of the Earnest could only be awarded for work defined by hard-boned Protestant misery, cleaned of joy or humour. A quasi-Kierkegaard position was willed – faith accessible only through thinking that accentuates guilt, heightens suffering, intensifies inwardness, and brings on the loneliness of Abraham. Humour, pleasure, and joy were false gods, cosmetic lies smeared on the face of the pain's truth. In these unbelievable rituals, actors and audiences collaborate in posing as pioneers on the tragic frontier, before returning to lives of well-upholstered comfort and plenty.

In truth, this was less a problem with the proscenium than with the theatre that followed, and O'Neill in his monumental seriousness is an outlier. Much of the proscenium had the saving grace of frivolity, and a boulevard charm, more honest to the soil from which it grew. And more honest to humanity itself, which is ever a blend of the grave and the silly, the madcap and the doughy, the glib and the heroic. Without him wishing it, O'Neill became an icon to legions of the *sérieux*, an honour which may disguise the breadth and variety of his work.

Measuring O'Neill's achievement, or perceiving his purpose, without understanding the wild daftness which preceded would be a folly. For centuries, the American theatre had proven steadfast in its resistance to any suspicion of depth. Sensational novelistic melodramas with cardboard characters were not the staple fare but pretty much the only fare. Wild West shows, garlanded with trick-rifle shooting and lariat twirling, were a strong narrative influence, as was any story involving train tracks with heroines or juveniles affixed. There were plenty of 'redface' representations of dastardly or dignified Native Americans, to go along with 'blackface' renditions of cheerful or chippy African Americans. *Ben-Hur* (the stage show which conquered the nation) was the epitome of success in its gargantuan size and equivalent simplicity. (The recent primacy of the Marvel Universe in the movies is as much a return to an old appetite as something new.)

Bad imitations of English comedies added a domestic element but did not reshape an art form whose primary aim, amid the sheet-metal thunder and the pictorial lightning, was defined by Tony Kushner as 'to lie effectively'. The seriousness, the realism, and the high art gravity which had taken root in European theatre over the last few decades had made a few tentative expeditions onto American soil but without gaining a foothold. So when O'Neill set out to create a serious American theatre, one which encompassed realism and modernism and expressionism, and whatever else was -isming, there was little to build on. He had to make roots, trunk, branches, twigs, and leaves all at once. An ambition requiring gravitas.

The attack on the previous theatre was more than an aesthetic takedown for O'Neill: it was an act of Oedipal reckoning. Modernism is sometimes described as a desire to kill off one's artistic forebears; rarely was this as literally true as it was for him. His father, James O'Neill, was a megastar of the romantic theatre. In 1883, after the company's star died in the wings at the premiere, James took over as the lead in *The Count of Monte Cristo*. An overnight sensation, he created a legend which eventually became an albatross. He played the part for forty years, giving over six thousand performances to packed houses across the nation. A fortune was made, but according to his son, a talent wasted. As James Tyrone, the avatar of O'Neill Senior, says in *Long Day's Journey into Night*, 'That God-damned play I bought for a song and made such a great success in – a great money success – it ruined me with its promise of an easy fortune . . . What the Hell was it I wanted to buy, I wonder . . .' When the son set out to reinvent the theatre, he was killing off the form that had glorified his father. Shortly after he saw his son's first play, James suffered a stroke, and was dead soon after from intestinal cancer. His final words encased a bitterness that haunted his son: 'Eugene – I'm going to a better sort of life – this sort of life – here – all froth – no good – rottenness!' His wife, Mary, and elder son passed soon after. A traumatic concatenation, which built a mausoleum of grief in the younger O'Neill, the weight of which it would take decades, and the writing of a masterpiece, to release.

O'Neill Junior was born in a hotel room in 1888, a just beginning for a life of transience. Throughout his early years he toured relentlessly with his alcoholic father and a mother addicted to opiates. Sent to boarding schools to acquire a stability home life could not offer, he secured a place at Princeton, but only lasted a year before dropping out. Wanderlust was sated by setting off to sea, working his passage and hitching rides to England and Argentina. Brief stints as a vaudeville actor and a newspaper reporter followed, and even a short adventure prospecting for gold in the Honduran jungle. Rootlessness brought misery, and he battled alcoholism and depression, before a brief bout of tuberculosis. While recovering in a sanatorium, he decided he wanted to be a playwright, cleaned himself off the booze, and uncovered a fury of endeavour to match his previous fecklessness. His work rate from then on was prodigious, as was his output, though the turmoil inside never found an exit. He spent his creative life trying to understand it, and putting it to good use to fuel his work.

At Harvard, he studied on a new playwriting course called the 47 Workshop, before falling in with a group of radicals, artists, and writers in Greenwich Village. This was the group, led by Susan Glaspell, who found their way to Provincetown in Cape Cod. There they formed a troupe that was passionate to overturn and remake American theatre. In the home of Glaspell, O'Neill retrieved from his trunk his first play, *Bound East for Cardiff*, and asked a friend to read it out to her and her husband, while he prowled around outside. It was the beginning of a beautiful relationship, first in the Atlantic wharf where the Provincetown Players premiered their shows, then in the Manhattan fringe theatre they leased, and soon on Broadway, where the plays transferred, before success broke the dream. His first plays were seafaring realism, then landlubber realism, before experimenting with a newly minted American expressionism. His first published play, *Beyond the Horizon*, transferred to Broadway and won the Pulitzer Prize (the first of four), and was soon followed onto the Great White Way by *The Emperor Jones*.

Success came early and hard, but never brought contentment. His mission to found a serious theatre, and his fealty to truth within it, were heavy burdens that cost him. He remained a spindle-shanks figure all his days, sometimes his Giacometti silhouette so slight as to be almost invisible. In photos and film, he often looks a ghost among the living, as if born with something dead inside. The plays can seem a tortured attempt to dream up an existence, to make life where nothing was before. His frequent checking in on himself in mirrors he passed once prompted a friend to say, 'You're the most conceited man I've ever known.' 'No,' O'Neill corrected, 'I'm just trying to make sure I'm still here.'

Most surprising within the work is the prevalence and the ferocity of its politics. Greenwich Village and Provincetown have been painted brightly bohemian, in part to disguise and dilute the strength of their political allegiances. The suffragist movement from Britain, the French syndicalist labour movement, and international progressive factions fighting for socialism and Marxism all had adherents in these communities. The influx of German and Russian Jews into New York, committed to labour reform and the above causes, as well as many converted to the new psychological science led by Freud and Jung, added to the ideological stew. Many were anarchist, at a time when anarchism wasn't benevolent and ecological but about killing czars in Russia and plotting the end of capitalist civilisation in the West. In 1900, America was the only 'great nation' without a state religion and had by far the most polyglot population. A heady concoction of ingredients, with a host of new futures simmering.

One of O'Neill's great friends was John Reed, who co-founded the short-lived Communist Labor Party of America. As a seaman, O'Neill had joined the Industrial Workers of the World (whose members were nicknamed 'Wobblies'), which promoted the idea of one comprehensive union, workers coming together to replace capitalism with industrial democracy. By the 1920s, almost 150,000 had joined up, a social democrat organisation unrecognisable from the tribal unions which monopolised the workforce later. From the vantage of America today, where to be called a 'socialist' is the ultimate smear, it is hard to imagine a country so widely and passionately committed to the ideals of the left. There were extensive and brutal crackdowns on radical movements, which makes O'Neill's public adherence all the more remarkable.

The IWW appears in a crucial scene in *The Hairy Ape*, an expressionist parable of labour and those who exploit it, set in its opening vignettes below and above decks on a steamship. This play, filled with Marxist speeches and anarchist agitating, has been neutered by many dubbing it an existential tale, seemingly in order to defang it. O'Neill is commended for putting lower-class characters on the stage, as if that was the extent of his daring, but he went further. A furious class war tirade, the story demonstrates how the violence contained within class corrupts whatever it touches. Throughout his work there is a constant cavilling against the wealthy and the dishonest tricks by which their power is acquired. Even the 'masterpieces' are underpinned by political argument. Part of the antagonism of the Tyrone family in *Long Day's Journey* revolves around the father's conservatism and the son's frequently invoked radical socialism. Though often played as character quirks, these oppositions are central to the dynamics.

Within the bunch of washed-up dreamers and misfits of *The Iceman Cometh*, attending their endless lock-in, there is an editor of anarchist periodicals, an anarcho-syndicalist, and the son of a celebrated anarchist (a storyline inspired by Emma Goldman). The betrayals and internecine struggles of this movement throw up one of the few strands of plot in the bleary five hours of chitter-chatter, and provide its denouement. Ideological neutering is again central to the standard psychological interpreting of *The Iceman Cometh*. The characters, it is said, are pipe dreamers, delusional and hopeless. A good production, and there have been great ones, highlights a different truth. The characters are activists and radicals whose spirits have been broken by the impossibility of political change. The pipe dreams aren't of wealth or power or personal fulfilment, they are of community and togetherness and a better America. It is what makes the characters sympathetic: rather than losers, they were believers who have lost the faith. As we watch their destruction, we see the play is about America and its perpetual stimulus of dissatisfaction, bearing out O'Neill's bitter dictum, 'I'm going on the theory that the US, instead of being the most successful country in the world, is the greatest failure.'

Nor did O'Neill shy from race. His methodology may not be pristine given today's standards but his determination to put black actors and stories onstage shifted the dial. His first big box office hit, *The Emperor Jones,* is a political fantasia where a Pullman Porter, who has killed another black man during a dice game, ends up as emperor of a small Caribbean island. Recounted in flashbacks as he runs from his former subjects through the jungle, the play amounts to the sort of topsy-turvy parable of which Brecht would have been proud. *All God's Chillun Got Wings* is an expressionist work about miscegenation, in which a woman who resents her husband's skin colour undermines his potential career as a lawyer. The play's virtue is that the unhappy marriage at its centre could be anyone's sour marriage, and in many ways it works as a trial run for *Long Day's Journey*. The role of the black husband was first taken by Paul Robeson, and when he kissed the hand of his white wife, it caused an almighty rumpus among the racists, posing then as ever as guardians of morality. The alliance with Robeson continued when the singer took on the role of Yank in a later production of *The Hairy Ape*, one of the first instances of colour-blind casting in a new play.

Two further Pulitzer Prizes were awarded for *Anna Christie*, a brooding and fogbound romance, and for *Strange Interlude*, a six-hour oddity, part sex comedy, part Strindbergian testament of toxic relationships, which unleashed O'Neill's determined experiment in internal monologue at inordinate length. In his whole career, with one-acts and protean experiments in form, with mask dramas and transpositions of Greek myth, O'Neill wrote fifty plays. The eggshell of American drama was cracked and a host of variegated chicks stumbled out. The prize winning was topped by the Nobel in 1936, accepted by O'Neill with a generous speech about a beloved Swedish playwright predecessor. He once told a friend that immortality would be worth it if it meant he could spend a day with Strindberg. All this success came in before he had written the three plays widely regarded as his finest, and the one considered his masterpiece, though the privileging of these above the early work is questionable.

The Iceman Cometh is a five-and-a-half-hour epic, set in a rank and beaten-up waterfront tavern, based on a downtown Manhattan dive where O'Neill once tried to kill himself as a youth. Beside the anarchists and revolutionaries, there are survivors of the Boer War, barkeepers, lawyers, policemen, and streetwalkers – all dank, dripping, and sodden with booze. Alcohol is one of the regular themes of the proscenium century, the most frequently abused drug of choice. Eccles in Tom Robertson's *Caste* set a high-water mark early for stage drunks, but there is no shortage of competition. Self-anaesthetising is one of the most regular rituals of the proscenium stage: Brick in Tennessee Williams's *Cat on a Hot Tin Roof* searches for 'the click', when he can let go of himself; Birdie in Lillian Hellman's *Little Foxes* is well down the road to self-obliteration; Edward Albee's George and Martha in *Who's Afraid of Virginia Woolf?* triangulate their feelings for each other through the third member of their marriage – the bottle; the doomed youth of R. C. Sherriff's *Journey's End* lash into the whisky; and every other moment of Harold Pinter's *Old Times* seems to involve someone fixing a drink. These are a scatter of instances in a century in which going to the drinks cabinet seemed to be a central part of the liturgy. What was so wrong with all these people that they needed to destroy self and memory so determinedly?

In *The Iceman Cometh*, their failings are laid out with sadistic cruelty, both by the author and by Hickey, the snake-oil salesman who whirlwinds into the play on a mission for letting go of dreams and meeting reality. For a while it seems he will save the dreamers from themselves, until he is unmasked as the greatest liar of all. The play is endless and profuse, not only writing about drunks but drunk writing. Madly verbose, full of self-serving intensity and a relentless push for some ill-defined truth, it has the charm and grandeur of the brilliant drunk, together with the haziness about where it is heading. There is no effective moral or structural compass, but you admire the enthusiasm of the treasure hunt, going after the golden truth which most boozers believe is out there somewhere. In the search fantastic, glittering insights bloom in random tangents branching off from the main themes, and pithy and perfect phrases flower on the edges of those branches. Like a drunkard's monologue, the words keep growing upwards, forced by incalculable rage and need, alive and fierce and desperately sad. A mystic elusiveness hovers in the heart of the play, the same evaporating core which makes lovers and families swirl with helpless love around addicts, always fleeting, always beyond. These are the unmoored, who can't bear the kindly oppression of anyone who might want to bind them back into the human community, however loving they may be. They will go to any lengths, even murder, to stay out of reach. The understanding of these souls and the reproduction of their dank pathology is pitiless and brilliant.

Addiction, and the sad dance of co-dependents around it, is also the heart of *Long Day's Journey*, the play which bears most of the 'masterpiece' garlands – maybe too many. The stakes are raised further by the mother's morphine addiction, a disease that has the rest of her family living on their nerves, and of which we see the fulfilment at the end when Mary Tyrone descends into the mental fog which matches the mist rolling off the sea. She crushes her husband and two sons with gentle and lost poetry.

O'Neill said *Long Day's Journey* was written 'in tears and blood . . . with deep pity and understanding and forgiveness'. Brutally frank in its autobiography, it relives his father's pride and weakness, his brother's self-delusion, and his own incapacity to help. Most unsparing about his mother, she is often played as a pathetic victim, though in truth she is 'a killer'. O'Neill left instructions it should not be performed or published until twenty-five years after his death. For good or ill, his wife Carlotta contravened his stipulation, and the play was soon in the world bearing its heavy freight of privacy. An open wound of a play, it achieves moments almost sacred in their merciless honesty about family and the corrosions of secrets and lies. 'Before the soul can fly, its wings must be washed in the blood of the heart,' was the playwright's mantra, and the wings get a rare old soaking here. It is far, far, far too much, but as with opera, the excess is part of the point, the marathon-running maximalism the correlative of the tumult in O'Neill. This is the prime altarpiece in the Church of the Earnest.

In performance, this is usually the worst of the steamrollers, the length of it rendered more crushing by the fact there are only essentially four characters. *The Iceman Cometh* and *Strange Interlude* at least provide a regular turnover of new characters to shift the rhythm. The word 'overwrought' cannot cover the endless recycling, and yet the characters' patent sincerity and desperate desire to avoid the inevitable tragedy make it hard not to watch. Attention must be paid. Here as elsewhere the writing is magisterial, and the witnessing penitential.

The third of the late greats, *A Moon for the Misbegotten*, is closer to unperformable, there being only three protagonists, but touched with the same greatness. James Tyrone from *Long Day's Journey* pops up again here, or rather slouches in, since like all of O'Neill's characters he is not much of a popper-up. Still drunk, still stifled by the self-laceration which marks the playwright's Rembrandtian self-portraits, he pursues with a lush's confusion a powerhouse Irish woman called Josie. The play gives limitless opportunities for high acting, and the pitch of focused intensity it requires carries off the laurels for those who prefer Olympian emotionality to haphazard, stippled truth. The play is incessant and undisciplined and sloppily repetitious, and yet we forgive it. Something in its quest, its search for an elusive transcendent somewhere beyond empathy, compassion, and outrage, for some tremendous meaning waving from a distant shore, holds our admiration. Jason Robards, one of the great actors of O'Neill plays, said that a couple of hours into *A Moon for the Misbegotten* or *The Iceman Cometh* or *Long Day's Journey*, when he felt he had nothing left to give, an invisible hand would appear at the small of his back and start pushing him forward. The remainder of the play would fly by. Hours would feel like minutes. As was told to him by Ralph Richardson, at those moments, 'You break time. You break space and time. If you do it right – it is time to dream.'

O'Neill's income and reputation went up and down as he floated on the unsteady ocean wave. His late plays were initially derided and then afforded excessive respect. Something about their appearance in the late 1940s and early 1950s, when the world was immersed in serious thinking – unsurprisingly – may account for the reverie. Reassessment of the earlier work may be overdue. Somehow, in a marketplace which respected trash and sensation, O'Neill brought grandeur and mystery, seized an audience with it, and created open spaces for others to spread their picnic cloths. He understood and gave poetic expression to the political ideas of his day, peopling his stage with the destitute and the left behind. He did not shy from the uglier side of life; he dealt with abortion and suicide and class violence, and – with a desperate truth – gave them dignity. He had no fear of failing and did not shrink from the greatest daring, alongside another chronicler of the ocean, Herman Melville, believing it was, 'Better to sink in boundless deeps than float on vulgar shoals.' As Kushner described him: 'A promethean'.

Above all, in his garrulous, wayward, lost plays, he makes us into family. He invites us to dwell in his dysfunctional crucibles of co-dependence, and as we bear witness we develop the tortured and reluctant intimacy we normally reserve for our closest dependents. 'The squeaky wheel gets the oil,' as the old saying goes, and in the course of these insufferable plays we find ourselves wanting to offer salve to the characters, to O'Neill, and even to our neighbours. We look after the wounded and broken, and offer solace to the unconsolable. We are drawn into the web.

O'Neill died in Boston's Sheraton Hotel in 1953 at the age of sixty-five. He whispered, as he died: 'I knew it. I knew it. Born in a hotel room and died in a hotel room.'

Dating as it used to be.
Carlotta Monterey O'Neill in *The Hairy Ape*, Plymouth Theater, USA, 1922.
Monterey later became O'Neill's wife

Clemence Dane
1888–1965

'Silly Novels by Lady Novelists' was George Eliot's title for an extended counterblast against much of the female fiction that came before her. The essay is an acid-sharp takedown of the clichés, stereotypes, and mannerisms that women novelists had fallen into – and their avid readership driven them towards – in preceding generations. As a cleansing of the Augean stables, it was effective, but its spry delight in making fun concealed a certain brutality, throwing a demeaning shadow across a host of writers who may have deserved better.

Something similar happened with the female playwrights of the first half of the twentieth century, a problem exposed by Maggie Gale in her brilliant book of cultural revisionism, *West End Women*. With a statistician's enthusiasm and care, she lists all the plays by women playwrights in London's commercial theatre written between the wars, an extensive and extraordinary catalogue. By her calculation, 21 per cent of all such plays were written by women. Though clearly no form of parity, it is almost equidistant from the myth that women's voices were absent. Jarringly, it is a considerably better ratio than similar figures for any decade since. We have gone backwards, our idea that history is always arcing towards social justice often proving wish fulfilment. The Royal Court and the Angry Young Men movement of 1956 was in many ways a radical one, it was also overwhelmingly (and grumpily) male and straight, in many ways a pushback against the gay and female culture that had preceded. The backlash is peculiar; stranger still is how this story of female success has been airbrushed from theatre history.

It is not only the angry playwrights and their male acolytes in the press and academia who are responsible. There has also been, as Gale delineates, a movement from feminist commentators and academics to downgrade the achievements of this moment. Much as Eliot ridiculed and belittled her predecessors, so there has been a sense that though these plays existed, they were the *wrong* sort of plays. They did too little to dismantle the patriarchal structure of the well-made play, too little to challenge governing cultural archetypes, and in fact many of these authors may have been, dare it be said, conservative. Thus their presence has been almost cancelled. It may be easier to claim that women never had a stake, than to allow that many did, but were not the *right* sort.

Of all the tales of subsequent neglect, Clemence Dane is one of the most unfortunate. Her nom de plume certainly didn't set her up for a life within the avant-garde. Born Winifred Ashton, a name that doesn't smack of the underground either, she chose her androgynous pseudonym in honour of St Clement Danes Church on the Strand. After a peripatetic schooling, placed hither and thither by a father who had little interest in her after her mother died, she kept on the move as a teacher in Geneva, Dresden, and Sligo, before deciding in 1910 that she was to be an actress. For this she chose another name, Diana Cortis – again not exactly streetwise. Acting was a brief detour, before she settled into her existence as the prodigy Clemence Dane – artist, sculptor, editor, journalist, campaigner, celebrity, friend to the stars, pioneering feminist, novelist, and above all, playwright. At her death, Dane had written thirty plays and sixteen novels and was the first British woman to win a Best Screenplay Academy Award, for *Perfect Strangers* in 1947.

My initial encounter with Winifred/Diana/Clemence was as a sculptor. Her bust of Shakespeare sits at the bottom of the art deco staircase in the Royal Shakespeare Theatre building in Stratford. One of her early playwright successes was a not-entirely-convincing biography of the Bard in verse after his style, and no doubt the commission followed. An elderly, retired Will broods in bronze, haunted by melancholy, hollow cheeks struggling to secure the heavy chin, with eyes sunken into the skull through the weight of their witnessing. Bold and masterly, it is a radical move away from the trim bank manager who ruled the roost for centuries. Another great bust is of her lifelong friend Noël Coward, which sits in the National Portrait Gallery. No other capturing of Coward reveals as much of the swirl of tensions, bordering on hysteria, which coursed through and sometimes broke him.

Coward adored her, and she formed a key part of his extended family. Dane lived for thirty years above a greengrocer's in Covent Garden, together with two successive partners, Elsie Arnold and Olwen Bowen-Davies, whom she referred to as her secretaries. She was convinced her flat had a resident ghost, demanding that visitors ascend the steep steps ahead of her, so they would encounter any spirits first. Coward took this spectral aspect of his 'lesbian muse' and exaggerated it into the immortal character Madame Arcati in *Blithe Spirit*, written both about her and for her to play. A genuine eccentric, Dane provided that special laughter from someone who has no idea they are funny. She once boomed a lunch invitation down the phone to Coward with the exhortation, 'Do come! I've got such a lovely cock.' 'I do wish you'd call it a hen,' he answered. She never worked out that the name John Thomas might have a hidden meaning, and was once heard expounding a peculiar psychological theory, 'Yes, every man has three John Thomases – the John Thomas he keeps to himself, the John Thomas he shares with his friends, and the John Thomas he shows to the world.'

For all her eccentricity, between the wars she was arguably Britain's most complete and versatile female creative force. Virginia Woolf wrote enviously in her diary of the press acclaim for Dane's 1919 novel *Legend*; she co-wrote detective stories with Agatha Christie and Dorothy L. Sayers; co-wrote the screenplay of *Anna Karenina* for Greta Garbo, another friend; and worked with Alfred Hitchcock on his 1930 film *Murder!* Renowned as one of the most notorious feminists of her generation, she wrote extensively for *Time and Tide*, the political journal founded by Lady Rhondda in 1920. Dane backed an early campaign against child abuse, and wrote in defence of the Six Point Group, an early activist organisation pushing for changes in the law towards equal rights. Even within this whirligig of achievement, it is for her plays she remains best known.

One of the many pleasures with encountering Dane is her honesty about her women characters. Neither the compulsory strong woman of recent dramaturgy, nor the fountain of virtue of nineteenth-century sentimentality, they do not represent anything but themselves, honestly realised. Here is a taster from an opening stage direction: '*HESTER FAIRFIELD is one of those twitching, high-minded, elderly ladies in black, who keep a grievance as they might keep a pet dog – as soon as it dies they replace it by another. The grievance of the moment seems to be the empty third chair, and MARGARET FAIRFIELD is, as usual, on the defensive. Such a little, pretty, helpless-looking woman as Margaret has generally half-a-dozen big sons and a husband to bully; but Margaret has only a daughter, and her way of looking at even the chair on which that daughter ought to be sitting, is the way of a child whose doll has suddenly come to life.*' When you read something like that, you know you are in the hands of someone who knows their creations and is excited by their potential, rather than trying to prove something.

In her delicately even-handed Oscar-winning script for *Perfect Strangers*, she tells an understanding story of how a married couple become ruptured by the lived experience of war. He was a dullard from the city for whom action on the frontline has scattered his previous self; she was a mousey housewife, who has developed a strong sense of her independent nature through service with the Women's Royal Naval Service. Their previous identities have been disrupted, and what they have reassembled is uncomfortably divergent from the previous self their partner knew and loved. Both presume they will divorce, but through the action of the drama, they learn a new respect for each other and develop a determination to rebuild their relationship. This theme, of selves broken asunder by war, was a theme of Dane's early stage success, though tragically from the previous war. Like many of her contemporaries, she had to witness the same catastrophe twice and, in doing so, try to find a language to discuss its recurrence that was not unmitigated despair.

Her first monster hit, *A Bill of Divorcement*, opened in 1921 at St Martin's Theatre, running for 402 performances. It was adapted three times into film within eighteen years. It is set ten years later, resetting the husband coming back from the war who everyone thought was dead scenario to a more troubling one. In this case, the husband has suffered disabling shell shock, which has tipped him far from sanity. His wife, pushing hard against the approval of her aunt, the local rector, and the culture of the day, has resolved to find love elsewhere and a divorce on the grounds of her husband's insanity. When his sanity reappears shortly before her second wedding day, it could be a set-up for farcical shenanigans, as in Maugham's *Home and Beauty*. But Dane eschews high spirits for a temper dissonant and troubling.

An immanent, barely restrained violence pervades the country cottage where the play is set: men grab women by the wrist; they steal kisses forcibly; push people down onto the sofa; block doorways with a jittery excess of excitement. There is something poisonous and spasmodic in this safe Home Counties setting, toxins bubbling away under the genteel surface. The war, and its jangling echoes, has travelled home, and the innate violence cannot be washed away from minds off-kilter. No character seems easy in their own skin, their language is broken and barging, flinging out bomblets in pre-emptive attack. The portrait of insanity in the returning husband, whose newfound clarity seems fragilely held, is horribly real. The conclusion is a plot twist which satisfies those hungry for narrative surprise but only maximises the queasiness. A high-wire act of maintaining tension, Dane keeps nerves jangled throughout. The central question, what are we to do with men saturated in violence now the war is over, must have jolted nerves in spectators still balancing mentally on a tightrope.

A later play, *Mariners*, features another young man whose cadence has been disrupted by conflict. In a smooth world reasserting its Edwardian rhythms, his body language and his verbal telegraphese signal very quickly that he is a disruptor, and not welcome when most are trying to shut out such realities. However, he is not the centre of the play, which revolves around a rector and his disastrous marriage to a woman from a different class. What could have been coarse and blunt becomes live and thrilling since the characters are so particular and well observed. It ends in high melodrama with violence, but the path has been laid by the same ugly atmosphere, the same culture reverberating to the echoing hurt of war.

Don't go down the stairs . . . Pauline Lord in *Mariners*, *Vogue*, 1927

Something is distinctly amiss here in the mythical Loamshire, which Kenneth Tynan would later satirise. No amount of small-town moralising centred around the church and the Sunday service can shut out the dark truths muttered by the rat in the skull. Just as no amount of chintz can cover the unsettling and articulate voice of Clemence Dane.

Sean O'Casey
1880–1964

Some people just love to prod and poke. They see a sleeping bear and find a stick to wake it. A cussedness and contrariness resides in them which cannot abide settled authority. If they read something complacent in its certainties, they feel the urge to argue; hear a clique parroting a party line and they want to close their ears; see a crowd walking one way and they want to walk against it. We should thank God, or behavioural evolution, for one of our most salutary human quirks, one of the few things that will render us irreproducible by AI. A quality vital in artists, and crucial in playwrights, no one exemplified it more at critical historical moments than Sean O'Casey.

Arriving fully on the theatre scene at a mature age, O'Casey was forty-one when his first play, *The Shadow of a Gunman*, was produced by the Abbey in 1923. Age had not lent him caution. The arena he entered was boiling hot. Ireland had just concluded the Civil War, which followed hard on its War of Independence and its emergence as a Free State. Having shucked off the yoke of colonial rule in a bitter and bloody struggle after centuries of oppression, the new state swiftly divided between those who consented to the peace treaty and those who felt betrayed. Families who had fought the British together a year before now turned on each other. By 1923 there was peace, but an uneasy one to say the least. A writer could have entered this arena with a degree of detachment, or to offer a diversion – a light entertainment, perhaps. Not O'Casey. He found the hottest topics and threw paraffin on them; he sought out well-buried secrets and dug them up; if there was a sacred cow to hand, he threw abuse. Splendid.

From a distance, it is easy to lose the sense of that heat. The Irish theatre had always been rambunctious, with a marked capacity for rioting and mayhem. In O'Casey's plays he was writing of history that was only a year or two old, of wounds that hadn't healed. When *The Shadow of a Gunman* played in the Abbey they had to put an armed guard on the door. When *The Plough and the Stars* opened, fists flew and the stage was stormed. As Captain Boyle says in *Juno and the Paycock*, 'Th' whole worl's in a terrible state o' chassis!' The trilogy arrived with the force of news and yet remained far from journalism. Writing in some sort of dream state – he bashed out four great plays in five years – he brought information about conflict, vainglory, and cowardice from the lower depths with a hard cynical clarity few have matched. One of the first dramatic chroniclers of the underclass, O'Casey wrote about life on the edge of the modern in Dublin. With a rich extravagance of cadence, he heard a new sort of person singing in the crucible of the tenements, alive and vivid in their scrabble for dignity. In a country under the thumb of its Church and its patriotic fervour, it was not a voice the newly forming Establishment always wanted to acknowledge.

O'Casey's father died when he was six (another playwright bereft at an early age), leaving a family of thirteen. Ulcerated eyes interfered with any normal education for Sean, and he had to teach himself to read and write, which he managed by the age of thirteen. He made up for lost time with voracious consumption. He was an avid consumer of Shakespeare, performing plays with his brother and learning four entire works, including *A Midsummer Night's Dream*, by heart. Thinking for himself early, and coming to his own conclusions, he wasn't conditioned by any school system or given pattern of thinking. From an early age he worked a variety of jobs, spending nine years on the railways, and working in retail and newspaper distribution.

Politics caught his heart early. For him, more compelling than the national cause were socialism and the unions. Frequently the two intersected, but he never doubted his own priorities, ever loyal to the red flag above the green. He was involved directly with the 1913 Lockout and strikes, an action against the English overseers, and starved alongside his fellow workers. In 1914, he became the General Secretary of the Irish Citizen Army, for which he had written a history. He fell out with them over their involvement with the more militant Irish Volunteers, arguing that his union, the ITGWU, was 'no longer the headquarters of the Irish labour movement but the centre of Irish national disaffection'. From that perspective, he watched the Citizen Army's participation in the Easter Rising against British Rule in 1916 with disquiet, and the conflagration filled him with pity for those he saw as its ultimate victims: Dublin's poor.

After the Easter Rising, he criticised those fighting for a new Ireland – rebels, patriots, and the Church – for forsaking the destitute, writing, 'In Dublin alone 20,000 families are wriggling together like worms in a putrid mass. In horror-filled one-room tenements, not in the shouts of the deluded volunteers, but in the hunger cry of the nation's poor, is heard the voice of Ireland.' He believed that nationalism had hijacked the radical forces in Dublin, and the needs of the working class were taking a back seat to independence. By those needs, he did not mean merely material necessities; from close acquaintance, he knew they needed imaginative and spiritual sustenance as well. And above all, dignity.

Soon after, he began to write plays, and his first was sent to the Abbey. They turned down *The Crimson and the Tricolour*, but feeling, as Lady Gregory noted in her journal, that the writer had 'something in him', they volunteered to type up the play and to meet. O'Casey was delighted, being a fervent fan of the institution. He told Gregory, 'All the thought in Ireland for years past has come through the Abbey. You have no idea what an education it has been to the country.' She encouraged him to play to a strength she had seen in his writing: character. A just prompt. Yeats, though he never felt easy with O'Casey, principally from old-fashioned caste snobbery, knew when his next play arrived that they had another Synge on their hands. Whatever he may have felt about this playwright's background, Yeats's instincts as a theatre manager kicked in. He saw quality, smelled scandal, and knew that ticket sales would follow.

As with O'Casey's other two masterpieces, *The Shadow of a Gunman* springs from his imaginative homeland, the Dublin tenements. He was not the first playwright to go into these slums, but no one had yet brought them to such full life. Following Lady Gregory's prompt, the essence to this is a delight in the quiddities of character. The single squalid room is shared by two lodgers – a salesman, Seumas Shields, and a wannabe poet, Donal Davoren – and soon a host of other residents are charging in and out. Few walk in shyly. Everyone, in that lovely Dublin phrase, gives themselves a big welcome. They go off like fireworks. This is circus naturalism, complex and honest, energetically performative and faithful to Synge's call for truth and joy. The play begins in the middle of the War of Independence, and though all are terrified by the violence outside, and constrained by poverty and circumstance, they never let it get in the way of expressing themselves. In the course of the play, Donal is mistaken for an IRA gunman and accepts the new identity, there is a terrifying raid by the Black and Tans – Churchill's lawless militia of thugs – and it ends with a tragic death. The mechanics of the plot are solid but they melt in the face of the people and their vivacity.

This was O'Casey's ultimate rebuff to the political rhetoric he despaired of: the voice he gave to these people rescued them from history's determination to eclipse them. Against a backdrop of death and sacrifice, we watch a daily struggle for life and see how much more important and *noble* it is than the posturing of politicians and soldiers. Born from a specific dialect and slang, the language has an overspilling humour and irreverence, too ebullient to accommodate the banalities of patriotism. For the audience, much of this would have been hard to take, hearing a rhetoric which had recently been a call to arms now harpooned, but to O'Casey little but humanity was sacred. The main voice of cynicism is the inveterate coward Seumas Shields: 'I believe in the freedom of Ireland, and that England has no right to be here, but I draw the line when I hear the gunmen blowing about dying for the people, when it's the people that are dying for the gunmen.' To the immense credit of the Abbey, and its audience, they had the courage to commit. The public (or a vast number of them) responded with enthusiasm, taking the characters to their hearts, liberated to hear fears and doubts writ large. The play had a short run, and by its third night was rammed to the rafters. A headline flatly summed up the achievement: 'Dublin Workingman Attains Success as Playwright; Lives in a Slum Tenement'.

Directing the play at the Tricycle in 2003, shortly after the long occupation of Iraq had begun, it was clear that further shadings complemented the play. Programmed at a time when small gestures were all we could manage in the face of war, at the point in the play when the Black and Tans stormed the tenement, rampaging up and down its stairways as people cowered in fear, it wasn't hard to read parallels. In one moment of excitement, a producer encouraged me to feed in the calls to prayer from a muezzin to underscore the connection. We felt that might leave people a little confused. But it was chilling to see that the play now had a wider application, a timelessness which came from its exposure of the corrosive mythmaking in war. Whether oppressors or cornered victims, everyone is shrouded in a fog of deceit. Yet the play kicks back against false pity by noting how its motley of dreamers, hotheads, fools and bigots go on being, rather gloriously, themselves. A triumph for the author, but also his producer. O'Casey said to Lady Gregory later, 'You gave me encouragement. It was you who said to me upstairs in the office – "Mr Casey, your gift is characterisation." And so I threw over my theories and worked at characters and that is the result.'

The same achievement undergirds the other two classics. *Juno and the Paycock* shifts its historical background to a couple of years later and the Irish Civil War, just as controversial. The internecine war which broke out in response to the treaty that let go of the North, and still required allegiance to the British Crown, pitted brother against brother, and created a division never entirely healed. With his play premiering only a year after the war had concluded, there was O'Casey prodding and probing, pushing at the rotten tooth and its exposed nerve ends. Even sending it to his producer would have stirred the pot, since Roxborough House in Galway, where Lady Gregory was born, had been burned down in the Civil War. In his tragicomic tale of delusional drunks, led by the trinity of dysfunctionality – Captain Boyle, Joxer Daly, and Juno herself – we see death and heartbreak jammed up violently against wild comedy. Pathos and laughter do not share the stage in O'Casey's world; they collide. Again we have the lampooning of ideals. When Juno's son brings up his principles, she replies sharply, 'You lost your best principle when you lost your right arm.' Nothing is sacred but the human, though she looks to an old source with her most desperate prayer as she cradles her bullet-ridden son: 'O sacred Heart o' Jesus, take away our hearts o' stone, and give us hearts o' flesh! Take away this murderin' hate, an' give us – give us Thine own – Thine own eternal love!'

Juno and the Paycock was a huge hit for the Abbey, and for O'Casey, who earned £25, enough for him to stop the manual labour and take up writing full-time. It also saved the Abbey, which had been in dire straits. Lady Gregory remembered, 'A long queue at the door, the theatre crowded, many turned away . . . One of the evenings at the Abbey that makes one glad to be born.' In this happy moment a friendship across several divides was cemented between O'Casey and Gregory. She stood with him at the front door to watch the happy surge of punters arriving, their eyes glinting with expectation, one of the rarest thrills known to man. As O'Casey put it, 'Our friendship – affinity – was an odd one: she from affluence, I from poverty; she an aristocrat, I a proletarian communist. Yet we understood each other well, talking, eating, and laughing easily together.' He remembered her in later days with fondness: 'She looked like an old, elegant nun of a new order, a blend of the Lord Jesus Christ and of Puck, an order that Ireland had never known before and wasn't likely to know again for a long time to come.'

All should have been plain sailing when he submitted his next play soon after, *The Plough and the Stars*, but O'Casey was O'Casey and could not help prodding the bear. The subject was further away in years, but only slightly – the Easter Rising of 1916, still bright in its burnished legend. This had become the lodestone of Irish heroism, already mythified in verse, onstage and in report. To write a play that criticised the rhetoric of rebels was especially blasphemous for the Abbey, since many of its company had been intimately involved in the rebellion and several lost their lives. But O'Casey was constant only to his own star. In the eyes of many, including the Abbey board, who asked for many changes, 1916 was too sacred and too fresh to be dramatised. O'Casey refused the changes, and the theatre stuck to (almost) his every word. When withdrawal of subsidy was threatened, Lady Gregory made a clear statement: 'If we have to choose between the subsidy and our freedom, it is our freedom we choose.'

When *The Plough and the Stars* opened in February 1926, there was an enormous excitement, and the theatre was again packed to the rafters. From the first night it was clear that new ground was being broken, even though some of the actors' doubts translated into them muttering or jumping over lines. The action moves around the tenements rather than being stuck in a single room, and the controversial crux came when it migrates to a bar, in which a prostitute, Rosie Redmond, is happy to talk and sing of her trade. This was crossing all sorts of boundaries. O'Casey had pushed hard against nationalism and the Church already, but now he was transgressing on territory of sexual propriety. That was too much. When the shenanigans in the pub are counterpointed by a speech overheard from outside about blood sacrifice, almost the same as the one given by Patrick Pearse, one of the executed leaders of the Easter Rising, it proved an incitement too explosive. The show held together for the first three nights, but by the fourth the forces of rage were ready. When the actress playing Rosie, Ria Mooney, came on for that scene, she later said, 'After the first couple of lines, I heard hissing in the theatre. And the next thing, a lump of coal hit me on the ankle. A young man on the balcony with dark hair and a pale face shouted at me to get off the stage as I was "a disgrace to my sex, my religion and my country".' Which is quite the trifecta.

More coal was thrown, the hissing amplified, and speeches by the wives of fallen heroes sounded from the gallery. Yeats was rung at home, and he rushed over from Merrion Square. The shouting made it harder and harder to perform, as did the flying coal. Several members of the audience tried to storm the stage, one of them sent backwards by a sock to the jaw from an actor. Another swung back and forth on a curtain. Yeats arrived and, after passing a text of his speech of spontaneous outrage to an assistant who took it to the press for the early editions, prepared himself backstage. Then he went out roaring. O'Casey takes up the story: 'Yeats came bounding out on to the stage to oppose the howling mob. And he's shouting out at them "You have disgraced yourselves again." And then when the roaring became worse and they shouted out against O'Casey he roared out at them with all the venom and vehemence that was in the great man, he shouted out at them, "This is O'Casey's apotheosis." I was wondering all the way home what in the name of God was the meaning of apotheosis and what had happened to O'Casey that he'd had such an honour conferred on him? It was only when I got home and, quietly and secretly you know, looked up the dictionary. I discovered that O'Casey was translated up into the gods!'

O'Casey was generous to Yeats for his roaring, because most there remembered him as inaudible below the volleys of shouts. But his speech has gone down in history owing to its report in the papers: 'You have disgraced yourselves again . . . Is this going to be a recurring celebration of Irish genius? Synge first and then O'Casey? The news of the happening of the last few minutes here will flash from country to country. Dublin has once more rocked the cradle of a reputation. From such a scene in this theatre went forth the fame of Synge. Equally the fame of O'Casey is born here tonight. This is his apotheosis.' You can't help feeling he loved all this. The Abbey had another riotous event on their hands. As with *The Playboy of the Western World*, it heralded a masterpiece. Sometimes it seems that greatness in artistic terms creates its own strange magnetism, pulling people and excitement and time towards itself, like a cultural singularity. The Abbey was blessed to have several such events in a short space of time, and deserved its luck.

O'Casey's fame grew abroad, where his plays were filling houses, and it drew him from home. He would have faced different forms of condescension everywhere, but not the particular sort he suffered at the hands of Yeats and Gregory. The tensions between himself and the senior echelons at the Abbey, both management and board, erupted over his next play, *The Silver Tassie*, which they rejected, and with a lack of grace. Lady Gregory, who was in the habit of sailing through life without qualm, regretted this deeply for the rest of her life. O'Casey wrote in an English newspaper, 'The Irish have no time for those who don't agree with their ideas, and I have no time for those who don't agree with mine.' The gaunt, fiery Sean never abandoned his faith in the dignity of man, nor his pleasure in opposition.

O'Casey was an inspiration. Not least among his admirers was the African American playwright Lorraine Hansberry, who credited him as her greatest influence. She wrote of 'the totality of personality' he achieved. An ability to engage with the whole of a person, with their flaws and sins and moments of pride and size of dreaming and pettiness, all wrapped up in one unholy but endearing mess. She was on the money. What marked him out was an ability to make characters larger than his own ideology, and to give them a new voice. He understood the history of his time and its allegiances, but they never occluded the pungency of his people.

O'Casey's three great plays were achievements of imaginative compassion. He found in the morass of compacted slum life, recreated with Shakespearean exuberance, a way to mirror the wild, careering hairpin bends Ireland was taking at the time. Our greatest theatre from Aeschylus through Shakespeare and Chekhov and O'Casey on down has been about appreciating a fuller idea of the human, about creating new potentials. We admire O'Casey always for his opposition and contrariness, but even more for his ability to swim in a new direction.

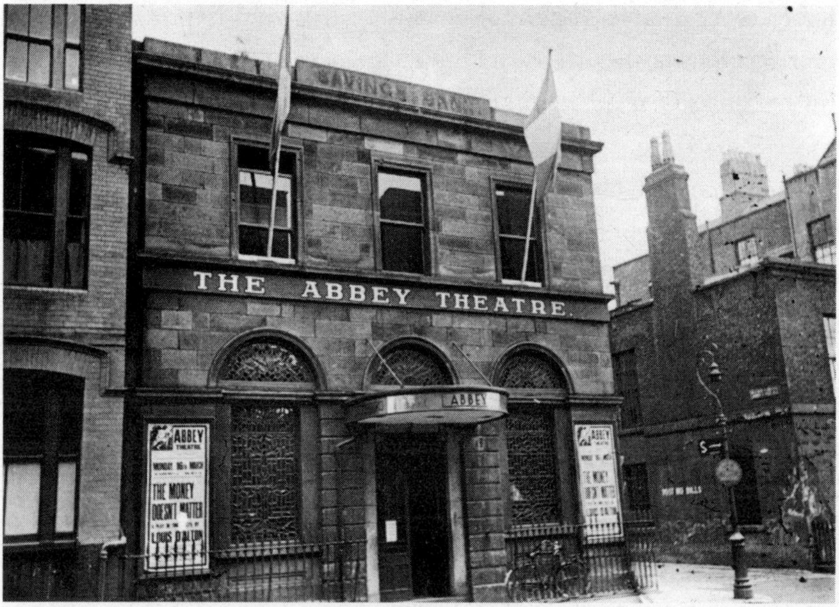

The room where it happened.
The Abbey Theatre in Dublin, *c.*1930

Mikhail Bulgakov
1891–1940

How do you put a chaotic and violent civil war raging across thousands of miles between multiple factions on a proscenium stage? Or the mass movement of refugees within a state of international anarchy? Or the revolutionary uprising of a whole continent? Or how to incorporate the enforcement of new economic policies onto a vast nation within a sex comedy? At about the same moment that Bertolt Brecht in Berlin was despairing of the proscenium theatre, and deciding it was too chocolate box, too mired in its own luxuriance to handle the demands of epic storytelling and of recording the movement of history at speed, another writer further east was achieving just that. Mikhail Bulgakov in Moscow found a way to pack more action onto the stage in a four-act play than James Cameron can squeeze into a blockbuster movie.

After training as a doctor, Bulgakov had served as a medical orderly in frontline field hospitals during the ructions that convulsed Ukraine at the end of the First World War. As with Brecht, who lived through the same hell on the Western Front, one senses that the full horror of war impacts as hard on those whose task is to heal as those who fight. For the Russian, the confusion of war was amplified by the speed and the savagery with which the battle for Ukraine metastasised from a monumental conflict between two nations – Germany and Russia – into a roil of madness between many factions – the Germans, the Hetmanate government they installed, the Ukrainian nationalists, the old Russian White Army, and the new Bolshevik force. Warlords, regions, and family members jumped from side to side with a shapeshifting celerity that mocked all logic. Bulgakov witnessed ten different coups, and each successive government commanded the young doctor to serve them. Within this parade of shifting power structures, reality itself began to dissolve, as did any idea of human consistency. Whirled around by the breakdown of order and logic, for Bulgakov the only solution was morphine, to which he soon became addicted. Happily, nothing impaired his fierce recall of what he had seen, and in later years he recreated on the page the living nightmare of history.

How did he do it? The achievement is often so miraculous it is hard to tell. One key quality is embracing the madness. Events go off like unforeseen explosions, as they must do in conflict. There is no signposting or artificial smoothness of construction. Wild and strange stuff just occurs. He knew the nature of people at war, their antic mirth, their attenuated nerves, their reallocation of emotion into unpredictable cul-de-sacs, their passionate temporary allegiances; even though the landscape is unfamiliar the behaviour feels awkwardly true. Key to this is a certain anarchic hilarity; as with Evelyn Waugh and later with *M*A*S*H*, Bulgakov knew how petty and comical behaviour in wartime can be. There are flashes of extraordinary heroism and courage, but most of the time there is venality and eccentricity. His characters have a combustible vitality – sometimes fuelled by vodka, sometimes evidence of a Slavic fondness for keeping the conversation lively – which matches the chaos of the world.

His key storytelling advantage is to place crucial scenes in communication centres, and always to keep telephones and telegram offices nearby. As with Shakespeare in his history plays, he knows about the wild horse of rumour in wartime, information flitting here and there at breakneck speed, and everyone clinging on to each new report as if it is the key to survival. The messenger in a Shakespeare play, though frequently mocked, is an important harbinger of news; in Bulgakov's plays it is conveyed at lightning speed across wires. Reports arrive at such different paces from such different distances it is impossible to map the true nature of any situation. Dramatically, it is also a great way for Bulgakov to share information, and to envelop the audience in the same crisis as his characters.

The other key is, of course, detail. These are not scenes where people make long and windy speeches, rather they are packed with dirt and small, grubby truths. In *Madame Zoyka's Apartment*, set in a Moscow struggling to contain the chaos following a new experiment with economic liberalism, the opening stage direction sets the scene for the small-scale feral capitalism which will ensue: 'Outside, the courtyard of the huge apartment house sounds like a musical-box gone mad. A gramophone is singing: *The Human Voice in All The World . . .*; a voice is shouting: *We buy second hand Primus stoves!*; another: *Broken samovars soldered!*; Tram-wheels grind, bells clang. Cars hoot. Cacophony. As the noise dies down slightly, an accordion plays a cheerful polka.' When, in the same play, we see a number of cloth cutters at work, their conversation is rich in details of tape measures and sewing machines and rolls of material. Whether in a bombed-out monastery or a Black Sea marketplace or a dilapidated apartment block, Bulgakov records his world with the vividness and accuracy of a film camera.

Within the topsy-turvy there is an acute fragility to all social hierarchies, often upended by the turbulence. Figures of great wealth and power dip to destitution and servitude at the flick of history's switch. Grand ladies of Russia become sex workers in Constantinople; military generals who have dispensed life and death judgements over cities become beggars on foreign shores; princes disguise themselves as injured soldiers to escape captivity. In *Madame Zoyka's Apartment*, Ametistov has lived under so many different aliases and in so many different social positions he has trouble remembering his true identity. Within these snake-and-ladder rearrangements, what quickly becomes transparent is the fragility of any form of civility. Living so close to the precipice, the characters find they are play-acting at governance and justice, and, since the structures that contain them are so flimsy, those who hold power briefly know no other way than through violence. These people understand the mechanics of oppression, they know torture, and the landscape they share is bleak. For Bulgakov and for his audience, having witnessed the Bolshevik Revolution, this madcap and violent performance of social order was both familiar and inflammatory.

Bulgakov's play *Flight* suspends any attempt at old-fashioned well-made-playness, and the eight narrative sections are called 'Dreams' rather than 'Acts', each sharing a horrible reality. Every scene finishes with the solemn declaration, 'The Dream Ends'. The Fifth Dream, set in Constantinople, where the motley crew of ex-colonels and madams and professors have washed up, is one of the most technicolour sections of stage poetry from the proscenium era. Eschewing conventional narrative, it presents a Bosch nightmare of naturalism around a Turkish market. It is a scene of social dementia which recalls Bulgakov's prose work *The Master and Margarita.* Charnota, a figure who we have previously seen on horseback as an avenging Cossack general striking fear into the hearts of men, transforms in a theatrical heartbeat into a trader flogging rubber dolls piled on a tray slung around his neck. He scrabbles around for cigarette butts, and waits for the big event of the day, a cockroach race. Both cockroaches and lice are leitmotifs in Bulgakov's work, and their presence one of the few reassuring constants in each new unpredictable environment. Sailors from many nations, and other drifters, gather to place their bets on the race, and their hysterical excitement descends into a brawl, pulling the whole theatre into its ugliness. As with King Lear on the barren heath, this is the moment where we witness the depths to which humanity can descend, a crazed convocation of 'bare, forked animals' slugging it out over competing cockroaches.

With a bitter irony, this imagery and the many other ways Bulgakov demonstrated the truth of his times was rarely seen by the Russian audiences who would have best understood it. His most successful play, known in the West as *The White Guard* and in Russia as *The Days of the Turbins*, opened on 5 October 1926 at the Moscow Art Theatre, directed by Konstantin Stanislavsky. Among the public it was a smash hit, running for an unprecedented 108 performances in its first season. Bulgakov's secretary recalled the response of those in the audience who had survived the horrors of the Civil War, 'All these things were still very much alive in the people's memories. There were fits of hysteria, people fainted, seven people were driven away by ambulance.' However, a large section of the ideologically pure (and theatrically jealous) took against its sympathetic portrait of White Army officers. They went after it in the press relentlessly, labelling Bulgakov 'neo-bourgeois scum'.

Soviet Theatre at its best, orchestrated by the master.
The Days of the Turbins, directed by Konstantin Stanislavsky, Moscow Art Theatre production, 1926

By 1929, the criticism had become so severe the Moscow Art Theatre folded under pressure and closed the show. In a funny twist of fate, the show was saved by its greatest fan, the last man anyone expected to defend a play which cast a generous gaze over the idiosyncrasies of the old aristocracy: Josef Stalin. Reportedly, he saw the play fifteen times, occasionally smuggling himself into the theatre in disguise. On his command the play carried on for another ten years. Thus began a strange and awkward relationship between dictator and playwright, which concluded with Bulgakov writing a distinctly poor play portraying the Georgian's early life, a year before his premature death in 1940.

The protection of the ultimate leader was not enough to help his other plays into the light, with many remaining unperformed, or languishing in the early Soviet form of development hell. Another play for the Moscow Art Theatre, *Molière*, a tale of how the French playwright coped with the Sun King (spot the parallel), was rehearsed for four long years, losing two directors, before it found its way to the stage. Adored by the public, it played seven sold-out performances before the grey apparatchiks of *Pravda* killed it with an article titled, 'Glamorous on the Surface, False Beneath'. The play was withdrawn immediately. *Flight*, one of the great masterpieces of the twentieth century, never made it out of the rehearsal room; the satire *Ivan Vasilievich* never made it into one.

Posterity was kinder, and these plays have made their way into the stage lights. Bulgakov had that stubborn faith in his work which marks out the artist. He wrote to his wife of one play, '"What's its future?" you ask? I don't know. Possibly, you will store the manuscript in one of the drawers, next to my "killed" plays, and occasionally it will be in your thoughts. Then again, you don't know the future. My own judgement of the book is already made.' Fortunately for us, the plays emerged from their drawers and brought us their uniquely vivid information about the darkest of times.

Sophie Treadwell
1885–1970

Machinal is a starburst of a play, breaking everything and making something brand new in the same instant. Living within the frame, but obeying few of its rules, it delivered all the deconstruction of patriarchal form which later writers retrospectively yearned to have seen from more playwrights of the era. Sophie Treadwell managed it, colliding expressionism and feminism within a personal vision of a dehumanising, mechanistic cityscape. Unique in the theatrical landscape of its age, it is also an outlier within Treadwell's work, stretching the boundaries of theatrical possibility further than her other works. It brought startling information about the impossibility of freedom or grace in a mechanised world, and created a heroine who exemplified that struggle not by any vainglorious victory but by a series of battling defeats.

Initial marketing sold *Machinal* as a riff on a famous murder case of the age, the Snyder–Gray killing. This squalid crime involved a pair of lovers trying to do away with the woman's husband, aiming to cash in on recently acquired insurance policies. They seem to have been very bad at murder, having made *seven* attempts, each of which the husband survived. He must have been rather slow on the uptake. Finally, and to make doubly sure, they stuffed his nose full of chloroform-soaked rags and strangled him with a picture wire. Then, to make triply sure, they beat him with a sash weight. Their bad alibis and confused stories fell apart with predictable speed, and before long both were executed by electric chair. The notoriety of the case helped Treadwell's play reach Broadway, where it opened in September 1928. The proximity to tabloid sensationalism did it a disservice, the inspiration being tangential at most. *Machinal* is a parable about modernity, and the resonance extends beyond one tawdry story.

A harsh and unremitting soundscape underscores the action. Where Chekhov is awash in the gentle chirruping of crickets and evening breezes moving through silver birches, *Machinal* assaults us with the nerve-shredding racket of city life. It resounds to the clang of the urban choir – machines whirring and clacking, automobiles screeching, snatches of sharp speech from passing strangers, dishes clattering in kitchen sinks. We are oppressed by what is called 'this purgatory of noise' as we watch the Everywoman at the centre in her descent towards doom. Even a maternity ward, a place which should offer sanctuary, is invaded by the slow, thumping beat of a riveting machine outside. Small wonder the heroine fixates on a still moment when she first listened to a seashell and heard its blend of silence and muffled roar.

The dialogue jazzes to the noise of this soundtrack. With few exceptions the lines are short and sharp, boxing with the abrasive energy of city speech, repetitious and brassy. 'Hot dog!' one character yelps out repetitively to punctuate the first extended passage of office badinage. The speed of the dialogue is rapacious and achieves a jazz poetry thirty years before the Beats, and an urban brutalism fifty years before David Mamet.

This whirling blend of jangly staccato and syncopated telegraphese is interrupted for disgorgings from the Young Woman at the centre, Helen. Her monologues are patchworks of words, phrases, and fragments (Samuel Beckett is given a run for his money twenty years in advance). They manage the balancing trick of being readily accessible and jarringly atomised. If a stream of consciousness can sometimes serve as a device for literary genii to talk without fear of interruption or comprehension, that is not the case here. We hear directly from a mind struggling to find truth and independence under the weight of a language constructed by a concrete and metal world.

Helen confronts a phalanx of male characters with the power to determine her life. Her only choice is to capitulate, though she resists. Her nausea at the matrix she is trapped within has a visionary intensity, and her shout-out against institutionalised misogyny – 'I will not submit' – still tolls a heavy bell. Many of the men we witness are also victims, unable to speak or think in any rhythm or grammar not pre-manufactured. They have collapsed into their given groove, and reserve a special loathing for those who do not surrender in the same way. Neither the materialistic husband nor the cavalier lover is the ultimate villain: the villain is the social edifice that leaves no room for sensibility.

Other physical elements combine to create Treadwell's bitter theatre poem. This is no well-made play, its nine scenes utilising minimal design and bold lighting to roam through the metropolis, gliding from office to apartment to honeymoon hotel to bar to courtroom to, finally, execution chamber. Neither melodrama nor docudrama, *Machinal* borrows expressionist techniques – a movement birthed by Strindberg's wilder experiments, and then nurtured in Germany by Oskar Kokoschka, Ernst Toller, and early Brecht, before migrating to the US with O'Neill's *The Hairy Ape* and Elmer Rice's *The Adding Machine*. The ambition for Treadwell was to summon the essence of modern life, closer to the nightmarish vision of Charlie Chaplin's *Modern Times* than the static interiors of domestic drama. The flatness of the characterisation, the repetitions, the hurtle of short scenes, the grating sounds all combine to present the journey of a woman who asks of a featureless world, 'How can I be free?'

The expressionism can lead productions down cul-de-sacs, where creative teams who want to make a mark lose sight of the inherent humanity in the writing. One scene in particular, with Helen on the first night of her honeymoon, is a terrifying record of the horrors attendant. The blundering husband is full of clichéd desires and taught expectations, while the bride does anything she can to delay the moment of encounter. She retreats to the bathroom to change and begs for a moment of pause or any softness or consideration to blunt the edge of collision, but none is forthcoming. Few other scenes have brought to such acute life the grisly ritual so many young couples had to endure.

The scene of seduction by her lover – played in the first Broadway production by a young Clark Gable – is hard and charmless. Yet the single scene after they have first made love is the briefest instance of solace in a loveless panorama. Helen remembers the seashell she listened to, and the vistas it opened up. Her lover hymns the authenticity he knows 'below the Rio Grande', a phrase repeated like a mantra. 'You're free down there,' he tells us, a place of uncertainties and 'quien sabe' (who knows). Treadwell was of part-Mexican heritage, and the contrast between economically developed, industrialised countries and the freedom of other worlds is underlined. For a brief moment while dressing, a stage direction informs us that she is 'innocent, relaxed, sure and full of natural grace'. She speaks of feeling 'purified'. The brief holiday of tenderness highlights the brutality elsewhere and – discreetly – touches the heart.

The conclusion is, as it should be, tragic. Helen, a sensibility-charged cog in a machine that cannot afford such irregularities, is bullied by her mother into a loveless marriage with her boss, with whom she has a baby. Momentarily liberated by her affair, she is driven to murdering her husband and ends up condemned to death. Plagued by machines throughout her life, she is at the last killed by one, the barbaric electric chair. The newspaper reporters take her tragedy and swallow it into the mechanical noises of typing and printing, regurgitating her at electric speed into another mini-legend of an ever-shifting construction.

Sophie Treadwell had been a journalist in her youth, interviewing Pancho Villa (an encounter which funded two of her plays), and travelling to Europe to cover the First World War. A modern in all areas of her life, she enjoyed a marriage which experimented with forms of openness, and fully embraced the feminism of her age, joining the suffragist movement in 1915. She walked the 150-mile march with the Lucy Stone League, which handed in a petition on women's suffrage to the legislature in New York. She also suffered some of the fragilities of the modern age, with various nervous conditions leading to extended stays in psychiatric hospitals. *Machinal* was the one big success of her life, being frequently anthologised and revived, though she wrote a number of other plays for Broadway. Their relative failure left a bitter taste.

What is remarkable is that so few at the time took the energy and invention of *Machinal* and ran with it to create a new language of theatre. It took almost half a century for the formal freedom of Treadwell's masterpiece to become a new model for how plays should be fashioned. The

Establishment of the time celebrated the play – though its initial run was brief – then folded it up, put it in the back of the chest of drawers, and returned to wearing the same old clothes.

Change can be very fast and then very slow.

Keeping it spare.
Cell of the condemned woman in the original Broadway production of *Machinal*, setting by Robert Edmond Jones, 1928

R. C. Sherriff
1896–1975

The life of Robert Cedric Sherriff proved a rather perverse fairy tale, sliding between suburban normality, the apocalyptic hell of trench warfare, and Hollywood. A man of almost Buddhist equanimity, little seemed to knock him off his plate. His pre-war vocation was as a £7-a-week insurance claims inspector, riding his bicycle around Surrey settling small claims. In 1916, he joined the East Surrey Regiment as a second lieutenant, serving a year in the godforsaken inferno of the trenches, before being wounded at Passchendaele and retiring from the fray. Once home, he calmly remounted his bike and resumed pedalling around the Home Counties, offering minor acts of mercy courtesy of Sun Insurance. Like many of his generation, he shrouded his trauma in the deepest silence, folding himself back into the embrace of hushed anonymity.

A few years after the war this placid life hit a minor snag. A committed member of the Kingston Rowing Club, his companions realised they needed a new boat but lacked the readies. Never having entertained the fancy before, Sherriff sat down and wrote a play for the Kingston Adventurers Dramatic Society. The proceeds went towards the boat. Several efforts later, none of them of great distinction, he intuited that their small stage was well shaped to recreate the dugout he'd lived in during the war. Settling down in his railway carriage bungalow in Selsey, he plunged into some sort of dissociative state. In a fever dream he summoned the ghosts of his past and wrote their hellish lives into a dramatic setting. The voices of the men he served with whispered over his shoulder as he wrote. All that was buried was unearthed, spilling up from below in the minutest detail. His boundless love for the comrades of his beleaguered battalion – many lost to war's cruel machine – would be honoured by bringing them back to precise, unsentimental life.

A professional production of *Journey's End* in 1928 soon outstripped its early amateur ambitions. A single performance was given by the Incorporated Stage Society at the Apollo Theatre with unknown actors, including a twenty-one-year-old Laurence Olivier, and directed by the neophyte James Whale (later of *Frankenstein* fame). The performance felt like an earthquake, cracking open a conspiracy of silence about what so many had endured. In a theatre scene of brittle romances and delicate comedies, it was as if a ghost Zeppelin had loomed into view, dispensing a motherload of truth. An audience who had lost husbands, sons, lovers, and friends witnessed onstage what few had spoken of. A flame was lit across the world. Opening for a long run at the Savoy in early 1929, by November the work was being played simultaneously by fourteen companies in English, and in seventeen other languages across the globe.

Barely a play written between 1914 and 1930 is not about the Great War, whether explicitly or implicitly. The conflict broke reality in many ways, and the idea of the world that existed before was shattered. Writing anything without the dark cloud looming overhead was impossible. In Shaw's *Heartbreak House*, the sound of distant guns from over the Channel reverberates; Maugham's *For Services Rendered* recounts with bitterness how the toxic ripples of violence follow the soldiers home, as do several works by Clemence Dane and Dodie Smith. Yet for all such multiple referencing, very few depicted the war itself.

Noël Coward, having briefly performed as Stanhope, the main role in *Journey's End* – the audience, he wrote, 'politely watched me take a fine part in a fine play and throw it into the alley' – wrote his own account, whose undigested bitterness made him ashamed. *Post-Mortem* is a ball of rage, starting and ending in the trenches, watching a soldier die, and in between imagining a future England not fit for such heroes. His embarrassment at its emotional directness conceals many virtues. Bizarrely, the story of this play straddled two wars. Coward initially refused performance, but did have it published. Its first rendering was by British prisoners of war in Eichstätt in 1944, led by Desmond Llewelyn (later

James Bond's Q). An honourable explosion of raw anger, it suffers from an undeniable lack of first-hand experience.

As does O'Casey's *The Silver Tassie*, one of the few other works to put the war onstage. The Irishman's play is a bold conflation of social realism and expressionism, perhaps in acknowledgement that he was writing away from his own experience – too bold for Yeats and the Abbey, who declined it. The play starts among the Dublin working class awaiting a football hero, although the rhythms already tend towards the literary. Its second act mixes music hall songs and semi-liturgical verse together with stark theatrical imagery to summon the horror of war. We are back in Dublin in Acts III and IV to see how the returning soldiers are rejected and betrayed. An explosion of anger at the catastrophic impact of war, the play has power and poetry, and the avoidance of any attempt at authenticity is an honourable path. As the playwright said, 'A generous handful of stones, aimed indiscriminately, with the aim of breaking a few windows. I don't think it makes a good play, but it's a remarkable one.'

The expressionism was taken further in probably the most celebrated proscenium attempt at summoning the spirit of the Great War: Joan Littlewood's *Oh! What a Lovely War*. This theatrical collage blending hymns, music hall songs, Pierrot, and satire is irresistible. Though no one died – under stern instructions from Littlewood – the lonely voices singing with pathos of the freight of grief, and the refusal to burden others with it, carried enormous emotional weight. All the while a ticker tape of information tells the story of the human losses: 'Sept 25 . . . British loss 8,236 men in 3 hours . . . German loss nil'; and 'Average life of a machine gunner under attack on the Western Front: 4 minutes'. Opening in 1963, it was an unlikely but massive success in the West End and on Broadway. The conflation of text and research and improvisation and variety is in some ways a denial of the writer's vision; a statement that only a collaborative process can match a subject. Perversely, it is also an assertion of the need for a writer. I have seen three noble attempts to make a revival of *Oh! What a Lovely War* work (I attempted one at school), and all failed. Littlewood's vision was a director's one, and what is on the page remains doughily on the page without her yeasty brilliance. As with other devised texts, there remains something flavourless without a writer, some lack of texture and the music of heard life.

Not a problem with *Journey's End*, which was heard and seen. Details hit the audience like a punch. The talk of rats, the hard drinking, the dirt, the exhaustion, the yellow soup, the cutlets of indeterminate origin, the clothes worn for a week, the snatched sleep, the khaki, and the candle grease – all would have shocked. The approach is cunning. Within this mudhole, flecked with old blood, the characters do their valiant best to recreate a distant corner of Blighty, planting seeds of England in French mud. They talk of old rugby games and of their gardens at home, and take tea, though it resembles onion soup. Small indignities become obsessions – 'War is bad enough with pepper, but without pepper – it's – it's bloody awful!' The argot is full of 'spiffing' and 'topping', which makes the surrounding grime and destruction all the more telling. The structure of the language – stiff, evasive, and oddly formal – transports you into the minds of scared young men trying to retain a civility in the face of humanity at its most barbarous, concealing terror with the language of fathers and teachers. Six of them we come to know as if they were family, and watch their immature masculinity, with its boasting and self-deception, under immense stress. With flailing attempts at sangfroid, we come to admire them, while hating the machine that sends them as lambs to the slaughter.

There is one passage of dialogue as subtle and deft and heartbreaking as anything written for the proscenium stage. Two soldiers try to avoid the subject before they head out for what they know is a suicidal raid towards enemy guns. (There are saddening correspondences to a passage in Tom Robertson's *Ours*, when a group of soldiers avoid the subject of danger in front of civilians.) We witness the desperate courage expressed in a song from Littlewood's show: 'And when they ask us, how dangerous it was/Oh, we'll never tell them. No, we'll never tell them.'

The final image of *Journey's End* is devastating: one character, an encapsulation of doomed youth, dies and others head out for a long-awaited push with the walls of their dugout shaking and crumbling under German shells. As the barrage intensifies, in a claustrophobic stage picture we see a whole world with its spiffings and arcane honour and cosy comforts coming to an end. Giving witness to quiet heroism, *Journey's End* becomes a theatrical cenotaph. And an open and undeniable rebuke to any callow fool who talks of the glories of combat. That the proscenium managed to encapsulate something so deranging within its elegant constraints is a testament to its framing power. Though writing the play must have been an extraordinary exorcism, it has shape and pattern and quiet detail, only possible within a rigorous form.

After the catharsis of creation, this remarkable man retreated to silence about his war experience. Having poured out memories, sitting at his typewriter in his railway carriage bungalow, he reburied the ghosts under the earth, and returned to his zen plateau. Not that his life was dull. He headed to Hollywood for a couple of decades, where he earned a handsome living working on all sorts, from *The Invisible Man* to *The Dam Busters*. He maintained a strictly Surrey life while living in the Hollywood Hills. He even brought his mother over to cook roast beef for him every Sunday in the California sunshine. After a while, he was back in Esher, cruising the Surrey lanes in his custom-made Rolls-Royce, before returning to write movies through the night in a home garlanded with rowing trophies and seed catalogues. With no desire to look at his demons again, nor for further stirring of the pot, he was happy to tend his azaleas and enjoy the quiet which so many of our grandfathers prayed for.

A radio journalist later found two dusty war journals at Sherriff's old school. Crammed with maps of the frontline he served on, and photos of his old comrades in arms, they were decorated with sketches of bomb craters, duckboards, and snapped trees. Within the pages lay a tiny pressed flower, browned by the years, and under it the caption, 'A scarlet pimpernel picked from the wall of my trench.'

Keep your helmets tilted.
David Manners, Billy Bevan and Colin Clive;
a publicity photo for *Journey's End*, 1927

Bertolt Brecht
1898–1956

Bertolt Brecht should be thought of not as an outlier from the proscenium tradition, but more accurately as its sworn enemy. The prettifying of human experience within baroque frames, the presentation of an achieved world behind a fourth wall, the invitation to an audience to identify uncritically with what unfurled within these chocolate boxes, all of these were shibboleths to Brecht, the walls of Jericho he determined to tumble with his discordant trumpet.

Brecht wanted a return to the public theatre of the Greeks and Shakespeare, to plays presented in open light where a democratic audience could judge with detachment the actions and choices within a story. He campaigned all his life to bring back the thrust stage, and to reinvigorate the connection between actor and audience. His pedagogy was successful and a significant factor in the eventual demise of the proscenium. Yet for most of his career, these theatres were where he learned his trade, they were the spaces he worked in, and the ones for which he left the greatest legacy. When Mother Courage trundles her cart the wrong way against a revolve, it proves a metaphor for her stubborn pushback against time. It is also a painterly image within the frame. When the Berliner Ensemble first came to the West in the 1950s, they not only demonstrated the possibilities of combining dialectics and storytelling but also exhibited a new aesthetic – uncluttered, focused, and relying on a stark functionalism. Brecht might not have wanted to be a proscenium playwright, but it would be hard to deny that he was.

History sweeps across the stage in Brecht's drama, just as it swept him up in its cross-currents, and scattered his life's story across the world. Onstage, we trundle with Mother Courage through the slaughter and chaos of the Thirty Years' War; we visit the early seventeenth-century Republic of Venice, where the Catholic Church and the scientific method fight for the soul of Galileo; in China, Shen Te argues with the gods over good and bad behaviour; and in Soviet Russia, an old folk tale is used by a community to help find its balance after the Second World War. This is not history used carefully to calibrate a moral argument: this is history on the attack. Choices and decisions are thrown at characters with no advance warning, and they have to react in the instant with the improvised confusion of life.

As was the case for Brecht. He was born in Augsburg in February 1898, into a provincial mindset whose Lutheran certainties were about to be detonated. A slight and highly strung child, he was rebelling from the get-go, revelling in his own uniqueness. The First World War dragged him from home. Initially a patriot, the realities soon burned that folly out of him and he became a disillusioned medical orderly. Drawn to Berlin after the war, he witnessed a city scattered into separate tribes, all driven by a kaleidoscope of beliefs. The communists had the upper hand in some corners, old Prussian patriots in others. Anarchists held sway at moments, conservatives for long periods. All the while the nascent threat of National Socialism lurked and bloomed and retreated and hardened and grew again. Brecht began his theatrical career against the backdrop of an ideological circus, and his early works – short plays, song cycles, musicals, sketches, variety routines – show all the colours of the rainbow.

Just as he was finding his mature voice and starting to write canonical pieces that would define him, his homeland became an alien place as Nazism swept into power. The morning after the burning of the Reichstag, he knew it was time to go. He had flirted with communism without joining the party but, communist or not, he was too contrary to live within the hysterical uniformity of Hitler's vision. Once his books had been added to the bonfire, he was left with little choice. He wandered Europe, 'changing countries more often than shoes', in his words. Preaching the dangers of fascism everywhere he landed, like Coleridge's Wedding Guest, he found much of Europe a closed ear. He went to Hollywood and was forced to sit out the Second World War within the exile community. After the war, just as fascism had hunted him down in Germany, capitalism came looking for him in America. He was brought before the House Un-American Activities Committee and interrogated about his political beliefs. Charming to the committee, he went into the meeting with an airplane ticket in his pocket, and the next morning was on the first flight back to Europe. There he founded a company, the Berliner Ensemble, within the Stalinist embrace of East Germany.

To call him a contrarian would be an understatement since he carved out a life in permanent opposition. Once he realised the barbarities of war, he was having no part of it. When he perceived that the establishment theatre of the Weimar stage was prettified and conservative, and absurdly at odds with the famine and disorder surrounding it, he screeched against the disjunction. Witnessing police firing on striking workers fuelled his rage, but his ideology never became doctrinaire. His anger retained a poetry, and his ideas a rootedness in his belly and his passions. His thinking was never sublimated into the abstract calculations of others. He could see that capitalism and anti-capitalism dealt not in reality but in fictions. For him, they should be attacked not with dusty analysis but with bolder fictions.

Early in his career Brecht achieved the rare distinction of nearly finding himself arrested in rehearsals for the crime of being irritating. He drove the director and manager of a theatre so furious with constant interruptions that a burly Prussian policeman was summoned. Brecht, a slight figure and a committed physical coward, scurried away. Half an hour later, with the policeman safely gone, he was back and giving out corrections again. His rage at fascism was inevitable, but he didn't slacken his irascibility when he got to Hollywood in 1941. Disappointed by the lack of enthusiasm in the American film industry for complex dialectical fables, he despaired noisily of Hollywood and its marketplace for lies. Once back in Berlin in 1947, he hardly knuckled under to the pro-Soviet regime. He wrote a couple of toadying letters to the authorities when the pressure became too hot but was no apparatchik. When all his Berliner Ensemble colleagues trooped off to lunch at the nearby workers' canteen, Brecht went to the best restaurant nearby to feast on caviar. There was no hunger to be a good Stalinist, he just wanted a theatre of his own to sculpt his dreams. He avoided a further test of his loyalties by dying shortly before the Soviets marched into Hungary to crush the 1956 rebellion. That action asked questions many a communist could not answer.

Unstinting opposition is exhausting, as per his last words to the doctors trying to prolong his life: 'Oh leave me alone, I'm so tired.' In death, he still desired to be set apart from the mob. Ever the poseur, he requested that a stiletto be placed in his heart and a steel coffin encase him, even his corpse set to frustrate the conservative expectations of worms. His exclusion from the herd would survive, he imagined, into the afterlife.

In this, as in many other ways, he helped in the styling of a twentieth-century archetype, the perma-rebel, the figure for whom discontent is a religion. Not given to bourgeois habits like cleanliness, he was remembered as a ratty little fellow. Under his black leather jacket, he shambled through a Dionysiac Berlin wearing a grey shirt, fraying slacks, and thick leather shoes. He was famous for the length of time he could keep wearing the same pair of long johns and socks without washing them. A strip of leather hung like a noose around his neck in place of a tie. Rarely shaven, fingernails packed with dirt, he had a sickly yellow complexion and rotten teeth – a punk fifty years before their time.

In spite of this assiduous slobbishness, he somehow gave the impression he was invulnerable and that nothing could touch him. An oddball smile floated on his lips, not so much a smirk as a hint at secret knowledge. There was a magnetism to him, one that drew women – a power he abused – and also colleagues, whom he exploited. Sometimes he combined the two, using lovers to 'help' him write his plays. One – Elisabeth Hauptmann – is said to have written 80 per cent of his first great hit, *The Threepenny Opera*. His capacity to collect and consume people like mushrooms is damnable but also amounts to a skill. He smelled of the truth, and everyone wanted a piece of that. Proudly aware of his value to others, he wrote in his journals, 'With me people live in the light, enjoy the drama, enjoy food, enjoy music, feel powerful, have something to work for, have adventures without travelling.'

His great virtue, and one that resonates powerfully today, was his unrelenting opposition to groupthink. He countered bourgeois self-satisfaction in *The Threepenny Opera*, which demonstrates the interchangeability of businessmen and criminals. He interrogated the improvisations of gangster capitalism in *The Resistible Rise of Arturo Ui*, the certainties of the Catholic Church in *Life of Galileo*, and the collateral horrors of warmongering in *Mother Courage and Her Children*. That is an achievement, but a collection of easy wins. More interesting was his loathing for those who revelled in facile moralising against these evils. He sets up no sweet avatars of virtue: most of those who oppose these sins are compromised themselves. His plays are cat's cradles of crossed arguments within which it is impossible to elucidate a static moral standpoint. Any stated ethical position is usually a false path, cunningly crafted to lead characters and audiences to a bad end.

The first major source of groupthink he opposes is that of the audience. He knows the bourgeois spectator sits waiting for a compelling argument, or for a virtuous character, something – anything – that might lead them towards a resolved ending. Something to send them home secure in providence. Brecht teases that expectation, casting out red herrings, false flags, and chimera. All titillate the audience's moral sense into anticipation of a happy teleological ending, before darting back into confusion and moral morass. Like a conjuror, he loves misdirecting the audience with ethical decoys and ideological cul-de-sacs.

In 2024, I directed *The Seven Deadly Sins*, the *Singspiel*–ballet Brecht co-wrote with Kurt Weill in the 1930s. When the intelligent producers, conductor and performers (and a perfectly sensible director in myself) gathered, we all made trenchant comments about the piece to each other. We spoke of the corrosive effects of money and the illusion of the American dream. All of us got it – in manifold ways – wrong. Although the purpose is staring you in the face (to our shame, it is laid out in Wikipedia), we found countless ways of missing it.

A young woman and her sister head off on an odyssey around America. One sister hectors the other with a morality she has inherited from their family. In each town a different sin is showcased. After staring at the piece for a long time and listening to its sinisterly beautiful music, the light bulb finally flicked on and we realised the morality was topsy-turvy. Each sin was in fact a virtue: when the moral sister drives the supposed sin out of the other, she is eradicating goodness. All the barracking sister's maxims and saws derive from the banging-on of their family, whose false ethics are a hotchpotch of religion, gossip, and newspaper punditry, all employed to suppress the honest impulses of these young women. A reverse fairy tale, the opera is crammed with morals that are bunkum. Once you understand, you marvel at the length of time it took to discern. And you hear Brecht the trickster snickering at you and others similarly smoke-screened.

Part of this obfuscation was the celebrated *Verfremdungseffekt*, sometimes translated drearily as the 'alienation effect'. This appellation has misled Brecht's followers down an aesthetic slip road, inspiring a lot of grey, disassociated studenty acting. A better translation is the desire to make the familiar strange. An urging to look with fresh eyes. The preceding Stanislavskian orthodoxies wanted actors and writers to look for emotion and truth, and for the audience to be swept up in the illusion. The Brechtian theatre wanted its collaborators not to be overwhelmed by feelings but to consider the behaviour of a character and situation informed by social conditions before psychological ones. Thus, someone's pay packet, class, upbringing, tribal loyalty, status and so on would inform choices more directly than an unspecific emotionality. Writers, actors, and audiences should all keep thinking, in a detached and critical fashion, rather than demonstrate their ability to rain down tears or shout with rage. The brain should be given primacy over the heart. The goal of such thinking should be a move towards a spread of understanding, and the goal of that understanding should be social justice. Brecht did not want to interpret the world; he wanted to change it.

There was much to change. He battled the monster of Nazism in a variety of works, most obviously in *Arturo Ui*. Under the shadow of Hiroshima and Nagasaki, he wrote *Galileo*, attempting to illuminate for his audience issues of scientific and technological advance, and the responsibilities that walked alongside. In 1949, he returned to a Berlin reduced to rubble and to the depravity that follows in desolation's wake. He didn't write a pious fairy tale about inspirational heroes; he wrote the twentieth century's toughest play about war. The foul-mouthed and comfortless Mother Courage trundles through the savagery of an earlier Germany, trying to turn a profit from destruction. People didn't need sanctimony; they needed to survive. Brecht proffered no false comfort and matched the moment.

His legacies are multiple. He cleared a path for writers to experiment with form while remaining socially relevant. He demonstrated how to oppose an oppressive regime and how to survive it. As with his adored Shakespeare, he knew how to wrap himself in riddling equivocations and mysteries to confound authorities. Both lived in times when words were lethally dangerous. Sometimes the solution to this is silence, sometimes it is profusion. Both chose the latter. A mordant wit, his plays are great fun – coarse, raucous, and anarchic. His narratives rampaged, bristling with events and filled with jokes. He wanted his theatre to be like sport, the animal pleasures of boxing and football. There is a recording of him directing the Berliner Ensemble where you can hear his voice crackling with energy, clarity, and excitement. A love for actors rings out.

Every age will find a different virtue to focus on in Brecht, dependent on their need. He never posed as anyone's saviour, and nor did his protagonists. 'Unhappy is the land that needs heroes' was a maxim of his, and he proffers none. Mother Courage thinks her greedy amorality a virtue in itself and is brought up short. Galileo fails at his moment of testing, just as most of us would. No one is morally superior, and nor are we, the witnesses to these spectacles. As Shakespeare understood, actors and audience are mired in sin and in need of forgiveness. All are complicit and confused.

Brecht loathed all public morality, and every coercive attempt by politicians or the media to corral people into tribes of opinion. How greatly we need him today.

Wild times.
Poster for *Die Dreigroschenoper*, *The Threepenny Opera*, 1928

Federico García Lorca
1898–1936

Lorca was born on 5 June 1898 into a Spain in the throes of an identity crisis. The once world-spanning empire, so laden with gold and silver it hardly knew where to lavish it, had shrunk century by century to the Iberian peninsula. In Lorca's year of birth, the last of its external colonies, Cuba and the Philippines, went in humiliating defeats to the USA. A cabal of artists – dubbed the Generation of '98 – talked with urgency about the importance of renovating a national sense of self through culture. Opposing cabals talked of murdering the artists. Throughout Lorca's short life, Spain grew further polarised as diverging regimes succeeded one another – a liberal government was overthrown by the de Rivera dictatorship in 1923, and that regime was in turn succeeded by the liberal Second Republic from 1931. An outbreak of democratic experiment followed, too bold for many. The fearful coalesced around a nationalist cause with fascist sympathies. Decades of tensions crystallised in a single antagonism: one faction looking back to the days of empire, the other forwards to a new identity carved out in step with a redefining Europe. The duality, and the passion of both sides, erupted into the Civil War.

An aficionado of bullfighting and a friend to matadors, Lorca hung close to the conflicts of his era most of his life, occasionally prodding them, sometimes dodging out of their way. Though his plays are rarely explicitly political, the tension in the air and the crackle of static around him makes each line stand to nervous attention. 'May you live in interesting times' was a saying often heard in the 1930s, purported to be a Chinese curse. Often a blight for humanity, interesting times can be a boon for dramatists. Tensions provide sturdy foundations for theatre-making: a state on the verge of collapse gives urgency to every phrase and movement. Lorca's work is about the heart and desire, but the conflicts and soul-searching of the polity around him pulse through. An accomplished political matador, before long he ran out of swerves and the age caught up with him. He was assassinated beside a ravine at the age of thirty-five, his body hurled into a ditch with two apprentice bullfighters.

One reason the proscenium theatre didn't fly as high in Spain was the adherence to the carnival energies and narrative freedoms of its Golden Age. Those sixteenth- and seventeenth-century plays by Lope de Vega, Pedro Calderón de la Barca, and Tirso de Molina – verse epics of rampaging ambition – were played out in *corral* theatres under an open sky. A prodigious, rambling energy remained the favoured item on the Spanish menu, and it had not yet undergone the same trapping into gilded boxes as occurred in France and England. Lorca saw the theatre as 'poetry in three dimensions', and the third dimension is always more present in a theatre in the open air or on a thrust stage. The living body is surrounded and at risk. Although the Spanish tradition was *al aire libre*, Lorca went further in his idealised theatre. He imagined one that came from 'beneath the sand'. His idea was of storytelling dug from the earth, a ritual arena telling telluric legends, uncovering buried truths and ancient passions.

During the Second Republic, just as FDR and his New Deal were ploughing money into the arts in the USA, so the Spanish government invested in public culture. As part of a mass programme whose aim was to eradicate rural illiteracy, Lorca and some of his comrades founded La Barraca. It would be, in his words, 'A wandering and free theater that will travel the torrid carts of Castile, and the dusty roads of Andalusia. It will penetrate into villages and hamlets, and will set up in the small squares its stages and puppet shows.' An old silent short shows these young people, all wearing quasi-Soviet boiler suits, crossing mountains and valleys in rickety lorries, setting out their stall in village plazas and building makeshift stages. They present roustabout productions of Spanish classics to audiences caught with wonder. The hope and joy shining from their faces is enchanting. Not unlike Joan Littlewood's early touring troupe – boiler suits and all – the correspondence was underlined by Littlewood's early attempts to produce Lorca's plays in Britain. Across Europe theatre was becoming an instrument of social regeneration, taking drama to those who had never encountered it before. Dynamically successful, the Barraca programme provoked the wrath of the right, who accused the company (not unjustly) of being an instrument of political propaganda.

Although Lorca's abiding fascination was the rural poor, he himself was born into a bourgeois family in Fuente Vaqueros, a village just outside Granada. He was said to get his passion from his father and his intelligence from his mother. The father was a wealthy landowner and a social progressive, the latter setting him apart from his own class; the mother was a retired schoolteacher in an age when to be an educated woman was a rarity. She lavished her pedagogical intentions on young Federico, teaching him to read early, to play the piano, and gifting him a toy theatre, a miniature proscenium he used to entertain the household. Later he put on mini-shows, dressing himself up as a priest and directing the family's staff, themselves costumed by the child prodigy, in the enactment of mini-rituals.

Fuente Vaqueros was a small community still steeped in folklore. In a land of harrowing poverty, peasants gave their life dignity with parochial legends of scandal and passion. Although Lorca found his maturity among the avant-garde in Madrid and Barcelona, the granary of imagery for his poetry was stocked up in childhood. In Fuente Vaqueros, he saw and stored away mules laden with sunflowers walking up a hill before dawn; death riding in and out of an inn courtyard on a black horse; a nun embroidering crocuses and moons on an altar cloth; the silence of myrtle and lime; and the songs of gypsies. Images living beyond explanation or category, they simply glowed in the sunshine.

A precocious youth, Lorca published travel journals and poetry volumes in his early twenties. Far from a sensation, these were substantially subsidised by his father. His first play, *The Butterfly's Evil Spell*, was a spectacular floperoo. Presented in 1920, at the Teatro Eslava in Madrid, it tells the story of a cockroach who suffers unrequited love for a butterfly. The performance met with a chorus of jeers, and one loud call for insecticide to be poured across the stage. Only playing four shows, Lorca swore never to write for the theatre again.

By this time, he had moved to a student zone in Madrid, and his life had flowered into a new milieu filled with the noise of science, Freud, and the music of the machine. Fuente Vaqueros was far away. Lorca's apartment became a centre of young radical Madrid life. Among his new coterie were the guerrillas of the avant-garde Luis Buñuel and Salvador Dalí. Their passion for surrealism and the news they brought from Paris of a new spirit of experimentation had a rich effect on Lorca. In notebooks filled with fragments, puppet plays sit alongside instructions for happenings, Beckettian shorts beside surrealist squibs, all exploratory gestures towards a new performance language. As in his verse, there is tension between the soil and *la máquina*, between a writer bursting with feeling and the modernist call for emotions to be impersonal. His attempt, and a noble one, is to include all.

The Love of Don Perlimplin and Belisa in the Garden, an early short play, draws on the puppet tradition, with Perlimplin akin to the British Mr Punch. A comical old man, he falls in love with Belisa, a young neighbour. On his wedding night, he is multiply cuckolded by Belisa's several lovers. Perlimplin, remaining formal and courteous throughout, dodges the humiliation by saying it has helped him to ascend to a higher love. To assist Belisa on the same journey, he invents and then impersonates an unattainably beautiful youth for her. On his death, the glories of metaphysical love over carnal desire become apparent to her. Not quite a play, *Don Perlimplin* is more a series of dramatic gestures coalescing into a story – Lorca subtitled it *An erotic lace-paper valentine in a prologue and three scenes*. By a peculiar magic of sincerity, through lush imagery and jagged non-naturalistic leaps, the fragments attain a touching and generative metaphorical space. What should be ridiculous is overwhelmed by tenderness and acquires a particular dignity. The intensity of these characters' attachments, within an unforgiving universe, becomes heroic. In a good production, it outweighs any industrial juggernaut of a musical in its ability to touch glancingly a quickened soul.

His supposed colleagues in avant-garde experiment, Buñuel and Dalí, were in the first audience for *Don Perlimplin*, and far from kind. They laughed loud and hurled abuse. For them – determined urban sophisticates – it revealed the worst side of Lorca's farmer primitivism. The folk traditions which fed into *Don Perlimplin*, and later *Blood Wedding* and *Yerma*, were too antique for them. They wanted to leap forward, towards Dadaesque happenings and surrealist subversion. Lorca recognised that much of the subterranean consciousness, which modernist forms strove to access, was already present in the ancient. His attachment to childhood imagery and rhythms was too inherent to let go, and he refused to succumb to the fashionable diktats of the metropolitans.

Lorca's breakthrough as a playwright came with *Mariana Pineda* in 1927. Given the frequency with which he foregrounded women's stories, it is fitting his first success should come from a story about a proper heroine. Pineda was a legend in Granada, a martyr to early nineteenth-century liberalism and love. She opposed the tyranny of the Spanish state under Ferdinand VII, assisting another rebel to escape by sneaking him away disguised in a friar's habit. Later she embroidered a flag for her lover with the words 'Equality, Freedom and Law'. Arrested, she refused to incriminate her comrades, and was garrotted, with the flag burned before her as she died. This melodramatic story was meat and drink for the poet, fertile with issues of gender and independence, and with a love story to relish at its centre. Mariana was a radical whose passions could not be squeezed into society's strictures, and for whom death was the only escape. The fable spoke to contemporary politics but also echoed the Golden Age dramas the Barraca company had played, with their twin obsessions of love and honour. Pineda believes her lover will rescue her from prison but is disappointed. She comes to realise that political freedom precedes, and often eclipses, erotic freedom. In its tale of someone assassinated by the state for their beliefs, *Mariana Pineda* prefigured Lorca's end.

The play was presented by the star and impresario, Margarita Xirgu. In Spain and Latin America, which enjoyed the same happy give-and-take relationship as London with New York, Xirgu was the Sarah Bernhardt of her day. The playwright directed it, with sets and costumes by Dalí, who seems to have been placed under the severest restraints of naturalism, though no doubt a little madness burbled up. First played at the Teatre Goya in Barcelona in June 1927, it soon moved to Madrid and elsewhere. Something about the blending of talents with a story which amplified rage at the de Rivera dictatorship, *Mariana Pineda* hit the moment and made money for the author for the first time.

In *Blood Wedding*, first performed in 1933, a blood feud between families and an illicit love affair explode into a wedding celebration. The escaping lovers and those who hunt them get lost in a forest full of allegorical figures. The Moon appears in the form of a young woodcutter with a face painted white. Death arrives disguised as a young beggar woman. Both pronounce the inevitability that blood will be spilled. In *Yerma*, first produced in 1934 in Madrid, again starring the loyal Xirgu, a woman is driven beyond sanity by her desire to have a child. Pagan rituals are sought for help, her community gives advice good and bad, and the Church restricts freedom to manoeuvre. Trapped within her own body and a punitive society, she is impelled to murder her husband. This act outraged the play's first audience, and its premiere was followed by a riot on a scale with the Abbey Theatre's nights of mayhem.

Dalí can't help squiggling.
Blood Wedding, Teatro Principal Palace, Barcelona, 1935

These plays made Lorca famous and he revelled in the limelight with a Noël Coward-like flamboyance. He hung out with toreadors and artists; he was photographed for newspapers; he was lionised by academics; and his home continued as party central for Madrid's brightest lights. He was burning fiercely, and his giddy display in a country split between those who revered peacocks and those who wanted to kill them invited disaster.

The House of Bernarda Alba remains his sturdiest classic, a frequently revived masterpiece which sadly Lorca never saw performed. An all-female play, something of a political act in itself, it describes a hermetically sealed existence, a house shut up by its matriarch to mourn the death of her husband. Her command is that her five daughters, the female staff, and a wandering grandmother should be incarcerated in a living death for eight years. The vivacity of the sisters and their dreams of flowering romance and unbridled erotic escape are overwhelming. The daughters are as ripe with desire as their mother is filled with controlling violence. This is the world in which Lorca grew up, a world of marriage enforced by elders, where unmarried maidens had little or no agency. The play contains a multitude of ingredients and potential forms. It encompasses a Gothic haunted house mystery, a whodunnit, a melodrama, a political allegory, and a poem freighted with hefty symbolism. No reading is right or wrong. Lorca himself wanted it to be 'realism, realism, realism', almost like a photographic document. There is a sobriety and consistency of register more controlled than in his other works.

Within a house simmering in the Granada heat and trapped in clothes of mourning, the daughters police each other with the same surveilling rigour as their mother. They have internalised her bullying methods, just as she has internalised broader social currents of repression. As with Brecht's *Seven Deadly Sins*, the dogmas of Church and State have created personae built on ethics unsustainable in the face of human experience. Few plays have exemplified better the inability of the human at any level – the individual, the family, or the state – to regulate sexuality. Here as elsewhere, Lorca sang with a keening voice of how desire must find its freedom.

Soon after the Civil War began he left Madrid and returned to his childhood home in Granada, already fallen to nationalists in a *coup d'état*. Though his heart seems to have been inalienably on the left, he had mixed with figures on the right, and at this moment chose to move in with a family of Falangists, believing they would protect him. Despite his outspoken queer identity, and his long-standing advocacy for the marginalised, whether women or homosexuals or the Roma, he believed old allegiances would save him. In fact, he was heading into the cross hairs of the reactionaries. Even at the start of the Civil War there was a determination to eliminate the dissident red gene, and Lorca was too great a lover of variety for the uniformity of fascists. Why did he not run? His work is a ceaseless *pas de deux* with death, and he may have felt it was an intimacy he could not withdraw from. A vigilante group arrested him one morning, and two days later he disappeared. One of the first notable instances of the fascist love of violence, it exposed their transparency in dealing with dissent through murder.

Lorca's body has never been located. His death certificate says he died of war wounds. No one would ever admit to the killing. In the absence of a grave or admissions, his ghost floats, as it were, both nowhere and everywhere. The lack of a resting place has helped him become a manifold icon: a gay martyr, a martyr of the left, and a representative of the estimated 130,000 civilians who were disappeared in the course of the Spanish Civil War. Lorca himself had foreseen and foretold his early death, but he probably didn't suspect its effect.

Refinding a home for his plays in Spanish theatres took time. *Bernarda Alba* did not see an audience until almost ten years after his death, when it was premiered in 1945 in Buenos Aires by his indefatigable champion Margarita Xirgu, by then herself an exile. The prestige and acclaim of the author grew rapidly in Latin America as he became a mainstay in the beautiful Spanish colonial theatres throughout the region. Lorca was first canonised within these temples, before becoming the most translated of all Spanish playwrights.

Although his work has travelled widely, one of the greatest problems for Lorca's translators was the difficulty of finding his register. First the dialogue, with its claggy, earthed texture and sparks of erotic fire, has defied cultural transfer. The Spanish language does such things with elegance and ease; most other languages don't. Productions suffer from a similar problem, either flattening the sierras into a featureless naturalism, or overcompensating with a phoney theatricality. The Spanish can access a style that is at one and the same moment rich and simple.

The term 'duende', first theorised by Lorca, is almost too elusive to define. It becomes most vividly manifest in the performance of flamenco dancers and musicians, where an ineffable aliveness occurs in electric communion with an audience. Each moment achieves its unrepeatable gleam, folding into itself an awareness of its own ephemerality, and in the same instant dies – the transient essence of performance writ in slashing colour. Lorca loved duende when he saw its quick bloom, whether in flamenco, bullfighting, his own young performances and later recitals, or in the passion of creation.

In his three rural tragedies – *Yerma*, *Blood Wedding*, and *The House of Bernarda Alba* – Lorca laid out his great achievement: the ability to put onstage a Spain both modern and ancient. The plays are written freely with a blend of lyricism, symbolism, and realism. Abstraction and naturalistic detail complement each other in a permissive universe which allows all houseroom. They resonate with Lorca's own life and the polarities of his moment: the push for freedom and the pain of breaking free; the impersonal art and the lyric voice; the avant-garde and the folkloric; the forward and the backward gaze.

So much hope.
Federico García Lorca, 1932

Ayn Rand
1905–1982

Everyone seems to call everyone else fascist these days. A friend from the realm of puppetry once told me any party (or gathering involving alcohol) that brought together the different modes of puppetry – marionette, rod and arm, shadow, glove – would usually descend into bitter factionalism. Each group would argue the others' chosen form was essentially anti-democratic. Once one group had hissed 'fascist', the game was a bogey and they would all start hurling it at each other. This image of a group of drunken puppeteers in an Islington basement shouting 'fascist' at each other has always seemed an eloquent allegory for the histrionic squabbles of wider society.

I once descended dumbly to the same line of attack during an argument with a meretricious young playwright, now a purveyor of smoothly liberal highbrow television. His plays had scant interest in real humanity, in heard dialogue, or in life, and were intricate little intellectual schemata with plot surprises to demonstrate how clever he was. He sneered at naturalism with the innate superiority of the overeducated and claimed to be aiming at something higher. Red rag to a bull for me, I descended to the F-word in a blundering attempt to state how appalled I was – and promptly lost the argument. As in the puppetry realm, the term has been rendered nigh on meaningless by overuse.

Imagine one's surprise and terror then to encounter a play that unapologetically flirts with fascism. Ayn Rand became an enormously influential figure late in life, her weighty novels – *The Fountainhead* and *Atlas Shrugged* – selling millions of copies. They fostered an army of acolytes in the interlocking worlds of extreme-right libertarians, neocons, and all those radical for capitalism. She produced books of argument and ideas as well, but it is less well known that her first literary forays were dramatic, including two plays on Broadway.

A naturalised American citizen, she grew up as Alisa Zinovyevna Rosenbaum from a Jewish bourgeois family in St Petersburg. Shortly after the Revolution, her family fled to Crimea, which was under the control of the White Army, before returning three years later to study at Petrograd University within the now communist state. Renaming herself Ayn Rand, with an instinct for the iconic, she obtained a visa to visit relatives in Chicago in 1926. Once there, she resolved never to return to the USSR. Her first hunger was for stardom, and that need propelled her to Hollywood. Making little progress as an actress, she resolved to write.

Her first play, *Night of January 16th* (the title needs an exclamation mark really), opened in New York in 1935. Its passage to the stage was troubled, not rendered any easier by its author. Her introduction to the published edition is a masterwork of unabashed arrogance. Her underlying assumption seems to be that everyone agrees thespians are half-witted lowlifes. This is not an attitude calculated to endear her to theatre folk. Rand divides the world categorically between 'Great men and small men'; everyone who helped her with the production falls into the latter category. A preview in Los Angeles she dismissed with a lordly, 'The production was competent but somewhat unexciting: unstylised and too naturalistic.' No gratitude here. Her work was then picked up by a hucksterish producer, and . . . 'the rest of the play's history was hell'.

She wanted the marketing to emphasise its unveiling of revolutionary 'sense-of-life' ideas; the producer wanted to sell tickets. ('Sense-of-life' is a nebulous thing distinct from ideology and philosophy, both of which are inadequate to envelop the radicalism of Rand's thinking.) A new title was forced on her, and casting and rewrites suggested, which Rand described as 'a junk heap of worn, irrelevant melodramatic devices'. Her relationship with her director can't have been helped by her describing him as 'a very ratty Broadway hanger-on'. On opening night, the playwright's enthusiasm was demonstrably withheld: 'I sat in the back row, yawning – not out of tension, but out of genuine boredom, since it was an event that had no value-meaning for me any longer.'

The play ran for seven months, though without the presence of its author: 'I could not bear to see the play again.' For all her loathing, she lists at some length the number of successful tours it enjoyed, and its enthusiastic taking up by summer stock companies. She despises critics for their praise as much as their condemnation: 'I learned to expect nothing from reviewers because of the so-called favourable reviews, not because of the illiterate smears.' Somehow she still finds space in her preface to quote at length from one who uses the G-word (genius), though his praise is for the play's potboiler construction rather than its 'sense-of-life' understanding.

Night of January 16th revolves around a gimmick – and a fun one – the sort of conceit the playwright I argued with would have been proud to call his own. The setting is a courthouse and the play is a murder trial, opening as the clerk of the court calls out twelve members of the audience, who troop up and form the onstage jury. At the end of each performance, they are free to cast their vote (though with scant time to do so). Two different codas follow for either a guilty or not guilty verdict. Celebrities crowded in to take part after the superstar boxer Jack Dempsey joined the jury on press night. One night there was a special performance for the blind, resulting in a blind jury whose forewoman was Helen Keller.

Trial scenes are of course central to the theatre, dating back to the democratic casting of stones for or against Orestes and his killing of his mother. The judgement in Aeschylus' play thrills, as do the legal shenanigans in Shakespeare's *Merchant of Venice* or Lope de Vega's *Fuenteovejuna*. A verdict is a reliable way to set pulses racing. But there is a special affinity between the trial scene and the proscenium arch, partly drawn from the latter's physical similarity to a courthouse. The judge sits on a raised platform beneath a tall wooden canopy; crests and regalia add pomp; bewigged clerks and barristers form a chorus arranged in a semicircle (as if badly blocked); and onlookers, many of them bearing opera glasses, are packed into ground-floor boxes and a high gallery. The fact that barristers are often failed actors, and vice versa, is hardly surprising.

The narrative for *Night of January 16th* was inspired by the 1932 suicide–murder of a Swedish industrial titan, Ivar Kreuger, known as the Match King. Many plays of the era were inspired by murders – often of overweening men. Kreuger was an international mogul who seems to have stepped straight out of an Ibsen play. His worldwide match empire was funded by a series of elaborate financial scams amounting to a Ponzi scheme. He was described by J. K. Galbraith as the 'Leonardo of larcenists'. This figure, repulsive to most, became an exemplar for Ayn Rand of the domineering, the-rules-don't-apply-to-me *Übermensch* she dreamed of. She invents a parallel figure (not subtly renamed), Bjorn Faulkner, whose death triggers the plot. His mistress, Karen Andre, is tried for his murder, and in the course of the trial all manner of skeletons come tumbling out of closets involving Faulkner, his mistress, his wife, his father-in-law, a gangster called 'Guts' Regan, Uncle Tom Cobley and all. The management of narrative is terrific, with surprises aplenty, great curtain moments, and every hoary old device from the melodramatic playbook. Credibility disappears on page one when the first character appears. Like all the others, he emerges from a catalogue of clichés. There is a faithful retainer, a straight-talking cop, a sinister and repressed Swedish Lutheran housekeeper, and a judge who says 'Order in the court' a lot.

The oddness of the play centres around Bjorn Faulkner and other people's reactions to him. His suicide note reads, 'I found only two enjoyable things on this earth whose every door was open to me: My whip over the world and Karen Andre.' This pound-shop Nietzsche turns out to have raped his mistress; sold himself in marriage in return for a large loan; defrauded investors the world over, and broken the law with impunity. For all these sins, his mistress loves him the more. As she puts it, 'When little people like you and me meet a man like Bjorn Faulkner, we take our hats off and bow, and sometimes we take orders: we don't ask questions.' In proof of their passion there is a section where the Lutheran housekeeper tells of their deluxe sex games with stern disapproval. She has to be read with an all-purpose Nordic accent: 'I tell you. He had a platinum gown made for her. Yes, I said platinum! Fine mesh, fine and soft as silk. She wore it on her naked body. He would make a fire in the fireplace and he would heat the dress and then put it on her. It cooled and you could see her body in silver sheen, and it been more decent if she had been naked. And she ask to put it on as hot as she can stand, and if it burned her shameless skin, she laughed like the pagan she is, and he kissed the burn, wild like tiger!' There is much that is inadvertently strange written for the proscenium stage, but little can top that.

Described in a somewhat confusing metaphor as 'A tiger in a vegetarian cafeteria', we hear how Bjorn celebrated each stage of his success with Karen: at an early stage, dinner at the finest restaurant in Vienna; at the next, on the shore of the Ganges, on the steps of 'an old temple where human slaves had been sacrificed to gods'; at the latter stage, in a biplane careering above the skyscrapers of Manhattan. The lifestyle dreams are straight from some kitsch 1980s Gordon Gekko wish list, a tacky Valhalla on earth for the capitalist superman. In this, as in much of the play, there is a weird prescience relating to the rise and rise, with no regard to known morality, of an American perma-tanned president. Throughout there is no sense of right or wrong: 'To him, it was only: you can or you can't.' Bjorn needed, 'no justifications for his actions: he was the justification; the man who said that laws were made for the fun of breaking them'.

When the attorneys come to sum up – and by this stage the plot twists have become so multiple it is hard to work out who is prosecuting whom and who defending whom – one of them tells us that this trial is not about Bjorn Faulkner! No, it is about us! Where do our sympathies lie, with the sad, half-hearted world as it is, or with the man who was born with 'life singing in his veins'? Have we felt 'a longing for greatness and for a sense of life beyond the lives around' us, or are we stuck in boring old grey contemporary morality? Can we recognise a conqueror who has 'a strength that is its own motor, an audacity that is its own law, a spirit that is its own vindication'? This heavily loaded question was put to New Yorkers night after night over seven months. Thankfully, though this was a time when America flirted with fascism, the New York audiences voted in a proportion of 3–2 against the *Übermensch*. A victory for 'the little people' in Rand's eyes. Still, worryingly close to call.

However troubling one may find her conclusions, it would be trite not to acknowledge the depth of her reading and the rigour of her thinking. She worked out her own philosophical system, Objectivism, which involved what she saw as a clear-eyed worship of pure reason and of ethical egoism as guiding moral principles. For her, the individual should 'exist for his own sake, neither sacrificing himself to others nor sacrificing others to himself'. As a system, it has proven attractive to millions and has birthed much of the world we live in.

The American theatre should be given credit that it gave ideas such as these room to breathe. Theatre, like any art form, gets moribund if it doesn't allow assumptions to be challenged. There are two problems with this play, and with Rand's later *The Unconquered*, an adaptation of her debut novel, *We the Living*. First, it is crummy art. The plot is all effect and no human truth, the dialogue is banal or rhetorical, and the characters have no existence independent of their narrative role. Second, there is a profound misunderstanding of the purpose of drama. Theatre is not tasked with enacting this or that social programme, of the right or the left or the centre. Nor is it an arena to discover how better to wrangle others into this or that shape to fulfil an ideological dream.

The task of theatre is to awaken an audience further to the existence of strangers, to sharpen their sense of the reality of others, and to respect their profound and winning unknowability. Placing a confusion of humans on the stage provokes a humility in the face of the multiplicity of existence. The first building bricks towards that confusion and humility are gathering moments of life, based on listening to others' speech, observing their behaviour, and understanding their needs.

The essential tools of playwriting. And the very qualities not readily accessible to . . . fascists.

They really do follow you around the room.
Broadway flyer, 1935

Clifford Odets
1906–1963

Appreciating fully the excitement of Christopher Marlowe took me a while. Sitting through rhetorical productions of *Tamburlaine* didn't advance his cause. Pained and tear-filled victim versions of *Edward II* didn't help much. And *The Jew of Malta* is pretty much a no-no on page or stage. Insight came down a surprising road.

At the Globe, once we had built our indoor Sam Wanamaker Playhouse, we created a young persons' company to perform the Jacobean plays written for young voices. Ignoring advice to hire a company of boys from private schools, we invited anyone under the age of eighteen to audition. Over five long days, more than a thousand kids trooped in and out of a dowdy church hall and delivered classical texts. Out of this we formed a company of fifteen youngsters as dazzling and diverse as London itself. Their attachment to the mission and each other proved a happy emotional uplift to our whole operation.

Their second show was Marlowe's *Dido, Queen of Carthage*. This decorative and gilded version of Virgil's myth habitually fails like a broken clock every time it hits the stage, largely as a result of actors' attempts to help the play. They try to act it, animate it, fill it with fascinating detail, and embellish it with rhythmic modulations and insightful surprises. In other words, they clot it. Young actors know in their bones a modesty their elders sometimes forget. Innocence instructs them just to say it, clearly and brightly, to let the language do the work and not interpose themselves between words and ears. In their unencumbered voices, *Dido*, with its long saga narratives, ornate declarations of love, and earnest declarations of intent, miraculously began to sing – a firework display of what language can do in a space. Suddenly, Marlowe's achievement became clear. He was the door-opener, the glass ceiling shatterer, the man who showed what was possible. Sitting in our oak theatre, young actors hitting consonants with precision and clarity, treading the iambic beat with unabashed relish, all within flickering candlelight, one felt for a second what Shakespeare and his contemporaries must have felt at their first hearing. The sheer joy of imbibing Marlowe's shameless audacity. Oh my lord, they must have thought, can you hear what is possible?

Much of the same mould-breaking applies to Clifford Odets, alongside a surprising multiple of further parallels. Both playwrights attached themselves to clandestine organisations challenging the status quo and were under close inspection from a shadowy branch of the authorities. Marlowe's underground club of atheists, the School of Night, was a thorn in the side of the Elizabethan Establishment and surveilled closely by the queen's spymaster, Sir Francis Walsingham. Odets was an unaffiliated member of the communist movement, widespread in the USA of the 1930s and watched under the panoptical gaze of J. Edgar Hoover and the burgeoning FBI. Both dramatists flickered with a dangerously exposed flame. Marlowe in many ways invented the celebrity playwright in the Elizabethan era. There were successes before his arrival, but audiences went for actors and stories; with Kit Marlowe, the audiences went for him. Odets was *the* American playwright of the 1930s, hitting the perfect intersection between commercial success, technical brilliance, and social commitment. Launched by the Group Theatre, a beacon of socially aware collaborative practice, his plays enjoyed long runs on Broadway.

Both torches blazed young: Marlowe's six-year career began with his first success at twenty-three; Odets had four plays on in New York at the age of twenty-nine. A punk freedom loosens the stays of both. Punk rock attitude is often typecast as solely about rage, but it is also about unfurling a range of colours – freedom and joy and possibility. Burning too bright for social permission, both were destroyed early. Marlowe was murdered in a brawl at an inn; Odets was ruined by success and Hollywood, the government and alcohol. Whether fate was kinder to Marlowe, since he did not have to watch his own slow and shameful demise, is moot. For me, Odets observing his extinction through the blear of booze is a crueller fate than the dispatching of Marlowe with a dagger – the 'great reckoning in a little room', which Shakespeare alludes to in *As You Like It.*

Both had the swagger of those whose flame dies young. Marlowe's freewheeling relish in language is matched by Odets's passion for phrase-making. Just as one can imagine Shakespeare sitting with ears pricked by his contemporary's work, one can see Arthur Miller and Tennessee Williams sitting in New York theatres listening to Odets's bristling energy and understanding anew a range of potentialities. Miller revelled in what he called 'the unashamed word-joy' of Odets, and remembered, 'An Odets play was awaited like news hot off the presses, as though through him we would know what to think of ourselves.'

Anger fuels part of the Odets swagger, but exuberance and ecstasy stoke the furnace equally. These and a collection of further textures opened windows for the audience; an apprehension of the allure of materialism – things and the obsession with things sing in his plays; a savouring of the vernacular on every street corner; a language tough and terse, with violence compressed into every verbal grenade; an understanding of human dignity both stoic and combustible; and an instinctive 'fuck you' to a malign world in each stance taken. All these colours pressure-cook in enclosed spaces, the characters piled one on another in tenements, sweating their way to new tempers. Together this amounted to a new poetics of the urban everyday.

Odets arose out of the Group Theatre, a constellation of talents including Elia Kazan, Harold Clurman, and Lee Strasberg, orbiting around each other and their historical moment, all sharing a passion for birthing a culture to reflect their struggles. As with many such movements, the Group was an assemblage of schematic ideas, unable to become flesh until they found a genius to ignite them. Along came this fiery and awkward boy – Odets. He manifested their dreams and, with the audacity of an artist, dug further into uncharted territory.

His tyro play, *Waiting for Lefty*, was not his greatest but it was his most incendiary. Short, blunt, and hitting like a hammer, it tells the story of the unionisation of the cabbies in New York City. Politics is in every stitch of the play, but not with the dour self-righteousness of the earnest: here it has the muscularity of a thrown punch, and the brightness of a Pete Seeger song. Odets later wrote romances where he captured with brute immediacy the heart swell of first love; in this play he captures the ecstasy of political discovery, the expansive joy one feels the first time one senses the world can perhaps be nudged towards justice, and that anyone can help. An instructive simplicity informs *Waiting for Lefty*, effective at its very first show when the audience chanted 'Strike! Strike! Strike!' and as the curtain fell, reeled out filled with a fresh sense of community. Odets said that 'new art works should shoot bullets': it does here. *Waiting for Lefty* is crude, vital, and a reinfusion of lifeblood.

Much of the discourse about 1930s America has become about communism, its influence, and the battles fought against it, but an equal if not more powerful energy of the age has been neglected: the fight against fascism. Though moving at pace elsewhere, the insidious influence of fascism was creeping into American life in ways hidden and explicit. One of the most articulate diagnoses of this drift appeared in Odets's neglected masterpiece *Till the Day I Die* (1935). Written in his customary Bronx-Broadway pop-culture lingo, the play is set in Nazi Germany, envisioning a step or two in the future after it has degraded further. A fascinating what-if, both of how Germany could develop and of how America could slide down the same dread slope. Borrowing some of the techniques of Berlin expressionism and vaulting through its story with disassociated images of brutality, the play has a consciously epic scope and shows terrifying prescience. The closest parallel to its chill brutality, surprisingly, is the work of Sarah Kane almost sixty years later. The alliance of American street-speak and fascist behaviour – the demonising of outsiders and the shutting down of free speech – has a toxic resonance that survives.

Elements of Odets's portrait of the state came true in his own lifetime when McCarthy's House Un-American Activities Committee (formed in 1938 in part to squash the Federal Theatre Project) forced the playwright to name fellow communists from his previous cohort. Although he had been named himself by Elia Kazan, and only confirmed names they already had, this act killed his reputation, his career, and his imaginative life. The committee was whipped along by the young Roy Cohn, the same lawyer who became the mentor to Donald Trump. Ah, the strange backwards and forwards soft shoe shuffle of history.

Till the Day I Die proved too bold and bleak to be embraced by a wide public, and it was with domestic dramas that Odets made his name. These are usually in tightly confined interiors, often revolving around families, where the political optics are absorbed into crucibles of human relationships. Their vitality is unmatched, busting open with life, enjoying the same delirium as French farce, with families, friends, neighbours, and strangers hurtling through doors that endlessly open and close. When anyone goes to leave there is almost always someone else bustling in. The old (and important) theatrical adage of never leaving a stage empty is in no danger here as seven or eight people dash across, exchanging brief and characterful greetings, creating complex lattices of quick chatter that stretch the audience's capacity to comprehend.

These cauldrons of flung comment wrench the audience out of itself and into the whirring centripetal energy. Every character has a hectic desire to speak, thereby affirming their hectic desire to exist. They all want a piece of the narrative, hungry to feel as alive as possible. Some characters carry heavy motives, some lighter; no matter, there are no hierarchies here – all are given weight. Each is entrenched in their own community, sharply aware of what the others are up to. A bright rapateta naturalism – the same staccato rhythms David Mamet relishes – is born here and has governed much of the American stage since. The same truth was present in O'Neill but sketched with a soft pencil in a drink-sodden fog – slow and repetitive and on a theme. Here chaos rules: all is life life life, and it gleams.

A rich confluence of streams flows in this river. The Yiddish theatre, which thrived in intimate spaces in downtown New York in the early part of the twentieth century, was a substantial influence. Here an immigrant population met to be entertained and stirred by the quirks and passions of humanity. This tradition's delight in contrariness fed into the zigzags and switchbacks of Odets's characters. Beside this gnarly perversity, he works in the polarities and dialectics of early Brecht, stirring it all together with, in Odets's own words, a 'poetry that was inherent in the chaff of the street'. The result is an exhilarating vitality.

The prime enemy was the life-draining force of the Depression and its poverty, a machine of demoralisation as inexorable as fate. Each of his characters defines themselves in opposition to this force as fiercely as Webster's Jacobean characters define themselves against death. The chief ally is joy. Following the example of Synge and O'Casey, Odets serves up great helpings of it, like tubs of ice cream on a summer's day. His young romantics take unbridled pleasure in shouting out their love. In *Awake and Sing!*, Moe and Hennie share a combustible energy – their declarations sing out like lines from popular music, and are all the better for the melodic, unabashed directness: 'The whole world's green grass and when you cry it's because you're happy'; 'No more pins and needles in your heart'; 'There'll be fruit trees where our ashes lie.' Young passion has little room for cleverness, and it is a relief to find a writer who understands that and joins in. A faction in theatre-making and criticism looks down on this sort of plain and unafraid writing, sneering at it as sentimental and sappy. We are the poorer for our snobbery.

An aura of shame hangs around Odets and obscures his brilliance. The drawn-out decline in Hollywood, his calamitous bullying by McCarthy, his capitulation to the committee, and the decline in the quality of his plays is a hard legacy. Yet his influence is everywhere. His language and syntax form a lexicon of phrase-making that has influenced any number of dash and elan writers. The song he sang became an archetypal melody: terse, snappy phrases like bullets; upward energy blended with a little downward weariness; surging hope mixed with ebbing cynicism; words impacted by the bruising of wounds; toughness mitigated by a single teardrop. This range of harmonics forms the template for much movie dialogue, a styling created by Odets.

In *Golden Boy*, he diagnosed one of the most paradigmatic crises in American masculinity. The hero, Joe, is torn between his desire to succeed in the boxing ring and the lure of the violin, for which he has an equal gift. The blood and thunder of the fight game is set against the transcendence of art. The confusion resulting from the two impulses wrecks him. This is the psychological trope that runs through many hero types, most notably Jack Nicholson's character in *Five Easy Pieces*. Its fissure between aggression and sensitivity, competition and meditation defines a conflict in the American soul, the same duality Odets sought to reconcile. The Group Theatre artist delighted in collaboration, community, and the chorus, while the competitive entrepreneur delighted in success, money, and the trappings of fame. As for Joe, so for Odets, resolution proved impossible by anything less than failure and death.

Feel the collective hope.
Group Theatre

However painful his ending, the quantity of joy he left behind redeems the long demise. As with Marlowe (and Wilde, who shared a similar precipitation in rise and fall), he left a profusion of zingers. Every page of each man's work is filled with lines that punch out delight and wisdom, such as, 'A dear true friend is more than love – the serge outlasts the silk.' Alongside Marlowe, and unlike Wilde, the achievement is lyric rather than epigrammatic. Each phrase is filled with emotion. Embarrassed by his own sensitivity, Odets seldom showed off his feelings, but his writing is as lyrically lavish as an opera. The aspiration behind it all is the embodiment of hope and an assertion of the sanctity of human dignity.

This was at the heart of the spirit of the age – a strong faith in the rights of *everyone* within a community to the full achievement of their own pride. His heroes question a society that devitalises all but the exceptional. Everyone is entitled to the same abundance. In their determination to achieve such richness of flavour – for themselves and others – Odets's heroes earn undying respect. And in the context of what came after, break our hearts.

Clare Boothe Luce
1903–1987

What one needs from theatre changes as one stumbles through life. As a youth, some sort of elevation is hungered after, some sort of enhancement; at later angry moments, it is a clarity about the politics of the world; at others, moral illumination; throughout, insight into others and oneself is hoped for. Recently, I have been treasuring the privilege of privacy, those evenings when one is given a glimpse into lives, or fragments of them, when a curtain is lifted on moments usually kept discreet.

This last factor is at the heart of *The Women*, the 1936 runaway hit by the wayward comet that was Clare Boothe Luce, which ran for 657 performances on Broadway. A play of forty female characters played by eighteen cast members, portraying the roundelay of chatter and infidelity and divorce and revenge among New York's female elite, it allows no trace of testosterone near the stage. For the spear side, it is a series of revelations, taking them to places they do not usually see and overhearing conversations normally unheard. For the distaff side, it was the liberation of seeing themselves as the subject, and the *only* subject, of the stage. Since these women are often talking about the men they pass from one to another, their dialogue might not pass the Bechdel Test. But I suspect Boothe Luce would have had a towering and toweringly offensive response to being asked to sit that virtue exam.

Ninety years after it was first performed, the play has an immaculate freshness and revelation. The women discuss the pain of childbirth in brutal detail; they swap notes on how to manage love affairs; they discuss the merits of hairdressers and manicurists; they compare the stature of their 'bazooms'; a mother talks to her prepubescent daughter about the changes she is undergoing; the same mother seeks maternal advice on how to handle her husband's infidelity. Trivial and significant matters are dished up with equally weighted seriousness and frivolity. Everything and nothing matters, and all discussed with the same dash. Throughout, the women aim for their natural climax – 'Orgasm by gossip' – all delivered with that relentless 1930s attack, attack, attack. The same linguistic storming of the barricades you see exemplified by Katharine Hepburn and Rosalind Russell in the rat-a-tat-tat dialogue of their screwball comedies. The period seems to have felt little need for interiority, or perhaps had resolved that if you had a private thought, you made a grenade-joke of it.

The information isn't only in what we hear, it is also in the intimate places we are given admittance to. An adulterous woman plots her manoeuvrings from a deluxe foam-filled bath; a quartet swaps barbs across the bridge table; a rumour flies around an exercise class. Across a split stage, and attended by an army of assistants, a wife and a mistress try on various haute couture outfits; we go backstage in a beauty parlour, hearing the workers kvetch about their customers; and in the most private of inner sanctums – a divorce resort in Reno – a group of women fall out spectacularly and end up in a fist fight. No one had put these settings onstage before – unmitigated by the inhibiting presence of chaps.

Boothe Luce was accused at the time, and since, of misogyny. This seems perverse for a number of reasons. The dialogue between these well-to-do New York matrons is labelled 'bitchy', whereas the same robust badinage between men would be called 'wit'. Their brutal competition for power and turf has been branded as demeaning, but with men it would be analysed as a portrait of power dynamics. These are real women, not saints. When men write this way of men, it is called honest; when a woman does the same, it is misogyny. Go figure.

Actresses have queued up to play these parts, then and now. Principally because *The Women* is a really efficient bit of entertainment. Boothe Luce excelled at creating forty fully realised bundles of energy, varying from complex leading characters to vivid passing caricatures. As a mosaic, it renders a panorama of 1930s New York. A taut story unfolds, neatly plotted in elegant jumps, incident to incident, as the women weave a daisy chain of infidelities and break-ups and sharing out of husbands and lovers, the men proving little more than raw meat with a wallet attached.

Even though there is no indulgence of sentiment, there is no shortage of it either. Among the innocent the pain of betrayal is deeply felt, before they learn how to exact revenge. And the jokes, from the school of Dorothy Parker's high and sharpened wit, are peerless.

Boothe Luce was described by the columnist Maureen Dowd as 'A woman who had more hyphens in her résumé than Barbra Streisand – actress-editrix-playwright-screenwriter-congresswoman-ambassador-presidential adviser.' She was born illegitimate, and into a loveless family, but little stood in her way. She married young to a rich man and divorced young to a poorer one. Before long, she was the managing editor of *Vanity Fair*, where she came to the attention of Henry R. Luce, the publisher of *Time*, *Fortune*, and soon after, at the suggestion of his new wife Clare Boothe, *Life*. They married only a month after he divorced his wife of twelve years, which implies a strain of autobiography in *The Women*. Their marriage was boldly open, with Boothe Luce collecting scalps among all the archetypes of patriarchal power, including Ambassador Joseph P. Kennedy, Randolph Churchill, and Major General Charles Willoughby. During the Second World War, the strapping Air Force pilot Roald Dahl was pimped out by British Intelligence to sleep with and gain the favour of powerful American women in Washington, DC. Dahl complained to the British ambassador that he found his affair with Boothe Luce more physically exhausting than his athletic frame could manage. Pleading for another assignment, he was told to think of Britain and carry on.

Boothe Luce wrote two further plays in the 1930s, *Kiss the Boys Goodbye*, a comedy inspired by the search for an actress to play Scarlett O'Hara in *Gone with the Wind*, and *Margin for Error*, a passionate denunciation of Nazi ethics and philosophy, framed rather awkwardly in the form of an Agatha Christie whodunnit. Both efficient entertainments, they were later adapted into movies. During the war, apart from sapping Roald Dahl, she sought more serious work than writing plays. A frontline correspondent of surpassing courage – often under fire and bombardment – she wrote despatches from Europe, Africa, China, and Burma.

Her trenchant criticisms of the British commander-in-chief General Auchinleck in the Middle East led to his dismissal. She was elected to Congress in 1942, and her experience at the Front had her promoted swiftly to the House Military Affairs Committee. After the war, she was the first woman to ascend to a senior diplomatic posting, becoming the US Ambassador to Italy. Wherever there was a glass ceiling, she was determined to smash her way through it. Republican politics and her take-no-prisoners outlook on life did not endear her to all. She was contrary in her attitudes, but steadfast in her refusal to let gender stand in the way. When she died, she left $50 million to the Clare Boothe Luce Program, for women to gain access to the science, engineering and technology fields traditionally reserved for men.

Like Falstaff, she could say, 'I am not only witty in myself, but the cause that wit is in other men,' proving the butt of as many jokes as she inflicted on others. When someone said to Dorothy Parker, 'Clare Boothe Luce is always kind to her inferiors,' the reply came, 'Yes . . . where does she find them?' Though she had no shortage of enemies, she mourned their passing since she believed they sharpened her act. But with a barrage of aphorisms up her sleeve, she almost always had the last word . . .

No good deed goes unpunished.

Widowhood is a fringe benefit of marriage.

I refuse the compliment that I think like a man, thought has no sex, one either thinks or one does not.

'It's all about men!'
Film poster, 1939

T. S. Eliot
1888–1965

The most baffling concern when reading the plays of T. S. Eliot is why they are so ineffably dull. The soil for great plays from Eliot was perfectly manured and tilled and should have borne forth orchards spilling over with various fruit. Instead, it creates an Eliot landscape: rubbly stone and cracked pavements stretching on for miles, broken only by the endurance and persistence of an occasional wildflower.

He knew what made a play, and a red-blooded one. He wrote at length about the Jacobean taste for rampaging plots and blood-stained storylines. Long, chewy essays about Middleton and Webster and Tourneur show his understanding of public theatre and its need for sensation. So why are the veins of his own plays filled with sawdust? He knew about diversity of voices and he could hear human speech. *Prufrock* and *The Waste Land* are full of vignettes alarming in their truthfulness, mini-dramas where taut women and hesitant men interrogate each other before indulging in fumbling embraces. *The Waste Land* is a cornucopia of heard voices – the women in the pub talking about abortion, Phlebas the Phoenician, the lady at a game of chess, Tiresias himself – which come alive, vivid and distinct. So why in the plays does everyone share the same tone, a steadily cadenced philosophical despair? Why does Eliot the poet enliven characters with such deft economy, while Eliot the playwright is determined everyone should inhabit the same looping lingo of salon sadness?

In one work in the 1930s he wrote an exhilarating collage that could have pointed the way to a brave new theatre. *Sweeney Agonistes* is a jazz-infused melange of dialogue, song, and monologue. Sweeney – an elemental, streetwise figure who ghosts through several of Eliot's poems – shares crude wisdoms with two prostitutes, a couple of Canadian soldiers, and two American businessmen. Plot is absent, but a foreboding of violence tightens the air, hovering over music hall insights about 'Birth, and copulation, and death'. He relished the popular variety show, and that voice is alive through Sweeney, cross-fertilised with expressionist experiments. Eliot understood the music hall was no arena for sentimentality and preferred the comfortless to the soft. Brutality lurks – 'I knew a man once did a girl in' a repeated refrain.

The verse calls for a drumbeat to usher along its sinister tempo – jazz composer Johnny Dankworth provided it with one for a concert version. When I directed *Sweeney Agonistes* at school, though performers, myself, and audience understood little, it had a mesmeric effect. Rehearsing it with young, affectless actors was one of those epiphanic moments when we discovered the power of rhythm to transfix. We worked it incessantly simply for the pleasure of being in the swing. The Group Theatre (London), a self-consciously experimental outfit run by a Home Counties Diaghilev called Rupert Doone, staged a version in 1935 with macabre touches of Grand Guignol. Play and production could have been the marker for a new approach to theatre – witty, pleasurable, suggestive, and strangely sexy. So how and why did this expressionist populism curdle into the strangulated refinements of *The Cocktail Party*, *The Family Reunion*, *The Confidential Clerk*, and *The Elder Statesman*? It is barely necessary to describe the milieux of those later plays: most can be imagined by brief contemplation of the titles.

Sweeney Agonistes exemplifies another quality Eliot was replete in, though rarely praised for, and that is humour. The nailing of the hesitant, inauthentic neurotics in *Prufrock* and *The Waste Land* is as comic in its observation as tragic. The mock-heroic resolution to 'wear the bottoms of my trousers rolled' is pathetic and funny. Oscillating between the grandiloquence of the private fantasy voice and the bathos of the everyday is everywhere in these works, and delicious. This is the humour of observation; a blunter humour electrifies the dark murmuring of *Sweeney Agonistes*. Eliot's greatest theatrical success showcases more of his vocal variety, the bouncing nursery school rhythm and rhyme that underpin *Cats*, based on his *Old Possum's Book of Practical Cats* (though a success he never witnessed). Where did the playfulness and fun go when he sat down to compose plays?

His most successful long-form dramatic offering is an outlier, written not for a theatre but a temple, his *Murder in the Cathedral*, which opened the Canterbury Festival in 1935. A sacred setting is maybe best suited to the sanctity of the writing. A telling of the martyrdom of Thomas Becket, performed near the spot where it happened eight centuries before, *Murder in the Cathedral* blends choric voices with theological arguments. Over its course, it manages to give a convincing account of the agonies of choosing self-sacrifice over worldly gain. The hero searches for access to transcendence in a disappointing reality. Psychological acuity penetrates here, beside grown-up politics. Somehow, it still doesn't fly.

The proscenium plays inhabit the London drawing rooms, country libraries, and dining rooms of the wealthy and super-sophisticated. In these settings Eliot ventriloquises his poetry of unruffled despair. Characters called Lord Claverton, Sir Claude Mulhammer, Celia Copplestone and Lord Harry Monchensey are the protagonists we are supposed to feel for, stuck in their cloud of inauthenticity and yearning for a life of commitment. Little disrupts the smoothly unfurled music with which they analyse themselves and each other and the death of civilisation. *The Family Reunion* premiered in 1939 before being reworked, but the other plays were written in the late 1940s and 1950s. They occupy the same spiritual arena of dank hopelessness as Sartre was diagnosing across the Channel. Where the Gallic misery-guts opined that 'Hell is other people,' Eliot believed that hell is oneself.

He was swift to criticise his own work but seems to have seen its failure as an incorrect arrangement of material rather than a problem with the material itself. The verse sails serenely forwards without pause or disruption, trapping the reader, spectator, and player within its steady passage. Unlike the jagged eruptions of *The Waste Land*, which liberate and energise, the plays enclose in a stilled chamber. Weighty passions are turned over, many recycling Eliot's troubled past, but lulled and stifled by a cataclysmic uniformity of tone. Sometimes you slip into the cadence as into a warm bath and find yourself transported to places of philosophical sublimity. But if you fall outside the cadence, and it is as easy to slip out as in, then it just translates as mad people droning wintry platitudes and priestly paradoxes. Each page is studded with a startling phrase or bleak insight, but there is no modulation controlling how to introduce them.

The aspiration to bring poetry into the theatre was a heroic one. Ibsen felt the passion, as did Strindberg; Thomas Hardy made interminable attempts, and Oscar Wilde a disastrous one; at the same time as Eliot, Christopher Fry charmed and beguiled audiences with several verse works, including *The Lady's Not for Burning*. Each struggled to find an idiom which felt urgently necessary; a strong whiff of the archaic and literary neutered the vitality. Tony Harrison, a later dramatist who relished arenas and amphitheatres more than the proscenium, is the one poet of recent times who has managed to make the pulse of metre and the bump of rhyme work in the theatre.

In truth, they were fighting an artificial battle against an outmoded distinction between prose and poetry. Simultaneous to Eliot and Fry, the work of Tennessee Williams in the USA was introducing audiences to a whole new idea of stage poetics, which didn't involve knowledge of alexandrine metre. With T. S., though one can admire the attempt, it was an impossible endeavour to splice together the apparatus of Athenian tragedy – choruses, Furies and the like – and the manners of drawing room comedy. It is hard to reconcile characters tragically intoning 'O this' and 'O that' with a glass of sherry in their hand.

The plays share a singularity of voice and linearity of intent with the classic French drama of Racine and Corneille. Given their provenance, shortly before and mainly after the Second World War, there may have been a determined commitment to refurnish a language of civility and sophistication in a world that had exploded both. Along with the burnished phrases of Anouilh and the overdecoration of Fry, Eliot's plays may have proved an attractive clutching at gilt and refinement in the face of their rending by history. A Romanian friend told me that he'd argued with his sister as they ran from the tanks during the revolution against Ceaușescu. She was determined to clutch her handbag and wear her high heels. He wanted her to run faster; she wanted to retain her dignity. People can grab for luxury items at the oddest moments. 'O, reason not the need . . .' as Lear says.

The somatic effect may have been deliberate as well. In a world in disarray, the mesmeric High Church calm of these plays, their determination to tamp down eruptive rhythms, might have been a balm. Attending a very long Roman Catholic funeral recently, I was reminded how effective an instrument its complex, careful, and slow rituals are to anaesthetise an audience reeling in loss. Outside the church before the service, the family were bewildered by grief, but after an hour of a liturgy as inexorable and slow as continental drift, they were quietened and able to walk slowly forwards into a future. Eliot's plays may have cushioned blows in a similar fashion. *The Cocktail Party* was a hit in London and New York. It is hard for us to comprehend the real needs of eras gone by. Where *The Waste Land* and *Sweeney Agonistes* seem so much of the world they inhabit, and reflect it piercingly, these plays seem to inhabit a hermetic chamber. That airless place of genteel refinement may have been a comfort.

The joy of new plays has always been about bringing news to the table and finding fresh voices for its articulation. The delight of an unheard voice is not in listening to an idiosyncratic way of talking, it is in discovering a gateway and connection to the present, revealing how people speak and think. A fresh voice is not an insulated achievement, appreciating its own flavour, it is a new key to the door of right now. Few found a more direct route into the mental and emotional landscape of the 1920s and 1930s than Eliot, as revealed in *Prufrock* and *The Waste Land*. No one had a more penetrating understanding of what distressed and grieved minds in the 1940s, as made manifest in the *Four Quartets*. Sadly, that understanding couldn't translate into the drama.

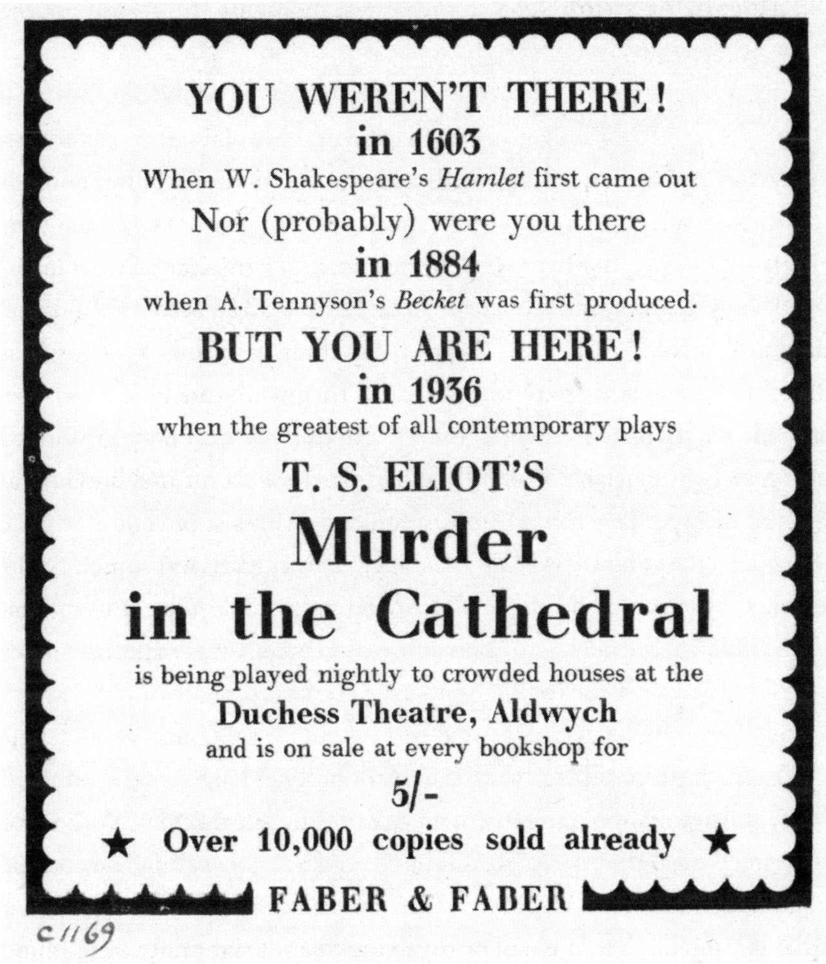

Faber leaflet, typically modest.

Langston Hughes
1901–1967

'If you want to die, be maladjusted, neurotic and psychotic, disappointed and disjointed . . . just write plays, go ahead' – the words of Langston Hughes to James Baldwin. Given the trials and tribulations Langston faced, they are not entirely surprising. His play *Mulatto: A Tragedy of the Deep South* should have been a crowning triumph. Opening on Broadway in 1935, it packed houses for almost a year. It was not the first full-length play by a black writer on Broadway; that honour went to *Appearances* by Garland Anderson in 1925, a story about a bellhop falsely accused of rape. But it was the first success on this scale, and one by a recognised poet and literary figure. Sadly, theme, tone, and content were hijacked by its white producer, who tipped a play cooking up a spicy stew of truth and nightmare into outright melodrama. And squeezed in an unnecessary rape scene for bad measure. The sensationalism was a crude denial of the quality of the writing.

The birth pains of black theatre in America were protracted and slow, rife with exploitation and frustrated desire. Theatres in New York were segregated until the 1930s. Blackface, the sad hangover of the minstrelsy tradition, remained a frequent occurrence onstage. But even the most racist sentiments are defeated by greed and the marketplace, and if there is an audience who will pay, producers and theatre owners will find a way. Musicals were the Trojan Horse black artists used to infiltrate Broadway. *In Dahomey*, a musical comedy written by and starring African Americans, was a hit in the 1900s and opened the door. *Shuffle Along*, a later musical, featuring Paul Robeson and Josephine Baker in small roles, was such a smash it was followed by nine more black musicals in three years. A new tradition was birthed here, rich with black talent, but the curation remained resolutely white.

To create a theatre not only performed by black actors but authored by an African American sensibility, there needed to be a greater revolution. This arrived in the form of the Harlem Renaissance, a movement which celebrated black lives and talent. Following the Great Migration from the South, and the arrival of others from the Caribbean diaspora, Harlem had become one of the most densely populated black spaces on earth. It required plays and a theatre to reflect its new modes of living. Starting uptown, a cultural energy was released and was determined to shatter stereotypes, increase visibility, and inspire. Black artists were not new, but their ability to collectivise and herald their own capacity was.

Many small and short-lived black theatre companies were created in an attempt to wrest the means of control. W. E. B. Du Bois founded *The Crisis* magazine in 1910, and from this he created Krigwa, a production entity housed in the basement of a public library, which lasted only three seasons but had a huge influence. They launched a playwriting competition, instructing applicants to 'Write about things as you know them . . . You do not have to confine your writings to the portrayal of beggars, scoundrels, and prostitutes; you can write about ordinary decent people if you want. On the other hand, do not fear the truth, plumb the depths . . . Be true, be sincere, be thorough, and do a beautiful job.' In *The Crisis*, Du Bois wrote a manifesto proclaiming African American theatre should be: '1) About us . . . 2) By us . . . 3) For us . . . 4) Near us'. The clarity and the line of attack inspire to this day.

Langston Hughes started a number of companies. He spent time in Spain and was in part inspired by the *teatro de urgencia* and the legacy of Lorca. With his own New York Suitcase Theater company, he wanted to produce a new translation of Lope de Vega's *Fuenteovejuna*, which Lorca's troupe had performed in 1933. Few of the companies lasted long: it would have been hard to contain the variety of Hughes's ambitions and voices within any single entity.

Mulatto, his disavowed success, is set in an old plantation mansion, described in an opening stage direction with classic proscenium detail. Twisted family dynamics play out in this pressure cooker between a white owner, his servant and mistress Cora, and their mixed-race children. One of them, Robert, has returned from college determined to act his white self and behave with the entitlement he has seen in his father. A toxic situation ensues, and the nakedly racist language and behaviour still wrench the gut. *Mulatto* flirts throughout with melodrama. In a thrilling finale to the first act, Robert walks with a stately pride out of his own front door, a forbidden portal for anyone who is not white. His father raises his cane, and then failing to use it, rushes to get his pistol. Cora sinks to her knees holding her master, and wails, 'He's our son, Tom. Remember, he's our son.' This might be ridiculous if it didn't ring true. As one of Hughes's early appreciators rightly countered in response to the slur of overheating: 'The South *is* melodramatic.' In a culture where violence – physical and psychological – is baked into the earth, it is hard for situations not to accelerate into extremity. A quiet rage thrums, as through all Langston's work. At one point the father asks Robert, 'What can you do about it?' After a scripted pause, he replies coolly, 'I'd like to kill all the white men in the world.' As the play closes, a white mob rampages into the home, seeking to lynch Robert. He foils them by taking his own life. Melodramatic certainly, overstated maybe not.

What is most surprising about *Simply Heavenly*, alongside *Little Ham* and others of his Harlem chronicle plays, is how tonally distinct it is from the seething angst of *Mulatto*, or from the brooding timbre of much of Hughes's poetry. A *jeu d'esprit*, it has a sassy swing and curve, sashaying and meandering its way through a flimsy plot while exploring the potentials of its own hybrid form. A play with music more than a musical, it wanders into blues songs or drifts into jazz before tipping back into speech. He was keen to escape categorisation, and his play comes ready-armed for critics who accuse it of pandering to types. When a self-appointed 'character' accuses the inhabitants of Paddy's Bar of being stereotypes, their biggest personality, Mamie, shoots back, 'Why, it's getting so colored folks can't do nothing no more without some other Negro calling you a stereotype. Stereotype, hah! If you like a little gin, you're a stereotype. You got to drink Scotch. If you wear a red dress, you're a stereotype. You got to wear beige or chartreuse. Lord have mercy, honey, do— don't like no blackeyed peas and rice! Then you're a down-home Negro for true – which I is – and proud of it! . . . I didn't come here to Harlem to get away from my people. I come here because there's more of 'em. I loves my race. I loves my people. Stereotype!' Here, as elsewhere in Hughes's free and easy lighter works, there is a sense of busting out of the straitjacket, pushing back against the heightened sensitivity of the academy, and refusing to give in to the cramps and confinements of self-censorship.

Jess Simple, the character at the heart of the play, appears in several works, and is a force buoyant. Colliding into misfortune on a regular basis, some mishaps of his own making, some accidental, he always gets back up. The community of Harlem swirls around his jittery centre, with lovers falling in and out of romances and each other's orbits, the mayhem accelerated by house parties and bar crawls and trips. All is held together by a swift reporting line of gossip. Proper jazz writing, with a loose sense of destination but a great deal of enjoying the journey, the stakes are kept laid-back and low, so you can drift in and out of scenes as if just passing through. Before long it feels as though you are within the community, relaxing in the same bars, spilling into the same rootin'-tootin' blues joints. Good-natured broad comedy, which floats its way to a happy ending. Who knew that was in Hughes's locker?

Living within racism is never far from the heart of the play, but the handling is so multifaceted it is impossible to settle on a single point of view. At one moment, there is impassioned complaint about racism in the American military, and then a spoof on racist complaint when Simple says that flying saucers never seem to appear to black folks. Here there is diagnosis of how racism comes to squat in the individual heart, and then over there a long wish-fulfilment fantasia on being a black general leading white troops. A firm moral base is never established, in keeping with the meandering haze of the plot. When it does dip into seriousness, it is all the more effective. Big questions about race, its uneasy dualities, and its never-ending pain are accommodated while keeping the swing easy.

In an entirely different register again was *Don't You Want to Be Free?*, a play–pageant Hughes wrote for his Suitcase Theater company. A bare stage at the beginning shows only a lynching tree and an auction block. An actor steps forward and says, 'We haven't got any scenery, or painted curtains, because we haven't got any money to buy them. But we've got something you can't buy with money, anyway. We've got faith in ourselves. And in you. So we're going to put on a show.' Along the way they walk you through what it means to be black in America. The narrative leaps from the first arrival of slaves in Jamestown in 1619, through the Civil War, sharecropping, Jim Crow and the Great Migration, to the Great Depression and the Harlem Renaissance. It culminates with the Harlem riot of 1935, when the residents stood against landlords and small business owners who discriminated against them. The fourth wall, the invisible barrier stretching across the proscenium, is barely present here as scene after fragmentary scene tells its story with urgent directness. Poems and hymns and spirituals punctuate the pageant, and keep it shored to a specifically black form. Here we see the minimalistic, free-flowing direct address style of the folk play, adapted for political purposes. Ending with a call to organise, to join unions and tenant leagues, and to combine with the white working class, we see the stirrings of later movements. It closes with a song as the cast join hands with each other and the audience, and all are exhorted to 'Fight, Fight, Fight'.

As with O'Neill, the achievement of Langston Hughes can only be measured with reference to the silence that preceded, though the historical vacuum for Hughes was more acute, given it was enforced by state and cultural racism. Yet, leaning on a tradition that had grown by increments over many decades in folk forms and the church pageant tradition, and blending it with the echoing jazz rhythms of his moment, there is a fertility and variety of invention here which astonishes.

The night is beautiful / So the faces of my people.
Langston Hughes (*c*.1925) by Winold Reiss

Dodie Smith
1896–1990

The epiphanies of the proscenium era are not marked out by grandeur or intensity; neither crescendos of slow-building pageantry, nor the climaxes of nail-biting cliffhangers. Quiet glimpses into privacy, they are the offbeat instances when life sidles onto the stage and takes up shy occupancy. Under the gaze of the Prozorov household in *Three Sisters*, the spinning top decelerates from transfixing whirl to toppling toy; Alison irons in *Look Back in Anger*, with Jimmy and Cliff swamped by the Sunday papers; Willie Loman is kept waiting in an outer office in *Death of a Salesman* – these are not grandiose but low-key invasions. One of the most potent examples of this diurnal magic occurs towards the end of Dodie Smith's *Call It a Day*.

One of those midsummer-madness plays that catch the shimmer of heatwave English days, when the sun power-boils a usually restrained psyche, *Call It a Day* opens with early morning tea and is finished by bedtime. Approaching evening, when a series of sun-baked passions have threatened to undermine the docility of the Hilton family, the scene moves to their central London back garden. Two young men lie bathing in the evening sun as they listen to a French tune 'Si oiseau j'étais' floating through a nearby window. One character, Martin, we know and have followed throughout the narrative. The other, Alistair, has just arrived, and will have fleeted away within a page or two. At quick speed we deduce through deft, oblique exchanges that he is gay, that he is silently and painfully in love with Martin, and that he will soon be betrayed and forgotten. Yet, while he listens to the music, and looks at the object of his adoration in the London twilight God is good . . . 'Queer how some moments crystallize themselves for one. I believe when I'm an old man I shall remember this garden and that tune.'

Surprisingly, another moment shortly after surpasses this. The housekeeper, Mrs Milson, is leaving through the garden, now empty of everyone but the paterfamilias. A seemingly imperturbable chartered accountant, Roger has been sent into a spiral by the attentions of a young actress and sits alone in the failing light. The certainties of the steady life he woke up with that morning have evanesced by cocktail hour. Mrs Milson, surprised by Roger's lonely presence, stumbles and drops her bag of groceries. Out tumbles an unseemly mass of food, including an 'ancient cabbage, several apples and an old bone'. They scrabble on hands and knees to gather everything up, their faces illuminated by a shaft of light from the kitchen door.

MRS MILSON	Thank you, sir. Just a few things cook had left over. It was me or the dustbin.
ROGER	You or the dustbin.
MRS MILSON	If I hadn't had them, they'd have gone in the dustbin. I don't like waste.
ROGER	Quite right.
MRS MILSON	(*retrieving the decrepit cabbage*) Course, they're not really fit for human consumption. But I thought they might do for my husband.
ROGER	(*returning a bruised apple*) That's the lot, I think.
MRS MILSON	Sorry to have troubled you.
ROGER	Not at all.

Class, power structures, disadvantaged but charitable lives, and privileged but lonely ones – all squeezed into a strange and numinous moment. Many may prefer impassioned speeches about politics or high-camp witticisms or moments of manufactured suspense, but for me, the real achievement of the proscenium theatre was allowing these loaded glimpses into the unruly triviality of life to become fleetingly sacred.

Actors love 'business', moments of beguiling ordinariness with kettles or drinks cabinets or new shoes, when they can disappear into the rituals of domestic life and the audience can follow the liturgy. Dodie Smith's work is full of such busy-ness. Family members and staff scurry around, criss-crossing hither and thither, attending to minute crises. We share in concerns about securing sandwiches for lunch or a loan for a business or cocoa for a child without wondering quite how or why. In the plays of the interwar period, in the shadow of titanic loss, with portraits of lost family members hanging on the walls and a new catastrophe looming ahead, the value of these small interactions acquires precious weight.

What surprises in Smith's work is her easy eroticism. This is not a matter of shedding clothes but more a shamelessness about unbridled female desire. In *Call It a Day*, a daughter and an actress are unabashed in expressing their wants, and a mother and a secretary tremble on the brink of revealing theirs too. All within a milieu where complaisant wives are happy for husbands to roam, sometimes lending them out on sexual errands to cheer up friends, and enjoying affairs of their own, which they take in their stride like a health cure. The hunger within these women is palpable. The actress jabs her pencil into a desk in frustration as her target stalls. She states herself tired of appearing in 'everlasting drawing-room comedies', and no longer wants to play 'pretty little parts in pretty little plays'. There is nothing pretty in the frustrations and cravings Smith gives licence to roam.

Call It a Day played over five hundred performances in the West End in 1935 before successfully transferring to Broadway and then becoming a film. There is also a delicious abridged radio version, starring the Broadway husband-and-wife legends Alfred Lunt and Lynn Fontanne. Dodie Smith is another of the female playwrights who dominated the West End in the interwar period and whose work was later dismissed as essentially trivial. She deserves more. It is doubtful she minded particularly, since she earned enormous acclaim in the theatre, and wrote two novels, one of which – *I Capture the Castle* – was taken to the hearts of the British public, and the other, *The Hundred and One Dalmatians*, became part of the iconography of children's literature across the world.

Born into respectability, her father's death when she was three led to an itinerant life parcelled out to different family members. Genteel vagrancy led, as it often does, to the theatre, and after training at RADA, her early career was filled with small roles in touring and repertory companies. Her first play, *Autumn Crocus*, written while she was a toy buyer at Heal & Son, went on under the pseudonym C. L. Anthony. The acclaim, and the discovery of her true identity by journalists, led to the unedifying newspaper headline, 'Shopgirl Writes Play'.

A Chekhov inheritance is transparent in Smith's best-regarded play, *Dear Octopus*, where admiration tips over into homage. What could charitably be called tropes from the Russian might be described more precisely as copying. Three sisters and an unwelcome sister-in-law sparring is not unfamiliar. Nor is the setting: a semi-grand house outside a large conurbation. A character with a neurotic obsession with flies feels like an imitative quirk. The strongest narrative tease in the piece is the difficulty a couple have in getting engaged, both sides too embarrassed and awkward to force the issue, which apes Lopakhin and Varya from *The Cherry Orchard*. In another scene, the characters all stop still in an upstairs nursery and hear church bells ringing from afar, just as the assembled playgoers hearken to music across a lake in *The Seagull*.

A family and its add-ons gather for a golden wedding anniversary. Their frequent comings and goings in a hectic first act prompt one character to observe, 'the house is restless'. In this very franticness we see the essence as well as the trappings of Chekhov as Smith captures the inability of a family, unreconciled to itself, to sit still. Setting a table in the third act is an action the three sisters share, and the simple domestic ritual calms the nerves of the family and allows what resolutions are possible. There is little of moment here, but much of life. No wars begin or end, but a family and their satellites figure out how to be good to each other. What else is necessary?

Characteristic of the age, time weighs heavy. J. B. Priestley with his quasi-scientific theorems and Eliot with his time-inside-out-and-back-to-front-and-upside-down versifying seem to have shared this obsession. Here the debate funds some relaxed thoughts about, 'Time and chance and love and all that' from one character, and a sense of urgency from another: 'You can't play ostriches with time in this house.' In discussion of the soul, the matriarch reassures that 'Nothing lovely can ever really be lost,' and goes on to quote Ecclesiastes: 'That which hath been is now; and that which is to be hath already been; and God requireth that which is past.' Such questions felt all the more acute in an age tormented by ghosts from the recent past and frightened by more to be made in a near future. The present tense had an amplified sense of the precious.

The final subject of the play is the dear octopus of the title, the family, 'from whose tentacles we never quite escape, nor, in our inmost hearts, ever quite wish to'. Though it explores unhappy dynamics with a British accent – 'Don't start to cry or you'll simply wreck your face!' – this is a family like any other, confusing the boundaries between hate and love, struggling to solve simple misunderstandings, and allowing them to fester. At the play's close, the awkward surviving son of the First World War (played by John Gielgud in the first production) makes a toast to kith and kin. The family, he says, is 'like nearly every British institution . . . adaptable; it bends, it stretches, but it never breaks'. The battered tribe raises its glasses to 'those we have lost and those still to come'.

The sense of fragility and foreboding in the play was justified. Despite the usual spate of condescending notices from the chaps, it ran for almost a year, before the run was halted by the outbreak of hostilities in September 1939. War could only pause it. After a short run in the provinces, it returned to the West End for two further long engagements. There are many reasons why the public might have felt the need to sit with this clan, but foremost was perhaps the reassurance in seeing decency, however troubled and complex, made manifest.

A smattering of British insouciance would have added comfort. One character's response as to why he had never sought high political office . . . 'You would be surprised, for instance, what a very large number of shelves I have put up and an almost equally large number I have taken down.'

Broadway bound.
Dodie Smith at Waterloo on her way to New York, 1937

Thornton Wilder
1897–1975

To suffer from too many productions seems an odd fortune, but if a play has a strong appeal to those who might perform it less well than it deserves, a peculiar fate is sealed. No play has suffered from this more than Thornton Wilder's *Our Town*, a play which on any given day is almost certainly being performed somewhere, from Vladivostok to Tierra del Fuego.

Wilder's imaginary New England town of Grover's Corners, crafted from fancy and memory and set in the earliest part of the twentieth century, speaks to small towns everywhere in every age. And illuminates that corner of everyone's inner geography imprinted by their first neighbourhoods. Originally considered a local American experience, it turned out to be an international one, gliding on air currents of recognition across cultures, time zones, and languages. The first foreign play to be performed in Berlin after the Second World War, it became part of the process of rebinding a shattered community. Yet for all its international prospering, its spiritual home is the USA. Wilder's nephew once had the dream of organising a reunion for every American actor – professional or amateur – who had acted in the play, but he soon realised there was no stadium large enough to contain them.

The play boasts the perfect variety of roles for a community group and, crucially, a simplicity of staging. Although a cosy and comfy aura has settled around this work, Wilder thought himself a radical modernist. He read his work aloud to Gertrude Stein and Alice B. Toklas in Paris; his other signature play, *The Skin of Our Teeth*, riffs on elements of Joyce's *Finnegans Wake*; and he strove to emulate the 'theatre-is-theatrical' stylings of Pirandello and Brecht. When *Our Town* opened on Broadway in 1938, it was greeted as the most radical experiment thus far in proscenium theatre. Wilder's ambition was to abandon the fourth wall and allow free communication between actors and audience. The mode of address, especially by the stage manager who ambles through the play stitching it together, is as direct as in the Shakespearean theatre Wilder loved. To summon up the details of Grover's Corners, it is specified sternly that there is to be no scenery, no curtain or props. Just a few chairs and benches, and nothing fancy to disturb the New England Shaker simplicity. Language, plain and dry, is all that is needed, alongside truthful acting and, above all, the imagination of the audience. The chorus at the beginning of *Henry V* asks spectators to participate in the creation of 'two mighty monarchies' and 'the very casques/That did affright the air at Agincourt'; Wilder invites collaboration on a more domestic plane.

The side effect of these instructions, particularly the absence of props, has been an outbreak of cataclysmic mime across the planet. Miming is an exquisitely demanding technical skill. Even in the best of productions of *Our Town*, it can be a trial watching experienced performers pretend to knead dough, shell peas, or play a church organ. In an amateur production, one can enter a confused dissociative state as you try to work out what this character is attempting to suggest with his twisted fingers, or that couple are up to playing a game of vertical Twister. When I was eight, I appeared in my local town's amateur production. I thought my version of a cheery youth on his paper round hurling the daily gazette to each porch passed muster, but I probably looked like I was suffering from a nervous spasm. I certainly had no idea what the grown-ups were up to as they flailed and floundered in the air around them. Wilder had little idea what he was setting loose.

The play passes through the rituals of a single day in Act I, before skipping years to concentrate on love and marriage in Act II, then contemplating death and the afterlife in the final act. We meet a gaggle of small-town archetypes, individuated through interactions chosen to feel both familiar and particular. In his early career, Wilder trained himself by writing a series of three-minute plays for three characters, an apprenticeship which taught the technique of compressing complex characters and dynamics into nuggets. His vision is shot through with empathy.

The play was written out of the Great Depression and first performed on Broadway in 1938. Wilder knew and cared for struggling families and desperate individuals. Relishing the minutiae of everyday existence, he illuminates human nature through precise observation of individual lives, creating a tapestry that could evoke the small Somerset town I performed the play in as a child, or the childhood home in Wisconsin he remembered, or your town, or anyone's.

Yet the play is not only written on the micro level, it also frequently pulls focus wider and with a dizzying speed. Characters give brief lectures on the geology of the rock formations on which they perch, the social and political history of the town (albeit favouring the Protestant colonisers in a way that now feels problematic), and giddily open out broader vistas to the universe. Wilder wished to write with 'an archaeologist's eyes combining the view of the telescope and the view of the microscope'. The round of the village's day is created against the slow turn of the stars. This expansive landscape does not dwarf the characters or their small actions but makes their definiteness, within a cosmic silence, both fragile and touchingly robust. He described *Our Town* to Stein and Toklas as 'a little play with all the big subjects in it; and it's a big play with all the little things of life lovingly impressed into it'.

A melancholy runs through his work, a sense of searching for life elsewhere, which could be explained by his being a twin who survived the birth that took his double. His brother, Amos, later said that being a twinless twin haunted him. A world view expanding beyond rural America could be attributed to his peripatetic childhood, which included a stint in Hong Kong, where his father was Consul General. The strangeness of *Our Town*, its fascination with the stars above and the ground beneath, alongside an excitement about the modest quietude of daily life, possibly owes something to the cosmic harmonics around him as a child in East Asia. The play evinces a yearning for stillness and rootedness, which may have come from a childhood spent on the move. His primary comfort was in voracious reading, with excursions into Shakespeare and the Greeks, but always from a home base of the King James Bible and *The Pilgrim's*

Progress, that primer for the Puritan obsession with orderly lives lived with modest ambition. Later in life he read drama with avidity, working his way through Ibsen's works and becoming so taken with J. M. Barrie that he read entire plays out loud to a barn full of cows. Whether from this experience or others, he resolved that 'the whole purport of literature . . . is the notation of the heart'. A rich literary background, it worked beside the eye of a man who studied everything around him. When asked of his technique, Wilder said simply, 'I looked and I listened.'

Our Town is a confounding blend of the banal and the odd, an unknowability which has kept it close to many hearts. The final act features characters we have come to know gathered in a graveyard for a funeral, alongside the ghosts of many we met earlier, who are now in the Tibetan Buddhist state of bardo, the liminal zone between death and rebirth. They flit and chatter and worry and wait for clarity, much in the manner of the transitional souls in George Saunders's *Lincoln in the Bardo*. One of them makes a despairing attempt to reintegrate herself into the temporal plane, only to realise the impossibility. This is Zen territory for American drama, and particularly for a piece often accused of folksy sentimentality. Only a bold sensibility could pull it off, and render the ghosts' concerns over eternity as unremarkable as the shelling of peas earlier. The stretching of our imagination before, the way we have filled empty spaces with horses and milk bottles and ink pens, opens the audience up to wilder fantastical jumps. The close proximity of death affirms Wilder's lesson that 'Each life can be felt to be inestimably precious though we all too seldom realise it at the time.'

As well as this generous parcelling out of dignity, there is respect for community. The small town or big village, that human unit that links those within it while remaining large enough to excite ambitions and curiosity, is an entity which provokes magnetic nostalgia, evoking memories of connectedness. Such feelings have an added piquancy now in the West as we see towns neglected and communities torn up and high streets deadened. From the perspective of our wastelands of fragmentation, *Our Town* serves as a rebuke from an age that valued community alongside the individual. There is nothing easy in the world Wilder presented – Grover's Corners is dully conventional and life is studded with pain and disappointment – but no matter, nothing is missed so sorely as belonging.

Classic mime-fail. Teacups?
Frank Craven, Martha Scott and John Craven in *Our Town* on Broadway, 1938

Lillian Hellman
1905–1984

History seems to chase some individuals around, or maybe they just have a nose for where it is kicking off. Lillian Hellman was one such. An unlikely blend of two distinct brands of aristocracy, New York Jewish and Louisiana Southern, she found her way into a series of vortices where history was dancing the quickstep. A member of the communist party in the 1930s, she remained pro-Soviet longer than many. She travelled to Spain during the Spanish Civil War and, as bombs fell on the capital, broadcast to the USA on Madrid Radio. During the Second World War, she reported on various anti-fascist fronts. According to her memoir *Pentimento*, she also delivered a tranche of cash to a friend in Berlin, travelling through Nazi Germany as a Jewish woman. After the war, she was dragged into the HUAC hearings – a blight afflicting Odets, Brecht, Miller and many others – and, after refusing to name names, was blacklisted by Hollywood.

Quite the charge sheet for a sensational life. Or it would be if it had all happened. Exactly how much did is questionable. Hellman later downgraded the import of her engagement in communism to joining a group 'sitting around a room talking of current events or discussing the books they had read'. Her tales of derring-do from the Spanish Civil War were disputed by Martha Gellhorn and Ernest Hemingway, both there at the same time. Gellhorn later claimed Hellman had waited for all the witnesses to die before making up a bunch of stories. The journey through Nazi Germany described in her memoir was later turned into the Oscar-winning film *Julia*, though the chapter describing her actions turned out to be part fictional and part purloined from the courage of an acquaintance. The director Fred Zinnemann said of her, 'Lillian Hellman in her own mind owned half the Spanish Civil War, while Hemingway owned the other half. She would portray herself in situations that were not true.

An extremely talented, brilliant writer, but she was a phony character, I'm sorry to say. My relations with her were very guarded and ended in pure hatred.' It is hard to dispute the accounts of the HUAC hearings since they were recorded and documented, though the extent of the blacklisting is open to discussion. All the blurring of fact and fiction climaxed in a long feud with Mary McCarthy, another public intellectual, who famously said of her, 'every word she writes is a lie, including "and" and "the"'.

Hellman was an assiduous creator of her own myth and, in relation to autobiography, she probably followed the director John Ford's dictum: 'When the legend becomes fact, print the legend.' Hellman's rackety love life included a turbulent thirty-year affair with Dashiell Hammett. Within their union, they fashioned a lifestyle as mythic as her adventures: living on a private island off the coast of Connecticut; countless parties at which Hellman, cigarette holder between her teeth, was the centre of attention; clusters of bohemians hooked on martinis and morphine; some hardcore transgressive politics to add danger; refugee and émigré intellectuals to add spice; and a lot of world-weary, raucous laughter. A mythic ideal of twentieth-century renegade artistic life. The fact that failure and pain walked alongside it deepened the textures, as did Hammett's long and agonised decline from lung cancer. Hellman was a storyteller and to judge her for fabrication is maybe to miss her point. She was there to live it large, and if life sometimes fell short, imagination filled the gap.

There is a huge amount to enjoy within the plays, and many did. *The Children's Hour*, *Little Foxes*, and *Watch on the Rhine* all proved massive commercial hits on Broadway. Such success was never going to escape censure. Something must be wrong if audiences were enjoying themselves so much, and a familiar barrage was aimed at her, the most reliable critique being her deployment of melodrama and elements of the well-made play. Despite this being appropriate to the architecture and the audience's expectations, indulging it was deemed bad form by the *sérieux*. Hellman's plays show a devilish amount of craft, storytelling filled with suspense that keeps you riveted. With a little extra gangster bravado, perhaps borrowed from her lover Hammett, she ramps up the tension in her work to explosive violence and death. For such shameless populism she loses points with the academy. Creaky old terms from the Eugène Scribe armoury are rolled out to punish her. She is condemned for using in *The Children's Hour* a *clou*, the small object on which a narrative pivots, in this case a stolen bracelet, and the denouement is denigrated as a clunky *scène à faire*, the well-made play's obligatory scene.

Hellman seems to have been judged to higher expectations because she was on the left, because she was an intellectual, and because she was a woman. If she had been a dour paragon of dullard artistry she might have won more esteem. The fact she wrote rip-roaring stories was letting the side down. She herself loathed classifications, declaring 'I don't like labels and isms. They are for people who raise or lower skirts because that's the thing you do for this year.' For her, one form was as good as another: 'There are a thousand ways to write, and each is as good as the other if it fits you.'

Adjacent to the problem may have been her fascination with evil. She disclaimed this, denying she wrote about good and bad people and claiming she only wrote of 'Goodness and badness'. This seems a tad disingenuous. Hellman fashioned some of the best villains since the glory days of mustachio-twizzling. Regina Giddens in *The Little Foxes*, the scheming Hubbard sister, who stands stock still as her disabled husband crawls for the medication that can save him, is not backwards in coming forwards on the wicked front, as Bette Davis on film made manifest. Her avaricious and deceitful brothers try to match her in malice, though they come short. Mary, the girl who wreaks havoc in *The Children's Hour*, is the epitome of the motiveless malignity of an angry child. Count Teck de Brancovis in *Watch on the Rhine* is a study in North America's suspicion of Old Europe and its phoney aristocracy, a blackmailing, wheeler-dealing psychopath who lives down to all expectations. As a rogues' gallery, this collection takes some beating.

Onstage, there is a modern tendency to downgrade moral polarity in an attempt to find – or at least understand – the good in everyone. For anyone motivated by a desire not to sink into the dumb binaries of social media and the internet, there is a virtue in this. For Lillian Hellman, a communist who witnessed the left massacred in Spain, a Jewish woman who watched the unopposed rise of the Nazis in Germany and a sympathetic movement in the USA, and a patriotic American who saw her country torn apart by McCarthyism, there was perhaps less grey. For her, a black-and-white morality was not simplistic, it was what was sometimes in her face. Hellman knew there were bad people among us, and made capital from the energy a villain could engender.

Her moral wrath was directed not only at the sinners, but more savagely at those who stood by. As one character states in *The Little Foxes*, 'There are people who eat the earth and eat all the people on it like in the Bible with the locusts. Then there are people who stand around and watch them eat it. Sometimes I think it ain't right to stand and watch.' *The Searching Wind*, set among the American diplomatic community, is a damning indictment of the complacency of those who watched the fascist takeover in Italy and the rise of Nazism in Germany without thinking it could impact their lives. Hellman later disowned the play's explicit politics and admitted, 'I meant only to write about nice, well-born people who, with good intentions, helped to sell out a world.' The most contemptible of her characters are those who wave evil through, turning their eyes away.

Hellman saw McCarthyism as an outbreak of circus horror, the oppressions of the state leading to behaviour squalid and comical. She wrote with wry amusement of those who telephoned old friends the night before they testified against them to ask for their toolset back. Her milieu was suddenly 'full of clowns talking their heads off, apologising, inventing sins to apologise for. And other clowns, liberals, who just took to the hills. Ugh, clowning is a hard thing to write about. Few people acted large enough for drama or pleasant enough for comedy.'

Subsequent commentators who didn't live through that roiling turbulence have condemned her for ideological confusion, one primly upbraiding her for failing 'to fully comprehend the subtleties and complexities of ideologies of the time'. Hellman lived in the world, felt its battles fiercely, and responded with matching ferocity. Who ever gets these things right? When she appeared before HUAC, under the pressure of threats which entwined friends, collaborators and her lover, she defied the committee and refused to speak about others. She defined her position clearly: 'to hurt innocent people whom I knew many years ago in order to save myself is, to me, inhuman and indecent and dishonorable. I cannot and will not cut my conscience to fit this year's fashions.' To see prim critics under the same pressure would be illuminating.

Few heroes people her plays, to counter the pervasive villainy. Hers is a world vulnerable to the predatory actions of the venal. But there are stumbling moments of goodness and small glimpses of solidarity. Much bad energy falls softly into the dissipating cushion of everyday survival. In *The Children's Hour*, the two central characters are morally redeemed at the end, though only after one has committed suicide. In *The Little Foxes*, Regina emerges triumphant but loses her daughter, who, like Nora in *A Doll's House*, slams the door on her past. In *Watch on the Rhine*, the family come together to conceal a murder committed by an anti-Nazi. The pivot for this moral choice is a short speech made by the matriarch, Fanny. She remembers what her husband told her before he died: 'He said, "Fanny, the complete American is dying." I said what do you mean, although I knew what he meant. I always knew. "A complete man," he said, "is a man who wants to know. He wants to know how fast a bird can fly, how thick is the crust of the earth, what made Iago evil, how to plough a field. He knows there is no dignity to a mountain, if there is no dignity to man. You can't put that in a man, but when it's there, put your trust in him."'

What a curious mix Hellman was, the disdain of the wannabe aristocrat and the vulnerable upward glance of the honest socialist. When she remembered the 1930s and the days of hope, she thought of much foolishness, but also of a time when goodness flourished. 'There were always X number of clowns, X number of simple-minded fools, X number of fashionables who just went along with what was being said and done, but there were also remarkable people, people of belief, people willing to live by their beliefs.' Her sense of the potential in people, and of their capacity for dignity, however obscured by the iniquities of the wicked, makes for drama – well-made drama – of effect.

Feel the evil. The Hubbards, one of the great villain families.
Tallulah Bankhead, Charles Dingle, Carl Benton Reid and Dan Duryea, *The Little Foxes* on Broadway, 1941

J. B. Priestley
1894–1984

'Epataying', presumably spoken with a long Southern drawl, is the verb Lillian Hellman extrapolated from the French phrase *épater la bourgeoisie* – to get under the skin of the middle class. Perversely, this was one of the prime missions of the proscenium: to make its audience feel uneasy about itself and accentuate a queasy feeling of unearned good fortune. In Shakespeare's farewell to his vocation speech, at the end of (almost) his last play, *The Tempest*, he says of the spectators, 'As you from crimes would pardoned be', assuming their universal guilt. Hamlet speaks of 'guilty creatures sitting at a play', when he is setting his snare for Claudius with his play 'The Mousetrap'. Proscenium plays were often set up to provoke these feelings of penitence, a shame more acute in those with more benefits than most. Few have approached the task of 'epataying' with the same blunt directness as the pipe-smoking sage of Yorkshire J. B. Priestley.

In work after work, Priestley holds up for inspection the venality of the well-to-do. Frequently we see a group takedown when either an outsider or the feral dynamics of the group itself work their way from character to character, exposing their flaws. In *Dangerous Corner*, a chance remark leads to a group unpeeling of their collective responsibility for the death of a friend and colleague. In the style of a sinister parlour game, each is shown to have behaved shabbily and covered up misdeeds. In *I Have Been Here Before*, a group of guests in a Yorkshire hotel, thrown together by a manipulated fate, watch the threads between them and their self-esteem dissolve. Most famously, in *An Inspector Calls*, a ghostly figure of moral inquisition, unsubtly named Goole, strips bare the pretences and sins of one after another of the Birling family. Occasionally, in Dickensian fashion, young women reveal charity and hope, but rarely sufficient to offset the cloud of cruelty that envelops the whole.

Successful at a young age, and seemingly in permanent pursuit of the honorific 'national treasure', J. B. cultivated the aura of the avuncular, sensible Yorkshireman – the permanently affixed pipe adding a seasoning of wise benevolence. As a public persona this reaped the reward of public affection, but any form of immersion in the plays reveals not just a loathing of the bourgeoisie, but a misanthropy which can feel hot to the touch. A journalist from a young age, with a quick and absorbing eye, Priestley saw much to tip a man towards rage. In 1916, he was buried alive by a trench mortar, and after months in hospital was sent back to the frontline, where he was gassed. The war, he said, had 'sliced my generation into sausage-meat held above a swill bucket'. In the 1930s, he decided to investigate the impact of the Depression at first hand and wrote a travelogue, *English Journey*, giving witness to the many methods for coping with hardship. His first successful novel, *The Good Companions*, which he turned into a stage play, recounts how an unemployed man goes in search of work, joining a travelling variety show, rather like the Crummles outfit from *Nicholas Nickleby*.

The inequity of the era between the wars is often contrasted in Priestley's sensibility with a nostalgia for a softer and kinder Edwardian age. Looking back is apposite for a writer who loved to play games with time, and who often seems to be a sort of socialist Dr Who, slipping between fixed points in a multiverse. *Time and the Conways* travels forwards and backwards in time to explore collisions of hope and reality; *I Have Been Here Before* extends déjà vu into his characters' ability to forecast their own fates. Both *Dangerous Corner* and *An Inspector Calls* feature similar games of temporal slippage. The plays were designed to exemplify the chronological theses of J. W. Dunne and P. D. Ouspensky, two speculative esoterics trying to find philosophical matches for the new understandings of time and space that physics had fostered. In his maturity, Priestley formulated his own pet theory in his extended essay *Man and Time*, which placed faith in precognitive dreaming and how other dimensions linked past, present, and future. This approach, alive to the science of the age, added a ludic touch to stories that could otherwise be mired in a mechanistic working out of sour truths.

Priestley admired Chekhov (who didn't?) and aspired to the same neutral recording of life, but his honesty tended towards the bitter. Illusions were always there to be torn down, and the flagellation of the middle class can seem diminishing. As part of a commercial contract with an audience it has a touch of cynical manipulation, the remorseless selling of by-the-yard bespoke self-loathing. *An Inspector Calls* pursues its argument with aplomb, but the fact every member of the family is venal, snobbish, and neglectful of the reality of others is reductive and finally strains credulity. Truth can also be kind.

Responsibilities as well as privileges. J. B. Priestley at work in his Highgate study, London, 1940

Priestley was no doubt aware of this bitterness, and sometimes fought against it. He always leaves room for a call to his characters and the audience to be better, to take account of their actions. Early in the war, he gave a series of radio broadcasts, *Postscripts*, full of a gentle wisdom articulating a creed of pulling together, demonstrating an eccentric and humane socialism. At its peak, the series had sixteen million listeners, and for many did as much as Churchill to define what the British were fighting for. He preached the creed with messianic fervour in *An Inspector Calls*: 'We don't live alone. We are members of one body. We are responsible for each other. And I tell you that the time will soon come when, if men will not learn that lesson, then they will be taught it in fire and blood and anguish.'

Agatha Christie
1890–1976

My first visit to the West End was not auspicious. In September 1979, at the age of fifteen, I sped with my family in an old Renault 5 to attend the opening night of a new play by Tony Shaffer, directed by my father. The glitterati were gathering at Her Majesty's Theatre, before it became colonised forever by *The Phantom of the Opera*. The play had a title which might not pass muster in our present day – *The Case of the Oily Levantine*. Shaffer had enjoyed one of the last monumental successes of the proscenium era with his twisty-turny whodunnit/who-is-it *Sleuth*, which ran for an extraordinary five years. His fortune was augmented by screenplays for film adaptations of Agatha Christie's *Poirot* books. *Levantine* was a meta-theatrical parody of the Christie opus, and of the supposedly stuffy shows that memorialised her work.

Even for a callow youth, it didn't take long to work out something was up. From the first syllable, a cold wind of disapproval gusted through the auditorium. Every joke died, every shock failed to raise an eyebrow, and each plot twist was greeted with a collective shrug. The decision to hate had preceded commencement. Our family barked with mad laughter in an auditorium that felt like a frigid mausoleum. At the interval, people muttered, 'Not my cup of tea', and avoided the eyes of those involved; at the concluding party in the theatre bar, the few who remained manically blabbed about anything but the show. I took the exit route from embarrassment most swiftly chosen by fifteen-year-olds and got howlingly drunk. Somehow I got to the after-party, where I passed out, waking to the arrival of the morning papers, which had been taxied over from Fleet Street. The reviews were uniquely savage, and the party did the time-honoured backwards flip from celebration to embittered wake. Looking back, it is a mystery why I chose the profession.

There is a collection of reasons not to try and parody the sainted

Agatha. The plays, as with the books, hover deliciously close to self-parody themselves, and there is only a wafer-thin space in which to manoeuvre. They are saved from the ridiculous by her reserves of dry, humourless solemnity. People occasionally try to ascribe a humour to her, which seems like much wasted effort. Her achievement is her patent sincerity, and the earnestness with which she proceeded. There are reasons why there is a statue of her in the middle of London's theatre district, why one of her plays is the longest-running show in the world, and why she is without doubt the most successful female playwright of all time. You mess with her at your peril.

In the 1950s, when the angry young men were storming the barricades of British culture, Agatha Christie had three plays on in the West End – *Witness for the Prosecution*, *The Mousetrap* and *Spider's Web*. One of them is still playing more than seventy years later, and another has been playing for the last eight in a revived production at the old County Hall in London. *Look Back in Anger* had a short and ill-attended run in a small theatre, the Royal Court. Arnold Wesker's trilogy played similarly brief runs. Yet those are the plays studied and declared to define the taste of the age. The Christie plays, which tens of thousands have witnessed and been obsessed with, are ushered off the literary roll call as if they are a collective embarrassment. Feminists condemn her as though her success was some sort of sinister collusion with the patriarchy, while the chauvinists in the academy can barely mention her name. The British have a peculiar relationship with success. One well-regarded critic once said he thought it 'highly dangerous if creators and critics surrender to the capricious tyranny of popular opinion'. George Bernard Shaw was on the same track, declaring, when attacked for disliking a successful Gallic boulevard comedy: 'Forty million Frenchmen can't be right.' What if they can be? And what if popular opinion is sharper and more radical than the gatekeepers?

The Mousetrap is a terrific show, which I am happy to have attended twice. Its appeal at present is as much institutional as dramatic. Watching the audience provides much of the pleasure, their excitement before, their interval deductions, and their contentment on departing, though it is a satisfaction spiked with a dash of Angostura bitters. Opening in London on 25 November 1952, the run was only interrupted briefly by Covid-19 and keeps on going. Christie often footled around with material between different forms, and *The Mousetrap* was no different. It larva'd as a radio play, then chrysalis'd as a novella, before butterflying into a play. The producers cannily opened it in the diminutive Ambassadors Theatre, and the presence of two stars, a young Richard Attenborough and his wife, Sheila Sim, made it the hottest of tickets. Both decisions helped to kickstart the run, though its gargantuan longevity depended on other factors.

Exceptionally modelled for its own moment, it spoke to post-war audiences drained by austerity. The period setting is flatly specific and specifically flat, evoking the world of rationing and restriction. Both times I saw it, the experience brought Proustian memories of that very British concoction, brown soup. (How many other dishes are named so suspiciously after a colour?) The setting feels pervasively beige, a country house, but not the gay, aristocratic type of the 1930s. The Second World War has broken luxury and decadence with an iron fist, and the family are trying to make a go of a guest house. The lady of the house crosses the stage with a vacuum cleaner. Instead of mixing cocktails, they wrestle with the fuse box and scurry out to feed the chickens. All these particulars pressed buttons of recognition for a middle-class audience going through straitened times. The familiar claustrophobia of the country house pertains, but with an extra patina of a class displaced, and a general mistrust of a new and uncertain settlement. For the present-day audience, it is like the opening of a time capsule containing pearl necklaces, tinned goods, and revolvers.

Beyond the specifics of time and place, there is the timeless pleasure of a detective story. One of the foundation stones of Western literature *Oedipus Tyrannus* is a whodunnit where the prime detective turns out, to his own revulsion, to be the culprit. Ancient Greece may seem an odd comparator for Agatha Christie, but not when it is remembered what an ardent amateur archaeologist she was, and how ancient history was another source of mystery she excavated for buried crime. As with the Sophocles, and with any great detective story, the discovery is one of genuine horror, a crime that crashes through taboos and the bounds of human decency. The crux of *The Mousetrap* is a backstory involving pitiless and hideous child abuse. When it invades the narrative, you realise that what you thought was pulp or pap has a furnace of outrage at its core. There would have been a particularly sharp resonance for a generation who had survived the war, and especially those who had entrusted their children for much of that time to foster parents. *The Mousetrap* plays on profound insecurities.

Much popular art has darkness and perversity at its centre. *Peter Pan*, a Christmas staple for over a hundred years, doesn't bear too much examination. Somehow its loaded tale of pirates preying on abducted children is nodded through, and its profound strangeness forgiven within its populism. Andrew Lloyd Webber is another case in point. *Aspects of Love* is one of the oddest stories I have ever witnessed, detailing a man's rather excessive admiration for his daughter. *The Phantom of the Opera* is no slouch on the strange front either, with the obsessive love of a masked man in the catacombs of Paris. For concentrated weirdness these two leave the avant-garde trailing behind. Agatha Christie creates in a similar zone, with child abuse, murder, and nihilism all sublimated into cockamamy murder mysteries. We kid ourselves when we say popular art has a soft centre. The coke in its stoves is often the charred remains of dark secrets and desires.

Another successful Christie work leaned heavily on the nihilism of her age. *And Then There Were None* is not unlike Sartre's *Huis Clos*, but garlanded with knitting needles stuck in jugulars. As well as selling over a hundred million books, once adapted for the stage this savagely bleak play enjoyed a long run in the West End and on Broadway. Eight visitors are stranded on a remote island, overseen by a ghoulish butler and housekeeper, all of them guilty of past murders. As they come to terms with their crimes, and as we hear accounts of the same cruelty dispensed to innocence as in *The Mousetrap*, one by one they drop dead to an unseen hand. Like zombies in elegant couture, they carry on the rituals of a weekend house party, as if convention is the only shield against impending chaos. Though its first title, with its easy racism, is appalling to us now, and its first book cover even more so, it is hard to conceive a more gruesome allegory for the doomed ship of the United Kingdom, drenched in collective sin and looking over its shoulder to past crimes. Amazingly, this bleak metaphor couldn't have been more popular. Screened by the distracting veil of light entertainment, people rushed to see their toxicity objectified. Popular art is strange stuff.

Many believe Christie prized her theatrical work more highly than her prose. Success came late, which may explain why. Her first play was produced in 1930, when she was forty, but she didn't hit the jackpot until the 1950s, when she was in her sixties. As far back as her teenage years she had wanted to write plays, and she was always highly invested in her productions, advising on casting, sitting in rehearsals, and on the case with producers. She loved the company of actors, delighting in their blithe priority-setting. She wrote approvingly of the passionate concern of one actress over which hat to wear in the middle of a world war. Her work, and sometimes her life, seems a shade loveless, and the giddy camaraderie of a troupe must have been a holiday from silence elsewhere.

One play, *A Daughter's a Daughter*, written under her favoured pseudonym, Mary Westmacott, lays out with brutality the kindless enmity between a hedonistic mother and an overcontrolling daughter. Without a trace of sentimentality, the play reveals a co-dependent pair destroying each other with misplaced duty and fake self-sacrifice. Unburdened by the murder and mayhem elsewhere in the opus, it takes a knife to the heart of the most sacred of relationships. Here as elsewhere, Christie had access to the quiet despair of those trying to fabricate conventions of dullness to alleviate a past shredded by loss.

The boys – Osborne, Wesker, Pinter – may have run off with all the highbrow attention, but few nailed the restlessness and confusion of the post-war period better than Christie. The scale of her success meant she was never going to attract the approval of the elite, no matter how rigorous her excavations of the buried, bleak, and gruesome anxieties of her age.

Lowbrow adulation was probably ample reward.

Agatha.
Ms Christie at Schiphol Airport, Amsterdam, 1964

Terence Rattigan

1911–1977

Every twenty years, Terrence Rattigan falls out of fashion. Ten years later he falls back in. One generation wonders how anyone could care for such stunted lives; the next at the obtuseness of those who have neglected his subtle emotional music. No matter how deep he gets buried, the pungent aroma of the work ensures truffle hunters dig him back up. The endurance is a rebuke to fashion, which once turned its back on him with stinging cruelty. Few writers' reputations have plummeted further faster than his did when John Osborne and his Young Men backing singers started chanting their angry song in 1956. Rattigan transformed in a heartbeat from being the most successful dramatist alive to being as chic as wearing a kaftan at a Sex Pistols gig. He committed no great crime. His work had lost none of its quality. Top-table taste simply did one of its quantum leaps and left him behind. The map was redrawn and he couldn't read it.

Identifying himself as the enemy was probably ill-advised. Famously, when asked on the steps of the Royal Court what he thought of *Look Back in Anger*, he tartly replied, 'I don't know why Mr Osborne didn't title it "Look how unlike Terence Rattigan I'm being."' Unlike his infuriatingly divine predecessor Noël Coward, who maintained a mask of amused disinterest towards the shallow wanderings of taste, Rattigan thrashed around trying to regain it. His was the celebrity wail: 'Why don't they love me any more?' To take on the young guns, he wrote a series of broadsides from a figure dubbed, in a peculiar act of self-sabotage, 'Aunt Edna'. The idea that Littlewood, Osborne, Pinter, Wesker, Jellicoe, Beckett, Behan and the rest, with their leather jackets and beanies, their CND marches and Coltrane collections, were going to run in fear from someone called Aunt Edna is so crazy it's endearing.

Reactions to critics were as calamitous as his response to his peers. Coward, who haunted Rattigan by walking ahead in all things and carrying himself ever-so-slightly better, maintained a calm state of war with the press. One evening in New York, Coward was dining alone in Sardi's when Kenneth Tynan wandered in, also alone. The critic had that day published in the *New Yorker* a demolition job of Coward's latest play. After five minutes of avoiding eye contact, Coward stood up and strode over. 'Mr Tynan, you are a cunt,' he said. 'Come and have dinner with me' – and they spent a delightful evening together. Rattigan lacked the steel and the style.

Writing angrily in public and offensively in private, he tortured himself into an unfortunate persona of injured vanity and angry waspishness. On occasion, he floundered around trying to be a hepcat, which wasn't the happiest fit for an Edwardian Harrovian. The nadir came in 1963. He was told by his doctors that he had just six months to live. Hurling himself back into high society in a state of beautiful despair, he glided from party to party proclaiming, 'Life is so sweet,' and, 'How can you know the value of life until you have looked death in the face?' Society fell in love with him again for his elegant stoicism. Then the doctors – with some embarrassment – told him they had misdiagnosed a cold. He went abroad for several years.

Before he did actually die in 1977, the Rattigan renaissance was showing signs of life. It took time to gain momentum. A posthumous biography by Michael Darlow pointed to the existence of an artist beneath the entertainer, and showed how the work provided a social chronicle of England from the 1930s to the 1950s. The later proselytising of academic Dan Rebellato on behalf of pre-1956 drama, together with his introductions to new scholarly editions of Rattigan's plays, helped wire-brush the sheen of shallowness that had accreted. More than anything it was keynote productions of *The Browning Version* at the National Theatre in 1980, and later in the 1990s *The Deep Blue Sea* at the Almeida, which brought into focus Rattigan's unique mix of emotional force and cold despair.

The most pat way of praising him has been as the peerless craftsman – the accomplished playmaker. The praise comes with the faintest sneer.

Rattigan was a first division storyteller, and after 1956 there was a suspicion of straightforward stories. As a reaction to the *Boy's Own* plots that swamped the theatre for so long, post-1956 much writing leaned more heavily on atmosphere and relationships than ripping yarns. Rattigan is a maestro of narrative, knowing exactly how to withhold and when to provide information. He misleads an audience with deft disguise, and with dexterity manipulates sympathy towards and away from characters. Most importantly, he knows how to bury his own mechanics. The storytelling remains unseen, mysterious. What passes by onstage is so relaxed and Southern Seaboard Chekhovian, it is only once the grip is firmly in place that you realise you're trapped in an arresting story. As the doyenne of theatrical agents Peggy Ramsay used to say, many writers could do with being 'rapped on the knuckles with the complete works of Rattigan'.

Beyond his technique, he is best known for soured romance. No writer is sharper on rotten, rancid relationships. Whether it's Hester's doomed sexual fixation in *The Deep Blue Sea*, the silent adoration of Joan in *After the Dance*, the major's impersonal groping in *Separate Tables*, or the Crocker-Harrises' dried-up marriage in *The Browning Version*, love has little to do with roses or violets. Rattigan was determined in his antipathy towards sentimental love. This is feel-bad work, a series of unflinching portrayals of stopped hearts, with a weight of negative emotion which is occasionally overwhelming. Little redeems the dour news beyond the Rattigan diagnosis, and his precision is matched by his ability not to blink. There is nothing affected in this sensibility, no aping of a willed misery. It is the real thing. Born from a yearning life in which he couldn't sustain a single relationship based on equality of respect, his work is a prolonged disquisition into failed love.

And why not? Much love is bad. For every day rolling in the sun there's a fortnight of muttering in the rain. No one needs a laureate for days of unrequited passion and self-disgust more than the English, and Rattigan turned out to be the ideal candidate. In these two qualities, craftsmanship and hard love, he ran the last leg of the relay team that sprinted off with Wilde, followed through with Maugham, and then Coward, who confidently took the last bend. Extraordinary how these four men, punished for the direction of their passion, revenged themselves on society by becoming the prime chroniclers of its emotional hollowness.

Rattigan's work offers distinctions from the rest of the relay team. Social and political concern is aired more explicitly. He flirted with communism in his youth, and despite later wealth and his love for the great and the good, he never lost an instinctive leaning to the left. He went on the stump for the Liberals late in life, and his plays always exemplified a loathing for Conservative ethics. He was probably more left wing than John Osborne, the firebrand who tore down the walls of his reputation. In many ways, Osborne was a celebrant of empire energy and empire rhetoric in a land that had lost its imperial influence, while Rattigan was probably happy to see the back of all that malarkey.

Beyond the politics, his work offers prolonged examination of an old-fashioned concept: virtue. Throughout there is a testing of what virtue is, and of how it survives in action. *Separate Tables* is an exquisite portrait of tolerance in a community, of how values are imperilled and then survive. Courage, generosity, and intransigence percolate to the surface in *The Browning Version* as a schoolboy dares to breach his fogeyish teacher's walls with the gift of a book, and the Crock determines to carry on true to himself. Self-sacrifice proves the base note of both *The Deep Blue Sea* and *After the Dance,* as two figures let go of sexual desire and accept a life of loss. *The Winslow Boy* is a testament to sheer pigheadedness, a refusal to be bullied, and an enduring independence. And *Flare Path* is the most haunting distillation of the patience and stoicism that helped Rattigan and his generation survive the Second World War.

Small acts of mercy pepper the work, relaxing the pressure exerted by emotional desolation. Tolerance, courage, self-sacrifice, independence, patience – different virtues for a different England. The gradualist virtues that used to glue the country together, before being swept away by various political whirlwinds, and which were never securely refound. When audiences bask in a nostalgic glow at a Rattigan play, it is not for tea sets or pencil skirts, but for a different quality of moral life. As well as craftsmanship, it is the continuing relevance of moral fortitude that endures.

History provides an incident which recommends tempering one's enthusiasm for Rattigan. One of his teachers at Oxford had become a professor of psychiatry, and established a reputation as a guru to young intellectuals, many of whom were held in thrall by this man's gnomic utterances. He announced with considerable aplomb in the early 1950s that he was going to conduct a psychological experiment: he would watch every performance of the next Rattigan play, from first to last. He would record every minute difference in the evolution of the company's execution and the changing nature of the audience's response. The harvest of his devoted attention would be an epoch-altering study of group psychology, artistic growth, and the mythic substructure of storytelling. The play was *The Deep Blue Sea*, one of Rattigan's greatest successes. It ran for seven hundred shows. The professor sat in the same seat throughout, fastidiously observing play and audience. At the end he produced no thesis. He was carried off babbling to an institution, where he resided for the remainder of his days, dreaming no doubt of pained romance and buttered crumpets.

Posture is everything.
Emlyn Williams in *The Winslow Boy* at the Lyric Theatre, Shaftesbury Avenue, London, 1946

Daphne du Maurier
1907–1989

Better known for her novels, Daphne du Maurier was very much a theatre animal, her provenance being close to the omphalos of the proscenium century. Her grandfather, George du Maurier, wrote one wildly successful novel, *Trilby*, which grew into a greater sensation as a play. This story gave the world the archetype of Svengali, a new ideal of bohemia, and after an actress adjusted her chapeau in stylish mode, a new name for a hat. *Trilby* also gave a first leading role to George's son, Gerald, an early master of chilled – almost casual – naturalism. Luxe hair middle-parted and highly brilliantined, Gerald ran the Wyndham's Theatre in the heart of the West End for fifteen years, charmed his way through many a role and became such an icon of slick urbanity he gave his surname to a popular brand of cigarette. Originating several roles for J. M. Barrie, he was the first actor to double George Darling and Captain Hook in *Peter Pan*. Daphne was the middle of his three daughters. Their cousins, the children of Gerald's sister, Sylvia Llewelyn Davies, were the inspiration for *Peter Pan* and other child characters of Barrie's fiction.

The heart of the Edwardian theatre world, however energetic the polishing of its gleam, had no little shading of darkness. Part of the charisma of the stage in any era relies on its ability to waft intimations of sexual licence. This magnetism was probably never greater than in this apparently repressed age. As discussed elsewhere, an odd energy seeps around J. M. Barrie: his gaze on the world makes one shift uneasily. Daphne, from a young age, had a moody sullenness that stares out from photos, compelling attention. Her later life was in many ways conventional, with an army-hero husband, three sons, and a life split between Hampstead and Cornwall. But a volcano of rumours erupted after her death about extramarital passion for the theatre star Gertrude Lawrence, and for Ellen Doubleday, the wife of her US publisher. Du Maurier wrote in her memoirs that her father had wanted a son, so she tomboyed her way through youth to compensate. She said her personae were split between the loving wife and 'the lover', who had 'a decidedly male energy'. Her final editor claimed Daphne confessed late in life that her father, beneath the polished veneer, was a violent alcoholic and that they'd had an incestuous relationship. Though hard to know the truth of such rumours, it is judicious to say these were wild times.

Sex is at the heart of du Maurier's achievement; an old-fashioned idea of sex which does not require shedding of clothes, playing more on the beam of intent in the eye and the slur of desire in the voice. Her first play was a theatrical adaptation of *Rebecca*, which came out in 1940, simultaneous with the Hitchcock film. The play was directed by George Devine, later to rebirth the Royal Court, and with the formidable Margaret Rutherford as Mrs Danvers. *Rebecca* is a magnificent potboiler and exudes sex from almost every pore. The scenes in the film when George Sanders slinks up to the window, intrusive and unabashed, his eyes sparkling with flirty excess, have an almost uncontainable, illicit naughtiness. Maxim de Winter is a bubbling volcano of repressed desire that looks ready to blow at any instant. Heaven knows what Mrs Danvers is after, certainly Rebecca for starters, but it could be anything for a main course. The final consumption of Manderley by fire seems the inevitable consequence of the sexual energies swirling around and twisting within it.

Her third play, *September Tide*, is no slouch on the saucy front either. We are again in Cornwall, within earshot of the crashing waves, a landscape that clearly stimulated du Maurier. At the sensual climax of this play, a young man rushes into the sea to save an unmoored boat. Returning in a wet shirt, a certain narrative inevitability comes with him. No one knows better than du Maurier the excitement that zinging skin, electrified by a quick plunge in a cold sea, can add to a flirtation. In this case the desire is transgressive, coursing between a young, arrogant artist and his new mother-in-law, a passion across the generations which has destiny in it from first encounter. What is remarkable, among crude plotting and coarse dialogue, is the directness and honesty of their desire.

Both parties move towards consummation with bold candour. There is some clumsy tying up of morals at the end, unnatural and forced, but it cannot occlude the crackle in the air preceding. Du Maurier knows a good narrative scenario and has the courage to show there are inner compulsions no one can control.

Her strongest play, *The Years Between*, has a reduced amount of atmospheric crackle, and relies on the spouse-gone-missing trope. Maugham exploited this in *Home and Beauty*, as did María de la O Lejárraga in *Take Two from One*. In a time of international conflict and poor communications, the idea that one might lose one's husband or wife, remarry, and then have to deal with a returning spouse must have been a perennial fear. In this piece, the desire motoring the plot is in part sexual, with the widow lusting for a local farmer, but more political. With a husband supposedly dead in a Mediterranean plane crash, the heroine takes on his constituency as an MP. Fired up by newfound freedom, she starts to find her voice, working on committees passing new education and housing bills through Parliament, and edging the world towards the Labour Party's New Jerusalem of 1945. When her husband returns from the dead, eager to resume marital duties, and to stop the spinning political clock, the stage is set for a vivid contemporary clash. The run of the play straddled the end of the war and the formation of Clement Attlee's government, opening in 1944 and continuing through VE Day with the bells of victory clanging in the background, and forward through 617 performances. Onstage, parallels with the movement of history must have electrified.

The returning hero is confounded to find his wife in his constituency seat, and reacts with raucous laughter. He is from old Cavalier stock, with a buccaneering 'to-hell-with-it-all' attitude. This rendered him a hero in the previous world but looks ugly and wilful in the new dispensation. Old and treasured iron gates have been melted down for munitions; the number of staff has been decimated; nobody laughs at jokes about 'buxom land girls' any more; and to his horror women are 'gadding around the country giving speeches'. The axis has shifted in his absence, and he is ill adapted for change. Before the war, he had spoken with dazzling brilliance for freedom and the individual and the right to do as you please: now his wife speaks with plainness and clarity for community and efficiency and taking care of others. Her appeal for 'Service, duty and obedience to the state' provokes his disbelief. This divide – between the individual and the community – survived this work, and its delineation here shows du Maurier's prescience.

Change invades an upper-middle-class marriage, as it did irreversibly for millions of men and women, and proves irresistible. Du Maurier had concerns of her own about how the enforced separations of war would affect her domestic situation with her soldier husband. She refracted her misgivings into a fictional scenario that would encompass the tensions of a society facing post-victory upheaval. There is creakiness in the writing here: plot shifts are transparent and overexposed, and several of the moments featuring trembling upper lips and stoical downplaying feel off the shelf. But many are also moving, and there is great skill. Melodrama is eschewed as painful moments are negotiated through miniature advances and retreats, taut verbal skirmishing, and nervous evasion. Tectonic shifts are rumbling, but subsumed within the quick, light fencing of an unhappy marriage.

One of du Maurier's great skills is for leaving chords unresolved. If endings tend towards the optimistic, they do so within a context of unsettlement and complexity. Problems that have been exposed remain, and conclusions offer methods of coping rather than tidy resolution. As in Hitchcock's film of her short story *The Birds*, the threat, whether inner or outer, remains hovering, perched on the telegraph wires, ready to strike.

Look Now! Those eyes. Daphne second left.
Gerald du Maurier with his three daughters, 1913

Tennessee Williams
1911–1983

Our culture often likes to lock a writer within a mannerism. Harold Pinter raged against being reduced to a purveyor of pauses. Tom Stoppard was box-ticked as a brilliant, crossword-puzzling wit-smith, yet his plays are fired up with heart and rich with substance. George Bernard Shaw has been pigeonholed as a speechifying, philosophical windbag (occasionally true), though his plays are frequently interrupted by delicate and precise naturalism. A by-product of our nervous need to squeeze art into box gardens, we won't allow artists to be the wilderness they are.

No one suffers more from this mania than Tennessee Williams. Public perception traps him within Southern States gentility – twittering women, fragile realities, and displaced camp – reinforced by a host of bad Southern accents from across the world. 'I have always relied on the kindness of strangers,' is a line distorted in strangulated contortions from Moscow to Montevideo. Actors and directors make attempts to seek out an ineffable Williams music, a search which neglects the hard facts of the narrative. His great interpreters, the actors he wrote for – Laurette Taylor, Anna Magnani, Marlon Brando – were roughhouse creatures of bruised humanity, workers who knew how to put over the information of a script. Both the acting and the public's desire to reduce him to a repertoire of gestures diminishes his landscape. A distortion which limits contrary and bulging energies – sexual, emotional, and social. Few tested the limits of the conventional as ambitiously as Tennessee Williams.

Two magnums are plucked from the crowd to represent the whole opus – *The Glass Menagerie* and *A Streetcar Named Desire*. 'His masterpieces', people mutter, as if throughout his whole life he only kept a single secret in his drawer. There are reasons for this: they are the plays that announced Williams to the world, arriving post-Second World War like a starburst of emotional honesty; they led a revolution that gave primacy to the politics of the soul; and, tellingly, they are the plays which fitted their proscenium midwife most sleekly. Something about their unity makes them manageable and easier to choose as representative. People want to make them a distillation, the ur-Williams. Chamber pieces, they drive down narrow channels towards tragic conclusions – Blanche DuBois's madness in *Streetcar*, the breaking of Amanda Wingfield's illusions in *Menagerie*. Their lack of digression, their purity of direction, helps them accelerate to an exemplary force.

A Streetcar Named Desire has elements of the classic pièce bien faite and is simultaneously a subversion of it. We have in Blanche the woman with a past, but never before did any work go into such detail about the ghosts that haunt her, or make us feel so acutely their debilitating effects on a woman's mind. The vestiges of the nineteenth century are present in the play, in the memory of the sisters' grand estate, Belle Reve, and in the affected refinement of Blanche's manners. They are brought into conflict, sharp and fierce, with the modern spirit of self-aggrandisement, as expressed by Stanley Kowalski. A melodramatic plot of past secrets, sexual tension, and rivalry for inheritance aggregate to bear down on Blanche's delicate psyche. In the time warp of stage time, hers is a mind we come to know, even in our fleeting acquaintance, almost as well as our own. Here, and in *The Glass Menagerie*, psychological fragility and an instinct for the undercurrents of history are thrown by Williams into the cauldron, and from this irresistible mix new potentials are created.

The effect of these two plays was seismic. Out of the personal life of this awkward, tortured, and proud gay man from St Louis came heart-bombs which sent out ever-widening ripples of emotional and sexual liberation. Williams took stories from his own life, incidents of confusion and cruelty, and put them onstage with an honesty unparalleled. His feckless father, his domineering mother, and his tragically vulnerable sister were mined for dramatic value and put onstage with zero, or at the most transparent, filters. As Gore Vidal said of him, 'He would have [a] play produced so he could, at relative leisure, like God, rearrange his original experience into something that was no longer God's and unpossessable, but his.' Lessons had been learned from Eugene O'Neill about the values of autofictional writing, but somehow Williams took it further into realms of naked and unashamed openness. He could be ruthless with this exploitation. Before he wrote *Suddenly Last Summer*, he regularly visited his institutionalised sister in order to accrue material. Alongside his guilt and indignation at how Rose was treated, he had enough of Graham Greene's 'splinter of ice in the heart' to realise its dramatic capital. The gleanings are intimate truth about human life on the half breath.

He wrote at a high pitch – gone was the repression, or self-control, or decorum of previous theatre. 'My approach to my work is hysterical,' Williams told his regular director Elia Kazan, 'it is infatuated and sometimes downright silly. I don't know what it is to take anything calmly.' The unabashed delirium was his particular gift, and it blew the top off a long-steaming pressure cooker. Within a claustrophobic theatre we see this sensibility afforded atomic density by being compacted into a tight space. The contrast with the rest of his output is as much spatial as spiritual. Elsewhere he is looser and less focused. *A Streetcar Named Desire* and *The Glass Menagerie* are his thin plays, but there is great virtue in the fat.

Many argue there is a falling-off in late-career Elvis Presley – that other Southern, mid-century icon. They lament his twilight persona, singing songs of redemption from inside a rhinestoned fortress. For some, including myself, they miss the high pathos of seeing a grown man searching inside his befuddlement for the purity of his youth. So with Tennessee, there is pleasure to be taken in his maturity, and in plays of mess that are rich with life. In *Summer and Smoke*, several different narratives are clumsily shunted into each other. The habitual hyperventilating woman, her fingernails clutching on to sanity, sits beside a subplot full of Mexican sensuality, a melodramatic sideline with gangsters and guns and social satire. Bold, bloody, and mixed up, all is kept spruce by a thumping narrative, and a painful insight of O'Neill proportions – that we rarely coincide with the ones we love. Though *Summer and Smoke* lacks the centripetal focus of *Streetcar* or *Menagerie*, it is a pleasure to roam in a landscape wider than a single fractured mind.

Looking at the whole body of work, it becomes clear just how unrepresentative the two thin and melodic plays are when set beside the fat and bellowing. *Cat on a Hot Tin Roof* is a dynastic drama full of the Mississippi Delta's equivalent of kings and queens. Five or six stories jostle for space over one steamy night. Similarly, *Night of the Iguana* is full of the bruised and battered carving each other up and drawing each other back from various abysses. *Orpheus Descending* dextrously weaves exposure of bigotry, a May–September love story, and an extended retelling of the Orpheus myth. The list goes on: *Camino Real* with its intellectual fantasia; *Suddenly Last Summer* with its Southern Gothic; *Sweet Bird of Youth* . . . all wild, all alive. No chamber tidiness here, this is good old thousand-acre sprawl.

As extraordinary as anything else is *The Rose Tattoo*. The play inhabits a working-class realm full of wandering goats, old witches, and truant children. It is Sicilian American, explosively sexualised, managing to be both clownish and operatic in its emotional range. A long way from the sealed and sewn-up world of the two classics, its fingers rake just as deep in the earth. The source for all these plays was of course Williams himself – he never failed to project himself into any landscape – but it is fascinating to see him so far from the hegemony of stylistic convention, joyously defying any critic's desire to fence him in.

His imagination teemed, and he created spatial environments, jungly and lush with life, barely containable in a seven-by-five-metre proscenium frame. Few stretched scenic possibilities as ambitiously. *The Rose Tattoo* creates an entire shanty town, with motorways passing on one side, and brass bands echoing in the distance. Firework displays light up the sky above the plantation of *Cat on a Hot Tin Roof*. A long hill slopes down from the plateau on which *Night of the Iguana* is perched, with a broad sea beyond. *Orpheus Descending* crowds the stage with a warren of rooms. An entire town is summoned up in *Summer and Smoke*. The manageability of the two chamber works comforts us; the expanse elsewhere bulges and alarms. As usual, one senses the strain of the form, the straitjacket tearing its seams as muscles expand within. This is an expanse to be celebrated, a mark of magnanimity.

The oscillation between contraction and expansion, the thin and the fat, is echoed in his journals. Early entries record the timidity of the adolescent imploding with pain, self-consciousness, and self-loathing. His sensitivity weighed him down, as did a family whose misfortunes were tragic, and whose pathologies were almost self-parodic in their Freudian casebook status. At a certain moment, coinciding with both the discovery of his own greedy sexuality and his sister's frontal lobotomy, all that inward pressure inverted itself. The energy that had been squeezing in and down, turned around and started pouring out. In his life he discovered the fleshpots of New York and Europe, and in his work the same switch from interiority to exteriority. He discovered the world with an appetite, and felt an equal hunger to reproduce it on stages, obese with delights and disappointments.

He celebrates his new freedom with the profligacy of a drunk. Sometimes a boozer will meet someone so prim they can't think of any appropriate response beyond getting even more smashed. The tighter the pursed lips of the puritan, the greater the drunk's desire for more liquor, and then more liquor, and on in a squalid spiral down. Williams sometimes feels like that in relation to the audience. Their sobriety determined him to be yet more drunk on sex and sadness and spirit, in a desperate bid to get the straights to loosen up.

Something woozy spreads like a gas across Williams's work. In the early plays, it is about the static heat of the South, and the brain-melt it induces; in the mid-period, it seems to be as much about booze and the way it makes the eyes swim; in the late fragmented works it is the record of a shattered brain. This very miasma, the dramatic equivalent of Da Vinci's hazy *sfumato*, is a large part of Tennessee's contribution. Where early writers preferred things clear and sharp – words hard and narratives pristine – he blurred the edges. Even Chekhov, who allows for chaos and confusion, ensures that a breeze is ever passing through the picture, keeping the outer lines brushed sharp.

Somehow functionality survived until the art–life balance got too entangled later in Williams's life. The bottle which had been his key to existence became his jailer, sousing his talent. His final plays are meagre, the expanse of his mid-period shrunken into the strained banalities of a lost gift. A short and late play, *And Tell Sad Stories of the Deaths of Queens*, tells its own story in the title, a desolate example of a talent's dissipation.

His influence was immense. He created a new language for characters in extremis, where perturbed minds have long mulled over words and phrases to give them vibrancy and polish. We know that Blanche has refined her 'kindness of strangers' line, and we appreciate her effort. He put queer experience and sensibility, if not front and centre, then much closer than any who preceded him. In this he showed determination and courage, given the context of his age and his background. Later generations punished him for not going further – yet another example of the historical narcissism which so bedevils progressives. Williams got to a hard-won place by pushing through thickets of brambles. Later avant-garde theatre-makers took advantage of the cleared path, and saw fit to criticise his efforts. Hey ho, the revolution eats its leaders.

Beyond gay or straight, he brought plain sex onto the stage in an unapologetic erotic manner no one had dared before. 'I cannot write any sort of story,' Williams said to Gore Vidal, 'unless there is at least one character in it for whom I have physical desire.' Stanley Kowalski is the first male sex object to be openly exploited onstage – his torn T-shirt, his frequent torso-revealing changes, his silk pyjamas are not far above the pornographic. Marlon Brando was an earthquake, the first actor (in alliance with his writer) to happily toy onstage with the desires of women and men. In a world now saturated in explicit sexuality, it is hard to realise the scale of this revolution. Kowalski was the first of a catwalk of sex objects, male and female, who blatantly flaunted their wares.

The greatest of his achievements may have been to allow emotional openness to flourish on the stage, and hence in the world. An openness which made the fragility of the heart, and of minds made vulnerable by the heart's stops and surges, the centre of the drama. The primacy given to the emotional self, for good or ill, opened portals which allowed in new material, later feeding into the poetry of the Beats, the counterculture of the 1960s, and a more inclusive bohemianism. He went into the world, the grand and the seedy, the fragrant and the rancid, heard sad stories and brought them to life for others.

Before the legend, when it was all still human. Jessica Tandy with Kim Hunter and Marlon Brando, *A Streetcar Named Desire*

Yet we would not trust in Williams's capacity for bustle and hysterical noise, and for mapping these erupting dynamics, if we did not also sense he saw something else. Whether in Blanche's line, 'Sometimes – there's God – so quickly', or in Laura Wingfield's luminous appreciation for her glass animals, there is a pathway to something beyond the movement and the greed, a place of rest and peace. Almost everyone in Williams, even the most destitute and desperate, are greedy for excess – too much rum, poetry, or hope – and for exposing too many nerve endings. At the same time they pray for the still, quiet place, only found by shedding and stopping. In that way, Williams pointed towards a future.

Jean-Paul Sartre
1905–1980

An old Irish friend visited Paris with a ne'er-do-well companion in the early 1960s. Keen to cover every site, they finished one day in the inner sanctum of the existentialists, the café Les Deux Magots. By this stage they were well tanked and downed a few more brandies. As if arranged by a heavenly travel agent, through an alcoholic haze they noticed a scowling and intense Jean-Paul Sartre settling on a banquette in a corner. My friend was all for distant admiration, his companion unfortunately less so. Hauling himself up, he lumbered across the room to stand before the Gauloises-smoking guru. He spoke with many decibels, and in the thickest of Dublin accents, with a rolled rrrr any Frenchman would envy.

'Hello, Sarrrtrre!'

The philosopher mumbled and looked down at his book. The Irishman paused, swayed a little, then boomed out, 'Give us an old song, Sarrrtrre.'

The Frenchman dragged on his cigarette and demurred.

'Go on, Sarrrtrre, give us an old song.'

With a wave of his hand and a glare, Sartre dismissed the Irishman. After a brief sway and before lumbering back, he announced to the café, 'Ah, you're no fucking good, Sarrrtrre!'

The Irish spirit of bonhomie, where the pub is a place for celebration and the elision of the individual into the communal, had met its quintessential opposite in history's unparalleled sage of despair.

Reading Sartre, after his plays have gone out of fashion, is still to be plunged into a queasy and nauseous dungeon of uncertainty. Even if feeling robust, vigour and spiritual health are stripped away, achievements feel illusory, connections fragile, and the ground under one's feet cracks a little. His capacity to immiserate remains unmatched. *Huis Clos*, Sartre's most celebrated play and an international sensation which hit the world's sweet spot of angst after the Second World War, locks three people in an enclosed chamber with Second Empire furniture. There are three sofas, an imposing bronze ornament on a mantelpiece, a sharp letter opener, and nothing more. The inmates are shown in by a sinister valet. Each, it quickly transpires, is deceased, and they cannot escape. This room is their bespoke hell. The story unreels the tawdry reasons for their sentencing, and in their manoeuvres around each other – sour negotiations of fear and need – they enact how they are set to torture one another for eternity. Dignity is absent, kindness is a joke, and connection only a matter of desire and punishment. The consequence of this premise is 'L'enfer, c'est les autres' – 'Hell is other people.'

Huis Clos and other works by Sartre set the template for much that followed, where strangers encounter each other in enclosed spaces and account for themselves, while waiting for unknown parties to pattern their futures. This matrix ushers in Beckett's sensibility and sums up a large part of Pinter's oeuvre. The latter played the lead in a television version entitled *In Camera*, and must have known the play inside out. *Huis Clos* opened in 1944, a few months before the Liberation of Paris, though it is hard to imagine anything less celebratory. Soon on Broadway, it played in London in 1946, directed by Peter Brook and starring Alec Guinness, a production broadcast to the nation by the BBC. There is something admirably clear-eyed in the way culture chose to speak brutal truths after 1945, rather than indulge in shallow triumphalism. The dank, comfortless world Sartre invoked, with lost men and women circling one another, mourning the loss of God and purpose, became a dominant tone. He set the tempo in books and in the influential journal *Les Temps Modernes*, established by Simone de Beauvoir and himself in 1945. They seeded a cloud which spread over the intellectual life of the West. Little sunlight found a way through. His philosophical influence is renowned, his importance to the theatre less marked.

Sartre always felt a passion for the stage, and it became an arena where he could transmit hidden messages, and a laboratory to explore human behaviour. When he was incarcerated at the beginning of the war, he wrote, acted in, and produced plays in his prisoner-of-war camp, Stalag 12. One was a nativity play, concealing a camouflaged appeal for resistance. Jesus became an exemplary rebel against the Romans, just as a messiah was yearned for against the Nazis. The Germans allowed him to write, and on his release and return to Paris, condoned further encoded messages around freedom. His play *Les Mouches* (*The Flies*), retells the Orestes myth, with Aegisthus quite plainly the usurping Germany and Clytemnestra a whorish France accommodating the invader. At rehearsals, Sartre met Albert Camus, beginning a friendship in great excitement which ended in bitterness. Camus was actively involved in the Resistance, Sartre less so. Though he liked the theory of having '*mains sales*', he was less prepared to dirty his hands in practice.

Some have criticised Sartre's conduct during the war and remained suspicious of the licence with which he was allowed to write. The Frenchman, contrary to a fault, declared later he felt his greatest emancipation during the occupation. For him, physical restrictions allowed for a liberation of consciousness, a sharpened sense of what freedom truly was. Though the philosophical perspective is comprehensible (just), this is the sort of sophistic contrariness – when men, women, and children were being shovelled alive onto trains and dead out of furnaces – that can make one look askance at les intellectuels.

Les Mains Sales premiered in 1948 and, like its predecessor *Huis Clos*, was soon being watched, read, and obsessed over by a generation smoking Gauloises and furrowing their brows in imitation of their pug-faced idol. The play is part of Sartre's project to marry existentialism and Marxism, no small task. An epic work of seven acts – yes, seven! Take that! – it outlines how a communist is tasked by a faction of hard-liners to assassinate a senior leader who is flirting with a policy of compromise. The theme is to distinguish those who live in ideological purity from those prepared to sully their hands in action. Each is tested. Who can act? Who can only think and worry? Over the seven acts, there are doubts, and false attempts, and persuasions, and losses of conviction, before the killing occurs almost by accident. This is a full-blown existentialist interrogation into the reasons of bad faith – ethical, religious, psychological, ideological – commonly supposed to drive our intentions, which are one by one revealed to be chimera. Finally, chance is the greatest enactor. Stuff just happens.

Here, as elsewhere, Sartre was keen to teach us how to give the slip to the various determinisms that enshroud us. Liberated from God, and detached from the moral codes prevailing over previous generations, men and women were now ethical orphans, free to make a way through the ruins and shreds of Europe. Saying 'I was only following orders' would no longer suffice, no more than 'It is God's will' or 'That's how I was brought up.' Old excuses had to be seen for the fictions they were, and men and women walk naked in the new state of being. Rejection of inherited identity was accelerated by the war, since so many had been thwarted and killed in the name of false creeds. Without predetermined carapaces, the characters may stumble along the way (they usually did), but they were making their own choices.

An inner self of psychological motivation was thought to be as great an illusion as any exterior creeds. For Sartre and his fellow intellectuals, the soul was a myth: there was no character or personality, just our activity in the world and our perception of it. Psychological journeys to change our inner substance were invented fictions. There is only how we act in this instant and then in that. To a degree this illuminates Sartre's passion for the stage. Actors are all about picking up new personas and values from one moment to another, walking shadows for whom nothing is ever achieved or finished.

Part of existentialism's discarding of old thinking lay in its phenomenological embrace of the object. In *Les Mains Sales* the lead character hymns the actuality of a coffee pot. He describes himself, with metatheatrical honesty, as being 'on a stage set', with the only reality being the cafetière. In a narrative which lurches between agonised speechifying and B-movie thrills (there are revolvers and bombs and tense face-offs), the coffee pot – both a prop and a real pot, part of the story in the theatre and equally a thing in a room – becomes a disorienting demonstration of theatre's slipped realities. Just as the object lives in adjacent dimensions, the plays slide between genres. There are moments of pure 'real', chunks of Shavian debate, lyrical surges, and tropes stolen from the boulevard theatre. Amusingly, there is a surprising propensity for people to climb in and out of windows. Barely an act goes by without someone jumping out of a window to hide or leaping in through one to surprise. While building a new theatre of seriousness, Sartre couldn't let go of the delicious vulgarities of farce.

The plays suffer from an excess of talk, in a rhetoric more authorial than character-based. Within a loquacious Gallic tradition – Jean Anouilh being the greatest circumlocutor – people often seem to talk simply for the sake of talking. *The Devil and the Good Lord*, set during the German Peasants' War of 1524, carries on for a testing four and a half hours of intense debate. Where Brecht would have used this setting for event, and encased it in vivid plastic moments, Sartre lets his spokespersons wang on at inordinate length. The hovering aura of violence galvanises some of the verbiage, but far from all. There are bursts of action, enough to fund a Bond film, but they arrive in isolated clusters, bombs going off in deserts of anguished chatter. Both a pleasure and a pain, it is rather like being stuck in the head of the philosopher. Noël Coward's characters could step off the stage and chat freely to whomever is sitting in the stalls; Sartre's creations are locked in the artifice.

Les Mains Sales, to his disappointment, was another international success. The accurate portrayal of how communist parties fought wars of ends and means, with purists attacking moderates and vice versa, was criticised by the left and celebrated by the right. To the latter it seemed an entertaining satire of how party machines self-combusted, and the narcissism of their small differences. The play was banned in Moscow, a bitter pill for Sartre, who had publicly thrown himself and *Les Temps Modernes* behind the Soviet Union, in full knowledge of Stalin's crimes. For Sartre, the Soviet Union was a lesser evil than the United States and the wrongs of unchecked capitalism. Again, he showed here a romantic attachment to the supposed freedom of consciousness possible within the authoritarian state – an attitude more plausible from a Left Bank café than a Siberian gulag. No matter his public attachments, the play was not seen in Russia and was a hit on Broadway. This unpredictability of response remains one of drama's abiding virtues, how it welcomes and celebrates plays in ways running counter to an author's stated intentions. The bitterness of this success, as well as his perception that the drama was drifting towards the abstract and away from the politically engaged, eventually disenchanted him.

For all the excess of rhetoric, and the alienating schematics, there is a terrifying pleasure to be taken in what Sartre offered. His characters often reassess who they are, wondering what has driven them to become archetypes. In *Les Mouches*, the mythical figures of the *Oresteia* – Aegisthus, Clytemnestra, Electra, and Orestes – reveal a dissatisfaction in being stuck in personalities fortified by millennia of myth. They attempt prison breaks from their set identities. As with many of the young emerging from the war, the Atreid family had no desire to receive a psychology: they wanted to reinvent.

In Sartre's theatre, as storytelling animals we observe the struggles of others to define themselves and refashion their narratives, and the lessons learned allow us the opportunity to recreate ourselves. Or at least tailor some minor adjustments. If we have the courage to face the everyday chaos with nothing locked down, we can embrace possibilities. In T. S. Eliot's phrase, we can dare to eat a peach. In the late 1940s, in a world wrecked by catastrophic folly, Sartre offered a generation the option of writing their own scripts. Even if most declined, it gave a delicious shiver to think it possible.

The final most insuperable challenge with Sartre is the insularity of tone. All the liberation he proffers leads to disappointment or despair. Other people can only ever be hell. Such a denial of the capacity of others to surprise with joy or illuminate with love smacks of someone fortressed within his own fixed perceptions, rather than someone unburdened by them. A thesis which can prosper in a philosophical exegesis, it survives less well on a stage. The theatre resists those who cannot be ambushed by the revelation of others. It endures as an arena where 'Le paradis, c'est les autres.'

Had he chosen to sing a song for the Irish ne'er-do-well in *Les Deux Magots*, he might have been taken aback by the joy it gave him.

Not War Horse, is it?
Olga Dominique in *Les Mouches*, directed by Raymond Hermantier, Paris, Theatre of Vieux-Colombier, 1951

Arthur Miller

1915–2005

When Arthur Miller, a totem pole of the proscenium era, died, not every reaction was adulatory. The *Wall Street Journal* obituary was headlined 'The Great Pretender: Arthur Miller wasn't well liked – and with good reason,' which lacks charm. *The New Criterion*, happy to rip open old wounds, ran with 'Communist Stooge'. A playwright's life (and death) can be an unkind business, but this was off the scale.

Miller's late career saw as much pain as glory. Alongside regular starry revivals of his classics, and his ascension to quasi-Mount Rushmore status as a sage, there were consistent disappointments. He kept turning out new work, and the American theatre kept turning its back. Though securing regional premieres and off-Broadway runs, Broadway shunned him. Several plays premiered in the UK before the US. If they were staged, critics hunted them down to belittle them. Like hyenas pursuing an old lion, they tracked him across the savannah, hungry for blood. Many bore grudges, some for his politics, some for his moral hauteur, some because they had loved him in their youth and were shamed by the spectre that shimmered in the mirror.

Miller's stature has been stoutly defended by his biographer, and chief disciple, Christopher Bigsby. Yet some of his lectures on Miller's behalf are such flagellating almanacs of all the abuse, they start to tell a counter-narrative questioning why anyone would defend him. Hysteria reigns on all sides, as in Miller's life. One truth becomes clear – that he could at some moments be great and at some not very great, and sometimes both. How could this be?

Arthur Miller didn't arrive as a meteor. He wrote nine stage plays between 1936 and 1943 before his first hit. One-act student plays and tyro experiments, they didn't go far. *The Man Who Had All the Luck* made it to Broadway but, despite its optimistic title, closed after four shows. Though scarring, this was a necessary apprenticeship as Miller experimented with form and content. Like many young artists, he shouted up hills and down valleys, waiting for an encouraging echo.

Then over an eight-year period, 1947 to 1955, he produced four of the twentieth century's great dramas, *All My Sons*, *Death of a Salesman*, *The Crucible*, and *A View from the Bridge.* An astonishing run, carried out in the eye of whirlwinds personal and political. As these plays appeared, the full force of the US government was cranking up to intimidate Miller and brand him a pariah, driving lifelong wedges between him and his comrades. To maximise the crisis, he met and fell in love with the most adored woman in the world, Marilyn Monroe. Under that burden, public and private, he smelted plays that redefined what theatre was, diagnosing the heart of the human experience in America. Staying alive would have been achievement enough. Somehow he stood steady. Far from crushed by the epochal pressure, he harnessed its force, and flung it back high into the air as exemplary art. Neither the crisis nor his defiance could last. The persecutions of Senator McCarthy crumbled to dust as America woke in sobriety to shame-faced regret at its first flirtation with totalitarianism. Shortly after, his first marriage collapsed and Miller wed Monroe. The weight lifted, and he never wrote a play as great again.

What happened during those eight years? Miller himself later prayed 'to catch the lightning again. A writer walks around with an iron rod in his hand pointing to heaven – hoping to be struck by that electricity – if you are, it's just a great piece of luck.' False modesty and solid insight blend here. A writer needs gifts, and substantial ones. An apprenticeship spent writing the wrong plays helps locate the right ones. But you also need well-tuned antennae. Everyone in any era knows there are tunes and truths floating among them, which no one has yet notated. Half hearing those whispers on the breeze is what makes artists listless, and all of us human. We spend our days twiddling with the radio frequency, trying to catch the song or the sense we need. It takes virtuosos of receptivity to hear them.

What is the proper response of writers to their era, according to Miller? For him, the major talents, among whom he counted himself, share 'a fierce moral sensibility which is unquenchable, they are all burning with the same anger. The little ones have made peace with it, and the bigger ones can't.' Rage then is a necessity, likewise courage. Giving a voice to thoughts hitherto unspoken risks punishment. Promethean fire burns the fingers, and it takes audacity to grasp it. In the film she made about her father, Rebecca Miller interviewed Mike Nichols, who had directed a revival of *Death of a Salesman* on Broadway in 2012. Nichols wondered if 'Arthur burned something out', when he wrote that play because 'he came so close to the target'. And she agreed: 'How do you write that first act in one night? It's almost a visitation. A raging fire that went through him.'

Miller believed that playwrights need the right moment to flourish, a coincidence of tensions and torques. 'Plays come out of a situation, it's no accident that at certain points in history you get a lot of plays – there's a confluence of things that bring about sufficient interest.' Miller came at the right moment for an America trapped within convulsions. Over the eighteen years preceding *All My Sons*, the country had faced two monumental tests of its mettle: the Depression and the Second World War. The Depression was the single formative experience for Miller. The son of two Jewish immigrants, his father, Isidore, arrived in New York at the age of six, with a luggage label around his neck. An illiterate man, he built up a substantial fortune from charm and grit and hustle. The young Arthur grew up surrounded by luxury and staff. Everything was lost in the crash of 1929. As Bigsby says, 'He learned that it can all go away, that you are on thin ice.'

As Miller delineates in his 1980 vaudeville, *The American Clock*, a panoramic sweep across the USA of 1929, it was a nationwide collapse of the spirit, parts of Manhattan like refugee camps, open fires lighting faces and warming hands, around which grew jerry-built shanty towns.

Families crammed into apartments. Starving men fainted on the streets. Beyond the sharp wound of poverty and unemployment there was a relentless falling away of purpose.

To cope, America engendered a spirit of shared endeavour. Imperfect, occasionally venal, riddled with hypocrisy – what human moment isn't? – the New Deal had a brightness. Its chief architect was Franklin Delano Roosevelt, with his rallying cry of 'The only thing to fear is fear itself,' and a majority joined hands to manifest a spirit of democratic, anti-authoritarian working together. Miller and his colleagues in the 1930s felt the benefit acutely in the Federal Theatre Project. This was sponsored by the Works Progress Administration – the Soviet flatness of those names speaks of a wholly different America. These were acts of determined public imagination to heal a national wound.

Though reluctant to join the Second World War, American troops were soon taking responsibility for subverting tyranny and fascism in Asia, in Africa, and throughout Europe. The interdependence fostered at home during the New Deal was now linked to the peoples of the world. Returning from sacrifices made in combat was never going to be easy without wanting to make the old world afresh. British troops came back from battlefields filled with enough zeal for a New Jerusalem to boot out Churchill and install the most radical British government of the twentieth century. GIs returning to America were ignited by similar feelings that a different future was possible. Chris Keller in *All My Sons* has witnessed the carnage and yet comes home with a renewed hope for mankind, a sense that, with everything destroyed, one thing would be made anew, 'A kind of . . . responsibility. Man for man.'

The brightness engendered by defeating the Depression and fascism was displaced by many evolving energies, two of which feature heavily in Miller's sensibility. Within a burgeoning economy, a blizzard of new materialism caught everyone's gaze. Attention that could or should have been paid to the human was wrenched away by the glimmer and glare of objects, glorious objects. In *Death of a Salesman*, the fetishising of the car blocks out the emotional capacity of the family. The Chevrolet was a potent symbol of suburbia, mobility, and the American dream, and rapidly becomes a substitute for self-worth for Willy Loman. At the play's climax he totals both himself and his motor. *All My Sons*, which basks in the back gardens of an apparently utopian suburbia, is packed with objects. The Kellers' factory churns out pressure cookers and washing machines. The chatter over the garden fence is a breathless one of toasters and malted mixers. In *A View from the Bridge*, the record player is an almost sacred object, occupying a space previously reserved for altars.

There was a sharper enemy than consumerism. Not everyone had bought into the New Deal. The Republican counter-revolution was in its infancy, and as full of violence as an angry infant. America was tearing itself into two tribes under the influence of Senator McCarthy and his House Un-American Activities Committee, a communist-hunting pogrom which had begun its life as a culture war tool to take down the Federal Theatre Project in the 1930s. Fact and decency were soon swept into a maelstrom of confusion familiar today.

Extremist individualism was birthing itself, and it rapidly became a creatively generative enemy for Miller. His cursed heroes, men swept up in a cult of success proven by status and the dollar, crave individual victories, triumphs to mark them out from the herd. (Willy Loman is so obsessed by proving his worth in cash, he kills himself to realise his insurance policy.) Loman stands in a long proscenium line of snake-oil hustlers whose souls are strip-mined by the human cost of selling. Like Hickey in O'Neill's *The Iceman Cometh*, or Shelley Levene and his cohort in David Mamet's *Glengarry Glen Ross*, these men have gutted themselves to keep the wheels of an unseen machine spinning. Salesmen whose exploitation of the self leaves denuded soil, they are the corporeal equivalent of Detroit after the car industry had vamoosed – empty human buildings of capitalism.

Joe Keller in *All My Sons* has seen a business partner sentenced to jail, and poisoned the heart of his family with lies to keep ahead. The tragedy of Eddie Carbone in *A View from the Bridge* is tied up in physical desires, but his determination for his niece to climb out of her own class seals their fate. Aware of his good fortune in gaining citizenship, Eddie has tightened his determination for his family to achieve at the cost of others. These men live in generous neighbourhoods, kindness rippling around them. But it cannot satisfy their hunger to win. The spirit of individualism manifests as violence, an idolatry which contains within it hatred of the collective. Even in *The Crucible*, greed and land-grabbing upset the harmony. Many of the families of those accused of witchcraft in Salem were engaged in lawsuits over land. John Proctor's first pushback against authority is his absence from the church, driven by the preacher's relentless sermonising about the acquisition of his parsonage.

The Crucible pushes further. Under the hot-to-touch influence of McCarthyism, Arthur Miller came to realise that individualism, in its capitalist guise, was backed by the apparatus of state power. And that, though it mouthed principles of freedom, it brooked no opposition. The villains in *The Crucible* are less the girls driven by their collective blindness than the officers of the state who exploit them. With suffocating plausibility *The Crucible* shows how, through group inertia and the coercion of a powerful few, old ties are broken and a community collaborates in acts of evil. The righteous shriek of the accuser is as old as humanity, yet its focus has rarely been sharper than in 1693 Salem, or Miller's America. The despair which erupts from John Proctor rebukes a culture given over to pointing the finger, and to conjuring villains from thin air. 'Is the accuser always holy now? Were they born this morning as clean as God's fingers? . . . We are what we always were in Salem, but now the little crazy children are jangling the keys of the kingdom, and common vengeance writes the law!' Potent then, it still serves today as the shrieks of left and right, of each and every binary, hurl accusations with little recourse to reason or proof.

Authoritarians thrive on moral simplicity; context and complexity dissolve their monochrome definitions. Their cry of 'With us or against us' has always been ignited by a desire to reduce human imagination. Deputy Governor Danforth strides into *The Crucible* determined to cement his influence. His prime weapon is moral certainty. 'You must understand, sir, that a person is either with this court or he must be counted against it, there be no road between.' The blank confidence of this statement had painful echoes in 1953. Miller saw the horror when morality is ascribed to prejudice. In Salem, as in his own time, it was about 'the delivery of conscience to the state . . . if the government said it was alright, it was alright . . .'

Miller was positioned to read and represent this moment. The Great Crash of 1929, the cataclysm which left his father and a generation grubbing for food in garbage cans, pushed Miller towards an understanding that society was not an illusion, it was everything. And that, to keep everyone afloat, society had to be remade constantly anew. He understood the desires of the individual – he admired his father's entrepreneurial instinct – yet he knew the necessity of a fully functioning commonwealth. He knew how to tell stories that addressed both.

Miller came from the urban culture of the East Coast with its fast street rhythms of thought and speech, and its nostalgic links to the Old World in Europe. Yet in his heart he looked west, and yearned for the slower, more taciturn and solid rhythms of the American heartland, of a life of the hands, of clean air, and open space. Willy Loman's most secure achievement is a porch he has built with his own hands, just as Miller constructed the shack in which he wrote his early work. Putting up the final wall, he said, was as satisfying as finishing a play. Willy Loman dismisses his son Biff's dream of working in the open air with the taunt, 'Go back to the West! Be a carpenter, a cowboy, enjoy yourself!' And yet later, in a mental fog, he talks of buying seeds and growing plants in his Brooklyn backyard, a myopic fumble for an older reality in an increasingly tarmacked world. Miller was the boy from Brooklyn who said he dreamed of being a farmer. In that duality lives the wrench between Loman's hand-built porch and his nervous spieling; the Midwest and New York; the wide-open sky and the concrete; the solid and the conceptual. Oppositions which divided America were painfully and productively alive within Arthur Miller.

What is intrinsic in these four buildings that is absent elsewhere? What in their brickwork makes them great? First and foremost, juice. There is an instinct for the sensational. The plays preceding and those that followed tinker with narrative and form. These stories just let rip, ransacking shopworn tropes from warhorses, thrillers, and boulevard entertainment. *All My Sons* is replete with old-fashioned theatrics, pilfered from the chickens-coming-home-to-roost cupboard. Mother is upstairs living in denial that her son is dead; the son's fiancée returns home after a long absence; her brother is making the same journey bearing revelations. The last stretch even revolves around that hoary old device – an unread letter. It would be risible if not so determinedly executed. Miller thought he was making a new drama of poetics, but he wasn't averse to exploiting nineteenth-century tricks. The work is the better for it.

A View from the Bridge self-consciously harks back to classical drama, inserting a chorus (the lawyer Alfieri) as homage. Predestination haunts the play as the seeds of its conclusion are planted early – the transgressive love of the uncle for the niece, the community's punishment for a snitch, the loneliness and pride of Eddie Carbone. The ingredients are laid out, and the direction they head in – tragedy – indicated. The hothouse atmosphere ensures the play never wavers. The inexorable raising of the oven's temperature owes much to the wilful hysteria of melodrama, but no one complains while enthralled.

Death of a Salesman starts at a high pitch as Loman returns home from what could have been a suicide attempt. It continues on a precipice. Present, past, and dream worlds fold into one another. Each fragment is caught at its moment of crisis, and sweated for potential suspense. It recalls the template of Shakespeare's *Henry VIII*, a play which brings on characters in succession – the Duke of Buckingham, Catherine of Aragon, Wolsey, then Cranmer – and takes pleasure in watching each walk the edge of a cliff, before toppling and falling. Shakespeare was an experienced playwright when he wrote *Henry VIII*; his powers may have been waning, but he knew his audience's fascination in watching great figures wobbling on a ledge. *Death of a Salesman* is one of the great sustained employments of this perverse fascination. Willy Loman falls and scrambles and clutches, each new incident sapping more of his strength for clinging to the cliff edge, each thinning the ropes. We watch his struggles appalled, and – in our sin – excited.

The reaction to the premiere of *Death of a Salesman* in Philadelphia is now legendary – the protracted three-minute silence, people standing and sitting back down, wandering dazed in the aisles, and then after the first tentative claps, the house coming down. Months later the reaction to the play started to irk Miller, the weeping and the wailing had become an affectation, and a missing of the point. '*Salesman* became too effective, or too affective,' he complained. People were using their emotional reaction to avoid necessary hard thought. Miller wanted people to be moved by Loman, but more importantly he wanted them to see the system destroying him. Tears obscured that.

'I wanted to write a tougher play than *Salesman*, and in *The Crucible*, I found the play that would resist *Salesman* for me.' If his dream was to clean off narrative excitement, he failed. *The Crucible* is as hoary a populist entertainment as any. Using tropes from film noir, and twisty-turny thrillers, it crystallises moral choices in cruxes of storytelling excitement. Though none of the play is clinically set in a trial, it makes capital use of courtroom drama devices – concealment, dramatic revelation, and volte-face. When Elizabeth Proctor is brought in to testify as to her husband's relations with Abigail Williams, the audience is frozen in a silent scream of expectation and fear. Though melodrama was sneered at throughout the proscenium era, its seams were industriously mined.

Miller may have been ashamed of such effects. Reflecting on his later unpopularity he described the writer in America as an entertainer, a tap dancer. 'We are not regarded as philosophers, moralists, leaders of any description . . . we tell stories and we divert the people.' Some of the bitterness might have been directed at himself. His own tap-dancing skills were pretty acute when he was keeping Broadway in thrall. The best playwrights have to remain a little whorish for effect. Brecht loathed melodrama; he also wrote *Mother Courage*.

Alongside the narrative roller coaster in his classics, there is an exhilarating sense of physical definition. As a director, reading a play triggers impressions of its potential plastic life. Something monumental and concrete plants these works of Miller's securely within the frame. Statuesque would be the right word if it didn't imply stiffness. The figures he sculpted in this, his purple patch, seem hyper-alive in their taut muscularity, rooted and securely foundationed. Though the drama is feverish, they do not feel excessively mobile. The sensation is of etched, gaunt figures, isolated in a hostile landscape with history, like a blasting wind, sharpening their features. Characters bring with them a declarative sense – I should stand here, I will leave this way, this is how I will hold this – which is a godsend to actors and directors.

Often overlooked, another gnawing question glued these works together, the asking of which ties Miller in with many other proscenium writers: how do you keep love alight when the flame has gone out? How long can embers glow? Miller liked to pay obeisance to Ibsen. His other play within his purple patch was a free adaptation of *An Enemy of the People*, Ibsen's classic about an individual isolated from his tribe. Proving as potent a rebuke to McCarthyism as *The Crucible*, it too enjoyed a long run on Broadway. This connection, together with his assumption of Old Testament moral authority, has forced a persona of Ibsen manqué on Miller, the stern issuer of Commandments. This has obscured what seem closer and more obsessive concerns, revolving around the jaundiced failure of love. Miller knew his forefathers well – respect for precedent was a powerful factor in the proscenium's capacity to endure. For me, Miller's greater debt was to Strindberg.

Miller was a frequent attendee at rehearsals and premieres of his work. He had a regular shtick in terms of notes. With three different plays, in three different theatres, I heard of him giving precisely the same note to correct the imbalance of a production: 'There's one simple problem, one thing you're not getting . . . it's a love story.' Something about the repetition begins to sound formulaic. It may have an element of *cri de coeur*. Every time he entered a room he was greeted as an ethical sage: what he had created in his plays were relationships.

The most celebrated relations in his work are between fathers and sons: Joe Keller and his son Chris in *All My Sons*; the two sons and the absent dead father in *The Price*; and above all, Willy and Biff Loman in *Death of a Salesman*. But beyond the father–son axis, there is a more recurrent pattern – the problems between husbands and wives. As with Strindberg, unhappy marriage sits at the heart of these plays. Between John and Elizabeth Proctor, between Joe and Kate Keller, Willy and Linda Loman, Eddie and Beatrice Carbone, each seems to have begun in fierce and celebratory love, and in each case the milk has curdled. Once you start to hear this tune, you hear it everywhere. The back gardens of suburbia in *All My Sons* aspire to some form of idyll, but tension seethes. Neighbours manifest love wars in a minor key. Husbands and wives carp at each other with thin humour, squabbling and scratching over responsibilities and household chores. Scrips and scraps of flirting and jealousy, done with bright smiles, ratchet up the unease. A skein of marital discontent spreads over the play, and – it is soon noticeable – all the other plays of his prime.

The cause, though muted, follows a similar path in each couple – sexual silence – the moment when they have nothing to offer each other any more. In *The Crucible*, John's transgression with Abigail occurs when Elizabeth is expecting a child and, as is awkwardly explained, she is unable to satisfy his needs. The chasm between Willy and Biff Loman opens up when the son discovers his father with a mistress. Between Willy and Linda, as between Joe and Kate Keller, there is the chasm between those sleeping in separate beds and living in separate realities. In *A View from the Bridge*, the subject is brought up directly by Beatrice Carbone in blunt language, shocking its contemporary audience. The sexual dysfunction here, where the niece, Catherine, has distracted the affections of Eddie, is raw and open. Beatrice's need and his masculine shame at being unable to satisfy her fuel the onrushing tragedy.

This theme, relationships undone, emerges as one of the keys that unlocked Miller's creativity. He returned to the theme of how a relationship falls silent, but never with the same innate force. Nor did the fragility and vulnerability of the family unit ever loom so large. It would be trite to say that later contentment diminished the depth of his need to write. But the process by which families corrode and love curdles was a powerful fuel for his storytelling in his prime.

After the Fall – Miller's kaleidoscope of fragments amounting to a play – offers a tipping point, for him and for the theatre. What came later would never match the previous works, nor would the proscenium regain its monumental authority. In several ways, in his purple patch, Miller perfected the possibilities of the proscenium, pulling politics and passion together into tightly constructed parables. With *After the Fall*, he pulled the pin and let what had previously compacted together be blown asunder in scattered shards. Premiering in 1964, after the death of Monroe and long after the demise of HUAC, it came eight years after his previous play. Both those subjects are addressed, together with the end of his first marriage, all with a blush-inducing nakedness. Friends, partners, and himself are dissected for the public gaze with a painfully awkward honesty. The sketched scenes which tell of the dayglo beginnings, the giddy rise and squalid fall of his love for Marilyn are raw, feeding his audience the celebrity gossip they already half knew.

A shift of gear occurs here, a discarding of reticence. No longer screening himself, he lets it all, in the lingo of the 1960s, hang out. Among a series of death knells for the proscenium tradition rung out by different authors, here we see one of its bulwarks – discretion – being torn apart. The quest of the play is a scramble to learn how to survive a world in which savagery flourishes, including in one's own heart.

Following the same drama-on-a-precipice dynamic as *Death of a Salesman*, all is at risk as we hurtle through the Depression, the Second World War, HUAC, and various marriages. Quentin – the avatar for Arthur – waits for his German lover to land at an airport. What is at stake as he trawls through his life is his own self-worth, hanging by a thread. The trigger for the quest is a recent visit to a concentration camp, in the company of a young German woman (transparently Inge Morath, Arthur's third and last wife). Before setting to work on the play, Miller had travelled through Germany with Morath and seen the camps in what he called 'their raw, uncleaned state'. This charnel house repository of the worst of the twentieth century prompts questions in the play, including: 'One day you faint because the gardener cuts his finger off, within a week you're climbing over corpses of children bombed in a subway. What hope can there be if that is so?'

Horrified as Quentin/Miller is by the crimes of the Holocaust, he is equally as shaken by his numbness, his feeling of complicity. This action, to share responsibility for crimes of that magnitude, struck some as moral grandstanding, but to me it appears exemplary. Many artists exploit atrocities as a means of gaining brownie points through the articulacy of their condemnation. Few have the courage to admit atrocity sits in their own hearts. Miller equates the cruelty Quentin shows to his father, to his first wife, to Maggie, all the turnings of his back, to that of mass murderers. There were few Holocaust plays then – unless you argue most plays after the Second World War are indirectly about that subject – because it remained a moral challenge to depict. Putting your hand up and saying you have the same capacity takes strength. Miller wanted to pay an honest debt to 'the destroyed, to the people who finally get it in the face'. A debt not paid by saying 'How tragic' or 'How terrible', but only honoured by saying 'I too am responsible.' In his words, 'There is in all of us a retrograde desire to kill, to destroy, a love of the dark. We have a lot of forces to keep us from doing it. The willingness to destroy others is very deep in the human mind.'

In his memoir *Timebends*, Miller calls mankind a 'denial machine'. No one exemplified denial more acutely than when he tried to protest that 'Maggie' in this play was not Marilyn. Everyone comes under the microscope here, but most savagely himself. Too much came out in this play, too much for him to put back in the cupboard. For me, this play – if it is one – broke him. Its openness shattered his capacity to imagine with tidy completeness from here on. Pandora's box was opened, all sorts of mess splattered over the auditorium, and all that was left in the box, with its self-interred cruelty, was hope.

After the Fall fits into no category – part confession, part testament, largely search. Miller earns the right to share – dread word – what quantum of wisdom he had gleaned, and he is worth listening to. Quentin's searchings come to an end as his girlfriend Olga's plane is about to land, and he speaks words from the heart of his author, words which cost character and playwright: 'What burning cities taught her, and the death of love taught me . . . that we are very . . . dangerous. Is the knowing all? To know, and even happily, that we meet unblessed; not in some garden of wax fruit and painted trees, that lie of Eden, but after, after the Fall, after many, many deaths. Is the knowing all? And the wish to kill is never killed but with some gift of courage we may look into its face when it appears, and with a stroke of love forgive it; again and again . . . forever? Now, it is not certainty. I do not feel that. But it does feel feasible not to be afraid. Perhaps it's all that one has.'

Olga arrives – 'Hello, Quentin', 'Hello, Olga' – and the play ends.

As Miller said, it's a love story. His life started anew.

The world hated it. They queued up to kick it. Miller had banked up much loathing, and it spilled over. His pretence that *After the Fall* was not based on his own life only fed the contempt. Hating came from all sides, from Monroe's fans, who had never forgiven him; trendsetters who thought drama had moved on; the right wing, who hated how Miller had stared them down; and the left wing, who hated his even-handedness. As he said, there was a 'ferocious reaction – it blew my image away for a lot of people'.

The theatrical community went sour on Miller, much as they did with Tennessee Williams. Rather than respecting the strides made by both in opening up potentials, they blamed them retrospectively for not going far enough. There is an ahistorical strain in the avant-garde which exhausts. Miller did little to court favour: 'We got an avant garde that was touting a dry hole . . . A seeking for sensation and a turning away from character and reality.' The reciprocal loathing from the vanguard was matched by the high priests of political wisdom – Miller's repudiation of the right, and his determination to avoid being squeezed into a leftist box, earned a plague from both houses. Tribes are inclined to hate other tribes and preserve a special contempt for those who choose to live in more than one. Or worse, try to make peace between them. He chose a tough road to walk – concerned with individuals rather than individualism, an internationalist without taking sides, and on the side of each and every human.

For all that the condemners deserve challenge, it is hard to block the fact that the later plays don't cut it. *After the Fall* really did prove a stop point – its openness and honesty an impossible act to recover from. Somehow the opposites Miller balanced carefully early in his writing now pulled him off-centre. Having walked the tightrope steadily under the pressure of history, somehow he wobbled without that weight on his shoulders. The watching crowd – envious of his previous insouciance, and excited by the prospect of a celebrity death – pursed their lips and started blowing.

Some animal capacity for hearing the tune had gone: 'playwriting is an auditory skill rather than a literary one. If I can't hear it, I can't write it.' Though never a recorder of speech as authentic or flavoursome as his contemporaries, particularly Clifford Odets, his source of inspiration dried up. When he was younger, he acted out the parts as he wrote, each character with a different voice but, looking back, remarked he'd not done this for twenty-five years. Some sort of ability for clownish exposure went too. Tellingly, Miller remarked, 'The best work that anybody ever writes is the work that is on the verge of embarrassing him.' Something happened that meant risks could no longer be taken. Some personal shift quietened his necessary rage. Who knows what that might have been. Few could have survived the burdens he carried in his shining moment and remained sanguine; only one in an era could have used that moment to forge such stories. We all know that Usain Bolt can't run 9.58 seconds all his life. Perhaps we should also allow artists to leave the racetrack gracefully.

An artist sits in the sun briefly, matching their historical moment. Though we project on them a need for consistency and purity, we have to appreciate that, like the rest of us, they are capable of a ripe state and a sour one. Miller, whose central theme was integrity, invited judgement on a higher plateau than most. But if he could observe his characters, and bring them to life, with no excess of sainthood or damnation, we should do the same for him.

His observation of the human comedy, including his own floundering self, was carried through straight and pitiless. Maybe cushioned a little by the belief that in knowing fully, we can find a way to be better to ourselves and each other. A process without end, for Miller: 'While my heart beats, my head is going to be asking questions.'

The price of that was a monumental loneliness. One carried out with grace.

Myths and misfits.
Marilyn Monroe and Arthur Miller at the April in Paris Ball, New York's Waldorf-Astoria, 1957

Jean Anouilh
1910–1987

'Dated' – traditionally bandied as an insult – can be a cause for celebration. As a slur it has all the intellectual curiosity of that deadening English phrase, 'Not my cup of tea'. Our age can often be guilty of historical presentism, with anything that fails to inhabit the culture of the now or next-to-be deemed unworthy. Exhibiting a heart-crushing lack of curiosity, this attitude proves an oddly wilful diminution of possibility. In that context, when people curse anything as dated, my curiosity is piqued.

In the late 1990s, there was a stilted production of J. B. Priestley's *Dangerous Corner* starring a line-up of old-school turns. The director Keith Baxter, a one-time matinee idol, had cast himself as one of the leads. On two occasions, he had to produce a cigarette. Each time he stopped the show for an elaborate display of old-school business. Leaning on his back foot, he patted the various pockets of his tuxedo in investigation. On finding the right one, he slowly extracted a cigarette case, flattened it in his palm at a languorous pace, sprung the top open, removed a single cigarette with elan, shut the top, and tapped the cigarette on the case thrice. Placing cigarette between pouting lips with precision, he returned the case to its pocket with little hurry. All achieved, he approached a table on which there sat a solid desktop lighter, which he lifted slowly. With cigarette held in his mouth exactly parallel to the floor, and the flame held at ninety degrees, he lit his cigarette, before replacing the lighter on the table. Then, and only then, he resumed the play. The entire rigmarole stopped the show for about three minutes each time. With no relation to character, plot or relationships, it was nothing but a demonstration of period styling. Though it drove sections of the audience bananas, and almost certainly the rest of the ensemble, I found it transfixing. The second time round I couldn't help applauding. Somehow the banal poetry of the ritual, the luxuriating in the past simply for its own sake, spoke more about the period than any number of history books.

Dated is an adjective often ascribed to the work of Jean Anouilh, but there is a fascination in diving into the epoch his plays inhabit. Most distinct is the prevalence of speech-making. Anouilh invites weighty historic and mythic figures to strut their stuff – Becket, Henry II, Joan of Arc, Antigone, Creon, Orpheus, and Eurydice. He wouldn't have been the first to allow such icons ample room to state a point of view. But in his plays, hardly a character appears who does not indulge in a degree of circumlocution and periphrasis previously unknown to the stage (and maybe humanity). Each action is justified, each thought qualified, each description amplified. An outbreak of logorrhoea provokes audiences to want to shapeshift into news interrogators and bark 'Get to the point.' Who out of Jean Anouilh and Eugene O'Neill indulges the higher degree of prolixity is unknown – a statistical survey has not been carried out – but it must be a close-run thing.

Where O'Neill stumbles forward towards forensic attempts at psychological truth, Anouilh prefers to sit still, seduced by the burnished phrase and an old-fashioned schoolbook use of simile. As with Keith Baxter and his cigarette unveiling, in Anouilh's speeches you hear 'like' or 'as' then sit back and settle in for the luxurious unfurling of a plush metaphor. High literary writing just waiting to be studied, it is the French prose equivalent of the outburst of verse drama in London in the late 1940s led by T. S. Eliot and Christopher Fry. Reacting to recent horrors, this clutching at gilt served as a veil of hyper-refined civility across a scarred visage. Each overdecorated phrase a pleated curtain to conceal the rubble left behind by war.

The verbal decoration is often pleasurable, as Anouilh used persiflage to add self-reflection to old stories. Using the prose of conversation rather than the verse of the elemental, he took the ancient tragedy of Antigone and replaced its blind propulsion with characters whose self-consciousness cushions the bluntness. Taking historical fulcra, such as Joan of Arc's trial and the antagonism of Becket and Henry II, where

Shakespeare or Brecht would have used epic action to show history hurtling by, Anouilh pauses for long reflection and focuses in tight close-up. He does not disappear other elements but foregrounds the thinking of individuals. Each is aware of their immediate context, and also conversant with their own place in history, literature, and art. In full knowledge of the ripples circling away from them, Anouilh shows how human history grows not more intelligent, but more self-aware.

Because they display a delicious combination of equivocation and moral elusiveness, it is hard for us to pin these protagonists down, as it is for them to work themselves out. Listening to their calculations between realpolitik and personal integrity, one can get exasperated, but there is an admirable desire from Anouilh to escape definition. Given several of his works were written and performed during the German occupation, this elusiveness became a mode of survival.

Several of Anouilh's plays deal with high stakes political power-broking; his two best known observe a disempowered woman carving out an identity within oppressive regimes. Both were no doubt influenced by the slippery act of surviving as an artist within the Vichy regime. *Antigone* rehearses at length the need for an individual to find a moral voice within a state trying to contain an ever-growing threat of chaos; *The Lark*, the tale of Joan of Arc (first translated by Fry in the UK, and adapted by Lillian Hellman in the US), observes how Joan finds her way towards an unasked-for exceptionalism, inflicted on her by the blundering of her captors. Both young women stumble flinchingly towards martyrdom, progressing from doubt and fear towards resolution. The climax in *Antigone* is a sustained agon between Creon and the heroine, where everything is put on the table in an argument between life-loving contingency and death-loving purity. In these exchanges, when Anouilh's lush prose matches the extremity of his situations, his work really does fly. At earlier moments in the same play, when the rhetoric is high but the stakes are low, it doesn't. *Antigone* was sufficiently balanced to appeal to both Resistance and collaborators; *The Lark*, produced in 1952, performed the same balancing act for a nation still riven by old sympathies.

Anouilh created work the keynote of which is ambiguity – achievement enough in a time of dangerous certainty.

Antigone's finest moment is its last, when, after the *Sturm und Drang*, a group of minor characters, who have witnessed the high drama, are left onstage to mooch around. There is little to animate the stage, until a game of cards is suggested. At which point they wholly engage with that diversion, completely forgetting the crisis just passed. In *Eurydice*, a play we presented in the West End in 1999, the highlight is an old Falstaffian character who, no matter the mythic rites swirling around him, cannot be diverted from itemising the menu of each railway station restaurant he has dined in. These miniature acts of diurnal hedonism are sufficient to distract from all the swirl.

The supreme of all Anouilh's truths, this is what he adds to the canon. No matter the depth of Orpheus' or Antigone's or Becket's tragedy, it can be wiped from the memory by a quality ice cream. A late friend once told me, after he had received his terminal cancer diagnosis, and once the buzz of sorrowing friends and family had departed, he was left at a loose end. Not knowing what to do, he checked out the football scores on Ceefax. Seeing that Arsenal had won, he cheered up and forgot he was dying.

Not quite the same as Brueghel's ploughman continuing his muddy progress as Icarus plunges into the sea, this is not a reference to the indifference of the universe. True to the proscenium ethos, it refers to how modest acts of pleasure can obliterate the catastrophes of titans, and how the small, good life can trump the grand tragic. As our world goes merrily mad, Anouilh's most abiding truth is perversely comforting.

No shortage of fabric.
Colombe, directed by Peter Brook at the
New Theatre, London, 1951

Ena Lamont Stewart
1912–2006

Each generation has its own cultural epitomes, zeitgeist-informing events which coalesce a cohort. For those of us in the early 1980s pursuing the earnest dream of changing the world through art – days of skinhead hairstyling, Doc Martens, and buckets shaken for miners' families – one event stood out. A clarion call was sounded in Scotland towards which fervent youth flocked. To suit the anti-chic of the age, it was fastidiously unglamorous: a revival by the radical theatre company 7:84 of a play by an unknown writer, Ena Lamont Stewart. Written in 1947, its subject was life in the Glasgow tenements in the late 1930s, focusing on the women and their struggles to maintain families oppressed by economic failures and the collapse of their patriarchs. The title was a perfect fit for an era of masculine self-abasement: *Men Should Weep*.

John McGrath, the gentle giant who ran 7:84, was already a cult figure thanks to his book *A Good Night Out*. This slim tome – a guide to creating popular, committed, subversive theatre – jutted out of our donkey-jacket pockets, dog-eared from midnight reading. The name '7:84' came from the statistic that 7 per cent of the UK population owned 84 per cent of the land, thus ensuring everyone was indignant before they had even bought a ticket. The company carved a niche touring the neglected small towns of Scotland. Their previous signal success had been McGrath's *The Cheviot, The Stag and the Black, Black Oil*, a loose Brechtian telling of how Highland communities had been displaced over centuries to free their land for first sheep farming, then hunting, then oil. Each show – a blend of cartoon and outrage, human transaction and lyric ballad – would end with a whisky and fiddle-based ceilidh. These reeled through to the early hours, with cast and audience spinning together and dreaming of utopias, before each morning's hangover reintroduced them to reality. *A Good Night Out* was a prescription for how others could reproduce this way of working. And for how to destroy the chocolate-box excesses of the proscenium tradition, a call for action not entirely urgent, since the form was already gasping for oxygen by the mid-1980s.

The iconic production of *Men Should Weep* originated at Glasgow's Citizens Theatre, and was directed by Giles Havergal, one of the triumvirate who ran that institution and who, ironically, were making a bold new case for the ailing proscenium. The minds behind the Citz shared a concern for social justice with 7:84, though their house pioneered in a different direction. Sitting decadent and beautiful in the middle of the impoverished Gorbals, it was a theatre that combined social purpose with louche extravagance of design and image. Their blend of cheap ticket prices and expressionist excess effected a collision of working-class audience and high artfulness that was unique and splendid. Peers watched *Men Should Weep* with wild enthusiasm when it opened, so when news arrived that it was transferring to London – and playing at the Theatre Royal Stratford East (another temple of sophisticated popular entertainment) – it felt like an apotheosis. Pilgrimages were organised. Unfortunately, my money had run out weeks before, and the prospect of spending my last pennies on anything other than speed and chips was inconceivable. So I waved goodbye to a bus full of fellow students and returned bedsit-wards to read a copy of the play borrowed from the library.

I picked it up expecting a Brechtian epic of incendiary agitprop. What I read confused initially. There was no speechifying call to arms, nor any pained argument about sexual politics: I was reading a gentle and human tale about characters surviving in grinding poverty. This was recorded not manipulated experience. Confusion soon turned to admiration, but the privacy of the pleasure seemed at odds with the brouhaha. Rereading the play twenty years later, when I was at the Oxford Stage Company, reinforced the impression that *Men Should Weep* is a classic of twentieth-century theatre. Oddly, having been rescued from neglect by 7:84, it had fallen back into literary oblivion, so we revived it for a touring production, with the National following suit. The ideal play for a period ravaged by Thatcher's monetarist experiments in social misery, the politics of the first revival may have obscured its quieter, more human qualities. *Men Should Weep* is a timeless play about family, survival, and dignity.

Ena Lamont Stewart was the daughter of a Church of Scotland minister. Her family was originally from the Highlands and reached Glasgow via a considerable detour to Canada, lending Ena the perspective of both outsider and insider. Theirs was an open house, filled with morality and noise. As she said: 'We laughed a lot, talked a lot and read a lot. We also sang a lot and had, in addition to the piano (which was played a lot), an organ, two sets of bagpipes and a penny whistle.' It's a music embedded in the language of her plays.

Although her family would have qualified as middle class, Lamont Stewart was disturbed by the poverty she saw around her in the Gorbals, still ravaged by the Depression. She was struck by the sight of working-class 'shawly women', who jostled into her father's jumble sales, rooting out the best bargains. Later, she was a receptionist at the Royal Hospital for Sick Children in Glasgow, where she saw at first hand the damage done by malnutrition and other diseases consequent on poor living conditions. Here she found the material for her second play, and here she first heard the phrase 'They've kep' him in,' muttered incessantly by a dazed mother affecting a scraggy bundle of clothes to be the child she'd been told to leave in hospital. The phrase becomes the emotional bedrock for the last act of *Men Should Weep*.

Her plays observe life with Sean O'Casey's lack of sentimentality and celebrate it with the same richness of language. Like the Irishman, her need to write was closely linked with a root-and-branch socialism. Her husband, an actor named Jack Stewart, worked for the Glasgow Unity Theatre, an idealistic company formed by working-class actors whose aim was to represent their lived experience. Strongly averse to the refined drawing room manners of the day, Ena herself wrote: 'One evening in the winter of 1942 I went to the theatre. I came home in a mood of red-hot revolt against cocktail time, glamorous gowns and underworked, about-to-be deceived husbands. I asked myself what I wanted to see on stage and the answer was Life. Real Life. Real People.'

She wrote *Men Should Weep* in two days flat. This is not one of those etiolated political plays with each phrase weighed carefully for ideological import; it poured out from imagination and memory. 'I wrote *Men Should Weep* at such a pitch of intensity I had no idea what the characters were going to do next . . . I think it was a kind of emotional release I needed at the time.' Her marriage was foundering, and she was about to become a single mother. Some of that desolation and fear fed into the work. She had something akin to a friendship with her avatars, claiming, 'I saw my characters – as if they really were in front of my eyes, and I wrote down what they said . . . they just arrived in my kitchen when I was doing a washing – as if they were saying, "Come on, we'll give her a couple of pages. She'll have to dry her hands and hunt for pencil and paper; then we'll buzz off" . . . Characters in full flow cannot be ignored.' The freshness of their voices, the truth of their manner, the explosive need-to-be-alive of each gives testament to the accuracy of her recording.

Lamont Stewart's later story was one of frustration. Subsequent plays were turned down – one with such force, by James Bridie at the Citizens Theatre, that she went home and tore up all the copies. The men's club has always had an ability for a brief welcome to outsiders before closing the door. Lamont Stewart lived out the twilight of her life in a Scottish nursing home, in a state further adumbrated by the clouds of Alzheimer's. One can only hope her characters were still chattering kindly to her.

A fastidious realism about presenting the life of the working class marked out the work of the Unity Theatre. They depicted their suffering, showed how heavily the odds were stacked against them, and admired the fortitude with which they deadpanned their way through each tough hand dealt. They were also unsparing in exposing flaws – the apathy and the lack of purpose that led to drink, gambling, and violence. And while Robert McLeish's *The Gorbals Story*, a companion play in many ways, dealt with racial and religious problems, *Men Should Weep* concentrated on the tough lives of the women. Amazingly, these two plays proved huge commercial successes for the Unity, and (before the company withered on the vine in London, detached from its Scottish roots) both ran for long periods in Glasgow, before transferring successfully to London's West End. In the brief socialist dream that gripped post-war Britain such things were possible.

The well she drew from.
Main Street, Gorbals, 1911

Jean Genet
1910–1986

The journey of Jean Genet's life, though often painful for him to navigate, offered prurient pleasure to copious observers. For more timid existentialists, it seemed a lurid fantasy of non-stop authenticity. Before Genet achieved much, Sartre had published a 750-page hagiography called *Saint Genet*. For the Deux Magots set (including his first sponsor, Jean Cocteau), Genet was the ideal of lively and rebellious action, a modus operandi they could only imagine, and sentimentalised greedily.

During a long guerrilla war with the French legal system, Genet was more often forced by circumstance into spaces of transgression than he might have wished for. In his secret heart, he may have hoped to be a suburban accountant. Born in 1910 in penury, he described the family as 'the first prison cell', and the justice system soon became his surrogate. Shunted from care institution to young offender's jail throughout a rickety childhood, he saw the state's capacity to exert power at its bluntest. By the age of twenty-four he had been incarcerated in almost every youth prison in France, serving ten different sentences. Relations between the directors of such institutions and their youthful inmates he described as one of performative submission. 'It formed a kind of theatrical event for the wardens – they were the first spectators and we were the first actors,' he recounted in a documentary. Exhibitionist abuse formed a template for his drama.

With glee at 'épataying', he defended authoritarian systems and balked at humane proposals of re-education. Declaring himself 'hot for crime', he worried that anything but the harshest of regimes would deprive the criminal youth of France of 'their violence, their vigour, their virility'. Invoking the precedent of Oscar Wilde, who extolled the releasing joy of sin, Genet celebrated the criminal class: 'I recognise in thieves, traitors and murderers, in the ruthless and the cunning, a deep beauty – a sunken beauty.' He defined his 'relation to society as an oblique one', and found that in embracing mayhem and robbery he achieved himself. His desire to provoke climaxed with him cheering the Germans into Paris, though this may have had less to do with enthusiasm for fascism and more with hatred for the elite of his mother country.

For these attitudes, articulated in grenades of punk shock, Genet became an icon, the counterculture hero of his day. His deranged, non-linear, psychotic output acquired a passionate claque. In a different era, misfit young (including myself) could drift to the corner of the bookshop, or the student studio production, or the after-midnight film show for some contraband Genet. The connection with David Bowie's 'Jean Genie' felt like important arcane knowledge. All his *matériel* thrived in the long-gone wonder world of 'the underground', a place where re-invention could occur. In a world before identity politics, with Genet in pocket, the young were no longer compelled to sequester within a racial or gender type or a given sexual preference. 'Genet' was a code word to gain entry to a basement of opportunities.

In a collection of memoir fragments written in overripe prose, in expressionist dramas, and most emphatically in the way he lived, Genet created a following, helping to shift the moral ambition of the educated towards a cult of contravention. In his allegiances, judged from the perspective of a present-day progressive, he was exemplary, a prophet, almost. He collaborated with the most active enemies of the Establishment – the French student rebellion of 1968, the Black Panther movement, the Baader-Meinhof Red Army Faction, and the Palestinian movement. His allegiance was early and fierce. When the *haute bourgeoisie* liberals signed up to the same causes, Genet found himself a hero to those he despised most. What does the rebel do when the mainstream co-opts their gestures and normalises them? As with punk rock, when nihilism meets approval it has little left to do but flail around in the void. Genet intuited that and fell silent, withdrawing from view after the événements of 1968.

In *The Blacks*, a white woman is tried and executed by a kangaroo court, while a queen and her entourage look on. Genet specified all parts should be played by black actors – in whiteface. The play opened in Paris in 1959 and went on to have a record-breaking off-Broadway run. Genet was savvy enough to know most of his audience would be white, but in a prefatory note he states that, in the unlikely event it has a black audience, one white person should sit in a spotlight. His diktat anticipated many of our present strictures around audience composition – including Black Out nights. In *The Balcony*, he analyses the rotten power structures of states, and the performative nature of class, within a series of vignettes in a brothel. Inflammatory gestures, all stumbling their way around acts of formal deconstruction, these scenic spasms are a gift for anyone searching out raw material for solemn monographs about performativity.

Largely unreadable, and almost unperformable, these plays are a procession of unmodulated, histrionic scenes bearing little relation to reality or each other. When asked about his playwriting in a late and mischievous interview, he smirks and remarks that although he had never been to the theatre and 'only read a few plays', he decided 'the theatre I prefer is the kind that seizes society at a diagonal'. Angularity is a wise approach. Proscenium theatre is defined by a straight-on collision between audience and art, so the diagonal is a good way to stir the pot. Genet took it further, claiming, 'I enjoyed making a clumsy (maladroit) kind of theatre, and in that clumsiness there was maybe something new.' Clumsiness can be refreshing, and a loathing for polish keeps the conversation lively. But Genet drove it to a place of provocative nonsense, which drains the spectator of any capacity to watch or listen. The impression that scenes are only there to demonstrate an outrage or provoke an appalled response soon becomes as meticulously dull as conversation with someone pursuing the same goals.

The Maids, his best-known work, is meat and drink to the semioticians. And a special sort of agony to watch. Two maids role-play the mistress–servant relationship while plotting to kill their employer, with myriad potential plot ramifications worked through. Each character speaks a stilted and camp parody of what it is to be human, and in the process forgoes one's sympathy at truly impressive speed. The ability to listen evaporates soon after. A quick glance at the programme then tells you there's another two hours to go. It feels like being persistently pestered to play by an angry child who has decided you are their special friend.

A host of energies disrupted France in the 1960s, the fight for independence in Algeria bringing most violence to the streets. At the height of that crisis, Genet wrote *The Screens*, an unplayable pageant of ninety characters. In scenes exposing the ugliness of France's imperial violence, it touched the nerve of colonial guilt at its most sensitive spot. Opening at the highly prestigious Odéon, one of France's designated national theatres, and lasting only a few performances, it created a storm of outrage and demonstrations. *The Screens* seemed to place Genet at the heart of revolution, yet it was his last play and close to the end of his public life.

One of the climaxes of the événements was the occupation of the same theatre, in May 1968. This proved one of several end points for the proscenium century, a moment that flattered the tradition by intimating insurrection could be nurtured there, and threw shadow by demonstrating how revolution was beyond its capacity. Genet was cautious about the movement, seeing it as little more than another bourgeois parlour game on a larger scale. 'If they had been real revolutionaries they certainly wouldn't have occupied a theatre. They would have occupied the law courts, the prisons, the radio . . . They should have conducted the revolution like Lenin.'

They asked Genet to join them in the Odéon. From archive footage, the scene is impressive, though it borders on self-parody. Panels on the stage, surrounded by signs and placards, make portentous statements about capitalism. The audience shout approval and look at one another to check out radical stylings. The leaflet which calls for attendance showcases the exquisite earnestness of the age. (It makes sense if you concentrate hard.) 'A group of artists and theater people, of students and workers, formed in a revolutionary action committee, tonight occupied after the show at the Theatre des Nations, the Theatre de France-

Odeon, symbol of a bourgeois culture they fundamentally contest in the same way that they contest capitalist society. From the moment of the occupation of the theater commissions open to all were created in order to undertake a labor of reflection concerning our refusal of the distribution of entertainment-as-merchandise and on the possibilities created by the newly established situation for the development of an art of combat.'

Genet went along to check it out, and his heart sank. He hoped for proper rebellion, for the countrywide violence he craved, for a full and physical expression of the rage he felt for a state which had so long kept its boot on his neck. Wanting Bolshevism and clarity of intention, he found long-haired kids who impressed only each other: 'In a circular movement, the speeches came from the stage to the audience, and back to the stage again. From the stage to the audience and back to the stage again. Continuing all the time. And never leaving the theatre.'

For all that his plays are indigestible, it is impossible to miss the punch of his insights, or the power of his example. In the story he tells of his night among the revolutionaries, he nails a truth about what the proscenium theatre did within the gilt and plush. At its best it enlightened, instructed, revivified, and repurposed. But often, it took a problem that needed direct action and instead shuttled it back and forth in a highly sophisticated circle jerk between stage and audience, draining an urgent issue of its pressing reality. Something of this anaesthetic quality infuriated Genet. His rage is hard to ignore.

Bliss was it in that dawn to be alive.
Odéon Theatre, France, occupied by students, 1968

Samuel Beckett
1906–1989

As light fails, you walk west, led by a friend, stumbling down a country path tapering from a narrow road towards the sea. Descending curved clefts of hills, you walk through the deep dark. At the end of the path, you come to a stretch of shingle and a rocky cove behind it, nature's monumental architecture stretching away to the north – spurs of black rock, battered plateaus of cliff. You sit on a pebbly beach washed by forever, and gaze into black-grey sea mingling with grey-black sky. A place of rough peace, where the war of wind, sea, shore, and crying bird sings to wars in the mind and heart.

You agree with your friend, yes, this is it, the thing itself, and sit there for an hour or two of silence, broken by an occasional salty word and some wild laughter. The wind in the lungs seems to push away a ration of pain, and you walk back thanking your friend for showing you this, feeling stronger for the punch of the experience.

You retire to a pub and have a few drinks, and find a new sort of warmth and a new sort of pleasure. Your friend seems disappointed. You are as happy with the pint as you were with the wind, you appreciate the steak sandwich as much as you did the sea air. For your friend, this seems a betrayal. For them, there is only the one authentic experience, only the one proper magic, only the one right purity. The seaside encounter was the thing, all else a falling away.

You try to explain that for you all experiences have different and equal validity. Walking through the gloaming to the shingle was great, an epiphany of the universe's tough beauty, but there are other events of value. Rather than slipping down that path, you could have stayed on the road and gone to a nearby funfair and thrilled to the sugar rush of a roller coaster. Rapture did come with the bleak poetry of the sea, but it can also be summoned by a dawn milkshake after a night buzzing on

MDMA. Or in a moment of intimacy at a dance or a bus stop. The truth of the great swirl is not only revealed in lost and alone places; it can be revealed in the manufactured and tawdry. Or anywhere. Your friend insists, no – that is the place, the place by the sea, that is the only one – it is higher, purer: nothing else can compare. A divide opens up.

The extended metaphor derives from a memory, but serves as an exemplar of many occasions attending the works of Samuel Beckett with friends and colleagues. For many, he is the ultimate, the master, the No. 1. Everyone else climbs the mountain to get close. For me, he has often been glorious, but one glory among many. To the acolytes, this seems a doctrinal lapse, a failure to understand the true nature of God. Moses-like, they castigate those who worship false idols. A *Paris Review* piece once said that theatre had nowhere to go after Beckett.

There is a problem with this sort of idolatry. A life-denying form of appreciation, it may also point to a failure in the work, an endothermic fault line. Theatre generally – its writing in particular – should be exothermic, creating energy and heat and enthusiasm. When you read *A Raisin in the Sun*, you love it and want to rush off and read other writers; when you read *Endgame*, you want to have a lie-down and ignore drama for a year. The Lorraine Hansberry play encourages you to enjoy a world of other things, the work fizzing with the energy of someone attentive and attuned. Beckett's work, and certainly when refracted through the glowering enthusiasm of his fan base, can make you feel that everything else has to be a disappointment.

To punish a writer for their disciples is unfair, just as judging Jesus by the doings of the Church would be a poor show. Beckett appeared at a moment of unmitigated despair as the world tried to absorb the horrors of the Second World War. Just as drama about the First World War took time to appear, as if a pause was required to draw breath, there was a corresponding silence after 1945. The effect could not be transmitted through addressing the facts head-on – there was no equivalent of *Journey's End*. The monstrosity felt uncontainable, and new forms were needed to fit new material. Largely this was achieved through a clear-out of old stuff. Kenneth Tynan wrote of *Waiting for Godot* that it 'jettisons everything by which we recognise theatre. It arrives at the custom house, as it were, with no luggage, no passport and nothing to declare; yet it gets through, as might a pilgrim from Mars.'

Beckett, and those who explored what came to be known as the Absurd, were not writing about the cohesive world around them, but about an abstract parallel reality – one fragmented, atomised. Their challenge was to show the madness to which Western civilisation had descended, the mania nations and cultures had become trapped within. They chose to junk the pre-war conventions, though within the same architecture. The ability of battered proscenium playhouses to handle the strangeness of these dynamics is testament to its durability.

Beckett's world-flipping signature work, *Waiting for Godot*, was written in French between 1948 and 1949, though chiselled out of stone may seem more apposite. First performed in Paris in 1953, under the direction of the visionary Roger Blin, it did not open in English until 1955, at the revolutionary Arts Theatre, a bijou hothouse of a miniature proscenium near Covent Garden, holding just over three hundred. In the unique transport of Beckett's imagination, two tramps rehearse dilatory conversations in the shadow of a possible visitation from an ever-elusive Godot. Their meander through the day is punctuated by the appearance of two circus figures, a master and slave duo, Pozzo and Lucky, encapsulating in their twisted double act a parody of Western civilisation. These bare elements are rooted in a gathering of soils accrued from various environments across Beckett's life. His poverty in Dublin and Paris, the strange blend of boredom and terror which comprised his time with the French Resistance, his perennial feeling of exile, and what he cheerfully described as his commitment to 'one's ultimate hard irreducible inorganic singleness'. Less frequently noted, but also immanent, was his perennial need for friendship. Beside these, a rumour of the end of possibilities whispers.

Perversely, in the ashes of destruction a new shoot of internationalism had grown, both with the United Nations and the Nuremberg trials, attempting to create universals of human justice. Beckett wasn't one for moral codes, but what influenced his form was the idea of a translatable theatre language. He wrote in French and translated his plays into English, but the form he created was a new international poetics – a plastic, physical dance of bodies and language in space and time – which could cross linguistic and cultural boundaries. His swift penetration into every corner of the world was formidable. Though he was the laureate of the wasteland, and may have had, as Sean O'Casey put it, 'a lust for despair', within that boundary-crossing generosity of form – a language more relatable than the old staples of a solicitor's office or a Sussex drawing room – there was a muted optimism.

More ink has been spilled on trying to find allusive meanings, hidden codes, and final understandings of *Godot* than is good and proper. Beckett remained silent and finally despaired at the neediness of others for answers. His riposte from his letters should be the final word: 'I do not know who Godot is. I do not even know if he exists. And I do not know if they believe in him or not – those two who are waiting for him . . . As for wanting to find in all that a broader, loftier meaning to carry away from the performance, along with the programme and the choc-ice, I cannot see the point of it. But it must be possible. I am no longer part of it, and never will be again. Estragon, Vladimir, Pozzo, Lucky . . . Maybe they owe you explanations. Let them get on with it. Without me. They and I have settled our accounts.'

The success of *Godot* disarmed Beckett as much as it alarmed the conservative audience. He had written the play, in part, as relaxation from the tortured exigencies of writing prose. It made him famous, and rich. Looking further for inspiration in the cracks and fissures of his imagination, he dusted off gems hidden in dark mental corners, to create mini-myths beyond character and location. *Endgame* features a co-dependent master and slave, akin to Pozzo and Lucky from *Godot*, eking out a bleak existence in a shabby room. Light seeps in from two windows looking out on a blasted land and a dead sea we do not glimpse. Hamm sits blind and immobile in a battered old armchair, trying to summon the authority of bygone decades: his amanuensis, Clov, scuttles about performing servility.

In Beckett's words, Hamm 'is a king in a chess game lost from the start. From the start he is making loud senseless moves.' A situation first and foremost generating games and languages, *Endgame* is also a critique. In Hamm (as with Pozzo from *Godot*), we hear the decadent strains of high Western culture, and in the way both treat Clov and Lucky we see the cruelty underfunding that languor. The games are inflected with a theatre flavour: Pozzo is a circus master and full of performative flourish, while Hamm the name literally plays on 'ham' acting. There is bracing anger here against establishments – literary, official, and theatrical.

As in *Godot*, the landscape in *Endgame* is stripped bare. Beckett was a poet of rejection, of denying the comforts of belongings. Enclosed in a room, we cannot witness the destitution as we did in *Godot*, but we are told that outside there are no more sugarplums, no more spring, bicycle wheels, nature, rugs, tides, navigators, and coffins. All is 'zero'. A flea tickles Clov, a rat lurks in the kitchen, and a boy may or may not be seen through the window. Here, as elsewhere, Beckett works one of his conjuring tricks: by stripping down, by voiding everything, he creates a hunger for and a powerful impression of the opposite, a paradoxical richness. Contemplating the vacuum before us, we sense the much we live within.

The spareness continues through *Krapp's Last Tape*, Beckett's most autobiographical work, where he contemplates extinction, and what he perceives as a life of failure. With the working title '*Magee Monologue*', it was written for the actor Patrick Magee and his bass rumble. A writer listens to a tape recording of his voice from thirty years before, talking with a cadence of energy and hope which has now flown away. For the director Robert Wilson, it is a love story between Krapp and the machine. There is something poetic and metaphoric about an old reel-to-reel. As one spool diminishes – Krapp himself obsesses over the word 'spool' – and the other enlarges in perfect proportion, there is the sense of a tipped hourglass.

Beckett's drive towards minimalism reaches its apotheosis with *Not I*, where we see nothing but a woman's mouth, eight feet elevated, hammering and clattering her way through a monologue, shooting verbal bullets from the arsenal of another wasted life. The delivery is rat-a-tat-tat, performed at the speed of synaptic thought, sharpening the nerves of the audience to a shriek. Pulling the theatre's focus into its most primal element, the mouth and the human voice, Beckett takes us to an elemental space. The sharpening of perspective within a proscenium towards a single spot works naturally with *Not I* to fill an auditorium with the firings of a panicked mind.

Contrary and surprising factors combine for Beckett's success. First, and most telling, is his humour. Through clowning and wit and human observation, they keep one sufficiently tickled to allay the boredom with which they flirt. In some cases, as in the lovely veteran production of *Godot* with Patrick Stewart and Ian McKellen, they can be uproarious, and all the better for it. Second, they feel perversely lifelike. These are not the stiff and stilted rhythms of the Ibsenian argument play; these are heard rhythms of human speech – abrupted, chaotic, self-contradictory. No matter how abstracted the setting, the speech could be real people talking. And the relationships feel true. Estragon and Vladimir sound in conversation like two friends saturated in too much knowledge of each other, mixed with an obliterating forgetfulness.

Third, the plays are oddly populist. Though the avant-garde has corralled them into exclusive spaces, they were written to be inclusive, filling big theatres with easy grace. I saw *Happy Days* staged comfortably in the ancient Greek theatre at Epidavros. While I was at the Globe, and musing on which plays from the repertoire to include alongside Shakespeare and new work, Beckett was always in the conversation. The test was whether we believed a play could be done in a field. If it could, as can Shakespeare's and the Greeks, then it could be done at the Globe. A Rattigan or an Osborne would look lost in a field: *Godot* would be in its element. Nothing is required beyond actors, text and audience. The plays communicate, they look out, they engage.

So why are they often so difficult in performance? Partly because of the excessive reverence of the audience, stifling the plays with a sacred hush. This is the madness of holy theatre, where any reaction beyond muted supplication is treated as bad form. Surely the opposite of what Beckett wanted. The distancing is exacerbated by a calculatedly strange style of performing. A sort of Beckettian otherness infects actors, which induces nothing but irritation. What is required is that they find the rhythm and truth, and talk with warmth and ease. When you hear that with Beckett, the effect is cataclysmic. When people set out to be cataclysmic, the result is dull.

Primarily the difficulty results from a sort of pre-emptive despair imbued in all elements of production. The oldest saw in the theatre, and one of the truest, is: don't play the end at the beginning. *King Lear* is not a tragedy until it is a tragedy. If you arrive into a world filled with glowering and gloom, there is nowhere for the play to go. This is sharply true of Beckett, where directors, designers, and actors check in hope and humour at the stage door. There is no reason why Godot shouldn't arrive at any moment. He could appear with a picnic of wine and fruit salad, full of songs and jokes, with offers of shelter and employment. Believing that this could occur, then finding that it doesn't, is a consistent heartbreak. A play has to live in possibility, or we would never listen.

When performed with excess reverence and inevitability, the experience mirrors the frigidity that deadened much of modernism. Beckett was a child of this movement, learning at the feet of his mentor James Joyce in Paris, before carving out fresh territory. The energies which funded the birth throes of modernism – a desire to reflect a world reshaping itself with convulsions, to link the march of technology and the machine with art, and to shuck off the previous excess of respect for 'classics' – all these energies brought refreshment. The world moves on and art must catch up. But the speed with which modernism ossified into an insular experimentation, and contempt for a wider audience, was bewildering. Once it unhitched itself from the public, it became the plaything of fanatics and the academy. Many of them claimed Beckett for their own, a patron saint beside Joyce, Woolf, and Eliot, and began the faith which excludes those who do not consent to the perfection of their idols.

There is, of course, a purpose in going to extremes, a value in searching out the lonely places of finality where Beckett dwells. Though all we see may be wastelands and dustbins and effaced humans, there is beauty there. But calling anywhere the *final* place, the end of the road, strikes me as arrogant and a little parochial. A sense of spiritual decay may have struck nerves in London and Paris and New York, but it would be rash and dishonest to posit the same crisis in Nairobi or Kathmandu or Rio. Life there was surging ahead in its own directions. Sometimes it seems that Beckett called end times a little early. For a Western, highly educated Protestant, the endgame may have seemed hard by, but it was not closing time for all. New identities and technologies and ways of loving and being cruel are always turning up and rejuvenating the story.

What the audience wanted from drama in the course of the century under discussion was new information. How are we living now? How are we feeling? What matters? The theatre was not placed to give answers, but to float energies, emotions, oppositions, and images that somehow mirrored passing confusions. At a moment of acute despair, Beckett conjured a collection of abstract fables which gave a voice to unheard cries and a shape to blurs.

He had no desire to be a prophet. When he won the Nobel Prize, his wife called it 'a catastrophe'. In fact, he entitled a play with that very name, *Catastrophe*, in appalled response to the Swedish Academy describing him as an 'idealistic' writer of 'compassion' and 'inner purification'. Yet however much he backed away from the limelight, we should be grateful for him bringing the information when the stage needed it most. And we should be as cautious as he was of those who announce him a prophet.

Mu – nothingness or the space between things.
En attendant Godot (*Waiting for Godot*), Théâtre de Babylone, Paris, 1953

Alice Childress
1916–1994

The battlegrounds where the Civil Rights Movement were fought in America were various. Public spaces in the South became electrified with potential bloodshed as entrances to schools, seats on buses, and humble water fountains became arenas of territorial aggression. But the battle was as concerned with perceptions, with ideas of what constituted reality, and it was here that Alice Childress had her effect. The realm whose prejudices she critiqued most directly was the theatre.

Childress didn't make it to Broadway in her lifetime. The pioneer status of being the first black woman writer on the Great White Way fell to her compañera Lorraine Hansberry, with *A Raisin in the Sun*. The two had a relationship which was part comrade on the barricades and part aunt–niece. Childress introduced her young friend to the theatre world, and to those who enabled her success. Both wrote columns for Paul Robeson's newspaper *Freedom*, and stuck by the singer when his passport was rescinded and others deserted him; both had FBI files detailing their leftist associations; and both were enabled in their careers by Sidney Poitier.

In the early 1950s, when she complained of the dearth of good parts for black actresses, Poitier challenged Childress to write herself something rich and interesting. She returned with her first play, *Florence*. The provocation was to defy a nostrum shared by Poitier and his friends that a successful black play could only be about 'life and death stuff like lynching'. Childress wanted to prove that a quieter domestic landscape, without recourse to violence or sensationalism, could have impact. As with Hansberry, she believed the ultimate weapon was expressing the totality of the human: 'My writing attempts to interpret the "ordinary" because they are not ordinary. Each human is uniquely different. Like snowflakes, the human pattern is never cast twice. We are uncommonly and marvellously intricate in thought and action, our problems are most complex and, too often, silently borne.'

Born in Charleston, South Carolina, Childress was brought up in New York by her grandmother, the daughter of a slave. Sitting at their Harlem window, they would look out and observe passers-by. Her grandmother challenged Alice to imagine stories behind the silent figures, asking her questions about the homes and families they walked towards. This ignited the first and fundamental requirement for any playwright: curiosity in the lives of others. School having failed to engage her, at a young age Childress joined the American Negro Theatre (ANT). She spent a decade in a communitarian atmosphere learning every aspect of theatre – playwriting, directing, managing, acting, and serving as a stagehand. The climax was a two-year run on Broadway in Philip Yordan's play *Anna Lucasta*. This tale of a prostitute's struggles with love and her community was written for a white company, but the ANT adapted it for an African American cast, and it became the first all-black play not directly concerned with race to run on Broadway. A seismic achievement rendered more unusual by the fact its co-adaptor and director went by the name Harry Wagstaff Gribble, who hailed from Sevenoaks, Kent.

At this time Alice was married to Alvin Childress, an actor who starred in the TV sitcom *Amos 'n' Andy*. For nearly three decades, this had been a long-running and mega-successful radio series, written by and starring two white actors from the minstrelsy tradition. Over 4,091 episodes they practised the aural equivalent of blackface, with America listening in to a show which with astonishing consistency, and seeming good cheer, demeaned the black population. The TV version – starring black actors – was relatively short-lived. Small wonder Childress was determined to address perceptions. One outlet for her concerns was a column in *Freedom*, consisting of conversations between Mildred, a black domestic, and her friend Marge, detailing the micro-aggressions and daily insults underpinning racial hierarchies. Mildred and Marge became, in minor form, an antidote to *Amos 'n' Andy*.

Florence opened in a small loft space, St Mark's, in Harlem in 1949, produced by the ANT. Set in a segregated train station, a black woman,

Mama Whitney, prepares to travel to New York to bring home her daughter, a struggling actress. The setting highlights how public spaces define the limitations of Jim Crow democracy. In a waiting room which segregates blacks and whites down the middle with a wooden railing, Mama, a black domestic worker, negotiates a relationship with a middle-class white woman, Mrs Carter, across the divide. Perceptions are challenged and re-understood. Mrs Carter believes she has insight into black experience from her sympathetic connection with a trashy book, which details how a young black woman committed suicide because of her identity. What is revealed to be sentimental and romanticised truths are challenged by Mama, harpooning a phoney empathy, which reeks of white do-gooderism and the arrogance of claiming private knowledge from bad art.

Critiquing standardised racial representation is at the heart of Childress's work. Her third play, *Gold Through the Trees*, was an historical pageant, leapfrogging with expansive freedom from ancient Africa to contemporary apartheid-ridden South Africa, taking in the Middle Passage, colonialism in the British West Indies, and racial violence in the Southern States. As with Lorraine Hansberry, Childress was determined to internationalise the narrative of struggle and demonstrate how domestic problems were part of wider patterns across history and geography.

Her signature play, *Trouble in Mind*, premiered on 3 November 1955 at the Greenwich Mews Theatre in New York City. The action begins at a moment of heightened tension familiar to any theatre worker as a company gather for the first morning of rehearsals. It doesn't take long to deduce that the play they are preparing – *Chaos in Belleville* – is of questionable merit, written and directed by white men, detailing life in a community of sharecroppers. Inevitably, it climaxes in a lynching. The creators have an awkwardly derivative understanding of the black world, though it doesn't seem to bother them unduly. However good their intentions, they are propelled by certainty that their comprehension of reality is of greater import than their black colleagues', no matter their neglect of detail.

The central conflict is between a black actress, Wiletta Mayer, a veteran of too many shows that falsify, and a white director, who plays manipulative games to release emotions he doesn't comprehend. Al Manners – the director – poses as a rule-breaker, but it becomes clear he is an old-fashioned bully using power games to tie people in straitjackets of self-consciousness. Gribble of Sevenoaks might conceivably have been the basis for the director; the source for Wiletta came from a co-star in *Anna Lucasta*, Georgia Burke. 'Georgia was a person who went along, went along, went along,' Childress said. 'And then some days she said, "I'm tired of it."'

Wiletta yearns for the excitement she found in the spotlights of her youth. Early in the story she has a moment of entrancing stillness, ambushed by the silent magic of an empty auditorium. We swiftly register the reverence she has held on to for the sacredness of her calling. To survive, Wiletta has confected a professional persona to ingratiate herself to her white directors, a carapace of goodwill and subservience, now tested and broken by this rehearsal process. We witness a woman waking up to the truth that the object of her life's passion has been the source of its despair. Her vocation is tainted by the same racism and inequality that corrode the rest of society. The simultaneous backdrops to the play are events in Montgomery, Alabama, an environment where militias are hired to get children to school. What is expressed with stones and torches in the South is articulated with manners and subtlety, but no less toxicity, in the North.

For Wiletta, the stage is a crucible where society can heal itself, but that can only be achieved when it speaks with a broad and comprehensive honesty. The tyranny of progressives, ever keen to speak on behalf of others when silence or curiosity would be better options, is seen to close rather than open avenues. Childress argues here, as elsewhere in her career, for the right of black creatives to define their own narrative. Her first productions went in front of an American public that was, in her words, 'not ready to see you the way you want to be seen because, one, they don't believe it, two, they don't want to believe it, and three, they're convinced they're superior'. However complex, the journey towards greater honesty in the playhouse requires tough self-criticism of motives and manners, and it is this that Childress serves up.

Wiletta talks of a show where, 'All I did was shout, "Lord, have mercy!" for almost two hours every night.' Another character is remembered for her range of roles: 'Gardenia! She was Gardenia! 'Nother thing . . . she was Magnolia. Chrysanthemum was another.' And the parade of potential attitudes in black plays is narrowed down to 'Shootin' and kissin', that's all you know . . . how big is your bust and murder, murder, murder'. Each of the actors has had to accommodate themselves to art in bad faith, and each has been diminished. Wiletta makes a stand and her defiance is thrilling, but we know further humiliations will come her way, and that the war is a long way off being won.

The play was a sensation in its off-Broadway initial run and generated considerable heat. The doors to Broadway seemed open, and it was due to run there in 1957. Then the producers asked for changes. And more changes. And more changes. Childress did her best to make it work, but when they asked for a new and brighter ending, they crossed a line in the sand and she refused. The mechanics of the play were played out in production.

Nothing good is ever easy. When Childress was asked whether she was ahead of her time, she replied brutally, 'People aren't ahead of their time; they're just choked during their time.'

Many barriers to cross.
At the bus station in Durham, North Carolina, 1940

Eugène Ionesco

1909–1994

Although *The Mousetrap* can rightly claim the longest commercial run for a play, it is trumped for the longest run in a single theatre. The Agatha Christie jumped across an alleyway from the Ambassadors to the St Martin's in 1974 (twenty-one years into its marathon), thus losing the prize. There is a double bill which opened in the Théâtre de la Huchette, on the Left Bank in Paris on 16 February 1957. Beyond belief, it is still there, opening its doors to an eager public. With an honourable exemption for Covid, *La Cantatrice chauve* (*The Bald Prima Donna* or *The Bald Soprano*) and *La Leçon* (*The Lesson*) have packed out the miniature theatre's eighty-five seats over twenty thousand times. While one can understand the commercial attraction of Agatha Christie's well-honed whodunnit, it is harder to see the perennial appeal of a work which features the exchange:

Mrs Martin *Bizarre, Balzac, bazooka.*
Mr Martin *Bizarre, Beaux-arts, brassieres.*
Mr Smith *A,e,i,o,u a,e,i,o,u a,e,i,o,u. I!*
Mrs Smith *Choo Choo, Choo Choo, Choo Choo, Choo Choo Choo Choo.*
Choo.

The French have always lived by different rules. The Huchette, a splendidly eccentric space, was one of a host of miniature Parisian prosceniums which bloomed in an explosion of creativity after the Liberation of 1944. Most remarkable about this production is not only its fixity in one venue, but the endurance of its cast, some of whom have been delivering its mad rhythms for thirty years. One, Monsieur Roger Défossez, played Mr Smith for over sixty years.

The production of *La Cantatrice chauve* was a revival, its premiere in 1950 having flopped. The play is a staple of the Theatre of the Absurd, the movement which predicated that since life under the shadow of the Holocaust and Hiroshima was drained of meaning, art should follow suit. In a series of short scenes, a bland couple called the Smiths welcome an equally bland couple called the Martins into their home. During stilted conversation, the Martin husband and wife, who initially appear not to recognise one another, discover that they live in the same apartment, share a child, and are in fact married. Before language breaks down entirely, we meet a fire chief and a maid, who are having an affair. I have seen this text performed as a school play, at the Edinburgh Fringe, and in a dazzlingly physical version in Târgu Mures in Romania. Somehow it always works, providing hooting laughter and the dizzying sensation of tightrope walks across the void.

Ionesco, who bore the aspect of a melancholy clown, believed in laughter as a proper response to the wilful craziness of the cosmos. The humour in *The Bald Soprano* doesn't only come from facing down an absurd universe; there is also school-revue satire on the daftness of English propriety. Deciding at the age of forty to learn the English language, Ionesco was parroting his way through the stiff and stilted sentences of a phrase book when he realised their comic potential. All the characters, in

a play set in England though written in French, live within the linguistic archness of a language course.

His intentions were often more serious, and gave honour to the words of Albert Camus from *The Myth of Sisyphus*, which helped inspire the movement: 'In a universe suddenly divested of illusions and lights, man feels an alien, a stranger. His exile is without remedy since he is deprived of the memory of a lost home, or the hope of a promised land. This divorce between man and his life, the actor and his setting, is properly the feeling of absurdity.' As prescribed for this brand of brow-furrowed deluxe despair, all is at odds with itself. Words don't carry meaning, nothing consequential happens, characters are not consistent, and narratives are disordered.

Happily, a wilder spirit presides in Ionesco at war with the sombre existential, one of antic carnival fun. In *The Chairs*, we have a lot of ostentatiously silly chatter, before a mad piece of circus as an elderly couple bring in chairs for an invisible audience to hear the man's speech. More and more chairs stack up as the pair usher in and chatter to attendees who are not there. We see the hysteria preceding a prestigious event without any public. In an emperor's-new-clothes dramatic image, the absence points up the emptiness of the grandeur.

In his masterpiece of political allegory, *Rhinoceros*, we watch the occupants of a small village one by one morph into megafauna. Ionesco was

Design 101. *Les chaises*, Théâtre des Champs-Elysées, Paris, 1956

born in Romania, oscillating in his early life between Eastern Europe and France. As a student in the 1930s and at the beginning of the war, it gradually dawned on him that the country of his birth was, in an almost imperceptible process, sliding towards fascism. 'University professors, students, intellectuals were turning Nazi, becoming Iron Guards one after another. We were fifteen people who used to get together to find arguments, to discuss, to try and uncover arguments opposing theirs. From time to time, one of the group would come out and say "I don't agree at all with them, to be sure, but on certain points, I must admit, for example the Jews . . ." And that kind of comment was a symptom. Three weeks later, that person would become a Nazi. He was caught in a mechanism, he accepted everything. Towards the end, it was only three or four of us who resisted.'

France was no refuge from this sinister creeping. In *Rhinoceros*, with a credible inevitability, humane and calm individuals one by one bypass their rationality and succumb to the seductions of the herd. They begin by telling others not to worry and muttering remarks of muted sympathy; before long they are transforming into rampaging ungulates. Fascism does not occur in thunderclaps, it approaches incrementally, step by step. What was once outrageous is first tolerated, then normalised, as individuals make choice after choice that lead them towards the blackest of moral holes. Ionesco's play renders the process chillingly natural. His everyman hero, Bérenger, who stumbles clumsily through several other plays, ends up with an against-the-odds dignity, spitting out the immortal words: 'Je ne capitule pas!' A surprising rebel, he came to mind when I watched the celebrated American journalist Jim Acosta leaving CNN with the words: 'I will not give in to the lies, I will not give in to the fear.'

For Ionesco, in a time of unquestioning Soviet allegiance among some of his compeers, the charging herd could be as worrying on the left as on the right. Socially committed playwrights (his contemporaries) attacked him for not writing with a message. Reviewing *The Chairs* and *The Lesson* in the *Observer*, Kenneth Tynan slammed the Romanian with the full array of his artillery for refusing to take a social position. Throughout the summer of 1958 a protracted spat followed on a succession of Sundays, when Ionesco replied in the *Observer*'s letters page. Tynan countered, and a series of heavyweights piled on, concluding with Orson Welles. The playwright accused his opponents of censorship, and other playwrights of a 'left-wing conformism', offering nothing 'that one does not know already through books and political speeches'.

For Ionesco, the theatre artist should promote nothing but his own created universe and leave the problems of politics to others. He admired the pataphysics of Alfred Jarry and the abstractions of Dadaism. Tynan believed in direct engagement. Whichever your point of view, to read the letters to and fro is to mourn a period when an excited readership thrilled to an ideological joust over the meanings of a proscenium play. A time when theatre – even if revelling in absurdity and meaninglessness – mattered.

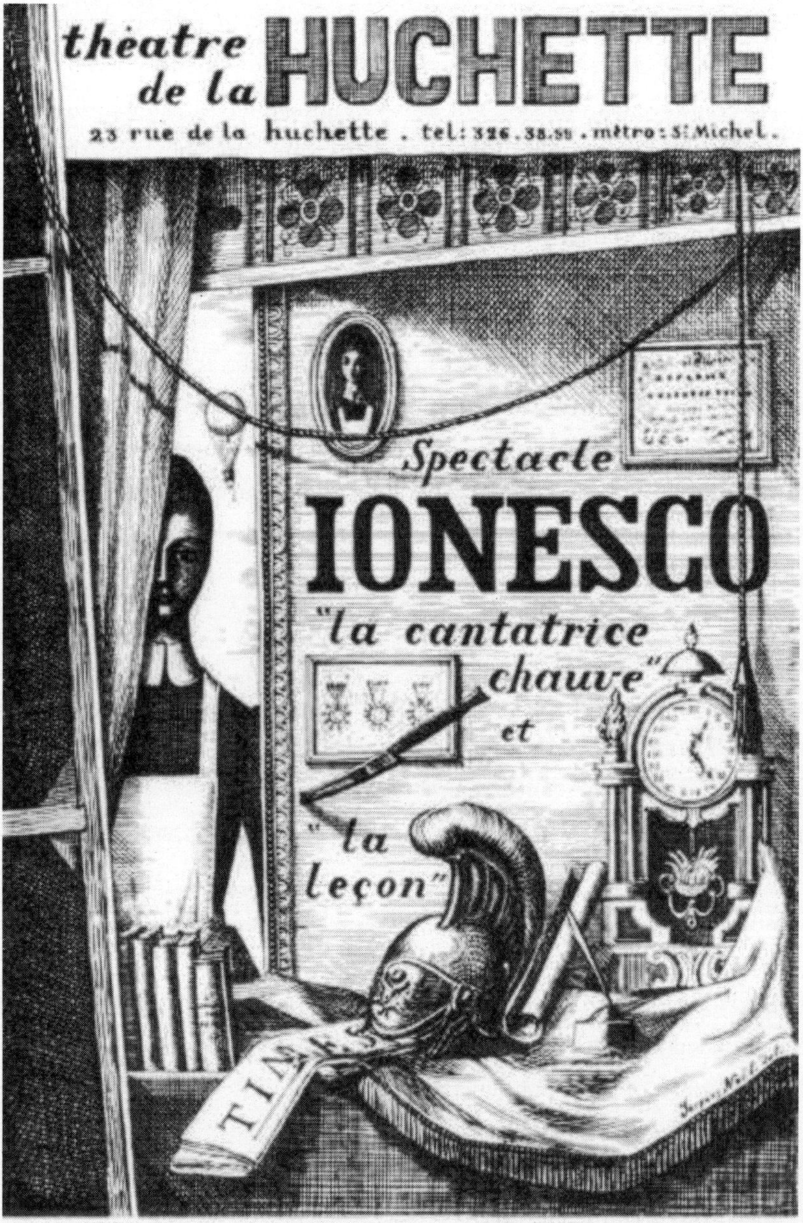

From such humble beginnings.
Poster for *La Cantatrice chauve* (*The Bald Prima Donna*) and *La Leçon* (*The Lesson*), Théâtre de la Huchette, Paris, 1950

Critics

Though the critic in some form has existed forever, whether the loudmouth barracking from the gallery or the sage in the salon, it is during the proscenium century they rose to a dominance historically unparalleled. We know from Sheridan's play *The Critic* the power of the judgemental voice in the eighteenth century, and the fury it aroused in the creative community. In the 1810s, William Hazlitt left accounts of the drama of his day, bringing to life, among others, the performances of the demonic dynamo Edmund Kean. Hazlitt's turbocharged prose was galvanised by the same romantic passion which fired the verse of his contemporaries Wordsworth and Coleridge. Late in life, Hazlitt described the precious joy of the theatregoer who 'views the pageant of the world played before him; sees human life, like a gaudy shadow, glance across the stage; and here tastes of all earth's bliss, the sweet without the bitter, the honey without the sting'.

Hazlitt was important, but the power of the critic came fully into its own later in the nineteenth century with the rise of the newspaper and the newfound gentility of the theatre. When Marie Bancroft completed the elimination of the thrust, and cemented the relationship between the train-travelling, journal-reading middle classes and the drama, she created a space for critics to thrive in. The review became a form of entertainment and provocation for new arenas – the early morning commuter train, the afternoon salon, or the Sunday armchair. Granted prominence, it set in place a pattern of co-dependence between the business and the reviewers. The drama needed the attention, welcomed the praise and was infuriated beyond apoplexy by anything negative. The critic loved the byline, relished the proximity to fame, and nursed resentments towards those in the glow. Each eyed the other warily from either side of the curtain.

In an ideal world, the division between the two would not be so great. Theatre needs good criticism. The best critics have a vision of what theatre should be, which the best practitioners define themselves against. New work redefines the critic's vision, just as new critical thinking will reshape the work. Each side's passion and insight will nudge the other forward.

In the 1890s, several critics took their trade beyond the awarding of points for technical achievement. Ibsen was never going to be a commercial success, because of his content and his provenance, yet his plays needed to be seen. His cause was taken up with all guns blazing by George Bernard Shaw. Writing in the *Saturday Review*, Shaw regularly unleashed his invective on Henry Irving and his actor-manager set-up at the Lyceum, and argued for a drama pursuing an ethical and social mission – the theatre of Ibsen. In this he was backed by his friend William Archer, writing for *The World*. Equally as strong an advocate for Ibsen, he went further and translated the Norwegian's plays. This was the best of campaigning advocacy, shaking up a complacent culture which hungered for the safe and similar and opening up new perspectives.

Little of the same prodding and poking came from their immediate successors. Max Beerbohm added to the gaiety of nations with immense wit, and good jokes, but apple carts remained un-overturned. James Agate, who wrote for the *Sunday Times* between 1923 and 1947, was pretty much the essence of everything that could irritate about the critic. Writing with an ostentatious otiosity, he puffed himself up as a connoisseur of great acting, much as one might be a connoisseur of caviar. Reading him now is rather like trying to get through the catalogue for an upmarket jeweller. An appreciation of technique is a good starting point for a critic, just as it is for an artist, but it is not a good stopping point. An idea of what to do with all that technique is also a necessity.

The sense of the moral importance of theatre returned to critical life in the UK after the Second World War. Most of it resided in the judgements of two prime entertainers of the Sunday armchair. Settling down with the Sundays became central to English intellectual life in the 1950s, and the twin biggest castles in this landscape were Kenneth Tynan of the *Observer* and Harold Hobson in the *Sunday Times*. The first act of

Look Back in Anger (a play saved by Tynan's glowing review) is set on the archetypal dank 1950s Sunday afternoon, as Jimmy Porter sinks into a sofa with the papers, raging at pundits and opiners. At the heart of that conversation were arts reviews, then treated with the seriousness of rabbinical scholars commenting on the Talmud.

Penelope Gilliatt wrote in 1959, 'One of the most characteristic sounds of the English Sunday is that of Harold Hobson barking up the wrong tree.' Wrong or right, both critics made their reputation by taking risks and backing the bold and the unfamiliar. Tynan was Hotspur to Hobson's Hal; the one all fire and flash and distemper, the other wit and solidity and judgement. Tynan defended his heroes like Horatius at the bridge – Osborne, Brecht and the Berliner Ensemble – his militant enthusiasm striking down hordes of light entertainers. Hobson went out to bat for Harold Pinter, raving about the first production of *The Birthday Party*, which every other critic derided. His tone is that of the willing martyr, 'I am willing to stake whatever reputation I have as a judge of plays by saying that Mr. Pinter, on the evidence of this work, possesses the most original, disturbing, and arresting talent in theatrical London.' The same lonely authority pervades his defence of *Waiting for Godot*, 'Mr Beckett has any amount of swagger. A dusty, coarse, irreverent, pessimistic, violent swagger? Possibly. But the genuine thing, the real McCoy.'

Hobson and Tynan wrote with dash and championed the new. They didn't shut the door on awkward guests, they invited them in, instructing the rest of the party to change their manners to accommodate. Rather than fearing the bold, they tried to understand it, and when they saw a nugget of truth, they went to war. They were wrong of course, often – and they lived in a time of radical reinvention when there was no absolute right (when is there ever?) – but they also contributed, helping to make a new theatre possible. As Kathleen Tynan wrote, they fought 'to make permanent the impermanent'.

Kenneth Tynan
1927–1980

Kenneth Tynan's great gift was one of ignition. An aesthetic terrorist, his arsonist ambitions went beyond the world of theatre: he wanted to burn down shibboleths, and inhibitions, and old forms. Considering what a monument to self-celebration he was – the veritable Sultan of Self – it is astonishing the amount he got done. When he began writing for the *Observer* in 1954, he had a clear-headed four-point plan. He wanted to abolish the ludicrous anachronism of the Lord Chamberlain, the censor who kept British theatre frozen in antiquity. He wanted to whip along the old dream of a National Theatre. He wanted to increase the amount of European work on England's parochial stages. And he wanted to drive English theatre away from Loamshire, his nickname for the fake idyll of drawing rooms, French windows, and cocktail cabinets. Amazingly, on his watch, he scored a result on all counts. Far from the only campaigner in these battles, he was their most articulate spokesman, and the lightning rod for their passion.

Beside that achievement, he loosened the restrictions on acceptable public language by proudly saying 'fuck' for the first time on British television. And he fought a one-person war against repressive sexual taboos, most openly expressed in his risqué revue, the muff-and-cock extravaganza *Oh! Calcutta!* All in all that amounts to a sizeable, if silly, effect on society. Placing what he did in its context, a world of post-war enforced placidity and an almost deliberate grey quietude, the wantonness of that silliness becomes almost heroic. In a world whose automatic reaction to the arrival of a peacock (Tynan's middle name, by happenstance) was to smother it, he had the courage to splay his feathers, over and over again. Every paragraph of his writing is a circus act of dazzling insight, humanity, and outrageous wordplay.

He had the courage to be properly and fully pretentious in an age that canonised common sense. He loved flourish, daring, and self-delighting artiness, when many thought all that 'a bit off'. He celebrated Beckett for rewriting the rules of theatre, Osborne for looking for a new England, Brecht for ignoring charm and burrowing towards truth, and Tennessee Williams for the tortured rhetoric of his prose. All are standard curriculum texts now, but at the time they needed a champion. Tynan was a crusading butterfly, yet one with a perverse need for weight and substance. He loved imaginative flight but wanted it freighted with truth. He understood the importance of marrying the light and the heavy in any successful dramatic moment.

His great weapon was his prose, a hybrid emerging from a boy who spent days having Augustan cadences thrashed into him and nights listening to Dizzy Gillespie spinning the sound fantastic on 78s. His style is the happy collision of Cicero and bebop. Small wonder that Tynan experienced multiple epiphanies when he first saw *Look Back in Anger*. The tension running through John Osborne was the same one that kept Tynan taut – a passionate nostalgia for the strong walls of Edwardian authority yoked with a romantic love for the sax and trumpet soloists intent on blowing the walls of that Jericho down. An irreconcilable blend, it electrified the prose of both.

For all his glories, he was a critic, and though he dignified that term to a height, he could also exemplify its smallness. He could be proper nasty. His remorseless hounding of Vivien Leigh, for whom he conceived a passionate loathing, is sour to witness. Laurence Olivier said later that Tynan's predatory destruction of Leigh's confidence, a tiger circling a fawn, helped tip her into mental illness. All great talent leaves wreckage – it can be the price of originality – but the violence was naked here, and ugly. Tynan paid a price, as made clear in his desolate journals. Towards the end the brutality rebounded. His last years, clinging to life and dignity and reputation, as success betrayed him and work deserted him, and lovers left, and money ran out, and the only thing that chose not to shun him was the cancer that crept closer and closer, those years proved a fairly vicious blowback for the damage done.

But he built more than he knocked down. The mischievous humour and sensual relish of his prose remain a pleasure, and we can take nostalgic delight in reliving, with eerie verisimilitude, moments in the theatre. Tynan sweated over his relationship with posterity, and felt it was vital to give later generations an impression of what effect performances and performers had on him. A mission in which he succeeded.

Critics really shouldn't be that svelte.
Kenneth Tynan with Claire Bloom at a
TV training school, *c.*1955

John Osborne

1929–1994

Look Back in Anger was born from the advertising section at the back of the *Stage* newspaper. This zone was usually the graveyard for antique variety acts, where lurid faces beamed out of grey newsprint, congratulating themselves or colleagues for their recent record takings in Yarmouth. But in 1955, amid all this vaudevillian decay, there was a small notice from a new organisation, the English Stage Company (based at the Royal Court), asking new writers to send in plays.

They received three hundred, the majority of which were of little interest. One, however, induced that funny skipped heartbeat in its first readers, which told them here was something emanating the incendiary paraffin perfume of the new. Those readers were George Devine, the director of the new company, and his young colleague, bristling with iconoclasm, Tony Richardson. They tracked down the author, John Osborne, to a telephone-free houseboat on the Thames, and Devine was rowed out to meet him at high tide. From such eccentric beginnings history was made.

The cliché runs that England was a theatrical desert in the early 1950s. London was certainly far from the dramatic capital of the world. Most of the dynamic energy of post-war proscenium theatre had been generated elsewhere. Paris had fostered the existential interrogations of Sartre and Camus, the burnished philosophical disquisitions of Anouilh, the arsonist gestures of Genet, and had set up laboratories for the absurdist experiments of Beckett and Ionesco. New York had midwifed a miraculous conjunction of commerce and conscience with Arthur Miller and the new poetics of Tennessee Williams, together with a muscular and ferocious style of acting. Broadway had been electrified by new voices that balanced heavy matter with populist brio, and by brighter entertainment, where the American musical was responding to the brash and booming energy of the 1950s with all the relish of 'Oh what a beautiful morning . . .'

Though the greatest excitement may have been overseas, the idea that London was a dead zone of zombies in evening dress shuffling between French windows and chaises longues has been significantly exaggerated. Largely by pundits who want to aggrandise the achievements of those who broke that mould (even if the mould didn't exist). The producer Binkie Beaumont's power over the commercial theatre was almost total, yet his aesthetic was not as comically archetypal as his name. The plays of Rodney Ackland – *Absolute Hell* and *A Dead Secret* among them – reveal with acid acuity a seedy, lubricious world of metropolitan despair. In *Waters of the Moon* by N. C. Hunter, a nervous Austrian sits shivering in the corner of a country hotel, provoking a dawning realisation in his hosts that the Holocaust may have created trauma that can't be solved by another gin and tonic, or a hearty walk with a dog. Rattigan was enjoying a purple patch, turning out further disquisitions into the British bipolar oscillation between repression and hysteria. And Eliot and Fry were sponsoring their last gasp burst of energy in verse drama, Eliot exploring drawing room ennui in burnished phrases, and Fry splashing around neo-romantic colour with linguistic dash. As discussed elsewhere, Agatha Christie and Enid Bagnold were ruling the populist roost with works more testing and contemporary than was allowed by their detractors.

But for all the camouflage – verse drama, classy Rattigan, imported French effusions – it could not disguise a central silence. Everyone lived in a world still scarred by rubble, ruins all around which served as a daily reminder of the Establishment's impotence before the violence of history. It was a world starting to dance to new rhythms, not only bebop and rock and roll, but also the noises of the new consumerism – the swirl of the washing machine, the skid of the fast car, and the crackle of the television coming to life. Few playwrights were addressing either that rubble or that rhythm.

England was looking for a play to answer that need, yet nobody knew what it would be until it appeared. The first season of the English Stage

Company at the Royal Court reflected that confusion in its eclecticism. Two pieces of verse drama came and went with astonishing speed; there was a new play by the novelist Angus Wilson, *The Mulberry Bush*; the British premiere of Arthur Miller's political allegory *The Crucible*; Brecht's parable *The Good Woman of Setzuan*; and, at the end of the season, a box office banker revival, the Restoration sex comedy *The Country Wife*. In the middle of all that variety sat *Look Back in Anger*, the play that would define the early Court, though no one knew it at the time. As with any great institution, there was no narrowing and confining policy – policy is a dangerous nonsense enforced by Arts Councils – but an abundance of cheek and ambition.

The impression you get of the early Court is of a ramshackle gathering of gifted individuals drawn together by rigorous aesthetic standards more than shared ideology. There was a desire for change, but it was of less weight than their elite craftsmanship and their simple love of doing and making. Revolution comes from the busy. Harriet Devine, George's daughter, speaks of spending her early life in the theatre, crafting props and creating hand-painted cardboard exit signs. Bill Gaskill, then a young assistant director, remembers the frequency with which marriages would collapse, unable to bear the strain of the bravado and excitement. The theatre soon became known as the Royal Divorce Court. After each press night there would be a party onstage and everyone would get drunk, until George Devine returned with the next morning's reviews. Invariably horrible, everyone would get even more drunk. A recent exhibition at the National Portrait Gallery captured in photographs the faces of that period – Devine, Richardson, Gaskill, Peter Gill, and Jocelyn Herbert. Decked out in polo necks and folk-singer caps, they all look callow, joyous, arrogant, and touched with the beauty of shared endeavour.

What of the work that defined that moment more than any other? *Look Back in Anger* has dated with the celerity of any work that catches its present moment – much groundbreaking art dates for a brief or long interlude – though it still blazes with life. Conventional in its structure, almost a pièce bien faite, it has a single box set, three acts, and powerful and contrived curtain moments at the end of each. The auditorium of the Court, as in its earlier heyday during the Vedrenne-Barker-Shaw era, has always been close to the Platonic ideal of proscenium perfection – close enough for intimacy, with enough height and depth for a sense of scale. The plays that thrive best in this shape – even if their content is radical – were and are those that understand the tradition encased within its architecture. The initial situation of *Look Back in Anger* is far from promising: a claustrophobic attic flat into which are squeezed a volcanically articulate working-class graduate, Jimmy Porter, with his posh and passive-aggressive wife, Alison, and the two friends who come and go. The set-up could have been the crucible for nothing but a prolonged whine and deadening philosophical onanism. Recent revivals have exhibited how close it floats to both, together with a dismaying streak of misogyny.

Yet something makes it more. A slash of pain runs clean through, the sense of a wound far from healed. Jimmy is alert to the moral imperative that no one should die unmourned – not his father, not his working-class substitute mum, nor the whole Edwardian world he pretends to despise but can't bear to see go. An enormous pulse of love sets its rhythm. Not sweet love, not the candyfloss capitalist version Osborne could see clogging up the arteries around the heart, but old-fashioned Strindbergian love – nasty, possessive, clumsy, crooked, and cruel – the jaundiced sort for which Jimmy Porter, and many others, would happily go to war.

The immediate impact of the play could have been negligible. The daily notices were by and large favourable, more like condescending pats on the head than roars of joy, the sort of notices that usually kill through muted kindness. It wasn't until the Sunday papers came out that the box office started to sing, when Kenneth Tynan, a man proudly and ostentatiously of the same generation, championed it with all guns blazing. His review – 'I doubt if I could love anyone who did not wish to see *Look Back in Anger*' – is a piece of prose young playwrights have dreamed of since, a hurl of excitement that the world had somehow produced a writer to match itself.

The Royal Court's press rep cooked up the phrase 'Angry Young Men'; the *Evening Standard* ran with it, then Osborne adopted it himself. They revived the play three times, having a section televised just as the Suez Crisis came to a head, and restyling Osborne as the flashiest and most *soigné* playwright since Noël Coward. Tynan led the march to invest meaning into the play, speaking of its 'instinctive leftishness'. Many followed, substituting a reflex political subversion, which had jaded recently following Khrushchev's denunciation of Stalin, with a reflex cultural subversion which helped fuel the Angry Young Man movement. But it was false to turn a yell into an argument, and the play has long outgrown the meanings attached.

As with many proscenium playwrights, spanning all the way back to Tom Robertson, Osborne got an early apprenticeship in the theatre at the grubbier end of the spectrum. As first a stage manager and then an actor, he worked with small touring and repertory companies. He was appearing in the unremembered classic *Seagulls over Sorrento* in Morecambe when he wrote his breakthrough play. Finding himself a comfy deckchair on the pier, he scribbled out a first draft in two weeks. His experience on such circuits, and his passion for old variety acts like Max Miller, fed into his second play, *The Entertainer.* Here the fading glories of the music hall and their usurpation by the energy of rock and roll stand in for the dimming star of the British Empire and the rising dominance of the American. In the background, young men leave the country to appear in the sour farce that was the Suez Crisis. As with *Look Back in Anger*, there are politics and symbols and malaises aplenty, but what distinguishes it is a lacerating honesty about a loveless and bitter family and their haunted patriarch, Archie Rice. Incarnated by Laurence Olivier in a terrifying portrayal of manic emptiness, Rice serves as an acetic metaphor not only for a nation, but also for a theatre tradition on its last legs and clinging desperately to past potencies.

The long-term impact of Osborne's work was in its insistence on the present moment as the ultimate food for drama. It emerged into a world that was ignoring its own present, and created a theatre, the Royal

Court, and a wider theatre culture that has never since dared to ignore its surrounding environment. Though vital to be aware of the past, and to dream a little of the future, theatre's most pressing concern is always its own moment. Osborne reminded everyone of that truth.

The passing of the torch.
Laurence Olivier and Joan Plowright,
The Entertainer, Broadway, 1958

Enid Bagnold
1889–1981

Loamshire, an imaginary county, was first invented by George Eliot as a setting for both *Adam Bede* and *Middlemarch.* Subsequently taken up by numerous English writers, including P. G. Wodehouse and Evelyn Waugh, it came to denote a classic Home Counties utopia, where there was always honey still for tea. The British military even adopted it when they needed an unspecific placeholder location. Its most famous use was a pejorative one by Kenneth Tynan. In his hands it became a satirical weapon against all that was supposedly wrong with the British theatre, a cosy, middle-class nowhere, where vicars bumbled and sandwiches curled in the sun and chaps were always playing fast and loose with the rules on the croquet lawn. Loamshire became the redoubt of all that was conservative and stuck.

Enid Bagnold should have been the quintessential representative of Loamshire, especially given her almost perfect name, and her signature play, *The Chalk Garden*, should have been the summation of all that was wrong. Set in a Sussex drawing room, there are butlers – two, in fact, one dying upstairs and one running a leaky ship downstairs – and three generations in the matrilineal line of a down-on-their-luck genteel family. A doddery judge totters through talking of 'incorruptible ritual'. Memories of former affluence plunge shamelessly into self-parody: 'The gold toothpicks, the green-handled ivory knives . . . We used to have celery with the Stilton – and the Bristol finger bowls and the épergne – and the sieve we served the Caraque on.' This is not a world of kitchen sinks, or none that are visible. The play opened in London almost contemporaneously with *Look Back in Anger*, setting itself up as the Aunt Edna of theatrical gentility at which Jimmy Porter and his chums could lob hand grenades.

So it comes as a surprise that Tynan, not given to lavish praise for works set in the Home Counties, hailed Bagnold's play as a glorious late flourish by the old brigade – a sort of last post bugled out for the West End in the sunset of its decline. He declared *The Chalk Garden* 'may well be the finest artificial comedy to have flowed from an English (as opposed to an Irish) pen since the death of Congreve'. Cecil Beaton, who designed the first production in New York, described the play as being, 'as whimsical as Sir James Barrie, as poetic as Giraudoux, sometimes as zany as the Marx Brothers, yet with all the elements of a detective story'. The variety of this praise is just since, though the physical setting is manor house deluxe, the play is unclassifiable.

The St Maugham family, working under the instructions of their first-floor bedridden butler, who supervises their efforts with binoculars and a spy network, are trying and failing to raise a garden of colour and joy from their unfavourable chalky soil. This serves as a heavy-handed, though deftly used, metaphor for their inability to pass love from generation to generation. Their emotional soil is also chalky: 'the lilies have rust – there is black spot on the roses – and the child is screaming in the garden'. Into this static environment, an immensely complex Mary Poppins figure, a governess called Miss Madrigal, steps in, dispensing wisdom on how to negotiate chalky soil and discreet truths on how to foster love. A nervous and hysterical substitute butler, Maitland (everyone's surname begins with M, which serves to confuse but also softens and crumbles the aural atmosphere), has served five years in prison for being a conscientious objector. Later, we discover that Madrigal has done a significant chunk of stir as well, and one of the meandering streams of plot is discovering why.

The detective element engages, but more profoundly engaging is the pervasive aura of guilt, and the sense there is much to forgive. Here again, in Shakespeare's phrase, we are 'guilty creatures sitting at a play'. In Osborne's work across town, this was being proven by the haranguing of Jimmy Porter; in Bagnold's, it is a density in the air, making us breathe more quickly and shallowly, hoping for the storm to pass and the barometer to shift. Each character has hurt or been hurt. There is no excuse for the damage they have done, but the story offers the possibility of renewal, just as the chalk garden, with thought and attention, may still become fertile. A tough optimism is offered in denial of easy judgements. One character says of what happens in a court, it 'is not my life. It is the shape and shadow of my life, with the accidents of truth taken out of it.'

Perhaps the most audacious of Bagnold's subversions was to wrap this tale of upper-class isolation and dissolution into a laugh-out-loud comedy. Each character speaks in borderline batty, extravagantly mandarin rhythms and switches of thought. Played at the right pace, these keep the audience constantly on guard. There is a detachment from reality here, but the kind that tickles rather than irritates. A very particular sort of madness, this is an emotional ambience where eccentricity flirts with psychosis, but just about holds on to the reins. Enid Bagnold's sensibility enfolds together a mindset of crested nostalgia, a vision of unchecked wisteria, and a soundscape of church bells and the scattered cries of children playing in walled gardens. Reminiscent of Eliot's *Four Quartets*, it lends itself to poetry as naturally as laughter. At its conclusion, Madrigal resolves, 'I shall continue to explore – the *astonishment* of living,' a resolution whose groundwork has been laid by the gentle madness preceding.

Why do some plays sink in public esteem and others soar? There are no hard and fast rules. Following Binkie Beaumont's rejection of *The Chalk Garden* (he found the symbolism 'muddling'), it took the surprising route of a Broadway opening, where it was a big success. It opened in London at the Theatre Royal Haymarket, in a John Gielgud production starring Peggy Ashcroft and Edith Evans, and was a smasheroo. Opening on 11 April 1956, it played for a year and a half. Four weeks later, on the 8 May 1956, in the scratchy Royal Court, *Look Back in Anger* opened. Playing only a short run, sensational reviews and a televised excerpt created the momentum to necessitate another run, again short. Both plays were turned into films, the Bagnold the more successful. Since then, there have been manifold revivals of the Osborne, and a smattering of *The Chalk Garden*, though it would be false to say it has disappeared.

So why is *Look Back in Anger* canonical and *The Chalk Garden* a charming oddity? Why does cultural history clutch certain artefacts tightly to its chest and keep others at arm's length, as though they smell a little off (or excessively fragrant)? Gender is the most obvious factor, the third word in Angry Young Men. The largely male academy and critical gatekeepers certainly had a hand in raising some plays and lowering others. The later revisionism of certain feminists, about which plays by women were acceptable and which were not, helped to undermine the case of many. A Marxist would hold that power promotes those works which support the cultural superstructure it needs to uphold itself. Though *Look Back in Anger* poses as an act of outsider rebellion, and *The Chalk Garden* seems on first sight the essence of conformist status, the gruff belligerence of the Osborne may finally be more of a comfort to the Establishment than the searching curiosity of the Bagnold.

Elegance personified. Enid Bagnold, 1910

The academy has an unfortunate habit of overpromoting and celebrating difference for its own sake – modishness, for want of a better word. The agent of change, preferably noisy and self-demonstrating change, is thrust into the limelight ahead of the agent of steadiness. No matter the quality of the work, or indeed what it is ultimately saying – politically, socially, or morally. Subverting some superficial hierarchies, with much *Sturm und Drang*, goes down better than sailing quietly forwards enquiring what reform might be necessary. Finally, it may simply be a suspicion of generosity. Where Jimmy Porter disparages, *The Chalk Garden*, in all its eccentricity, embraces. Sometimes it becomes necessary to correct the prejudices of history and rescue a play from neglect. To that end, it seems worthwhile to fix our gaze on the *Chalk Garden*s a little longer.

When Hamlet returns from having met his father as a ghost, he is questioned and disbelieved by his friend. 'O day and night, but this is wondrous strange!' Horatio blurts in fear. Hamlet replies with two statements. The second has become canonical: 'There are more things in Heaven and Earth, Horatio, / Than are dreamt of in your philosophy.' This superior, faintly contemptuous commonplace has become a branding watermark for who Hamlet is. It sounds very like Jimmy Porter putting down his sidekick, Cliff. But Hamlet's first response has been largely ignored by the quotation industry. It is the statement close to the heart of both Shakespeare's and Bagnold's plays – 'And therefore as a stranger give it welcome.'

Brendan Behan
1923–1964

A renowned dispenser of stories during his life, more have stuck to Brendan Behan since his death in 1964. Some say the energy and imagination he put into storytelling – the hours and years spent entrancing boozy audiences in London, Dublin, Paris, and New York – led to the smallness of his literary output and the shortness of his term. To go into a bar and throw a spell with wit and wisdom wasn't just killing an afternoon for Behan, it was a calling. To tell a story wasn't just fun, it was his work. He was enamoured by the memory of the eighteenth-century Gaelic poets, whose court had been exiled, and who plied a trade of high sophistication in hedge schools, small bars, and cottages. Behan followed in their line when he lost a day in verbal creation and performance. A linguistic Miles Davis in a saloon bar, his was a non-stop, porter-fuelled live jazz improvisation. Flann O'Brien hailed him as 'a delightful rowdy, a wit, a reckless drinker, a fearsome denouncer of humbug and pretence, and sole proprietor of the biggest heart that has beaten in Ireland for the last forty years'.

Though his life was short, it didn't lack mileage. Born in the slums of Dublin in 1923, his home was his school, where he was stuffed with literature, the Irish having been forced for centuries to develop an education system outside the umbrella of a state which refused to help the majority of its population. He joined the IRA at a tender age, carried out a couple of tragicomic missions, and paid the price with long spells behind bars in Ireland and England. Violence was never his vocation. As he said, 'If my plays show anything, it's that no ideal is worth the shedding of one drop of human blood.' Exiled to Paris, he did the Left Bank thing, hanging out with Camus and Sartre, and summing up their thinking with a beautiful acuity, 'Existentialism is teaching that man is sentinel to the null.'

Once an international celebrity, he tore around the television studios of the world, keeping just ahead of the debt he owed his creditors and his internal organs. His output was small but ripe. His two great plays, *The Quare Fellow* and *The Hostage*, were international successes and have stood the tests of time and fashion. His honest and beautiful memoir of prison life *Borstal Boy* is a masterpiece. Beyond that are short stories, songs, articles, and even books of rambling anecdotage, all wrapped in Behan's unique salt, seagull, and Guinness aura.

He was a staggering drunk. Starting at the age of eight, sinking pints with his granny, acquainted with the gutters of the world throughout his twenties, convulsing in his thirties, and killed by alcohol at forty-one, he leaves most other booze legends trailing behind. Actors used to like to cultivate a reputation for heavy drinking. But those who follow others' scripts never have quite the same thirst as those who write them. On the top of alcohol's Mount Olympus are the writers, those with the worst orc-ish demons to drown – Hemingway, Fitzgerald, Faulkner, and in a special place, Behan. He was an ugly drunk. When he wasn't enchanting, he was horrible. He fought, he abused, he rambled, he fell over, he bored, he fell over again. Those who airily accused him of being a stage drunk never found themselves on the end of a punch, or a tirade, or wiped his vomit off the floor. And would a stage drunk die of it? Behan knew what he was doing – 'I'm committing suicide on the instalment plan.' By the time of his death, hardly a bar in Dublin would admit him. Yet they all turned out for his funeral.

Many of the stories about him are about his drinking. If you work on a play of his, these stories start spilling out of the ground. An Irish writer told how Behan was once asked by the Guinness brewery to come up with a new slogan. He requested a large fee, a crate of Guinness, and to be left alone in a hotel room. The nervous execs paced the corridors listening to Behan in the throes of creativity – mumbling, singing, and crashing around. After a considerable silence, they ventured in. They found Behan fast asleep on the floor, surrounded by empty bottles. On a table, on a piece of paper, a short scrawl: 'Guinness makes you drunk.'

An old raincoat of urban myth has been wrapped around Behan. In part this is Brendan performing some atavistic function. Every tribe needs a banshee, a wild one who destroys himself and others. He was one of the first stars of TV. From the moment he stumbled out of his drunken interview with Malcolm Muggeridge and realised that people loved him for being outrageous on the prim and proper BBC, he knew he had a persona that was profitable. There is little doubt he played up to the image of the ex-IRA carouser. There is also little doubt that is who he was. The mask was an extension of himself. The problem came when he wanted to move on and take the mask off. And the crowd wouldn't let him.

His relationship with his home country is complicated. For some audiences he was the model Irishman: a republican, who twice went to jail for the cause, and as gifted in Gaelic as he was in English. Yet Ireland, though it can be more generous and freewheeling than England, can be as deadly in its fastidious snobbery. Behan fell victim to that. Literary Dublin turned its back on him. As Hugh Leonard, a boulevard playwright, sniffed, 'His place in the pantheon seems to be founded on the axiom that loutishness and chronic drunkenness are evidence of genius.' The warmth of the Irish working class, and the eccentricity of its upper class, can disguise a deadly conformity emanating from its middle class. Behan was a walking affront to that, particularly in its rigid post-war guise. In New York, the third-generation genteel Irish wouldn't allow him to join the St Patrick's Day parade. The Abbey wouldn't open its doors to Behan during his lifetime. Even forty years after his death, the programme of work the Abbey produced to mark its centenary included not a mention of Behan. As Ireland has sought to Disney up its propensity for the craic, and to commodify its mayhem, it has had less time for the real thing. The renegade spirit many associate with Ireland was exemplified in Behan, but renegades hurt both themselves and others.

What has been hidden by the clouds of notoriety, the stories and myths? A great playwright. No polished dramatist, but a great one. Behan is in the punk tradition that runs from Euripides through Webster through Rimbaud and on into Shane MacGowan – the writers quoted more often by the young than at high table. The writers of any age who understand that the future is more likely to be found among freaks and criminals than in the drawing room. The way ahead is often invented on the margins, and that is where Behan, whether in prison or shebeen, was his happiest. As he said, 'Pity is my vice and my downfall. I pity every sort and size of sinner. I stand by the damned anywhere in this world and in the next. If there are people put out of heaven, put me out with them.'

His play *The Quare Fellow* is a beautiful piece of construction. The easy, rolling, naturalistic surface conceals a seriousness of purpose, and a careful architecture. While posing as a documentary photograph, Behan is in fact revealing art of careful composition. Slowly, through the course of twenty-four hours leading up to the execution of an inmate at Mountjoy Prison, Behan reveals the terror contained in certain death. The jokes, the insight, and the stories of the inmates fill the stage with a firecracker display of life, yet it is clear at every instant that they are whistling in the wind. Their furious energy is as purposeless as that of their more abstract contemporaries, Vladimir and Estragon in *Waiting for Godot*. Beckett had helped Behan home from many a drunken night in Paris, and though the two writers are on the surface chalk and cheese, their substance is not so far apart.

The Quare Fellow appeared on the London stage around the same time as *Godot* and *Look Back in Anger.* Beckett's play articulated nihilism and fortitude in the abstract, while Osborne's brought rage into the listless world of the disentitled lower middle class. Both expanded the language and possibilities of the proscenium. But Behan pushed the envelope just as far. In *The Quare Fellow*, he brings us to a prison; in *The Hostage*, to a brothel. Behan brought working-class life, with all its sardonic humour, stoical acceptance, and unsentimental realism onto the polite stages of the mid-century. The prison of *The Quare Fellow* is dank with the stink of piss and shit, topped off with the occasional whiff of frying rashers. Behan brings us the excited noise of the day, and then, within that, when the uncanny quiet of the hangman haunts the stage, the cool breeze of death. When the warder looks up at the stars and wonders at the empty hysteria of it all, he brings us something else. Something grander – life and the wide dark – glimpsed by a mystic drunk, opening us out to colder, emptier vistas.

The Quare Fellow helped make the reputation of Behan and its director, Joan Littlewood, and the legend of her theatre, Stratford East. She gave it a painstaking production, drilling her actors with a rigorous brutality to recreate the realities of life inside. She honoured the play, and its art. At the opening, Behan made a speech and said, 'Joan Littlewood has directed a better play than I wrote.'

'Fuck Joan Littlewood,' was the statement Behan shouted from the back of the stalls at a late performance of *The Hostage*, their next collaboration. Something had clearly gone wrong. *The Hostage* had begun life as *An Giall*, written in Gaelic and, in its style, a quiet exercise in lyrical realism. Set in a brothel, it tells the story of an English soldier kidnapped by the IRA and held as a hostage to try and stay the execution of a republican fighter. The soldier and a working girl fall tenderly in love, a potentially melodramatic storyline told with restrained modesty.

The play is caustically unsentimental about nationalism, of both the Irish and British strains, manifesting Behan's stance, 'An author's first duty is to let down his country.' (This may be another reason why the Irish held Behan at arm's length.) The most arch of the republicans, Monsewer, turns out to be an Englishman educated at Oxford and the archetype of many an Aran-sweater-wearing public-school chap, who strains to be more Irish than the Irish. About republicanism and political violence, Behan was writing from the inside, just as with the prison depicted in his earlier play. There is no romanticism here, nor any displaced attachment; old IRA man Pat assesses violence with a chilling accuracy: 'There's always two kinds of gunmen . . . the religious man and the man with a sense of humour. Always the man with the sense of humour was the worst gunman – the more venomous maybe.' Not even O'Casey, in *Shadow of a Gunman*, gives you inside track like that.

It is uncertain how much of a translation was brought into the rehearsal room with Joan Littlewood, but what is certain is that the eventual play, *The Hostage*, bears scant resemblance to *An Giall*. A delicate tragedy was transformed through improvisation and devising into a music hall extravaganza. The same humour in the face of death which distinguished *The Quare Fellow* survives into *The Hostage*, but confused with a forced variety jolliness. An unfortunate strain of Paddy-whackery abounds. The worst of the coarsening occurs with the love story, which becomes a *Carry On* romp full of saucy gags. In *An Giall*, the pathos is enhanced by a shy sincerity; in *The Hostage*, the end is abrupt and alienating but goes for little beyond shock value.

When Behan cried out 'Fuck Joan Littlewood,' it was at the end of a long commercial run, which made him a lot of money, and brought kudos and dosh to the Theatre Royal, Stratford East. But success is a corrupter, and both playwright and company lost soul and spirit as the money rolled in. Littlewood's actors, previously a praetorian guard for her and the cause of rigorous populism, started losing their cohesion amid commercial fanfares and offers of work in television and cinema. Behan came apart at the seams. With its anarchic brouhaha, *The Hostage* was certainly present and in the moment, but it's hard not to see it as a mutual loss for Littlewood and Behan, both being forced into a mannerism of hyper-roughhouse-spontaneity when both were careful and considered artists.

Twin rebels, kindred spirits. Brendan Behan seated behind Joan Littlewood, *The Hostage*, 1959

Behan is often patronised as being little more than a purveyor of rich sing-song dialogue. In fact, he was a once-in-a-generation original, bringing new form and content to the stage. He was a dirty dandy, an Oscar Wilde of the gutter, who brought information from the whorehouse and the gaol, and with that news, new ways of talking and thinking. He brought colour to a 1950s world that was grey and bleak and cold. As Norman Mailer said of him, 'New York was dead in those days. It was the end of the Eisenhower regime, a puritan period. Brendan was an ice-breaker and the times needed an ice-breaker.'

Or, as his mother put it more simply, 'He swung the world by the tail.'

Lads, lads, lads.
Brendan Behan drinking, 1962

Friedrich Dürrenmatt

1921–1990

While many in England were aspiring to write for a maybe not entirely necessary genre, the state of the nation play, Friedrich Dürrenmatt was going a step further. He aimed for state of the world. He felt himself well positioned to scale this mountain from his homeland, neutral (or quasi-neutral) Switzerland. As the Cold War reduced the world to binaries, the Swiss, he thought, were afforded a detached point of view. From there, they could view from aloft the onrush of capitalism in the West and authoritarianism in the East, the farcical self-importance of the intelligence war, and the lunacies of the arms race. As the citizen of a small state, he felt neutrality lent a hot-air balloon perspective, from which he could look down on the ground plan of Europe and diagnose its nuttiness.

A natural refusenik late in life (earlier he had been a little too keen on the Nazi perspective), Dürrenmatt was determined to escape categorisation. In his work, he blended elements of realism, the grotesque, the absurd, classical tragedy, and satire. Rather than an arena for the working out of theorems, he felt theatre should be a laboratory for continual experiment, for trying a little more of this or a big helping of that, ever in pursuit of enhanced vividness. Much of the latter half of his career was spent revising and redirecting his own work. Like the whizzing atom, he thought life in Heraclitean flux, a volatility the theatre should mirror rather than aiming for settled states. Inspired as a young man by Georg Büchner's *Woyzeck*, he aimed for the same supercharged vibrancy; drama barrelling along at a fever pitch, where tragic intensity clashes with comic grotesquerie. All needed to be exaggerated, the febrility and the caricature; nothing sketched with a soft pencil, all clash and clatter, scattered within a narrative of fits and starts. To maximise the insecurity, neither the play's construction nor the acting should take itself too seriously.

This chaos finds its most thrilling ramshackle unity in *The Visit*. The play was premiered as *Der Besuch der alten Dame* at the Schauspielhaus Zürich in 1956; it was first presented in London and New York by Peter Brook, and has since been translated into twenty-five languages. Adapted into a series of film and television versions, it is frequently revived by auteurish directors who fancy a bit of showing off. A chilling parable about man's greed, the play showcases social passivity in the face of the willpower of tyrants, and how small-town smugness is just a hair's breadth away from moral collapse.

It opens as the solid burghers of Güllen – a fictitious name meaning 'liquid manure' – await the arrival by train of Claire Zachanassian. Their municipality is in dire financial straits, and they hope she will help. Having left as a young woman in disgrace, she is returning as one of the super-rich, an oligarch status achieved by a succession of marriages. (Her name is a compendium of Zaharoff, a renowned arms dealer, Onassis, and Gulbenkian, the shipping and oil magnates, all superstars of wealth in the dowdy 1950s.) Her purpose is revenge – not on the whole populace, though her loathing for all is capacious – but on Alfred Ill, the man who deserted her when she was a pregnant youth, leading to her expulsion from the town. Alfred is a simple, popular, and rather dull chap now, the keeper of the general store. If the townsfolk want her money, they must kill him. This is the moral quandary that imperils the play.

What most excites the auteurs is the zoo entourage which trails onstage behind Zachanassian. There is a butler called Boby (the ex-chief justice of Güllen); a panther, who escapes in the course of the play and roams the town (not the subtlest of symbols, but subtlety is out of the window here); husbands, present, past and to be; two gum-chewing heavies called Roby and Toby, purchased from death row in Sing Sing; and two blind eunuchs called Koby and Loby. The two heavies carry Claire in a sedan chair and, to raise the stakes of narrative inevitability, two further servants carry a black coffin. An ornate statement of comic expressionism, directors and designers find it irresistible. Audiences can do as well, if it's austerely pitched. Claire, a glorious role taken by a succession of great actresses from Ingrid Bergman to Lauren Bacall to Kathryn Hunter to Lesley Manville, is an amalgam of prostheses, the result of accidents that have battered her along the way. The mix of wounds from the gutter alongside towering imperiousness is catnip for actors.

The comic fantasia is exhilarating, but not the whole story. There are moments of loose almost documentary realism in Alfred's shop as customers come and go; tableaux of frenzied public hysteria which chill the blood; and a lyrical tenderness in scenes in the woods between the two ex-lovers. No formal unity resides here, just as the world contains none. Alongside this Aristophanic grab bag of styles, an abundance of ideas spill over about guilt by neglect, political decay, and evasion of moral responsibility. Claire understands the greed of the townsfolk, and utilises that insight to corrode their veneer of morality. Preaching justice, she in fact wants vengeance, wreaking the same chaos on the town as it inflicted on her. Through scale and freedom, the story blooms to prove a multipurpose allegory for Nazi Germany, for post-war Europe with its sacrifice of community for capitalism, and beyond for a universe in entropy. All spiced with wild laughter.

His second celebrated work, *The Physicists*, is set in that old Mitteleuropean allegorical staple, the sanatorium, or 'madhouse'. An ingenious Pirandellian set-up ensues where, in a decaying mansion, three distinguished physicists have been locked away. One deludes himself he is Newton, another Einstein, and a third Möbius. At the beginning of the play the police are present, investigating the strangling of a nurse, the second such occurrence in a matter of months. By the climax of the first act, a third nurse is strangled. In further Pirandellian plagiarism, it turns out the physicists are not mad but pretending. One is a KGB agent, another works for the CIA, and both are trying to get their hands on the third, who has cracked the theory of Universal Discovery, whatever that may be. In a further twist (by which time the audience may be tiring of being deceived), the director of the madhouse, Dr Mathilde von Zahnd, turns into something between a Bond villain and a lunatic, incarcerating the physicists, and stealing their work to destroy the world. Here, the private sanatorium in the Swiss mountains stands in for a world locked in the madness of the Cold War, with battle lines drawn between a Soviet system promising justice without freedom, and an American one offering freedom without justice. Into this philosophical brew is stirred the technological acceleration of nuclear physics and its capacity for universal destruction.

Fiendishly clever would be one description of *The Physicists*. Slightly irritating might be another. The cleverness dazzles, turning its own logic into a sort of Möbius strip which keeps turning back in on itself. The whole amounts to the type of boffin drama students inflict on each other at university, where escalating crossword puzzle connections are meant to indicate increasing depth. Or, more often, ever higher Tower of Babel edifices of piffle. Though hard not to honour Dürrenmatt's ambition, the sheer absence of independent life in his characters, not to mention the casual way he dispatches three nurses as a sort of dark joke, leaves it weightless.

That *The Physicists* feels a little lost is perhaps a side effect of the delusional smallness of its age, which reduced so much to reductive oppositions, allowing a presumption that the richness of the world could be wrapped up in schematic art. And so we return to the circus anarchy of *The Visit*, shored up as it is by an ample sprinkling of surprise moments where life simply dances before us, its wild expeditions delighting audiences to this day.

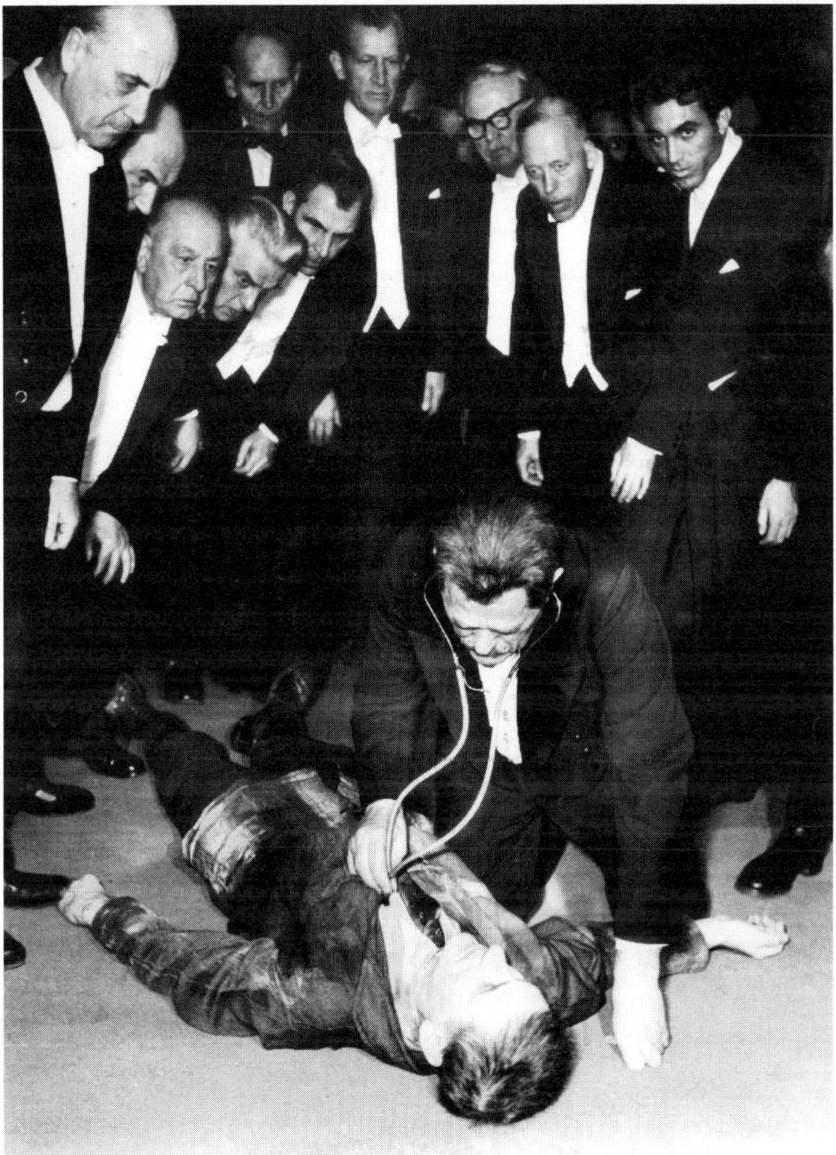

I blame his tailor.
Bernhard Minetti in *Der Besuch der alten Dame* (*The Visit*)

James Baldwin
1924–1987

History can be meagre to its sages.

After the toughest of early lives, and a hard scrabble to get early work published, James Baldwin achieved literary fame and enjoyed focus in the spotlight. One apotheosis came when he debated the conservative grandstander William F. Buckley at the Cambridge Union in 1965, and electrified a room packed with the next generation of opinion makers, earning a long-lasting ovation. He hovered close to the heart of the Civil Rights Movement, though never invited into its innermost sanctums. Partly because of class – Baldwin was from the Harlem ghetto – and partly because he was gay, which was not uncommon, and unapologetic, which was. Partly also because of his radicalism – though present on the podium at the March on Washington in 1963, his proposed speech was deemed too inflammatory.

For a long time, he was a figure of great note in American cultural life, before history with its great caprice subjected him to its final weapon, neglect. I met him briefly at a revival of *The Amen Corner* in the late 1980s, and from the way everyone moved round and past him, and from the lightness of his benign curiosity, it took me a while to work out this was James Baldwin, the man who upset the hierarchies. Following his death in 1987, his work drifted from centre stage, and his voice grew fainter. However, truths as concrete as his and insights as sharp can never be fully erased, and when the Black Lives Matter movement grew in hunger for voices to define its arguments, Baldwin the ghost glided elegantly back to centre stage.

He has now ascended to the status of a secular saint, quoted on any and every issue, with a reverence he might find excessive. His acute sense of the absurd, and his suspicion of any form of adulation, might be moved to a little light laughter when earnest middle-class white folk intone his words with teary eyes as if gospel. He may well fade from view again, before another resurrection. However much his aura ebbs and flows, it can never be extinct.

Baldwin approached the theatre with trepidation. He was finding it hard enough to gain respect for his prose without venturing into an alien medium, especially one with its drawbridge so firmly down. He felt, with justice, that the theatre was closed to black work and its audiences. The walls of white Jericho were built high and strong, and it would take a mighty horn to blow them down. His first play, *The Amen Corner*, was published in 1954, and it took eleven years and a circuitous route for it to reach Broadway. He found the time to write it only after a gift of a cash donation from his friend Marlon Brando. By the time of his second, *Blues for Mister Charlie*, he would have seen nudges of improvement. Watching his great ally Lorraine Hansberry's play at a try-out in Philadelphia, he was astonished by both play and audience: 'I had never in my life seen so many black people in the theater. And the reason was that never in the history of the American theater had so much truth of black people's lives been seen on stage. Black people ignored the theater because the theater had always ignored them.'

The chief virtue of Baldwin's work was once described as its ability 'to fold back in on itself'. You see this at a micro and a macro level. His elegant prose – written or spoken – has a Latinate capacity to drill down in subclause after subclause, to find the right word, the right formulation, to ensure that no argument or justification is omitted. Though his stepfather was a Baptist preacher, this is not the rolling upward inflection of the orator: it is the steady and calm pursuit of the well-buttressed castle of thought. His narratives 'fold back in' with their attempt to reassemble the pieces of lives blown apart by trauma. They try to secure selves and to leave them, if not whole, then on the journey to becoming so. He was always looking for the history behind the present moment and wrapping that into the fabric. As the stories move forwards, we search backwards into the crises that fostered the conditions. The present is a millefeuille (if not too effete a metaphor for tales of blood and cruelty), a lattice of lost moments regathered to present the fullest truth.

Baldwin's theme, by necessity, was race. In his view, white America had created a false reality, based on partial history and the excluding of competing realities that reflected other perspectives. The moral and aesthetic aim was to redress the balance. From his own odyssey, he had a wider collection of viewpoints to call on than most. Born and raised in a ghetto, he emigrated to Paris at the age of twenty-four with no more than $40 in his pocket. He lived in Europe for a long time, mixing with an elite group of exiles. As with Oscar Wilde, and the pantheon of other gay playwrights, his queerness sharpened his outsider's eye. A voracious reader, as a child he tore through Dickens and Shakespeare and the King James Bible, and these voices he managed to blend with the rhythms of gospel and jazz and the blues to compose his own cadence. He didn't cast aside old voices for new ones, he threaded them into a richer weave.

For Baldwin, drama was always a public forum: 'I was born in the church. I knew that out of the ritual of the church, historically speaking, comes the act of the theater, the communion which is the theater.' *The Amen Corner* is set in a church, switching between front-of-house services and backstage machinations. Singing – sublime and wrenching – fills stage and auditorium, as gospel tunes make the spirit soar. There is no sentimentality about the music's effect. Beautiful harmonies do nothing to wash away the pain of a lost child, nor do they invest morality in the singers. No sooner have characters finished quivering the souls of the audience with their outpouring, than they are squabbling with petty viciousness over church expenses. Nor does music clarify the confusion of those in darkness.

Into the church Baldwin invades Luke, an old jazz musician coming to the end of his life. A wandering soul and the husband of the church's leader, Margaret, he carries a strong moral voice. These two go to war over their son. Two competing calls fight for the young man's soul: the church and the jazz club; moral fervour and the allure of the cool; music that gives uplift and music that sets a groove. With no winners possible, the pressure of competing ideals breaks both. Finally, they realise a redemption in love and self-knowledge: 'A man only survives if he has a sense of himself – that's what pulls him through no matter how much he has lost – and that sense of himself can only be revealed through love.'

Blues for Mister Charlie revolves around an act of violence. Loosely based on the abduction and lynching of fourteen-year-old Emmett Till, it was written on a promise to the assassinated civil rights activist Medgar Evers, to whom it is dedicated. A story which spills across a ranging landscape, it is loosely held for the first two acts within a church, and for the last in a courthouse. As in *The Amen Corner*, everything is worked out in public forums and their rituals, with narrative events woven into their liturgies. Both arenas fit hand in glove into the proscenium. A young black man, returning from the North to his community in the Deep South, has been murdered by a white racist, a murder we witness. A complex lattice is constructed – love stories, family dynamics, communities closing in on themselves, marriages falling apart, and lost souls drifting in confusion – as the play moves towards a trial.

Baldwin sets out to get under the skin and into the mind of a white racist, and manages it. There is no caricaturing here – the killer, like the other characters, is contrary and identifiable, and somehow, in a stroke of authorial generosity, even sympathetic. A bold act of dramatic imagination, it is at the core of what Baldwin was attempting to achieve. By demonstrating such empathy, he provokes his audience to attempt the same.

More surprising, and particular to Baldwin, is the boldness with which he brings desire onstage. There is tragedy here and high-flown rhetoric, but what grounds it is a feeling for sexual excitements and needs. The pious atmosphere of *The Amen Corner* is punctuated by one character remarking spikily of the church's leader, 'I tell you, honey, you been married once, it ain't so easy to get along single . . . no wonder that woman make so much noise when she get up in the pulpit.' The tension between the returning jazzer and his pious ex-wife crackles with powerful cravings. The love here is not sweet or coy, it is obsessive and destructive: 'I ain't never held no man until I felt his pain coming into me like little drops of acid.' In *Blues for Mister Charlie*, sex is much of the problem between black and white communities. Powerful feelings of attraction cross the divides, and disorienting fears about the greater potency of others. Desire hazes the air in both plays, lifting them to an original plane. Baldwin understood all this from a queer perspective, with a strain of homosexual desire running through the second. His honesty about sexuality within the matrix of racial confusions is a truth few others dared to voice.

Both plays feature sermons at a climactic point, around which the plays symphonically arrange themselves. Given Baldwin's stepfather's preaching and his own flirtation with the church, it seems natural the pulpit should prove pivotal. In both works, the sermons fail in their intentions, with the preacher either not finding the language, or being so blinded by hatred of others or the wrongness of history they cannot prevail. There are no false victories here. Baldwin understood what it cost to take a public position, in a pulpit to a small community or broadcasting to the nation. In these sermons he demonstrates the weight and responsibility of trying to carry the souls of others.

Baldwin's works succeeded on Broadway, but there have been few subsequent productions (admittedly they require large casts, but then so does the endlessly revived *The Crucible*). One can't help wishing he had written further for the stage. The stagecraft is faulty, with little sense of how to frame one scene against another. Though the excess of their ambition is a joy – their surging, uncontainable energy – some moments block each other out. With a talent of his size, it is a loss that no one gave him a theatre home in which to relish the technical challenges. But we can be grateful for what we have, two plays that brought into the public arena information about black lives, and about the heat of the confrontation between communities when that heat was fierce. These plays brought secrets into the light and made the private public.

Feel the spirit.
The Amen Corner, 1965

Shelagh Delaney
1938–2011

Shelagh Delaney whirled through London theatre as a teenage tornado. Having written her first play at the age of eighteen, it was staged at Joan Littlewood's Theatre Workshop in Stratford East before she was twenty. The inverse of the brooding, imploding angry young men, she was a tonic, free with opinions, insights, and the unfiltered bubbling up of her inner self – and soon she was every young journalist's favourite source of copy. As Jo says in *A Taste of Honey*, 'Me, I'm contemporary . . . I really do live at the same time as myself, don't I?' The play opened in 1958, was in the West End within a year, and on Broadway within two. Her presence as a personality, alongside the play that served as her magic carpet into the world's esteem, proved pivotal in London's emergence from post-war gloom and into the vivacity of the 1960s.

Delaney was part of a long tradition of voices coming down to London from the North, with bracing news about sex for neurotic Southerners. It's a tradition that later extended to Andrea Dunbar and Jonathan Harvey. Each in their own era burst into rooms full of people strangled by tortured etiquettes and denied desires, to announce: 'Oh, come on, it's only sex! Get on with it!'

Delaney's play brings us a mother, Helen, a Salford courtesan who flirts with prostitution, while staying just the right side. She lives with her daughter, Jo, born from a five-minute fling outside wedlock. She in turn, while claiming to be older than her fifteen years, is romanced by a sweet-souled black merchant sailor. When Jo gets pregnant, her mother having run off with a shambolic car salesman, she shacks up with a gay art student. They begin a hybrid relationship, a modern mix of friendship, dependence, and not-quite-sex. The frankness here about homosexuality, relationships across races, and people using sex for personal gain comes as a blast of sleety cold wind rushing through a fusty drawing room. What Rattigan and Coward and Maugham had muttered discreetly about for a century, Delaney presented breezily and fearlessly.

Rattigan was the perverse inspiration for Delaney's writing. She went to see a touring production of his *Variation on a Theme*, a piece of elegant suffering, garlanded with costumes by Norman Hartnell. The sheer distance between this coutured wallow in self-pity set on the Riviera and the raw-boned life surrounding her in Salford, enraged the young Delaney. She went home, bunked off work for two weeks, and dashed off her tangy masterwork.

Having read in the newspapers of a confrontation between the Lord Chamberlain's censors and Joan Littlewood's outfit, she decided that Stratford East was the place for her. Their reciprocal enthusiasm for play was instantaneous, and before long Delaney was in rehearsals. Littlewood fought a long war against the fourth wall and what she saw as the deadening stuffiness of the proscenium. Being much enamoured of the direct communication of variety and music hall, she always looked to create an open relationship between play and audience. *A Taste of Honey* – with wisecracks drawn from the vaults of old comedy and Delaney's characters' desire to bring the audience onside – was the ideal match for Littlewood's show-bones. Though the setting was realistic, with a dingy flat in Salford recreated fastidiously, and with acting as real as the wallpaper, the characters weren't stuck within it: they were free to share thoughts outwards. For an extra splash of sauce, Littlewood added a jazz trio to accompany the goings-on. Here and with *The Quare Fellow*, she collided truth and a knees-up to the benefit of both.

What anchors *A Taste of Honey* is the easy naturalness of the dialogue, the contrary truth of the relationships, and a fascination with stuff. Only the best writers can make a whole play revolve around an object. In *Othello*, a juggernaut of a plot and the eyes of three thousand spectators in the Globe revolved around a lace handkerchief. That flimsy object magnetised the story to itself. In Delaney's play, a Woolworths ring fulfils a similar function: it is given in an act of proposal, worn on a necklace throughout, and later cruelly ripped from Jo's neck. Much emotion gets invested in this crystallising object. Later, there is a fierce stand-off over two objects. The art student has found a woven Moses basket for the new baby, with which Jo is much taken. When her mother returns to the family home, she scorns the basket as dirty, saying she has acquired a mail-order cot with 'pink curtains, you know, and frills . . . A proper cot of the latest design. It's got all the etceteras and everything.' Stuff is the concern for a dawning consumer age. In this stand-off over cots, we see new class uneasiness breaking out over taste.

The dialogue refreshes because it never overreaches, it has the confidence of the young person who has zero interest in being anything other than who she is. Statements have a plain punch, such as this quick exchange between mother and daughter:

I don't suppose you're sorry to see me go.
I'm not sorry and I'm not glad.

There are subtleties in the double negatives and the contradictions, but it is the directness that is striking, especially in a proscenium form given to tortured circumlocutions. For someone simply to say what they feel, quickly and accurately, must have felt like heaven. Similarly, when the two young lovers have a brief holiday in joy before separation, the giddy fullness with which they declare love exhilarates. Both know their relationship is not forever, and that much is performative – but, praise God, there are not a thousand little ironies clogging up the arteries of feeling. Lie it may be, but it is allowed its own sweetness.

Delaney's characters shift, turn, and rearrange positions two or three times a page. They rile, attack, and squabble from ever-changing points. Every speech from the mother contains a mound of internal contradictions. Sometimes they pull themselves together and resolve on a single position, usually a heroic one, based on love rather than self-interest. Then, on a sixpence, they switch again. Inconsistencies exasperate but also lend them vitality. It feels like Delaney is putting a new sort of human on the stage, definite in immediate standpoints and bewildering in changeability. Something modern brews within these oscillations – personalities that are not fixed, positions not held.

The new often doesn't come in the shape we expect. The academy would have us believe that cultural shifts can only be delivered by tortured souls cooking them up for decades in laboratories of modernist experiment. Abstract formulations will trickle down from temples of applied learning. Change is, in fact, likelier to come from a funny young woman from Salford. Putting this content onstage at Stratford East – dispossessed families, unmarried young mothers, biracial relationships, openly gay characters – was the first step towards normalising them. Delaney and Littlewood posited no scheme of improvement, they simply said, 'Look, this is happening.'

A New York take on British working-class fashion. Angela Lansbury as Helen and Joan Plowright as her daughter, Jo; *A Taste of Honey*, Broadway, 1961

A Taste of Honey bounced into the West End, across to New York, and onto film – proof that this was news people were conscious of in the back of their minds but waiting to hear said out loud. That it was encased in a shapely play, spilling over with good humour, was an immense help. Its artlessness was a challenge to the deliberacy of the academy, and its healthy sexuality a rebuke to the timidity of the educated middle class. Ways were soon found to patronise and diminish its achievement. Thankfully it has a rock-solid heart and the gleam of the natural. The snobs can't touch it.

John Arden

1930–2012

In 2003, just as the British Army was joining the invasion of Iraq, we thought it apposite at the Oxford Stage Company to revive and tour John Arden's *Serjeant Musgrave's Dance*. His play from 1959 is a chilling parable about the destructive blowback from colonial aggression. As the United Kingdom, against the wishes of an overwhelming number of its citizens, prepared to join an army of occupation, we thought some form of response was necessary. Not from any crazed delusion we could make a difference, it was more a matter of 'What else can we do?' As Arden put it at the time, 'You don't write to stop things. You write to show people there are things that need to be stopped.'

The production by Sean Holmes was sterling. It had a mighty cast, including Tobias Menzies and Maxine Peake, and the reviews were stellar, all proclaiming it as work that needed to be seen both for political reasons and to hear Arden's voice again. Watching it, there was a sense of witnessing something rare and substantial, muscular and knotted with life. Nobody came. Nobody. We limped around some of our most beautiful old theatres, and emptied them. 'You could graze a cow in the stalls,' in the old thespian saying. Rheumy-eyed elders – venerable socialists and anarchists and peaceniks in fraying donkey jackets – attended in tiny numbers. You could almost see monochrome memories of marches and speeches and disputatious committees floating through their mind's eye as they watched.

Arden's plays were never popular – he has survived more through the loyalty of artists than audiences – but this felt sadly terminal. Our very purpose as a touring company, compelled by the Arts Council to tour neglected theatres for thirty-two weeks a year, felt an anachronism. An act of social responsibility in an age of competitive hustling. Watching this earnest and vivid old epic, human and troubled, playing out in front of empty seats, reinforced the suspicion we were worshipping dead gods. Something substantial had left the building a while before.

When *Musgrave* opened at the Royal Court in 1959, the critics were largely enraged or bewildered. A tale set in the Victorian era, it follows four army deserters, kitted out in redcoats like 'swaggering lobsters', who turn up in a bleak, strike-bound colliery town. The townsfolk assume they must be strike-breakers, but their purpose is darker. Driven by the merciless logic of 'Black Jack' Musgrave, they are resolved to exact revenge for an act of colonial violence, to bring home the merciless cruelty of war. In a distant colony, the killing of a British soldier, from the same mining town, has been followed by the tit-for-tat murder of five innocent civilians. (The play is based on an incident from 1958, when British soldiers killed five innocent Cypriots in an antiterrorist reprisal.) Musgrave wants with mathematical exactitude to kill twenty-five innocent English and thus 'to work that guilt back to where it began', to render to the source the savage cost of colonialism.

As with all Arden's plays, it is written in his brand of epic chaotic. A theatrical magpie, he stole freely: ballads from music hall; routines from vaudeville; Shakespearean verse; satirical doggerel; songs of elemental beauty. His prose is as textured and bloody as a great black pudding; in Michael Billington's phrase, the language 'ricocheted off the walls of the theatre like a ball in a squash court'. Annie, a barmaid, tells Musgrave, as testament to his obduracy, that 'the north wind in a pair of millstones was your father and your mother.' She rebukes the other soldiers, 'that serjeant squats in your gobs like an old wife stuck in a fireplace.' In *Live Like Pigs*, two council households – one lower middle class and one Romany – pursue a neighbour feud of epic dimensions. A daughter recounts her ma's romantic memories of her dad; after work, he would be 'home like a traction engine and revel her three times down to Rio without he'd even take off his boots'. There is an unabashed richness of prose here unmatched since the Restoration age.

Yet his work never found an audience. In its first run, *Serjeant Musgrave's Dance* only sold a fifth of its tickets; *The Happy Haven* an inglorious tenth. He wrote other plays just as rich – *The Waters of Babylon* is a rambunctious Jonsonian comedy about a slum landlord in 1950s London; *The Workhouse Donkey* a Dionysiac pageant about municipal corruption – and they fared no better. But then it would be true to say of all the Royal Court cadre – Arden, Wesker, and Bond – that they failed to secure a true popular audience. In a way they disdained it. Little of the boulevard inflects their plays. This rendered them heroes to a minority but fatally undermined an ancient compact between the theatre and the public. It is right not to be a slave of the public: it is wrong not to care about them. Somewhere between the two is a moving target of a solution that playwrights have to keep an eye on. This generation of writers, perhaps aware the form was a dying beast, lost sight of it.

To compound the problem, they went to war with their hosts. After his sojourn at the Court, Arden migrated to the Royal Shakespeare Company, a relationship which ended as badly as it could have done when he and his wife, Margaretta D'Arcy, picketed the audience at their own play *The Island of the Mighty* in 1972. They believed the director had shifted the play's perspective towards favouring imperialism. Edward Bond decided he was done with others interpreting his plays, and made it a condition he should direct his own work, a stipulation from this less than easy man – a curious mix of Olympian aesthetics and Stalinist control – which left numerous actors and theatres traumatised for years. Arnold Wesker was involved with various groups – Centre 42 and the Writers & Readers Publishing Cooperative Ltd – whose aim was to subvert structures and democratise the means of production. His dreams foundered again at the RSC in 1972, when a group of actors influenced by the Socialist Labour League refused to perform his play *The Journalists.* The journey from dismantling the hierarchy to not doing anything at all proved surprisingly swift. There was a misunderstanding of the role of the director here, which, at its best, is not there to exercise control but to mediate it, not to enforce ego but to dissolve it. Whichever, it amounted to more thrashing around of a dying animal.

Maybe a day will come when audiences are ready for Arden's work; one would hope so, since it is remarkable. Finally, what stymied it was a singular virtue, his own determination not to take a point of view. Nothing in his plays is simple, no character is admirably heroic or comfortingly villainous: all are compromised. As he put it: 'A play, by offering a complex image of human beings reacting among themselves, can offer contradictions.' This is not moral ambivalence, it is a moral commitment to seeing the world as it is. To letting a play be what it wants to be.

Arden was a lyricist of brilliance, following in the dramatists' tradition which stretches back to Shakespeare. His songs trace threads relating to each play they feature in, but also stand alone, not relying on the interconnection. A great lyric is an event, a little grenade of compacted resonance, as much as it ferries a message. The word 'hallelujah' has a meaning, but primarily a forceful existence as a sound. Arden took this principle, the independent haunting strangeness of a beautifully rendered ballad and applied it to the whole of his work. As Chekhov said in response to a query from his wife just before he died: 'You ask what life is. That is like asking what a carrot is. A carrot is a carrot and nothing more is known.' Arden aimed as high as simple existence and, whether it attracted an audience or not, the work stands up.

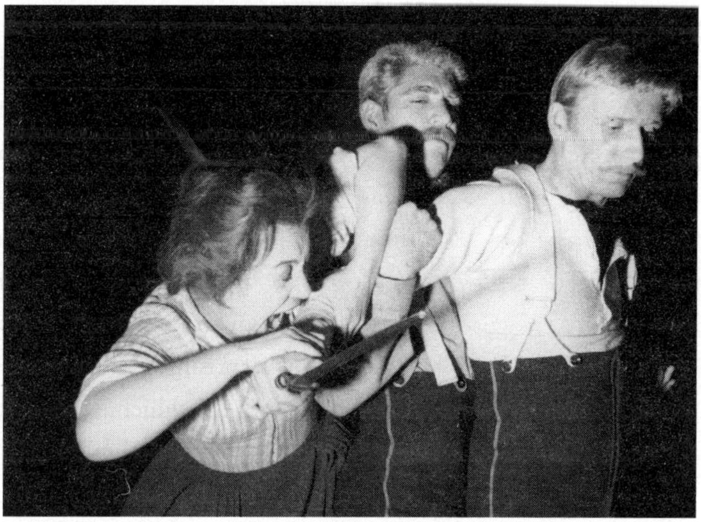

Twister gone wrong.
In rehearsal for *Sergeant Musgrave's Dance* at the Royal Court Theatre, London, 1959

Arnold Wesker
1932–2016

'I'm not an angry young man: I'm a happy young man,' said Arnold Wesker, with that pinch of unctuousness which bedevilled his pronouncements. When does an artist not object to being incorporated into a movement? When do you hear a playwright or novelist saying, 'Yes, I am part of that gang, and delighted to be so! I am pleased for my participation to define me for now and posterity! And if there are any other gangs going, I would be delighted to sign up for them!' That would be the real surprise. Wesker, as with them all, pushed hard against all such characterisations. He refused the 'angry' soubriquet, though he did no shortage of protesting, at one point ending up in prison. He protested with the same vehemence against being described as part of the 'kitchen sink' movement, a pushback which strains credibility. His first play was called *The Kitchen* and featured more sinks than had ever been seen on a stage; his next two successes boasted single sinks. Sometimes people could maybe fall into the welcoming arms of the collective.

His claim for happiness has basis in fact. Wesker was born in 1932 in Mother Levy's, an East End Jewish maternity home, and brought up in an attic flat on Fashion Street nearby. He was born into poverty, bathing in a tin bath, his industrious mother on one occasion selling their chairs to pay for food. The lack of authority from his work-shy father, Joe, was more than compensated by strong women – his mother, sister, and aunts. The cradle of love they constructed fostered an emotional security which carried him through life. The attachment of the Jewish community, its web of ties and connections, also secured him. Both brought belonging, as did their politics. Communism was in the air he breathed, and in every other word he heard. A street corner nearby was the meeting place for the party. Marxism provided a substitute faith for the secular Jewish community, and they committed with the same ferocity as others attended to

Jehovah. His home was a stone's throw from Cable Street, where in 1936 a fighting alliance of the Jewish, the Irish, and the trades unions, among others, drove out Oswald Mosley's fascist mob and their police accomplices. The sounds of these battles rang in the ears of the four-year-old boy, his home a refuge for members of his family and others as they took a breather before returning to the fray. Cable Street stories mutated rapidly into legend and became the myth-system of Wesker's youth.

University was never on the cards for Arnold: his education was more various. In short order, he was apprenticed to a furniture maker, worked as a carpenter's mate, and served as a bookshop assistant before undertaking his national service in the RAF. He tried to write a novel based on that experience, which later morphed into *Chips with Everything*. Drifting on through the university of life, he accumulated further credits as plumber's mate, seed sorter, and farm labourer. All provided material for later scenarios, all advanced his ear for the language of struggle, and for the poetry of prosaic transactions. Perhaps most igniting was his time working in his first great medium – pastry – as a patissier in a Parisian restaurant, Le Rallye. (He remained proud of his apple strudel for the rest of his days.) Something about the mechanical repetition of the daily toil, and the balletic frenzy with which kitchen staff and front of house danced around each other, delivering food to hundreds, sparked his imagination. When he came to write his first play – his passion triggered by a viewing of *Look Back in Anger* in Streatham – it was to the kitchen he returned.

The workplace he presents is a hellhole, the dehumanised factory reimagined in a service industry. The action crescendoes to a maelstrom of babble and cacophony as waitresses shriek orders, knives click and clack, trays clang and clatter, and bodies swirl in patterns of function erasing the individuality of each. The kitchen becomes a monster of purpose, eating its workers and spitting them out. In quiet moments we get to know the diverse cast of characters, a blend of young people drawn from across the world, rife with nationalist aggressions and differing dreams of the future. Once service is called, such differences dissolve in the crush of co-ordinated action. Some break down under the pressure, others erupt into antagonism.

The allegorical nature of the action is trowelled on in heavy helpings. 'This is life, isn't it?' one character comments; 'You have stopped my whole world,' the owner wails when the tension of the kitchen boils over into the restaurant; 'What is there more?' he questions repeatedly, trying to understand why his workers are dissatisfied. Yet overblown questions do not damage the integrity of the picture. The play has required little adaptation to travel around the world, with over fifty productions in different cities, and even inspiring a musical in Japan.

Having cannibalised work experience for *The Kitchen*, Wesker did the same with family for the trilogy that made his name. The Kahns of *Chicken Soup with Barley* lived in the basement rather than the attic, but that seems the single and signal difference between them and the Weskers. He disclaimed any ability to come up with stories: 'I can't invent plots or characters.' He believed most writers began with ideas and found characters to suit, whereas he began with characters who became animated by ideas. He didn't travel far to find them: 'I find the people I know more interesting than anything I can invent.'

Chicken Soup with Barley opens with excited characters rushing in from having seen off the Mosleyites on Cable Street, exhilarated by their own violence: 'We threw stones and bottles at them'; 'We made the policemen surrender!' In this instant, their allegiance to communism means glory and freedom and brotherhood, and it is hard not to share their excitement. Over two acts, and twenty years, we watch the shine of their gleaming faces fade to pallor, blanched by the Second World War and Stalinism and the brutal repression of the Hungarian Revolution of 1956. We see a family's disintegration set against the collapse of an ideology. The tensions between different generations cannot be borne; husband and wife are at war; and it is harder for all to vault the disillusion which followed the evidence of the crimes within Sovietism. Wesker deftly sketches the onset of 1950s capitalism, and the powerful opiate of material possessions. As the matriarch, Sarah, bemoans of lost comrades,

'You give them a few shillings in the bank and they can buy a television, so they think it's all over . . . Is that what you want? Is that what you want me to be satisfied with? A television set?'

Heroically, against evidence and history, Sarah keeps the faith, even in the most bitter arguments with her son, Ronnie (a transparency of Arnold, and his own name an anagram of Ronald). Though Ronnie cannot be persuaded, his mother is afforded the strongest argument: 'If the electrician who comes to mend my fuse blows it instead, so I should stop having electricity? I should cut off my light? Socialism is my light, can you understand that?' And she is given a tolling bell of a final rebuke – 'Ronnie, if you don't care, you'll die' – which chimes soft but long. Wesker was sympathetically concerned with failure and how those who lose learn to survive. We feel for them and for the preservation of their dignity. This is political writing but not alienated; where Brecht eschews sympathy, Wesker with his sensitive observational writing invites it. These voices, talking in a working-class idiom rooted in their vernacular and vivified by radical ideas, were new to the stage, and Wesker held his characters' hands kindly as they stepped forward. Not from sentimentality but from loyalty.

Having consumed and regurgitated work and family in these two, in his third great play, *Roots*, he made good use of love. While attempting yet another job in his peripatetic existence (much like Bluebottle in *The Goon Show*), that of kitchen porter in a Norwich hotel, he met and fell in love with Doreen Bicker, whom he rechristened Dusty, because of her 'gold-dust' hair. An Arts Council bursary of £500 was diverted to cover the cost of their wedding in 1958. Having entered his universe, Dusty must have known she would end up as a character. Wesker went further, appropriating the entirety of her East Anglian farming family. (Later in life, he sternly said he had *never* written about his children, as if that excused the rest of the thieving.) By now he was shameless about his larceny, sitting in the farmhouse kitchen of his in-laws and typing out everything they said. By some miracle, probably that of naked fidelity, Wesker manages to achieve his ventriloquism without it feeling exploitative. Partly this is because these voices – working class and unprettified – were new to the playhouse and there was a feeling of simple revolution in that. And partly through the author's generosity – he took neglected people and let them speak for themselves with big and independent voices.

For this, the second part of his trilogy, which transferred to the Royal Court in 1959, Wesker executes a neat sidestep. The Kahns do not appear but are an offstage presence. Beatie Bryant, the avatar of Dusty, returns from London to Norfolk, where she and her family await the arrival of her beloved, Ronnie Kahn. Throughout she drives her family up the wall with second-hand maxims and opinions hyping mass education, all drilled into her by Ronnie, most of which imply criticism of the uneducated Bryants. Beatie's own voice starts to sound increasingly shrill, especially when surrounded by the slow, taciturn, and grounded rhythms of agricultural life. This is naturalism at its zenith, with a real stove cooking liver and onions – how they gasped in Sloane Square!

The apotheosis comes at the end of the third act when the family gathers for a splashing-out tea to welcome Ronnie, and in place of the promised boyfriend a letter arrives dumping Beatie. She wavers but does not break: in a long and astonishing jumble of speech, she finds her own unaided voice, one with a verbal vitality beyond Ronnie. In a beautifully observed moment, we feel for Beatie in her jilting, are thrilled by her assumption of herself, and in the background see the family sitting down for dinner, leaving the freshly glowing Beatie alone. She has risen, and at the same time she has lost. As with Eliza Doolittle, though she is transformed and can now outstrip her teacher, something rooted inside has flown away.

As in *Chicken Soup*, we see a woman suffer a serious disappointment but resolve to carry on. There is a social optimism in these moments, which rendered Wesker the nearest writer Britain ever came to a Clifford Odets. Obstacles happen, and there are stop points when death blocks the road, but there is a visionary desire to keep looking towards the future. And it occurs within a context, whether an East End basement or an East Anglian farmhouse, where there is security and support and attachment. As is said in *Roots*, 'You can't change people, he say, you can only give them some love and hope they'll take it.'

Wesker had a complicated relationship with the Royal Court. They were permanently turning down his plays, and only when they were successful elsewhere (usually in the Belgrade Theatre in Coventry) did they express enthusiasm. They turned down *Roots* after the acclaimed *Chicken Soup*, because Wesker rightly refused to accept their daft note that Ronnie should appear at the end of the play. But Joan Plowright popped up insisting she do it, and in her performance as Beatie she brought stardom to herself and Wesker. There seems a pretty clear subtext in the Court's interactions with Wesker that they were uncomfortable with his lack of university manners, his avowed and unapologetic Jewishness, and his occasional pugilism. His regular and loyal director John Dexter wasn't always at ease with him, once famously snapping when Wesker tried to contribute a bit too much in rehearsal – 'If you don't shut the fuck up, Arnold, I'll direct the play you wrote.'

Wesker had a tangled relationship with most of the people he encountered. A lifetime of righteous protest began with the infant Arnold greeting the warriors of Cable Street. In the late 1950s and early 1960s he joined the Direct Action Committee in marches on the nuclear weapons research station at Aldermaston. The second of these, led by the Committee of 100, ended with him in a police van alongside Bertrand Russell. Together with several other writers, he was sentenced to a month in an open prison. To his credit, his righteousness (occasionally with a 'self' prefix added) was sprayed in all directions, not just against his own government. He made scenes and created discomfort in East Germany when he visited there, and again at the Iranian Embassy over their country's authoritarianism. Later, he became the object of protest himself when a group of hard-left actors refused to perform his play *The Journalists*. His decision to sue the company and write jeremiads against the institution might not have helped his career. He called it the nail in the coffin and described his subsequent years as literary leprosy.

Ever an awkward presence, though he may have rejected the label 'angry young man', he proved an angry old one, firing off missives bemoaning his neglect. I suffered a painful hour in the small and grubby meeting room of the Bush Theatre, where I tried to explain to him why we couldn't produce one of his plays, and how our subsidy was intended for writers at the start of their careers. His discomfort was unsettling to witness – he deserved a home for his plays, but there was none forthcoming. His greatest virtue was an almost childlike enthusiasm, manifesting as a writer in his open-hearted receptivity to the speech he heard and the life rhythms he witnessed. That unworldly simplicity did not sit easily beside the young firebrand, or the embittered mid-career crisis, or indeed the knighted grand old man of letters. An artist of gravid honesty did not sit comfortably in these costumes.

He had a remarkable access to Keats's idea of negative capability, the notion that a poet can disappear their self and work in a state of openness to experience, and identification with the object contemplated. The state when, in Keats's words, the artist is 'capable of being in uncertainties, mysteries, doubts, without any irritable reaching after fact and reason'. Wesker described it as the same art as a diamond cutter's. Having acquired a rough stone, the cutter places it on a table and walks obsessively around it, staring intently, for three days. Then at the moment when theory and prejudice and preconceptions and mannerisms and style have all eroded away, and all that is seen is the object itself and alone, the craftsman steps in and cuts swiftly this way and that, revealing its hidden shape. As with his own rough stones – his kitchen work, his family, his love – 'you look at the material and you let it dictate what the shape should be – you don't say I want it to be this or that. The material is what it is.'

As an artist he had a symphonic ability to arrange the life he heard into three-act structures and stage imagery, yet his most prodigious skill remained that spongelike capacity to record and reproduce. When asked late in life how he wanted to be remembered, he eschewed all labels –

a Jewish writer, a socialist writer, a 1950s or a 1960s writer – and said repeatedly he wanted to be remembered as someone who had contributed to the mainstream of the English theatre tradition. Though he came right at the end of the proscenium century, it was the one artistic community of which he was a more than willing member.

Joy abounding.
Robert Stephens and Mary Peach during rehearsals for *The Kitchen* at the Royal Court Theatre, London, 1961

Lorraine Hansberry
1930–1965

With a form as free as theatre, where the work and the world feed on each other, and writers swap influence as freely as schoolchildren spreading germs around a playground, it is tempting to create hypotheticals. What if certain infecting strains had not appeared, or others had flourished? What if some powerful woman had taken George Bernard Shaw under her wing, absorbed his neuroses, and left us without his prolix agonising? What if Stanislavsky's faltering new playhouse had closed before the last show of their first season – *The Seagull* – which rescued the Moscow Art and the reputation of the play? What if Yeats and his Abbey colleagues had accepted O'Casey's *The Silver Tassie* and secured the socialist's future in Ireland? What if George Devine had decided that Osborne's moany mutterings were too callow and singular and left *Look Back in Anger* to rot in obscurity? How would post-war theatre have developed without Jimmy Porter's rantings? Would Ireland have grown differently with O'Casey as a thorn in its side? What reduction in the sum of human empathy would we suffer from without Chekhov's later plays? And what calm without Shaw's agitations?

What is certain, among all these alternative histories, is that three heartbreaks were inflicted that left unknowable gaps. The vilification and scapegoating of Oscar Wilde was one. Though sometimes his life seems strangely of a piece, as if shaped to his tragic will, had he not been crushed by the fury of his enemies what might he have gone on to create? Another is the disappearance of D. H. Lawrence's domestic dramas, which lived in bizarre neglect until being unearthed by the Royal Court in the late 1960s. If these object lessons in how to make working-class life vivid on the stage had appeared when they were written, in the Edwardian age, they could have changed the possibilities of the form. The greatest tragedy is the third, the death at thirty-four of Lorraine Hansberry, a visionary whose career, had she survived, could have transformed not only the stage but wider society.

Regular contact with her work is to be admitted into a community blinded by her grace. One scholar lists her students' responses to exposure to Hansberry, which boil down to repeated refrains of 'Why did no one tell me about this before?' The lack of noise tells a story of neglect, yet the heartache comes from the sense of what was left unachieved. She left behind three major plays, a gaggle of minor ones, and a host of speeches, articles, and essays. This is no mean corpus for someone finding her voice in a hostile environment and only given a decade of creation. Yet what more could she have produced?

One of the greatest achievements of *A Raisin in the Sun*, her signature work, is its lightness of step. Conceived on the weightiest of themes, the permanence of racial discrimination in the heart of America, it dances with the floating elegance of Gene Kelly or the Nicholas Brothers. The framework is that of farce, a small room with various doors, characters hurtling in and out, flying through the space with comments flung hither and thither, bodies swerving and shimmying to accommodate the abundance. Hansberry was a student of the theatre, reading Ibsen and Strindberg avidly, and acting in Lorca's *Yerma*. Her theatrical idol was Sean O'Casey, whom she praised for writing characters with a totality of personality, flaws and all. The inheritance appears as much in the delirious mayhem she recreates. This is not naturalism turgid with misery, it is proximate to the delighted madness of Feydeau, and to Synge's prescription of 'reality with joy'. Real life moves at speed. The Stygian slowness of an O'Neill play is hard to watch, and false to the world we whir in.

Speed is close to the heart of the proscenium achievement. The central axiom of its acting is 'picking up your cues'. This means leaving only the slightest gap – or none – at the end of one character's line before the commencement of the next. Though maligned by schools of intensity and emotional exhibitionism, it is hard to express how important this is.

Partly because it corresponds to the nature of most conversation, where chat moves at the speed of synaptic thought. Partly because it helps actors stop holding on to themselves, to ensure they are listening and responding to colleagues. Principally, because it is the main weapon in drawing an audience into a centrifugal whizz of different perspectives, where they let go fully of their own and enter the confusion. Theatre (though many believe the opposite) is essentially an egoless business. Actors and audiences lose themselves in the words and actions of others. If each actor leaves long pauses while they act furiously, gearing themselves up for their next important utterance, then ego congeals like solidified vapour on the stage, and the act of dissolution is lost. When old pros bark 'Cueing, darlings! Cueing!' they are not being camp or effete, they are enforcing something necessary for the central trick to occur. Theatre depends on an unconscious state of mind. Speed is the principal highway to that destination.

Hansberry understood this, hurtling characters and thoughts across her stage in *A Raisin in the Sun*. Her second major play, *The Sign in Sidney Brustein's Window*, is an explosion of self-involved blather in the bohemian Greenwich Village of the early 1960s. A group of young artists, playwrights, sex workers, and hangers-on explore what a new articulacy might be, with an onrush of confession, divulging, and whacked-out self-analysis. Taken slowly or with self-importance, this would be deathly; taken at the speed of tumbling thought shared by its supercharged youth, it reflects the excitations of a generation on the cusp of a new rhetoric. One character describes himself as 'A fool who believes that death is waste and love is sweet and that the earth turns and men change every day and that rivers run that people wanna be better than they are and that flowers smell good and that I hurt terribly today, and that hurt is desperation and desperation is – energy and energy can *move* things'. This is the swirling writing of the Beats, of Charlie Parker's riffing, transposed to the stage: it can't dawdle or ponder. Crucially for Hansberry, there is an optimism within its toughness, an energy pushing through despair. Neither the hope nor the energy can survive at snail's pace.

Her other gift, expressing another central proscenium tenet, was her commitment to the ensemble. Someone (my daughter Cara) once described her as 'an ensemble thinker' in opposition to her comrade James Baldwin, who was 'a soul-centred one'. Theatre intrinsically slants towards the collective, where each and every voice must be heard. Hansberry was the exemplar of that generosity to a spectrum of perspectives. As *A Raisin in the Sun* toured, before arrival in New York, battles raged between its box office draw, Sidney Poitier, and its matriarch, Claudia McNeil, over whose part was at the centre. Both essentially missed the point. Everyone matters with Hansberry. No one is neglected. Her narratives need each vital contribution, all influencing the outcome. Within a framework of dizzying speed, she telescopes together generations and histories – all mattering. The centre is not grabbed, it is shared, an open space around which energies collide.

Racial tension, expressed in the play through the battle of a black family to buy a house in a segregated white community, is no small energy to contain within the plush and gilt. Yet the problems of America were not the whole of Hansberry's concerns. The end of colonialism and the onset of the African independence movement were always part of her political purpose. Within the domestic naturalism, Africa blows into the room with the character Asagai, and in the language used and behaviour enacted by the Younger family. When Walter Younger is drunk, he leaps on the kitchen table, crying out 'FLAMING SPEAR . . . THE LION IS WAKING.' The stage direction indicates Walter 'sees what we cannot see, that he is a leader of his people, a great chief, a descendant of Chaka'. For the Youngers, the fate of Africa was inextricable from their struggles.

Lorraine's uncle Professor William Leo Hansberry was one of the world's foremost scholars of African antiquity. Through his classroom and home passed Nnamdi Azikiwe, the first president of Nigeria, and Kwame Nkrumah, the first president of Ghana, along with others soon at the forefront of independence. After moving from Chicago to New York, Hansberry worked in the offices of W. E. B. Du Bois and Paul Robeson's newspaper, *Freedom*, whose standpoint was always to link the injustices felt by African Americans with the crimes inflicted on their lands of origin. Through these offices in the early 1950s passed exiles from South Africa, Rhodesia, and other countries who later returned to their homelands to fight, only to die in colonial jails. Throughout her notebooks, Hansberry reveals a vision binding the continents together: 'I cannot allow the devious purposes of white supremacy to lead me to any conclusion other than . . . that the ultimate destiny and aspirations of the African peoples and twenty million American Negroes are inextricably and magnificently bound up together forever.'

The specific trigger for her final masterpiece, *Les Blancs*, was her visceral response on attending the US production of Jean Genet's *Les Nègres*. A generous critic, she appreciated Genet's outsider boldness and his attempt to set down experience previously neglected. Yet she found it to be 'a conversation between white men about themselves', and a conversation too marinated in racial exoticism to shed light. 'In *The Blacks*, the oppressed remain unique. The blacks remain the exotic . . . we were spared the ultimate anguish of man's oppression of man.' By othering the victims within the play, Hansberry felt that Genet evaded a full diagnosis of how humans oppress one another and failed to establish a necessity for action. (She abhorred the idea of 'absurdism', seeing it as too quick a route to despair, and too easy an excuse to avoid the washing-up.)

For her, the hurt inflicted on Africans and black Americans was disproportionate, yet there was nowhere humans were not oppressing each other. In the spirit of post-war internationalism, she saw that a ghetto in Warsaw or India was the result of the same inhumanity as a ghetto in Chicago. All resulted from a sickness to be diagnosed and cured, not turned into burlesque porn-pain. As a character says in *Les Blancs*, 'I have seen the slums of Liverpool and Dublin and the caves above Naples. I have seen Dachau and Anne Frank's attic in Amsterdam. I have seen too many raw-knuckled Frenchmen coming out of the Metro at dawn and too many hungry Italian children to believe that those who raided Africa for three centuries ever "loved" the white race either.'

Hansberry worked on *Les Blancs* up to her death, carrying her manuscript in and out of hospitals as cancer besieged her. The question it asked was enormous: could liberation be achieved without violence? Here as elsewhere, she kept the biggest of questions grounded in a specific setting and in characters bursting with complex life. To that end she pondered, wove and knotted in search of a multi-tiered structure flexible and taut enough to illuminate her mesh of ideas. Against the deadline of her life it was not finally achievable, but her ex-husband and devoted high priest, Robert Nemiroff, picked up the fragments and, following her intentions with fidelity, finished the work.

The setting is a mission compound in Africa, somewhere very like Kenya. A white American journalist has come to write a piece on the legendary missionary who presides over the camp. As in *Godot* and *Lefty*, we remain waiting for him throughout. The journalist meets a gaggle of white expat misfits presiding over a black population on the verge of revolt. Each of these characters, styled like Graham Greene's *The Comedians*, negotiates their self-loathing with varying degrees of pain – the kickback from their explicit or implicit racism.

A tribal elder has recently died and his two sons return for the funeral. One is a European-educated Marxist reluctant to assume the robes of authority his community wish him to don, the other a priest who has bought entirely into white and Christian thinking. The former, Tshembe (in part modelled on Jomo Kenyatta), is a Hamlet figure uncertain whether to move forward into a fuller self defined by action, or to remain in pause and reflection. A proper stew is cooked, the various antagonisms between whites and whites, blacks and whites and blacks and blacks creating a rich flavour. Any seasoning of good or bad is burned away by human mess. When action is finally taken, it is violent and radical. Too violent for some, and at the first performance on Broadway many were shocked. Given where Hansberry was in her thinking, it could not have been anything else. At the end, Tshembe can no longer avoid the pressure of the present moment and takes action against immediate injustice. In her progression through the 1950s and 1960s, Lorraine walked a path from the existentialist confusion of whether to act, to a civil rights belief in peaceful agitation, and finally to the 'by any means necessary' activism of her comrade Malcolm X. With an artist's obliquity, she patterns the same journey for Tshembe.

Race, in her description, is a device which becomes a reality through universal enactment. Through her work she burrowed as deep as she could to undo that enactment and expose that device. Had she lived for a hundred years, her quest may still have ended in defeat since it was a grail she was chasing, and the core of any grail myth is failure. Yet how much closer to full understanding she might have nudged us. We are lucky she was with us at all, and that she chose theatre to encase her boundless humanity. Spurred on by her mentor Du Bois, who believed all art was propaganda, Hansberry felt rage for those who dismissed the idea of marrying art and social purpose. For her, they were inseparable.

The form she chose was one naturally generous at its best. She left behind more grain in the store.

'We come from people who had a lot of pride.'
A Raisin in the Sun. Ruby Dee, Claudia McNeil, Glynn Turman, Sidney Poitier and John Fielder, Barrymore Theater, NYC, 1959

Harold Pinter
1930–2008

Harold Pinter's career straddles the last flails of the proscenium era, and the more splintered spaces which succeeded and superseded. He thrived in both – in all – and was a small part of the process that killed off the hegemony of the playhouses. Pinter was first and foremost a poet, who found the ideal frame for his voice in drama, though his vision could be adapted to a range of media. A natural for radio, he was an early star of the BBC; a great screenwriter, he wrote extensively for television and film; as a playwright, he adapted to the studio black boxes, the converted old industrial buildings (like the Donmar and the Almeida), the thrust arenas and in-the-round spaces that came to dominate the terrain. His fluency across media was common to a generation who stopped thinking of themselves (and their earning power) as reliant on commercial theatre. Opportunities in TV and radio freed them from the exigencies of writing for a live audience. Many had written for film throughout the preceding century, but there was now a profusion of other platforms. Taking a holiday from a discipline as technically exacting as the proscenium became an alluring prospect.

The transition from theatre to television is part of the mythology of Pinter's first major play, *The Birthday Party*. While on tour playing a character named Tops in an unremembered classic called *A Horse! A Horse!* (double exclamation mark! – that will pull in the punters), he found himself in stinky digs in Eastbourne. He turned the sad fried breakfast, the wrap-around dinge, and the strange dynamics between guests and hosts into a play. An enterprising young producer, Michael Codron – later champion of Orton, Stoppard, Ayckbourn and more – gave him a £50 advance, and opened it at the Lyric Hammersmith, on 19 May 1958. The critics massacred it, the *Guardian* pitching in with, 'What all this means, only Mr Pinter knows, for as his characters speak in non-sequiturs, half-gibberish, and lunatic ravings, they are unable to explain.' Even Kenneth Tynan, the friend of the new, murdered it.

Codron was relying on the attendance of Harold Hobson, the esteemed *Sunday Times* critic, who had previously expressed enthusiasm for a one-act play, but he was absent. When he eventually came to the Thursday matinee, he joined an audience of seven in an auditorium built for six hundred. Among the others was the forlorn playwright, contemplating oblivion. That Sunday, Hobson wrote of 'the most original, disturbing, and arresting talent in theatrical London'. Too late, too late – the play had closed the night before. By a strange quirk of fate, the new medium came to the rescue. A television producer, Peter Willes (a later champion of Orton), read the play and called Pinter. 'How dare you?' he said. 'I've read your bloody play and haven't had a wink of sleep for four nights.' The TV version went out in March 1960, and was seen by eleven million viewers. The *Daily Herald* came up with the penetrating headline, 'Stage Flop is Big Hit,' and a Rubicon of some sort was crossed.

Harold Pinter graduated from a Hackney grammar-school boy to become a living legend, political activist, and Nobel laureate. Born in 1930 into a Jewish family, he grew up in an environment flush with violence. Antisemitic gangs roamed his area, and met with whirring fists from a young Harold and his gang. Newspapers and public meetings spouting the same racist poison gave him early tastes of socialised threat and menace, as did the storm cloud of Nazism hovering in memory. A refusenik at a young age, he balked at National Service, reasoning at his tribunal that he would have fought in World War Two but saw no present necessity for a standing army. A loathing for authority continued through an unhappy period at RADA, where he spent more hours reading in libraries than in workshops learning how to be a blazered young gentleman. He and his cadre preferred to meet in coffee houses, discussing European intellectual ideas and politics.

Pinter's first play, a one-act called *The Room*, was written in four days, while acting in Rattigan's *Separate Tables* in Torquay. My father, producing radio in Bristol at the time, went along to see the premiere in a university studio. He entered reluctantly with a group of friends, all wondering noisily why they were there. From three lines in they shut up, holding their breath, trying to discern the pattern carved out in front of them. The dialogue electrified – every line was a surprise, not a single one following the logic established for drama, or habitual patterns of speech. Each word emerged from a suspicious music of its own, with language used to shadow-box and to dig nervously for hidden intentions. Beside the talk, there was the unknowability of the locale. Called *The Room*, and set in a room, there shouldn't have been too much confusion. But somehow the space was rendered uncertain, liminal, hard to read on its own terms, or as whatever it potentially could be.

Written towards the end of the proscenium century, *The Dumb Waiter*, *The Caretaker*, and *The Homecoming* retained the claustrophobic single room. Pinter locked his imagination in the sealed container he learned from Sartre (and *Huis Clos*, in which he acted), and which mapped an inner landscape. Specific locales, imagined with dense detail, they also occupy Pinterland, a separate realm. Miniature territorial acts and mutual vigilance unsettle the atmosphere. The chat is blighted with failed communication and queasy subtexts as characters manoeuvre like a pack of animals in a nature documentary. The pauses and silences – a celebrated feature – had been part of theatrical language before, but never so precisely annotated nor so loaded with dark electricity. In the context of a form that prided itself on the fluent and the fleet ('Cueing, darlings!'), they generated all the more power.

In these tight spaces, Pinter created an ambience of insecurity, in which all have spent much time since. The pervasiveness of his effect is a surprise, given the degree to which he was swiftly fortressed by the academy. The aura of mystery around Pinter, together with his pugnacious refusal to respond to enquiries about the meaning of his work, soon repainted him in the sombre hues of high art. After the runaway success of *The Caretaker*, critics and academics soon began to construct Castle Pinter, a grim and forbidding bulwark.

This seems a misdirection, since his early actor salad days were spent in the tawdry gloss of the lowbrow, and flakes of garish paint remain sprinkled across the oeuvre. Many of the sources he drew inspiration from were unavowedly populist, several from the world of variety. He was a devotee of the old music hall theatres which dotted the landscape around Hackney. Double acts like Jewel and Warriss, quick-fire verbal tightrope walkers who ping-pong banter back and forth at lightning speed, resurface in plays such as *The Dumb Waiter*, and in the two heavies Goldberg and McCann from *The Birthday Party*, a work offering a potpourri of patter routines. Pinter understood from those acts, as from the linguistic jousting he relished with his cohort of street-fighting schoolboy exuberants, the rhythms of like minds. He enjoyed the way partners get in each other's heads, knowing what they will say before they say it, playing with that expectation and using it to wind the other up to breaking point. This was verbal music, riffing at speed and accelerating beyond comprehension towards something more felicitous and perilous.

An ambitious young actor, Pinter spent four years in the early 1950s schlepping around repertory theatres playing stock roles – family solicitors, psychotic maniacs, and policemen with important notebooks. He would learn his parts for weekly rep with swift absorption, each leaving a smudge on his subconscious. The effects survive. He emerged from the same dingy milieu as John Osborne: seedy digs, lascivious landladies, and a trunk full of costumes. Both were labelled subversives, destroying the etiolated refinement of post-war theatre, but they made sure they were soaked in that tradition before they started subverting. Dramatic curtains at the end of acts, the thriller element from murder mysteries, the maintenance of suspense, and the slow striptease delivery of information were all carried over from the neverland delights of weekly rep. As an actor, he may have been pitching lines to a gentle susurrus of chinking teacups, snoring colonels, and chattering ladies, but they left a mark. Touring the country as Sir Lancelot Spratt in a version of *Doctor in the*

House might not have felt worthwhile, but he learned how to listen to an audience.

More was absorbed from working with two of the self-aggrandising actor-managers of his day, the reasonably civilised Anew McMaster, with whose troupe he toured Ireland, and the beast of the populist jungle, Donald Wolfit. The young Pinter had a brief but telling engagement with Wolfit in Camden in the early 1950s, rising through the ranks to play Iago opposite the great shouter's *Othello*. These dinosaurs gave demonstrations, by the brute imposition of dark imagination and raw will, of the sheer animal weight any moment can bear. Pinter's later moments of oppressive silence, or unknowable grief, or blind terror, could be traced back to the glaring stares or elongated gestures of these wonderful hams. Pinter blew smoke in front of such hoary old tropes, but the appreciation of powerful connection never left him.

Nor did his writing career begin in obscurity. He wrote revue sketches for the West End, one of the most popular forms of the day. Here he followed a standard path – Noël Coward had done the same forty years before. This is a form of apprenticeship we have lost. Probably the only writer with a similar contemporary experience is Patrick Marber, who wrote sketch comedy before exercising his gift on a wider canvas. It's a wonderful way of learning. The sketch teaches economy, accuracy, timing, and the importance of hearing. Pinter's sketches are remarkable for their annotation of the high-definition lunacy of everyday speech. A sketch is funny only in so far as it rings true. We judge in a moment whether a writer is tuned in to the world. If they are, we enter. Pinter has a curious ear, with a relish for the sublime banalities of the demotic, and a lethally exact ability to reproduce the heard.

Much of his early work met outsized audiences. He fell early for the limitations and the possibilities of radio, realising the importance of the dialogue's music, and the potential of suggestion in a medium that understands most of an atom is space. Much of what he learned about understatement and the power of the audience's imagination, he learned from radio. In those pioneer days, it was that marvellous compact: a serious artistic medium with huge reach. Pinter-speech was soon being heard by millions. Following *The Birthday Party*, he gained swift access to another outsized public through television. Hard to imagine now, but this was once a medium that allowed itself pauses, with oblique and angular writing, where people were allowed to be stuck and scared within brooding silence. Pinter adapted his radio play *A Night Out* for TV, and it went out as part of ABC's Armchair Theatre. These days such an event might attract twenty thousand lonely souls drawn to the wastelands of BBC Four; in 1960 it was number one in the week's top ten ratings, proving more popular than Bruce Forsyth's gurning in *Sunday Night at the London Palladium*.

Pinter's work in the proscenium began to populist acclaim. *The Caretaker* played 444 performances in its first run, and transferred to Broadway, with *The Homecoming* making a splash on both sides of the Atlantic. Together with *The Birthday Party*, they became part of the international repertoire, baffling and delighting audiences in a range of languages, and in each fresh place speaking private and local truths. These early works did not achieve success because of their cold austerity, nor their stiletto insights into the pain we cause each other, nor their exposure of the nothingness that lurks in an empty envelope. What sold tickets was the elegant play construction, the potboiler tricks from old thrillers, the front-cloth jokes, the ear for speech, and the brooding, melodramatic silences. Pinter closed out the proscenium century with what seems a repudiation of its light charm and ingratiating manners, but if you look hard at the DNA, there's a lot of the boulevard ghosting around in there.

Pinter used to visit the Bush Theatre regularly when I worked there in the early 1990s. One evening he came into the pub below the theatre on his own, his usual prickly charisma crackling around him. A force field of restrained aggression always seemed to tighten the air in his vicinity. It was an aura prepared for arenas of competitive status, such as the Ivy restaurant, or a West End first night, or a gathering of the great and the good. But our pub was filled with its usual motley of feral addicts, plain-clothes coppers, and festive Jamaican grandads. None of them paid the slightest attention to the future Nobel winner. I watched as he pushed his way through the crush to the bar and ordered a pint. Drink in hand, his shoulders slumped and all the tension fell from his face, replaced by a simple and lively humility. His whole body seemed to say, 'Thank God, I can stop being Harold Pinter for five minutes.'

After a few happy sups, his party arrived. And the tension returned.

The masters.
Donald Pleasence and Harold Pinter rehearse
The Caretaker, *c.*1965

Edward Albee

1928–2016

After a century of stories about miserable marriages and straight couples slowly killing each other – the proscenium's most reliable diet – that template reached its climacteric with *Who's Afraid of Virginia Woolf?* After Edgar and Alice, Nora and Torvald, Elyot and Amanda, Jimmy and Alison, and lord knows how many other partnerships soused in sourness, Edward Albee served up George and Martha, and left everyone else nowhere to go. This was the Thrilla in Manila and the Rumble in the Jungle all wrapped up in one, two heavyweights of emotional damage, punching the souls out of each other, body shot for body shot.

The one-time doyen of West End producers Michael Codron once explained to me his reason for declining to invest in a hit gay play we had produced at the Bush. 'It's a wonderful play, but it will only last three months. That's the length of run you get for a gay play. What you want is a play about couples who loathe each other. They last for years.' The image he summoned up was of couples, fallen into mutual loathing decades before, travelling in from the suburbs to watch and laugh as their antipathies and neuroses were played out within the frame, before taking the train back to Surbiton to sleep fitfully, dreaming of garrotting each other. Though it made commercial sense, the image wasn't the best advert for the spiritual health of the form.

Albee's play bore out the Codron dictum. It opened on Broadway in October 1962, and, despite being described by one critic as 'a sick play for sick people', ran for a princely 664 shows. A printed edition sold seventy thousand copies, a recording of the original cast rapidly sold out, and post-haste it was turned into a feature film, the directing debut of Mike Nichols. Despite being in downbeat black and white, and unhelpfully labelled a 'dirty picture' by its own producers, the film did mind-boggling business, vying for the biggest box office figures of its year beside two bits of grandiose hokum, *Hawaii* and *The Bible*. All this for a text that prides itself on unsparing viciousness, lack of sentiment, and academic rigour. And for an evening that is overlong, with a narrative that swirls more than propels. The legendary Uta Hagen playing Martha in the first production would have kickstarted it; Richard Burton and Elizabeth Taylor letting their demons rage gave the film an added incandescence; and many other stars have queued up to perform since then in productions that return like an angry hamster on a wheel. Yet star wattage alone cannot explain the appeal.

Having a great title doesn't hurt. Albee saw the phrase scrawled with soap on a mirror in a Greenwich Village bar: 'When I started to write the play it cropped up in my mind again. And of course, *who's afraid of* Virginia Woolf means who's afraid of the big *bad* wolf – who's afraid of living life without false illusions.' The banner has musicality, which is a tick, an intriguing question, another tick, intellectual snob quotient, major tick, and above all mystery, the biggest tick of all. If its final meaning is elusive, the riddle adds rocket fuel to the trajectory.

An element of sport is central. The most compelling sporting occasions are when two equally matched titans go at it hammer and tongs, both stretched to the limit of ability and endurance by the adrenalising drug of combat. Federer and Nadal in their prime, Evert versus Navratilova, Tendulkar against Warne, Prost versus Senna, and of course Ali and Frazier. Literary commentators have even compared George's tactics in *Who's Afraid of Virginia Woolf?* to Muhammad Ali's rope-a-dope strategy against George Foreman in Zaire. The idea is to cushion yourself on the ropes and let your opponent drain their life force, throwing punches into your body, as Martha does throughout Acts I and II, before you bounce off the ropes and finish them with a one-two combination, as George does in Act III.

The couple play mini-games, announcing them for our benefit – Humiliate the Host, Hump the Hostess, Get the Guests – and have a special power not given to sportspeople: they give a running commentary on their own performance, becoming both participant and pundit. The larger game, of course, is their eternal wrestle with each other. Here we see two supreme athletes of marital loathing, having honed a formidable array of techniques over years of bickering, enjoying one final night of showtime combat. People may take pleasure in rooting for one or the other, they may split on gender lines (though rarely the case), but it is the spectacle of two people stretched to breaking point that compels.

A case is sometimes made for the humour of the play, but this doesn't quite stand up. Its author once named it 'a grotesque comedy', and there are jokes, but those present are on the austere side. This lack is in some ways a surprise since a comic author was clearly a model. Coming from Greenwich Village, a scene overflowing with artists and composers, Albee always liked to raise the tone when discussing influences, with sombre nods to abstract expressionist painters, to Beckett and Ionesco. Much of his previous work was of that ilk. With reference to *Virginia Woolf*, he was generous enough to namecheck a less fashionable figure (at the time), Noël Coward.

The correspondences are telling. What Albee titles 'Get the Guests' is the entire plot mainspring for *Hay Fever*, a work for which the American author later wrote an introduction. Strangers are invited over to be used and humiliated, soon caught helpless in the maelstrom of family dynamics. The distinction between hosts and guests in Albee and Coward is the same – the first stage themselves, the latter simply live. Like actors, George and Martha are aware of what they are doing, critiquing their own performance. They live in E. M. Forster's round dimension; their victims, Nick and Honey, live in a flat plane. The same delineation operates in Coward's weekend of mayhem, where the Bliss family enact themselves, and the guests try to keep up. If *Hay Fever* is an influence on Albee, *Private Lives* is a template. In this quartet, an older couple are locked in a pained romance where they can neither let go nor spend five unflustered moments together. They teach the same push and pull, obsession and loathing, to a younger couple. The similarities are indecent. Coward was way out of fashion when it was written, yet Albee's play amounts to significant homage.

There is no shortage of intellectual high jinks in *Virginia Woolf* to satisfy his Greenwich Village constituency. We are on a university campus and the characters are overeducated adult children, flaying each other because there is little else for which they can take responsibility. The weapons they use are debate and wit. Albee claimed to write with no plan or structure, no outline or notes, saying he spent a long time getting to know his characters and, once he trusted them, let them write the play. A freewheeling element spins here, but the play misleads with an impression of exhausting mess, since there is control in arc and tone, and a symphonic music. A host of phrases are picked up and repeated, until through repetition they acquire some of the force of a mantra. The music provides a hidden, underlying shape, an architecture which is needed so the clashing of genres – symbolist and realist and boulevard – can sit together.

The central theme (and it seems fair to spot it since it is very much asking to be spotted) is that old American standby: truth and illusion. All the characters circle this duality, and George repeatedly states it. O'Neill was a major influence (one acknowledged), but where *Long Day's Journey into Night* and *The Iceman Cometh* come down on the necessity of illusions to make one's way through the hard day, Albee is determined to see them stripped away: 'How people cheat themselves, that's my basic concern.' A smokescreen of fictions and fibs cloud George and Martha's life, and within their game-playing it is hard to name what is true. Even they get confused, giving rise to one of the great insults: 'I swear, if you existed I'd divorce you.' For them the imagined is as concrete as the real.

The most towering cathedral of falsehood they have built is their child. His whereabouts is a well-blurred story, and many are left none the wiser as to whether he exists or not. The film producers wanted to make him real, which rather wrecks the endeavour. The final exorcism is of their greatest untruth, and collapsing such an edifice takes significant violence. The lie is so hard-baked that dismantling it is the task of the whole long night. As the truth is finally revealed, the author ushers characters and audience to a numb, battered quiet space of honesty. The final moments in the grey light of dawn, as hostilities cease and – spent and subdued –

they face up to a future without lies, have a bruised end-of-war dignity. Birdsong is sprinkled across a no man's land of a marriage.

In this bomb-blasted coda we perceive that, however perverse, we have witnessed a love story. Martha's explosions and acts of sabotage, George's strategies and manoeuvres, all are attempts to stop a guttering candle from petering out. They tear at scabs, but only to keep the blood flowing. Though their twenty-five years together have curdled into sourness, there is still a quantum of connection, however meagre. In this sense, they follow in the tradition of an earlier couple, who meet ill by moonlight, Shakespeare's Oberon and Titania. The king and queen of the fairies arrive in a state of warfare in *A Midsummer Night's Dream*. Much of their rage is displaced into a quarrel over a son, as with Albee's play, and much derived from infidelities. Their struggle is a by-product of a central problem – if you are together for eternity, how do you keep the conversation exciting? Oberon and Titania resort to some kooky games in the wood to keep things lively – love potions, madness, cavorting with a half-man half-donkey, but if anyone was in the four thousandth year of a love affair, they might be moving to the weirder items on the menu. Shakespeare and Albee both ask the hardest question, the one to which Codron was referring with those suburban couples taking the train for their cultural meal of emotional dysfunction: what do you do when the flame dies but the embers still smoulder?

Albee, adopted after his father abandoned him, was brought up by respectable parents in an environment he deemed stultifying. Though the walls of his home were lined with books, he was admonished by his adoptive father when he took down a volume of Turgenev – for the crime of leaving a gap in the shelf. Discerning quickly that he was in the wrong tribe, he left home young, never to see the father again, and only contacting the mother who raised him after another twenty years. With such a background, he was no fan of the conventional family. *Who's Afraid of Virginia Woolf?* was written while Kennedy was still alive, and its wrath is partly directed at the claustrophobic image of the wholesome nuclear family nurtured during the Eisenhower years. The construction of an imaginary son is in part due to the social stigma of being childless, a toxic nostrum of the age.

Families are an older dramatic staple than romantic love, and the killing of close family members dates back to the *Oresteia*. Albee's particular spin is that it occurs in a virtual world. George has turned his possible killing of his parents into a novel, and the sacrifice of their son to rescue their marriage spills fictional blood. We are in no rational world here, and old music thrums beneath the hyperarticulacy. Albee believed that 'Art is not pacification, it's disturbance.' He was determined to dig under the surface of a bright, positivist America and see what the creepy-crawlies were up to underneath.

Marriage and family were two of the principal constructs of the proscenium century, enforced by law and by social convention. Throughout we see those institutions tested. By the early 1960s, a multitude of new dynamics was pushing against these constraints, new ideas of sexuality and gender and love. The centre, an artificial and oppressive construct denying messy instincts, could not hold.

When we watch *Who's Afraid of Virginia Woolf?* we see, alongside the bitter compulsion of blood sport, the social fabric being torn.

The legendary Uta Hagen surfing the wave.
Who's Afraid of Virginia Woolf? at the
Piccadilly Theatre, London, 1964

Wole Soyinka

1934–

In many ways, Wole Soyinka is a post-proscenium author as much as he is a post-colonial author (the two are awkwardly adjacent). His best-known work, *Death and the King's Horseman*, premiered in 1975, and much of his later work was composed for the expansive thrust stages built in newly independent African states. Born in 1934, and educated in Nigeria, he left for university in Leeds in 1954. One of the short plays he wrote there came to the attention of the Royal Court, and they offered him an apprenticeship as a script reader. Though he returned to Nigeria in 1960, the connection stayed live, and they produced a couple of his plays. Soyinka's work was soon spreading fast on stages, radio, and television in the West and across Africa.

Shorter and more lethal than later epics, his early efforts show evidence of their proscenium antecedents. Each new scene is prefaced by a short description of the setting, like a Samuel French Acting Edition of old, detailing where each door and window is placed, stage right and left. The difference, and an extraordinary one, is that we are envisioning not genteel drawing rooms, nor depressing kitchen-sink attics, but African villages with red mud flooring, beaches beside the Atlantic Ocean, and homes raised on stilts above flooded swamps. The theatre had ignored African life: Soyinka was determined his stage should see nothing else.

The plastic life of a Soyinka play is vibrant: backstories are summarised by 'mummers' shows involving Yoruban dance, mime, and caricature; with ululating song, characters approach and depart in procession, accompanied by drummers; and protagonists are ever sensitive to one another's physical presence, either from territorial fear or in excitement at erotic possibility. Entrances and exits are conceived with a choreographer's instinct to criss and cross the straight lines and diagonals of the stage. Soyinka's imagination operates within proscenium geometry, exploring physical as much as political or spiritual conundrums. Theatre, he said, 'is one arena, one of the earliest that we know of, in which man has attempted to come to terms with the spatial phenomenon of his being'.

He uses carnival exuberance to tell stories about the encroachment of modernity and the outside world on Yoruban culture. Traditions are in flux here as the urgent present and the transformative future clash with a world steeped in the charisma of its past. Soyinka is a beguilingly neutral witness, and it would be a brave interpreter who claimed to know where his sympathies lie. He is no follower of the literary Negritude movement, criticising it in essays as a nostalgic movement idealising a utopian black African past, which ignored the possibilities of progress. Or as he put it, 'A tiger doesn't proclaim his tigritude, he pounces.'

In *The Lion and the Jewel*, we see the shift in dynamics inflicted on an ancient village by a photographer who has come down from Lagos and taken a set of pictures. When the glossy magazine containing the images arrives, with images of the villagers glaring shinily, it disturbs political and gender hierarchies, until their forcible reassertion. The camera and the magazine show technologies at their most potent and disruptive, reorganising social patterns in their wake. The Jewel of the title – a beautiful young woman – hovers her hands over the magazine's pages as if over a sacred icon. In *The Swamp Dwellers*, we watch a young man returning from the vibrant city to a village still eking out subsistence from resistant soil. His contact with modernity, and the treatment he received from a brother who thrives there, throw a shadow across his psyche and the village. In *Kongi's Harvest*, a dictator tries to push his country forward into modernity, while calling on a deposed king to present him with a ceremonial yam at a state dinner, an ancient ritual to embody a healthy transition. Old and new are held in turbulent equipoise, with no answers as to which road to travel.

Short and fashioned parables, these works stir up eddies of emotional confusion and a perversely ebullient tragedy. They are reminiscent of J. M. Synge's short bulletins from another section of the Atlantic coastline, far further north. Both authors cram extraordinary amounts – of

Irish life pre-independence and of Nigerian life after it – into modest stew pots. It is, or was, the particular virtue of the proscenium that it could enable a rich collation of ingredients to come together and meld. Soyinka's work is concerned with the difficulty of welcoming new narratives into communities held together by loyalty to old stories. It is ironic that such collisions are framed in a form created by an alien culture, and one with a questionable influence. An irony he toys with happily. His colonial characters complain about the speech patterns of the indigenous characters, their swirling roundabouts and curlicues, their frequent dips and dives into myth and nature, but the outsiders end up defeated by the thinness and glibness of their own verbiage. No one can control a narrative when confronted by such rich obfuscation.

The novelist Ben Okri has described Soyinka as the parent of Nigerian literature, birthing a tradition with a stroke of his pen. Possibly his greatest act of resistance, and achievement, was to write about nothing but his own country. The rewards have been substantial, with visiting professorships, a legendary status in Nigeria, several films – fictional and documentary – made about him, and the Nobel Prize for Literature in 1986, the first awarded to a sub-Saharan writer. Yet the costs were substantial, his political influence resulting in spells in prison and exile, a death sentence at one time, and silencing by the state at others. Soyinka has never been shy of a fight, co-founding an anti-corruption student organisation in his youth, the Pyrates Confraternity, and, in his maturity, going so far as to hijack a radio station at gunpoint in order to play a tape with accusations of electoral fraud.

The Nigeria presented in his plays is undiluted, full of its own contradictions and affronts to European values. The humour is brutal, the sexual relations are challenging for some, and there is no sentimentality in the satire. Priests and prophets are exposed as money-grubbing frauds with the same glee as in a Jacobean comedy; old marriages calcify into bitterness and occasional violence; old chieftains are afflicted by a Benny Hill-like degree of sexual rapacity; and old concubines scheme and deceive. No virtue signalling here. A particular joy resides in seeing a culture onstage unmitigated by filtering. No arena can deliver information about fleshy humans in their contemporary environment quite as vividly as the stage. Not newspaper articles, not glamourising cinema, not overly plotted television, not even painting – nowhere can deliver people to other people, in their charming petty comedy, as vividly.

At a recent production of *Death and the King's Horseman* in Sheffield, graced by the presence of the author (who had travelled up by cab from Heathrow, fuelled at his request by a bottle of red wine and a packet of crisps), I wept with happiness when a whole community burst onto the stage, rich with the details of Yoruba life, reincarnated in a way only theatre can achieve.

'The man dies in all who keep silent in the face of tyranny.'
Akinwande Oluwole Soyinka at his residence in Ibadan, the week he was released after two years' detention for alleged involvement in the Nigeria crisis

Joe Orton
1933–1967

Travelling through the Mediterranean on a cut-price cruise ship in 1967, my father was sitting on deck when he spotted something curious on the front page of a Norwegian newspaper being read by a fellow passenger. It was two photographs: one of Joe Orton and the other of Kenneth Halliwell. Having directed the first production of *Entertaining Mr Sloane*, and having had intense and turbulent interactions with both the playwright and his lover, he was intrigued. Had they come out? Been outed? Had Joe won another award? Had he signed another deal to top the £10,000 he had been offered to write a film for The Beatles? He asked the elderly and respectable Norwegian woman what the story could be. She gave him a wary look. 'Those two are my friends,' he explained cheerfully. The look got warier, and she explained in halting English, 'This man . . . has hit this man in the head many times with a hammer . . . and killed him. Then the same man has swallowed many pills . . . and killed himself.' 'Ah . . . right . . . thank you,' my father said, stumped to find the appropriate words, and, ashen-faced, looked out to sea.

Orton was once described by the *Observer* as 'The Oscar Wilde of Welfare State gentility', cementing a series of parallels between the two subversive stylists. Both loved the surprising epigram, both relished innuendo, and both loved the inversion of contemporary morality. 'The British police force used to be run by men of integrity,' exclaims Fay in *Loot*. When Inspector Truscott solemnly replies, 'That is a mistake which has been rectified,' we laugh and hear Oscar's gleeful flipping of ethical codes. We have left the drawing rooms of the well-to-do, but part of Orton's territorial claim is that the lower middle and upper working classes are allowed the same aspirations to verbal grandeur as the demimonde of Wilde's day. Kath's grandiose claim in *Entertaining Mr Sloane*, 'I'd the upbringing a nun would envy and that's the truth. Until I was fifteen I was more familiar with Africa than my own body,' has the same rhythm as one of Wilde's self-deluding duchesses.

Both went to prison, but there were few parallels there: their experiences were starkly contrary. Wilde was broken by it – coming at the end of his writing career, his comic spirit didn't survive. The shame, the isolation, and the back-breaking physical labour were more than he could bear. He found scant amusement in the world thereafter. He wrote the scorching prose of *De Profundis*, and the mesmerising incantation of *The Ballad of Reading Gaol*, but there were no more wry quips. (Aside from his last words about his dank Parisian hotel: 'My wallpaper and I are fighting a duel to the death. One or the other of us has to go.') Joe Orton, on the other hand, was energised by prison. Somehow it clarified. In his diaries, he made a plea: 'Cleanse my heart . . . Give me the ability to rage correctly.' Prison seems to have answered that plea and helped to focus his anger. He wrote to his sister Leonie about how much he was enjoying it, and its illumination – 'The old whore society really lifted up her skirts and the stench was pretty foul.' Though his lover Halliwell was damaged almost beyond repair by their six months inside, and attempted suicide twice, Orton discovered a buoyancy and an attack, which bounced him into the West End within eighteen months of being released.

Orton is at the end of the long sequence of queer writers who throughout the proscenium century wrote in code about gay love, life and identity, without ever being allowed to state the perfectly obvious. Wilde led the charge, Maugham followed with elegance, Coward dazzled, and Rattigan battened down the hatches. For each, the effort of disguising became further strained by the distance between desire and the language permitted to talk about it. By the time it came to Orton, writing on the verge of an age of sexual liberation, the chasm was so vast the only language to bridge it was the rhetoric of the absurd. Communal insanity rules in his plays, brought to a climax in *What the Butler Saw*, which is set in an asylum. This final destination is the logical end point for a society whose hypocrisy ran so rampant it could only be matched by arch craziness. Characters in Orton's plays vault well over the far side of self-parody, appropriate to a world living in psychosis.

Wilde gloried in sin, seeing it as a spiritual freedom within a dishonest ethical system, and Orton found the same expressive joy in gleeful amorality. He and Halliwell were brought together by natural subversion. When they were on their uppers, living in a small Islington bedsit (the one they died in) and scraping by on benefits, their first field of mischief-making was the local library. They sneaked out books, rewrote their blurbs, manipulated their illustrations, and crudely photoshopped the covers, each alteration tending towards the obscene. They then waited for library users to pick out their adulterated books, and observed their shock with suppressed hysteria. This was the crime that got them sent to prison. Once their tricks were uncovered by the sleuthing work of Islington's chief librarian, they were both sent down for a Gothically punitive six months.

The experiment with books set the template for what Orton did to la pièce bien faite. A voracious reader of drama from first- to third-rate, he knew all the common tropes of exposition and set-up and crisis and denouement. He took those and inserted a barely concealed depravity, constantly testing the boundaries of what the frame could take. The strain of the containing vessel is what exhilarates, the proscenium and the well-made form serving as allegories for the tension in a society unable to constrain its unruly energies.

The watchdogs of that society were exemplified by one Mrs Edna Welthorpe, an upright conservative who wrote a stream of letters of complaint to the newspapers and authorities on a variety of topics, principally concerning the plays of Joe Orton, which she condemned as brutal, sick, and disgusting. Edna Welthorpe was, of course, Orton himself, pranking a world he found laughable. Only a couple of years ago, I sent *What the Butler Saw* to a theatre manager who wanted to produce a play with a well-known comic actor. After a weekend of reading, we did a collective Zoom, which began with an appalled rant: 'Dominic, I have spent the weekend sunk in the filth of this revolting play. Incest, rape, predatory sexuality, revolting perversion. I feel like I need to swim in the sea for a month to wash all the dirt off.' Nearly sixty years after Orton's death, here was the unequivocal voice of Edna Welthorpe, rebooted by contemporary censoriousness.

Exhilaration courses through his plays, a freedom that seems too gaudy, too delightedly vulgar. They reverberate with the exuberance of those old lurid seaside postcards. Orton's creations want to bust out of their casement and return the stage to the direct to-and-fro connection of vaudeville. The nudge-nudge wink-wink relentlessness of the innuendo becomes frenetic, virtuosic in its inventiveness, a tightrope act risking whether it can sustain itself and stay vertical. Our old carnival, merrymaking seditiousness survives here. The unlikeliness of squeezing such energies into a three-act structure lends Orton's major works their exhilarating oddity. End-of-the-pier cheek decked out in elegant West End attire.

There is an ebullience of appetite as well as a cavalier verbal energy, the same delight in cottaging sex which Orton details in his diaries. *Entertaining Mr Sloane* is a dance of appetites between three different exploiters. The young and handsome Sloane seems at first to be calling the shots, but he is first bedded by his landlady Kath, and later by her predatory and sinister brother Ed. The elderly father of Kath and Ed, a bewildered hangover from a different generation, ends up kicked to death behind a sofa. In *Loot*, a demented policeman, Truscott, gets in the way of a plot to dispose of money stolen in a bank raid. The timidity and caution of tradition seems to be blown offstage here by a joyful Zephyr of hunger and desire. People simply go after what they want. Orton was one of the first significant writers to come of intellectual age after the war, someone who could sense the logic in Harold Macmillan's famous cry, 'You've never had it so good!' We start to see the lurid colours of the Swinging Sixties, an age of unabashed materialism, with shiny new objects provoking the same thrill as sex.

The relationship between history and the lives of authors is complex, with an ever-present temptation to affix a false patterning, and to see a collection of links, where there was only ever chance and stuff happening. Historical ironies abound around Orton. His death came only two weeks after the decriminalisation of homosexuality, and a year later the arcane and obsolete power of the Lord Chamberlain to censor plays was gone. For someone who tested the boundaries of both, it is particular of history to have kept these dates so close. Maybe some sort of ghoulish sacrifice was necessary before such freedoms could be attained. Or maybe the pressure of history's hypocrisy contributed to the tragedy. Did Orton have that much more to write? Or had he – again like Wilde – put together the perfect lean corpus? In some terrifying way was Halliwell fulfilling a destiny with his violence, ensuring there was no falling away? *What the Butler Saw* finishes with a mysteriously apposite exit as the gaggle of seaside-postcard grotesques become transformed into mythic deities. The roof of the asylum opens up, a bright light descends, and they all climb up into the sun. A self-consciously Greek climax, a stage act of transcendence at the end of tawdry farce, it is as elegant in the theatre as Orton's end was hideous in life.

In a first edition of *Entertaining Mr Sloane* Joe wrote a simple inscription to my father, a quote from the play: 'I got over it though; you do, don't you?' Simple words – banal even – but containing multitudes. They had had a stormy time, my father asking Kenneth Halliwell to leave rehearsals on several occasions, when his interference became a block to progress. Their backgrounds and styles were different, but they respected each other, and my father gave Joe a production that pierced its moment and sent Orton's career skywards. When the next play, *Loot*, got in trouble on the road, Joe and their producer Michael Codron asked my father to take over directing duties, but he declined. In the screenplay Orton wrote for The Beatles, *Up Against It*, each member of the band flirts with and tries to bed a lubricious secretary called Miss Patricia Drumgoold. Some sort of revenge was being enacted here, though it was never clear for what. Rehearsals are often intense because of a terror of exposure. Nerves and tempers fray, and ugliness can spark. But in the theatre we find a way to forgive, wash the pain clean, and move on. The inscription is a miniature and potent act of forgiveness.

Joe Orton had more to get over than most, a hardscrabble upbringing on a Leicester council estate, scraping by in London on next to nothing, failure as an actor, the fear of living as a gay man in a society in which it was illegal, prison for book tampering and then, often the hardest to handle, fame and success. His capacity to sink and then bob back up, refreshed and ready for action was remarkable. Even after his brutal death he flourished, his story and his style lending him iconic status, and his plays retaining their wildness and beauty.

In his own limpid words: 'I got over it though; you do, don't you?'

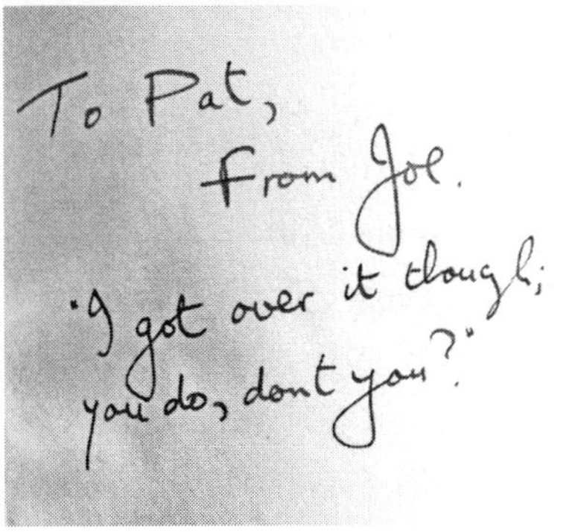

Edward Bond

1934–2024

Towards the beginning of this chronicle was Tom Robertson, whose signature success *Caste* (1867) features a moment when its comic creation of ribald anarchy, George Eccles, is left alone with a baby. Eschewing the fawning of kindly grandparents from the previous century's theatre, Eccles has no soft feelings towards the mewling infant. He curses it, begrudging the affection it receives, and blows cigar smoke into its face. Before long he steals the baby's necklace, the only remembrance of his lost father, in order to buy booze. The whole episode is a disturbing vignette of neglect and abuse, though its wrapping in comic extravagance and salty monologue softens the chill.

A hundred years later, at the end of the proscenium century, 1965, in Edward Bond's *Saved*, which premiered at the Royal Court, a group of youths gather in a South London park. An angry mother leaves them in charge of a baby in a pram. Each of the young men is an essay in affectlessness: as a group, their disconnection amalgamates into pathology. At first, they tease the baby with curiosity, and then with speculative cruelty. As with many of the worst forms of evil, their actions have the horror logic of an open-ended game, spinning out of control as it competes with itself. The baby fouls its nappy, and the youths rub its face in the excrement. As the baby screams, in mock outrage one kid throws a stone to shut it up, and then another, until soon all are hailing stones into the pram. The baby is stoned to death. We never see the target, we only hear its cries. Here there is none of the comedy or connecting context of Robertson's *Caste*: it is a heartless episode in a loveless landscape.

This is André Gide's *acte gratuit* – a seemingly random act which defies routine, custom, and normal explanation – migrated from the novel to the stage. It is the extension of Dostoevsky's claim that 'If there is no God, then everything is permitted.' For a long time, the theatre held out against such violence. Sociopathy is naturally alien to a form that requires depth of connection. In theatre, collaborators assemble to make something; actors meet to rehearse; an audience gathers to witness; all share in the storytelling. Webs of connection and community push back against lonely lovelessness. Edward Bond fractures each with an instant of exemplary vacancy.

As a kid, I played one of the lost young men in a Somerset youth theatre production. I have almost no memory of the stoning, as if I had fallen into some sort of fugue state. One of the actors from the original production, Tony Selby, is adamant that he 'didn't throw a stone', yet there are photos of him doing so. Although its gradation from curiosity to bloodlust is handled with delicate care, and though meticulously truthful throughout, either to perform or watch it amounts to a bad dream, a year zero phantasm of psychopathy. Bond was a dedicated Marxist humanist, and though the acte appears gratuit, it is encased in his intentions. It mattered to him that we did not shut ourselves off from the great outrages of the twentieth century, from Auschwitz and Hiroshima, and that we understood that violence was not a thing of the past but embedded in the warp and weft of who we are.

The Royal Court took a risk in mounting the play. Though on its last legs, the Theatres Act of 1843 was still in force, and scripts had to be submitted to the anachronism of the Lord Chamberlain's Office, the head of the Queen's Household and still the official censor. Unsurprisingly, the Office balked at the stoning scene and pushed back. Bond quite rightly refused to alter a word, and the English Stage Company had to present the play under club conditions, thereby avoiding censorship. The first night was an uproar, with booing within and fist fights outside. 'It is not often in that hardened audience you hear the cry "Revolting" and "Dreadful" and the smack of seats vacated, but you did last night,' the *Daily Mail*'s Peter Lewis wrote. The critics rained scorn and disapproval on the show and inflamed the passions of moral arbiters. Defenders argued its cause with the same passion, Laurence Olivier at their head: '*Saved* is not a play for children but it is for grown-ups, and the grown-ups of this country should have the courage to look at it.' Several of the theatre's executives were arrested on technicalities and went to court. A guilty verdict against them spelled the end of club status for avant-garde productions – a loophole which had lasted almost the whole proscenium century. This proved a pyrrhic victory for the forces of reaction. The publicity and the heat around the case highlighted the absurdity of Britain's licensing laws in an age moving swiftly forward, and the Lord Chamberlain's Office passed into oblivion in 1968.

Edward Bond was a rich and imaginative writer whose work traversed a variety of forms. He knew theatre history well and explored its different stylings. In *Bingo*, he writes one of the most cool and telling assessments of Shakespeare in his retirement in Stratford, a weary and jaded veteran, out of love with anything but hard business. He asks over and over again the question that shivers us all: 'Was anything done?' The Restoration theatre with its exuberance and flummery is invoked in Bond's twisted homage, unsubtly titled *Restoration*. And he knew Edwardian drama well, riffing on its mannerisms and tropes in his delightful and dotty comedy *The Sea*.

With such knowledge, and being such a conscious artist, there seems little doubt he understood what he was doing with his scene of atrocity in *Saved*. He was gobbing in the eye of the proscenium tradition, exposing its many hypocrisies. *Saved* placed a cruel reality in the harsh light centre stage. Hiding truths behind the curtain would no longer be possible. It was some sort of stop point, a bitter end.

All in a blur.
Saved at the Royal Court Theatre, London, 1965

Afterword

The Old Vic, that venerable old maiden south of the River Thames, has sometimes been viewed as holding the soul of our nation's theatre. Opening in 1818 and housing the last gasps of the romantic drama movement, including the electric galvanism of Edmund Kean's performances of Shakespeare, the Vic grew to be one of the great homes for melodrama, before becoming a classic proscenium house. The Vic has not featured in this volume, as it was more often a home for great acting than new writing. Olivier, Thorndike, Gielgud, Ashcroft and more all delivered their charismatic truth within its hallowed auditorium. Its status as national spirit house was confirmed in 1963 when it became temporary lodging to the National Theatre, a company still awaiting a permanent home on the South Bank. For this grand opening and in the years before, it underwent architectural adjustments which heralded the end of the proscenium century.

In the late 1950s, following a visit from Brecht's Berliner Ensemble, and in keeping with how fashion was moving, there was a movement to de-prettify. Decoration was removed or painted over in search of a plain, neutral ambience that would not distract from the hard-hitting focus onstage. Soon after, the last remaining boxes were pulled down and the frame radically reduced. The last artistic director before the National, Michael Elliott, designed a new apron stage which jutted out beyond the frame. When the National moved in, its boss, Laurence Olivier, joined in alliance with the designer Sean Kenny – both sworn enemies of the proscenium. Kenny said if he had his way he would put a bomb under the place. He didn't go that far but he did destroy what little of the proscenium survived. Olivier determined to push the thrust further, taking out several rows of the stalls and declaring, 'We are rebuilding the stage again, bringing it more forward. We shall be playing in the foyer eventually, with the public outside in the New Cut.' His logic was impeccable:

'As each and every family in Britain has a baby proscenium arch in their "through lounge" [*a television*], it would seem wise to offer them another sort of experience.' To rub out any remaining traces of Victorian elegance, he had the whole place painted sludge green. As he later admitted, he ruined the place.

The Old Vic was the trendsetter of its day, an authority augmented by national theatre status. As it reversed the centuries-long process that had fostered the proscenium, other theatres followed, jutting thrust and apron stages out beyond the frame to reconnect with the audience. Michael Elliott later left London to open the Royal Exchange in Manchester, one of the most elegant and enduring examples of theatre-in-the-round. This trend birthed notable spaces in Stoke-on-Trent and in Scarborough, where the prolific Alan Ayckbourn premiered his work. Elsewhere, Tanya Moiseiwitsch, having progressed from stage designer to architect, changed the idea of what was possible in the 1950s and 1960s with broad open thrust stages in Stratford, Ontario, in the Guthrie Theater in Minneapolis, and the Crucible in Sheffield. No longer was the energy to be contained within a defined frame: now all was openness and clarity, with the audience in democratic wrap-around.

Other practical factors led to the decline of old models. Television and film became a powerful lure, not only for writers, since it offered a bigger income and a quick route to a huge audience, but also for actors. The requirement for the latter to be contracted to a play for a year or more – even the biggest stars – no longer worked, and their desire to sign up for only a few months necessitated different economics. Directors proclaimed themselves auteurs, an adjustment which led not only to battles with playwrights such as Bond, Arden, and Wesker, but also a demand for a slowing down of preparation. This necessitated further remodelling of old budgets, largely derived from an antiquated bung-it-on school of production. An enforced stasis about working conditions had endured for a surprisingly long time. Television and film offered opportunities and a freedom to manoeuvre too light-footed for the juggernaut structures of traditional theatre.

Elsewhere, fringe and alternative companies began to colonise the old dining rooms of pubs, and to seek out battered industrial spaces to present staging within and around and intermingling with its audience. The studio or black box with its guaranteed focus – with nothing to look at beyond the lit action – maximised intensity and was soon favoured by actors and directors. Many were now eager to play to audiences as small as possible, giving a primacy to intimacy. Underground groups ran in horror from the decadence of bygone rococo excesses, as – naked – they rolled around in paint in dank basements and empty wastelands. With the end of theatrical censorship, and the burgeoning counterculture of the 1960s, the position of many artists was that their content was simply too radical to be contained within traditional architecture. New platforms and outlets were required.

Whether these movements into fragmented spaces were symptomatic of, reflected or even perhaps accelerated a social breakdown into atomised units is moot, but it is hard to deny it occurred. Where previously society had been reflected and criticised and lampooned onstage from the centre within, it was now under attack from the margins without. Which of these two methods of cultural critique led to the most useful social reform is again moot. It is hard not to see the end of the proscenium era as adjacent to the end of the soft power of the West, a moment when an assumption of cultural supremacy started to crumble as coming generations with curious minds started to look to other perspectives, and to respect different histories and aesthetics.

A confidence of self-presentation eroded in both society and the theatre, a host of certainties having come under such consistent barrage they now looked antiquated and often risible. The confidence was not necessarily something spoken, rather it was borne for decades within the textures of the design and the carriage of the characters, saturated in everything from wallpaper to upright posture. An assurance crystallised from savoir faire and sangfroid – lending theatre and society their stoical carapace – now dissolved into confusion and tears. A charm went with it – a brightness and wit and gaiety and refusal to be downcast – whether expressed in the brilliance of Wilde's aphorists, Feydeau's mischievous adulterers, Maugham's confected personae, or Coward's dizzy ditzes. The complacency came under fire from the angry, and the lightness was rendered trivial by the *sérieux*, all crying out against paradigms inherited from parents and grandparents.

The dissolution was inevitable. From the moment of its creation, the proscenium had contained within it the seeds of its own decline – an inbuilt irony that kept it interesting. All too aware of the demons seething beneath the blithe, those tensions would one day finally undermine its dominance. In the circumstances, it is amazing it lasted so long.

Of course, we are talking about decline rather than destruction. The theatres (or most of them) survived, and playwrights carried on fashioning work for their requirements. Tom Stoppard played marvellous ludic games with the form; Pinter carried on chiselling out charismatic works of glowering granite; Brian Friel (who sometimes kept a model proscenium beside him as he wrote) explored the slippage and the glow of memory; and August Wilson set down his decade-by-decade proscenium chronicle of African American experience. Each of these and many others were conscious of the tradition they wrote for, and the potency of framed spaces.

The influence survives to this day. New writing squeezes in (just) beside steamroller musicals and the endless versioning of novels, game shows, and podcasts. The plays of the great Lynn Nottage are sturdily proscenium – real-time narratives depicting social turmoil playing out on single sets. The success of Mark Rosenblatt's *Giant* is another striking example of roiling content poured into a classic mould. David Eldridge's trilogy of tortured romances – *Beginning*, *Middle*, and *End* – in addition to its strict adherence to real time, demonstrates the dividends of Lawrentian detail in its setting. With these writers and others, the blend of turbulent substance in a form built for elegant style retains its static electricity.

I spent a happy year at the Old Vic putting on new plays, alongside theatre giant Peter Hall, as he ran a company reviving classics. At my urging, he included a play in his repertory which offers within itself a commentary on the story of proscenium theatre and its inheritance, Caryl Churchill's *Cloud Nine.*

Her satirical fantasia on gender and much more premiered at the Royal Court in 1980. The first half is set in Africa in the late nineteenth century, a demented sex farce playing out within a colonial community as they pursue each other with wilful and bug-eyed appetite. The narrative gallops down purposeful and maniacally driven straight lines. The linearity serves as a parody of the strictures of Victorian society, and of its storytelling. The second act is set in a London park in 1979, though the characters have aged by only twenty-five years. The straitjacketed gender patterning of the first act has loosened and been subverted. In the modern world, women occupy with confidence the stage and their own lives, and homosexuality is not buried under stifling layers of sexual hypocrisy. Here the rhythm of the narrative is distinct. Scenes happen in still ponds, offering tangents and resonance, their relation to each other almost accidental. (Caryl told us they could be laid out in any order.)

The idea of story is reinvented here – the first act propulsive and destination oriented, the second moments in time sitting beside each other, coexisting in different planes. The first act chimes with the artificial unities of the proscenium, the second with the less causal theatre that followed. With her customary formal imagination, Caryl tells a story, illustrates a theme, and proffers a discreet masterclass on the many eloquences of the theatre.

Forever loyal to that perfect proscenium, the Royal Court, she has carved out a career in response to the passing crises and neuroses of the age. Whatever the subject may be, she has conjured up – with a magician's lightness of manoeuvre – the appropriate form to illustrate her content. Whether feminism in *Top Girls*, the rampages of deregulated capitalism in *Serious Money*, the emergence from communism in Eastern Europe in *Mad Forest*, a dystopian vision of a world paralysed by fear in *Far Away*, or the dangers of human cloning in *A Number*, Caryl Churchill has felt the pulse on the wrist of our time and reported on its health. Her last long play, a cornucopia of vignettes offering glimpses of life passing by, all with a fleet evanescence suitable to an age of overload, has a title that sums up much of what we do – *Love and Information*.

History dances on, and the theatre keeps in step.

Epilogue

In 1999, I directed a production of Chekhov's peerless *Three Sisters*, which opened in Frank Matcham's almost perfect Royal Theatre in Northampton, before touring into the West End. Casting a young company, with the three sisters – Olga, Masha, and Irina – all at the ages they are supposed to be – twenty-eight, twenty-four, and twenty – we were lucky to happen on a superabundance of talent, all in the full flush of enthusiasm and hope, before cresting waves had crashed on the rocks of fame and success. Even the smallest part was taken by a young Michael Fassbender.

Rehearsal was a joy supreme, the company's open hearts and boundless energy searching out every nook and cranny of the play's dynamics before bringing them to life. There was a sense of constant revelation and ceaseless easy creativity, doing what we do in excelsis. On the road, we would meet up each afternoon in whichever town we landed in to rerehearse. Sometimes this was to sharpen or revive or redefine; more often it was simply for the pleasure of enacting the life of it.

One moment in Act II we regularly returned to, a scene where the household fills the empty moment between dinner and late-night excursions. Downstage in a drawing room, Tuzenbach and Vershinin discuss the future with philosophical largesse – one stolid with optimism, the other charismatic with despair – while Masha asks the big questions and falls for Vershinin. Upstage at a dinner table, the elderly Chebutykin reads a paper and passes on some news – 'Balzac got married in Berdichev.' Irina, playing patience, repeats in an absent murmur, 'Balzac got married in Berdichev.' Fassbender as Fedotik, one of a couple of freeloading soldiers, strummed lightly on a guitar and hummed.

This scene blending gossip and sweeping statement (a vital theatrical conjunction) became a lodestar for the company. Locking it into place, finding its loose music, was our equivalent of tuning an instrument. In repetition after repetition, we entered – almost trance-like – a happier state, one rich and ripe with humanity.

In a long – and determinedly secular – life, it was the closest I have come to the practice of faith.

Bibliography

Finding plays from the past can be an arduous quest today.

Surveying proscenium theatres and the relative scarceness of plays is one small heartbreak; heading towards the drama section of a bookshop is another. Where one used to find two stacks of shelves bursting with single plays, collections, biographies of playwrights, critical studies, and practical guides, there is a meagre and muted single shelf dominated by a few Shakespeares, one or two contemporary plays, maybe *Hedda Gabler* and *Death of a Salesman*, and a couple of brain-crushing amalgamations of jargon about semiotics. The sheer paucity looks apologetic.

There are exceptions. In London, there exist compendious emporia like Foyles, which house as much as possible, and the excellent National Theatre Bookshop. Sadly, the almost cult-like French's has gone the way of all flesh. Happily steadfast is the John Calder bookshop, an anachronistic haven on The Cut, opposite the Young Vic. Once a diminutive temple to the avant-garde, this is now the best place to burrow out old plays, many of them generously donated from the library of Sam Walters, once director of the Orange Tree Theatre, where he resuscitated a host of neglected classics. Here you will find many of the writers mentioned in this book, as well as an excellent collection of books on the period.

If you are further afield, I can heartily recommend the delights of the Internet Archive, a non-profit online gathering of old books, all photographed with loving, if haphazard, care. Though online, the format retains the aura of an old library, with books borrowed for an hour at a time rather than downloaded. A very pleasing dustiness somehow clings to the platform. This is a good deed in a naughty world, on a par with Wikipedia. The latter remains the information source par excellence, and though it can lead you down excessively fascinating rabbit holes, we would be lost without it. I pay a small yearly stipend in gratitude, as we all should.

A number of books served as an overview for the century under discussion, affording both close-up details and a sense of the wider panorama. These include *Century of Innovation: A History of European and American Theatre and Drama since 1870* by Oscar G. Brockett and Robert R. Findlay (Prentice-Hall, 1973), which covers the same period; *Modern British Drama: The Twentieth Century* by Christopher Innes (CUP, 2002); *Mid-Century Drama* by Laurence Kitchin (Faber, 1962); *A Pocket Guide to 20th Century Drama* by Stephen Unwin with Carole Woddis (Faber, 2001); Michael Billington's two wide surveys, *The 101 Greatest Plays: From Antiquity to the Present* (Faber, 2015), and *State of the Nation: British Theatre Since 1945* (Faber, 2007); *The Cambridge Companion to Victorian and Edwardian Theatre* edited by Kerry Powell (CUP, 2004).

For an understanding of cultural contexts from a Marxist perspective, and there are still few better lines of approach, it was a pleasure to reread Raymond Williams's *Drama from Ibsen to Brecht* (Chatto & Windus, 1968). John Russell Taylor's *The Rise and Fall of the Well-Made Play* (Methuen, 1967) helped shape some of the arguments that thread through these pages. As did Dan Rebellato's *1956 and All That: The Making of Modern British Drama* (Routledge, 1999). Particular thanks to Benedict Nightingale for pleasurable lunches and for his shrewd and comprehensive *An Introduction to Fifty Modern British Plays* (Pan, 1982).

Certain books threw a captivating spotlight on cultural moments within this century. These include ripe insights into modernist Paris in *The Banquet Years: The Arts in France, 1885–1918* by Roger Shattuck (Vintage, 1958); into avant-garde New York and Provincetown in *The Shores of Bohemia: A Cape Cod Story 1910–1960* by John Taylor Williams (Farrar, Straus and Giroux, 2022); and into the early shadow-boxing of McCarthyism in James Shapiro's *The Playbook: A Story of Theatre, Democracy and the Making of a Culture War* (Faber, 2024). An inspiration for the project was Michael Holroyd's incomparable *A Strange Eventful History* (Chatto & Windus, 2008), which alongside a close-up portrait of Henry Irving, Ellen Terry, and Edward Gordon Craig, gives a novelistic impression of the Lyceum Theatre story, and a window into late-Victorian and Edwardian theatre.

Special mention must go to *West End Women: Women and the London Stage 1918–1962* by Maggie B. Gale (Routledge, 1996), which prompted further study into many of the authors here. This seems to me an ideal form of scholarship – unearthing long-buried knowledge, and accounting for a long-neglected phenomenon with precision and cool analysis. Also to Rebecca D'Monte, whose *British Theatre and Performance 1900–1950* (Bloomsbury, 2015) is an invaluable guide to the hidden cul-de-sacs of the period, and manages to combine critical acumen with nuggety details. And to John Lahr, who writes like a dream and understands like an analyst. His definitive biographies of Tennessee Williams, *Mad Pilgrimage of the Flesh* (Norton, 2014), and Joe Orton, *Prick Up Your Ears* (Penguin, 1986), his *New Yorker* profiles, and his essay collections afford almost as much pleasure as the best nights at the theatre. The chapters herein on Williams, Miller, Orton, and others are indebted to him.

To get a better handle on the astonishing Irish efflorescence around the Abbey Theatre, I was grateful for time spent with Christopher Morash, Tony Roche, and the Abbey's archivist, Mairéad Delaney. The pleasure in conversation was extended in reading Morash's *A History of Irish Theatre 1601–2000* (CUP, 2002), and Roche's *The Irish Dramatic Revival 1899–1939* (Methuen, 2015).

Throughout I was grateful to Robert Whelan, a fount of knowledge on England's proscenium theatres, exemplified by his *The Other National Theatre: 350 years of Shows in Drury Lane* (Jacob Tonson, 2013). He contributed elegant programme essays for our Oscar Wilde season, and his understanding of Wilde, his contemporaries, and the history of London's commercial theatre is extraordinary.

The opinions of many critics resonate throughout these chapters, together with those of Lahr, Billington, and Nightingale mentioned above. Kenneth Tynan – as the chapter on critics manifests – is a perennial inspiration, and his *A View of the English Stage, 1944–1965* (Davis-Poynter, 1975) together with his journals and letters are a marvellous way of relishing the elegance onstage and the furies offstage of his time. Among others, it is worth dipping into the work of James Agate – particularly *At Half-Past Eight: Essays of the Theatre 1921–1922* (Blom, 1923) – to perceive how irritating a theatre critic can be, and to read J. C. Trewin – particularly *The Theatre Since 1900* (Dakers, 1951) – to see how subtly illuminating.

At the less scholastic end of the spectrum, a small word for the wonders of oft-maligned YouTube. There is a marvellous series called *Crash Course Theater*, which over fifty episodes using witty animation, apt quotation, and acute insights manages to tell the story of theatre in comprehensive and surprising style. They have helped with historical details and with links between writers and epochs. Their channel has nearly two billion views, and deserves it.

Elsewhere on YouTube it is still possible to find documentaries which have long disappeared from now largely philistine mainstream platforms. Richard Eyre's great overview programmes *Changing Stages* are there, as are brilliant documentaries on Pirandello, Miller, Hansberry, Genet, and many more that have informed this book. Within these documentaries and elsewhere in scattered fragments, it is helpful to see and hear the authors themselves. To hear anecdotes at first hand and opinions unfiltered is a privilege. Actors love to have writers in the rehearsal room, since their presence offers insights into the work – how they dress, how they relate to people physically, how they speak, all help open windows into the plays. As a single 'for instance', check out the old BBC *Monitor* programme '1960: A Taste of Salford with Shelagh Delaney' to get a sense of her charm, which few words can convey. We are lucky such clues are extant and available on YouTube.

Equally useful and informative are the ubiquitous and diverse podcasts. Many individual authors are covered in great detail in this format. Of particular help is the incomparable Radio 4 series *In Our Time*, which it is hard to imagine being bettered for breadth of insight. There is also *The Play Podcast*, an excellent series on individual plays convened by Douglas Schatz.

The following are some of the books which provided insights into particular writers. Many of these have been consumed greedily, some have been dipped into. No source of knowledge is as important as the vital one of reading the plays themselves – ever the best route to the heart of a writer and their moment.

Eugène Scribe by Helene Koon and Richard Switzer (Twayne, 1980).

The Bancrofts: Recollections of Sixty Years by Marie and Squire Bancroft (John Murray, 1909). Hard to read without falling in love with the pair of them. *Victorian Theatricals: From menageries to melodrama* by Sara Hudston (Methuen, 2000).

Plays by Tom Robertson edited by William Tydeman (CUP, 1982). This collection has a great introduction, a summary of the theatre preceding the proscenium century, and a biographical sketch of Robertson. There is a loving chapter on Robertson in the Bancrofts' book as well. *Victorian Theatricals* by Sara Hudston.

Emile Zola by Angus Wilson (Mercury, 1965). *Documentary Theatre and Performance* by Andy Lavender (Methuen, 2024).

Ibsen (Doubleday, 1971), Michael Meyer's towering biography is hard to move beyond. There are good further provocations from a variety of sources, including Shaw, Forster, and Miller in the Bloom's Major Dramatists study on *Henrik Ibsen* edited by Harold Bloom (Chelsea House, 1999).

Georges Feydeau by Manuel A. Esteban (Twayne, 1983). *Georges Feydeau and the Aesthetics of Farce* by Stuart Baker (Ann Arbor, 1981).

The Social Plays of Arthur Wing Pinero (Dutton, 1922) features the idolatrous introductory essay by Clayton Hamilton, which I have drawn on. There is a more measured introduction in *Pinero: Three Plays* by Stephen Wyatt (Methuen, 1985). *Victorian Theatricals* by Sara Hudston.

Strindberg (Random House, 1985) – again Michael Meyer's monumental biography dominates the landscape. Meyer was a formidable scholar, and his work as a distinguished (if not lively) translator of the plays gives his insights an in-depth intuition into the writing process. *Replay: Classic Modern Drama Reimagined* by Toby Zinman (Methuen, 2015).

Hauptmann, Wedekind and Schnitzler by Peter Skrine (Palgrave Macmillan, 1989) gives a good account of each writer and of the connections between the three.

Oscar Wilde – each year brings a new and enjoyable biography, including Matthew Sturgis's *Oscar: A Life* (Apollo, 2022). Uncritically, I love them all, reaching back to Richard Ellmann's *Oscar Wilde* (Penguin, 1988). More recently, I leaned on angular approaches, which reveal Wilde through those closest to him. *The Fall of the House of Wilde: Oscar Wilde and His Family* by Emer O'Sullivan (Bloomsbury, 2017) was one way in, exploring the family dynamics. *Constance: The Tragic and Scandalous Life of Mrs Oscar Wilde* by Franny Moyle (John Murray, 2011) was another.

The Man Who Was Cyrano: A Life of Edmond Rostand by Sue Lloyd (Genge Press, 2003).

The Director and the Stage: From Naturalism to Grotowski by Edward Braun (Methuen, 1982). In addition, there is brilliant writing about Jarry and his bohemian Paris context in *The Banquet Years* by Roger Shattuck.

As an entrée to the early days of the Abbey, Colm Tóibín's *Lady Gregory's Toothbrush* (Picador, 2003) is the ideal short book, a beautiful and funny introduction to the narrative, characters, and period. Ellmann opened the door to understanding Yeats long ago, and more recently Roy Foster has thrown fresh light. If you are in Dublin, seek out the Yeats exhibition under the National Library of Ireland. It is a wonder and demonstrates how Yeats thought of himself as a man of the theatre above all else.

Bernard Shaw by Michael Holroyd (Chatto & Windus, 1991) is so all-encompassing and wise it rather defeats the need for further comment. The single volume is best for all but the fanatic.

As above, *Hauptmann, Wedekind and Schnitzler* by Peter Skrine.

Captivated: J. M. Barrie, Daphne du Maurier and the Dark Side of Neverland by Piers Dudgeon (Vintage, 2009) brings together two of the authors herein. *The Dark Side of Peter Pan: J. M. Barrie, the Man Who Couldn't Grow Up* by Olivia Camozzi (Pen & Sword, 2024) ploughs a similar furrow. No one seems to have written a book about the bright side.

John Galsworthy by R. H. Mottram (Longmans, 1963). There is an excellent introduction by Benedict Nightingale to *Five Plays* (Methuen, 1984). *British Theatre and Performance 1900–1950* by Rebecca D'Monte.

The Synge story is well covered in Colm Tóibín's book, and there is an excellent introductory essay by T. R. Henn in *Synge: Complete Plays* (Methuen, 1981). *Modern Tragedy* by James Moran (Methuen, 2023). *The Irish Dramatic Revival 1899–1939* by Anthony Roche.

Harley Granville Barker by C. B. Purdom (Rockliff, 1955). *Granville Barker On Theatre: Selected Essays* edited by Colin Chambers and Richard Nelson (Methuen, 2017) has great stuff on his attitude to theatre and reflections on Chekhov, Ibsen, and the European theatre of his day.

Elizabeth Robins: Staging a Life by Angela John (Routledge, 1995).

It is hard to know where to start with David Herbert, and Geoff Dyer's *Out of Sheer Rage: Wrestling with D. H. Lawrence* (North Point, 1998) casts a serio-comic shadow, which is hard to evade. *The Theatre of D.H. Lawrence: Dramatic Modernist and Theatrical Innovator* by James Moran (Methuen, 2015). There is an excellent introduction by Raymond Williams to the *Collected Plays of D. H. Lawrence* (Penguin, 1969).

Looking for Githa by Patricia Riley (Stairwell, 2019). There is also surprising pleasure in dipping into *The Social Significance of the Modern Drama* by Emma Goldman (Gorham Press, 1914). The legendary anarchist was a passionate student of the theatre, and her book spills over with enthusiasm. She is interesting on Galsworthy too.

The Secret Lives of Somerset Maugham by Selina Hastings (John Murray, 2010) is a great match of subject and writer, as stylish and witty and enjoyable as Maugham's plays.

Susan Glaspell: Her Life and Times by Linda Ben-Zvi (OUP, 2005). And John Taylor Williams's *The Shores of Bohemia*. *Visions of Tragedy in Modern American Drama: From O'Neill to the Twenty-First Century* edited by David Palmer (Methuen, 2018).

Luigi Pirandello: In Search of an Author (1987) is a brilliant documentary from the old days of shamelessly intelligent television. Playful and insightful and proudly pretentious, it offers huge illumination. There is also a good chapter in Eric Bentley's *The Playwright as Thinker: A Study of Drama in Modern Times* (Harcourt, Brace & World, 1967).

I'm grateful to Paula Paz, who ran the late lamented Cervantes Theatre in Southwark, for introducing me to this writer. *María Martínez Sierra: A Great Playwright Hidden in Plain Sight* (Methuen, 2022) is a revelation, a brilliant edition of selected plays put together by Colin Chambers and Richard Nelson, with attached essays on the plays and her life.

As with Wilde, Noël Coward is an endlessly fertile subject for biography. I rather shamelessly love them all, from the showbizzy anecdotes of Sheridan Morley to the acute perception of Philip Hoare. Oliver Soden's *Masquerade: The Lives of Noël Coward* (W&N, 2023) is the most recent treat. On the plays, *Coward the Playwright* by John Lahr (Methuen, 1982) is exceptional.

Eugene O'Neill: A Life in Four Acts by Robert Dowling (Yale, 1970). *The Theatre of Eugene O'Neill: American Modernism on the World Stage* by Kurt Eisen (Methuen, 2018). *Visions of Tragedy in Modern American Drama* edited by David Palmer.

Thanks to Maggie Gale whose *West End Women* pointed me towards Clemence Dane. *Clemence Dane: Forgotten Feminist Writer of the Inter-War Years* by Louise McDonald (Routledge, 2021). *British Theatre and Performance 1900–1950* by Rebecca D'Monte.

Sean O'Casey: A Life by Garry O'Connor (Paladin, 1989) is a great introduction. O'Casey wrote a series of memoirs which are worth a look – eminently readable if not entirely trustworthy. I am also grateful for conversations with his daughter, Shivaun, and for watching her documentary on her father. *The Theatre of Sean O'Casey*, by James Moran (Methuen, 2013).

Manuscripts Don't Burn: Mikhail Bulgakov – A Life in Letters and Diaries edited by J. A. E. Curtis (Harvill, 1992). *Soviet Theatre during the Thaw: Aesthetics, Politics and Performance* by Jesse Gardiner (Methuen, 2023).

Susan Glaspell and Sophie Treadwell by Barbara Ozieblo and Jerry Dickey (Routledge, 2008).

From Journey's End to the Dam Busters: The Life of R.C. Sherriff, Playwright of the Trenches, by Roland Wales (Pen & Sword, 2016).

Brecht: A Biography by Ronald Hayman (OUP, 1983). And anything by John Willett, primarily *The Theatre of Bertolt Brecht: A study from eight aspects* (Methuen, 1977). And the Raymond Williams book mentioned earlier. Brecht's journals are always a subversive delight, and his ethics and aesthetics are set down in riddling fashion in *Brecht on Theatre* edited and translated by John Willett (Methuen, 1964).

Federico García Lorca: A Life by Ian Gibson (Faber, 1989) is both comprehensive and lively, which is all you can wish for.

Three Plays by Ayn Rand, edited by Richard Ralston (Signet, 2005) is a strange delight, principally for the unabashed toxicity of her own introduction.

Odets the Playwright by Gerald Weales (Methuen, 1985). Plus a brilliant essay by John Lahr in the *New Yorker* (2006). *Modern American Drama: Playwriting in the 1930s: Voices, Documents, New Interpretations* by Anne Fletcher (Methuen, 2018).

Rage for Fame: The Ascent of Clare Boothe Luce (Random House, 1997) and *Price of Fame: The Honorable Clare Boothe Luce* (Random House, 2014), both by Sylvia Jukes Morris, provide a great jaunt through the rapacious life of Clare Boothe Luce.

T. S. Eliot by Peter Ackroyd (Abacus, 1985). *Modernists and the Theatre:*

The Drama of W. B. Yeats, Ezra Pound, D. H. Lawrence, James Joyce, T. S. Eliot and Virginia Woolf by James Moran (Methuen, 2022). *Verse Drama in England, 1900–2015: Art, Modernity and the National Stage* by Irene Morra (Methuen, 2016).

The Political Plays of Langston Hughes, with Introductions and Analyses by Susan Duffy (Carbondale, 2000). *Modern American Drama* by Anne Fletcher. *Visions of Tragedy in Modern American Drama* edited by David Palmer.

Dear Dodie: The Life of Dodie Smith by Valerie Grove (Pimlico, 2002). *British Theatre and Performance 1900–1950* by Rebecca D'Monte.

Thornton Wilder: A Life by Penelope Niven (Harper, 2012). *Replay* by Toby Zinman.

Lillian Hellman's memoirs are worth a dip for their raciness, if approached with caution. There are various biographies for a life liberally covered. For a more focused attention on her drama, there is *Lillian Hellman: Rebel Playwright* by Ruth Turk (Lerner, 1995). *Modern American Drama* by Anne Fletcher.

J. B. Priestley: An Informal Study of His Work by David Hughes (Freeport, 1970). *The Contemporary Political Play: Rethinking Dramaturgical Structure* by Sarah Grochala (Methuen, 2017) has a great chapter on time in the theatre.

Agatha Christie: A Life in Theatre: Curtain Up by Julius Green (HarperCollins, 2015) continues Green's ardent endeavour to get people to take his hero seriously – his endless devotion has had its desired effect. *Good Nights Out* by Aleks Sierz (Methuen, 2019).

Terence Rattigan by Michael Darlow (Quartet, 1999). Darlow has been a devoted champion, and Rattigan was lucky in his disciple and this exemplary biography. *Replay* by Toby Zinman.

Daphne du Maurier by Margaret Forster (Arrow, 1994). *British Theatre and Performance 1900–1950* by Rebecca D'Monte.

Tennessee Williams: Mad Pilgrimage of the Flesh by John Lahr. You can't do any better. Williams's *Memoirs* (Doubleday, 1975) has all the slapdash, wayward brilliance of his late writing. And his *Notebooks*

(Yale, 2006) are as naked as one would hope for (and fear), brilliantly edited by Margaret Bradham Thornton.

The Theatre of Jean-Paul Sartre by Dorothy McCall (Columbia, 1969). Eric Bentley's *The Playwright as Thinker* is worth looking at here.

Timebends: A Life by Arthur Miller (Methuen, 1987) and *Arthur Miller* by Christopher Bigsby (W&N, 1995) are excellent starting points. Though many (to my surprise) find Miller's tome irksome, I think it's one of the great autobiographies. Since Miller was a fabulous interviewee, he sprayed aperçus and insights liberally on television and radio. They are all over the virtual world, and unlike many a rabbit hole this one is nourishing and a pleasure to fall down.

Jean Anouilh: Five Plays with a great introduction by Ned Chaillet (Methuen, 1987). *Anouilh: A Study in Theatrics* by John E. Harvey (Yale, 1964).

Ena Lamont Stewart in *British Theatre and Performance 1900–1950* by Rebecca D'Monte.

Genet: A Biography by Edmund White (Random House, 1993). Genet's memoirs are worth a look. I am indebted to the brilliant *Arena* documentary '*Saint Genet*' of 1985, where the novelist Nigel Williams invited Genet into his own home for an interview. Genet agreed, in return for reputedly £10,000, and then proceeded to grill and interrogate Williams.

Samuel Beckett: A Biography by Deirdre Bair (Vintage, 1978) is unbeatable for the life. *Samuel Beckett: The Last Modernist* by Anthony Cronin (Flamingo, 1997) clarifies the achievement.

Alice Childress by La Vinia Delois Jennings (Twayne, 1995).

Eugene Ionesco edited by Harold Bloom in the Bloom's Major Dramatists series (Chelsea House, 2003). *Replay* by Toby Zinman.

The Life of Kenneth Tynan by Kathleen Tynan (Phoenix, 1995); *The Diaries of Kenneth Tynan* edited by John Lahr (Bloomsbury, 2001); and *Kenneth Tynan: A Life* by Dominic Shellard (Yale, 2003). Like Falstaff, Tynan is witty in himself and the cause of great wit in others. All that surrounds him is enjoyable.

For John Osborne – his own memoirs, *A Better Class of Person: An Autobiography, 1929–1956* (Faber, 1981), and *Almost a Gentleman: An Autobiography, 1955–1966* (Faber, 1992). Both are brilliant reads and also give an unmatched sense of the theatre of the time, including the grubby and arduous touring circuit from which he and Pinter emerged, as well as the early years of the Royal Court. *Modern British Playwriting: The 1950s* by David Pattie (Methuen, 2012). *Obedience, Struggle & Revolt* by David Hare (Faber, 2005) mounts a brilliant defence of Osborne against his critics.

Enid Bagnold's Autobiography (Century, 1985). *British Theatre and Performance 1900–1950* by Rebecca D'Monte.

Borstal Boy (Hutchinson, 1958), from Behan himself. And Ulick O'Connor's short introduction – *Brendan Behan* (Abacus, 1985). *Irish Drama and Theatre Since 1950* by Patrick Lonergan (Methuen, 2019). *Joan's Book: The Autobiography of Joan Littlewood* edited by Philip Hedley (Methuen, 2016).

Friedrich Dürrenmatt has left little trace, apart from the plays.

The Fire Next Time (Dell, 1963) by James Baldwin, alongside many essays and fragments. *Talking at the Gates: A Life of James Baldwin* by James Campbell (Penguin, 1991).

Sweetly Sings Delaney: A Study of Shelagh Delaney's Work 1958–68 by John Harding (Greenwich Exchange, 2014). *Joan's Book* edited by Philip Hedley.

John Arden by Simon Trussler (Columbia, 1973). And *Theatre Language: A Study of Arden, Osborne, Pinter and Wesker* by John Russell Brown (Taplinger, 1972) is strong on Arden and the others. *Modern British Playwriting: The 1960s* by Steve Nicholson (Methuen, 2012).

Looking for Lorraine: The Radiant and Radical Life of Lorraine Hansberry by Imani Perry (Beacon, 2018) is a delight. It maybe errs on the side of idolatry, like myself, but it is hard not to. *To Be Young Gifted and Black* (Vintage, 1995) collated by Lorraine's husband, Robert Nemiroff, from her writings is a great introduction to the woman and the times. Lovely essay by Deirdre Osborne in *Visions of Tragedy in Modern American Drama* edited by David Palmer.

Harold Pinter by Michael Billington (Faber, 1997) – unimprovable. *Harold Pinter: Stages, Networks, Collaborations* edited by Basil Chaisson and Catriona Fallow (Methuen, 2021).

Edward Albee: A Singular Journey by Mel Gussow (Applause, 2001). *Visions of Tragedy in Modern American Drama* edited by David Palmer. *Modern American Drama: Playwriting in the 1960s* edited by Mike Sell (Methuen, 2019).

Biography of Wole Soyinka: A Tapestry of Words and Courage by Lynne Addison (Independent, 2024). There are several lyrical memoirs as well. *Modern and Contemporary World Drama* edited by Esther Kim Lee (Bloomsbury Academic, 2022).

Prick Up Your Ears: The Biography of Joe Orton by John Lahr (Penguin, 1986), and *The Orton Diaries* (Da Capo, 1986) edited by the same.

Bond: A study of his plays by Malcolm Hay (Methuen, 1980). *Edward Bond: The Playwright Speaks* by David Tuaillon (Methuen, 2015).

Image credits

p. 10: The Swan Theatre, Wikimedia Commons.

p. 12: Theatre Royal, Wikimedia Commons.

p. 16: Englert Theatre, Wikimedia Commons.

p. 22: Eugène Scribe, *documents iconographiques*, Wikimedia Commons / Bibliothèque nationale de France.

p. 29: Effie Bancroft, Wikimedia Commons / Boston Public Library via the Digital Public Library of America.

p. 39: Sir John Hare, Wikimedia Commons / National Library of Scotland.

p. 44: Giacinta Pezzana, Wikimedia Commons / Oslo Museum.

p. 57: Henrik Klausen, Wikimedia Commons / Oslo Museum.

p. 62: *La puce à l'oreille*, Wikimedia Commons / Bibliothèque nationale de France.

p. 68: *The Magistrate*, Wikimedia Commons / National Library of Scotland.

p. 74: August Strindberg, Wikimedia Commons.

p. 79: *Die Weber*, Wikimedia Commons / Emil Orlik.

p. 92: George Alexander and Rose Leclercq, Wikimedia Commons.

p. 95: *Cyrano de Bergerac*, Wikimedia Commons / Frédéric de Haenen.

p. 99: *Ubu Roi*, Wikimedia Commons / Alfred Jarry.

p. 106: *Cathleen ni Houlihan*, Wikimedia Commons / Cornelius Weygandt.

p. 108: *Three Sisters*, Chronicle / Alamy.

p. 118: Harley Granville Barker, Ernest H. Mills / Hulton Archive / Getty Images.

p. 123: *Pandora's Box*, Wikimedia Commons.

p. 126: J. M. Barrie, Wikimedia Commons.

p. 133: *The Skin Game*, Wikimedia Commons.

p. 142: Pat Mac Donagh's cottage, Wikimedia Commons / Trinity College.

p. 149: *Androcles and the Lion*, Smith Archive / Alamy.

p. 154: American Women's Club, Universal History Archive / Universal Images Group / Getty Images.

p. 162: D. H. Lawrence, Wikimedia Commons.

p. 165: New Theatre, Wikimedia Commons / Imperial War Museum.

p. 170: Katherine Githa Sowerby, Wikimedia Commons / *Illustrated Sporting and Dramatic News*.

p. 176: *The Circle*, Wikimedia Commons, *Theatre Magazine*.

p. 182: Lewis Wharf, Wikimedia Commons.

p. 188: *Six Characters in Search of an Author*, Wikimedia Commons / Special Sphere Pictures.

p. 193: María Martínez, Album / Archivo ABC / Virgilio Muro / Alamy.

p. 202: *Private Lives*, Wikimedia Commons / *Theatre Magazine* / Vandamm Studio.

p. 214: *The Hairy Ape*, Wikimedia Commons / James Abbe / Beinecke Rare Book & Manuscript Library, Yale University.

p. 220: *Mariners*, Wikimedia Commons / Florence Vandamm / *Vogue*.

p. 230: Abbey Theatre, Hulton Archive / Getty Images.

p. 235: *The Days of the Turbins*, Wikimedia Commons.

p. 241: *Machinal*, Wikimedia Commons / *Theatre Arts Monthly*.

p. 247: *Journey's End*, Wikimedia Commons / Tiffany Gainsborough and Welsh-Pearson.

p. 255: *The Threepenny Opera*, Wikimedia Commons.

p. 261: *Blood Wedding*, Wikimedia Commons / Colección Fundación Federico García Lorca.

p. 265: Federico García Lorca, Wikimedia Commons / Museo Nacional Centro de Arte Reina Sofía.

p. 272: *Night of January 16th*, Wikimedia Commons.

p. 279: Group Theatre, Wikimedia Commons / *Theatre Magazine Company* / Alfredo Valente.

p. 285: *The Women*, Wikimedia Commons / MGM.

p. 291: *Murder in the Cathedral*, Faber & Faber Ltd.

p. 297: Langston Hughes, Wikimedia Commons / Winold Reiss.

p. 303: Dodie Smith, Keystone / Getty Images.

p. 308: *Our Town*, Wikimedia Commons / Vandamm Studio.

p. 314: *The Little Foxes*, Wikimedia Commons / Vandamm Studio.

p. 317: J. B. Priestley, Wikimedia Commons / National Science and Media Museum @ Flickr Commons.

p. 323: Agatha Christie, Wikimedia Commons / Joop van Bilsen for Anefo / Nationaal Archief.

p. 329: *The Wilmslow Boy*, Denis De Marney / Hulton Archive / Getty Images.

p. 334: Gerald and Daphne du Maurier, Wikimedia Commons.

p. 341: *A Streetcar Named Desire*, Wikimedia Commons / Eileen Darby / Graphic House.

p. 348: *Les Mouches*, Roger Viollet / Getty Images.

p. 364: Marilyn Monroe and Arthur Miller, Wikimedia Commons / Associated Press / *Kingsport Times-News*.

p. 369: *Colombe*, Roger Wood / *Picture Post* / Hulton Archive / Getty Images.

p. 374: Gorbals, Wikimedia Commons.

p. 380: Odéon Theatre, Wikimedia Commons / Eric Koch for Anefo / Nationaal Archief.

p. 389: *Waiting for Godot*, Wikimedia Commons / Roger Pic / Bibliothèque nationale de France.

p. 394: Durham, North Carolina, Wikimedia Commons / Jack Delano / Library of Congress Prints and Photographs Division.

pp. 396–7: *Les chaises*, Wikimedia Commons / Roger Pic / Bibliothèque nationale de France.

p. 400: *La Cantatrice chauve* and *La Leçon*, Wikimedia Commons / Eugène Ionesco.

p. 406: Kenneth Tynan and Clare Bloom, Hulton-Deutsch Collection / Corbis / Getty Images.

p. 412: *The Entertainer,* Wikimedia Commons, Associated Press.

p. 416: Enid Bagnold, Wikimedia Commons.

p. 423: *The Hostage*, Wikimedia Commons / Roger Pic / Bibliothèque nationale de France.

p. 424: Brendan Behan, Wikimedia Commons.

p. 429: *The Visit*, Ullstein Bild / Getty Images.

p. 435: *The Amen Corner*, Wikimedia Commons / Roger Pic / Bibliothèque nationale de France.

p. 439: *A Taste of Honey*, Wikimedia Commons / Bill Doll and Company.

p. 443: *Sergeant Musgrave's Dance*, Chris Ware / Keystone / Hulton Archive / Getty Images.

p. 451: *The Kitchen*, Keystone / Hulton Archive / Getty Images.

p. 458: *A Raisin in the Sun*, Wikimedia Commons / Friedman-Abeles.

p. 465: *The Caretaker*, Hulton-Deutsch Collection / Corbis / Getty Images.

p. 471: *Who's Afraid of Virginia Woolf?*, *Evening Standard* / Hulton Archive / Getty Images.

p. 475: Akinwande Oluwole Soyinka, Keystone / Getty Images.

p. 481: *Entertaining Mr Sloane*, courtesy of the author.

p. 485: *Saved* © Zoë Dominic / Dominic Photography.

Acknowledgements

Various provocations led to this book. The company I worked at between 1998 and 2005 – the Oxford Stage Company – toured many of the proscenium theatres of the country with a diet of plays drawn from their century: Strindberg, Chekhov, Coward, Rattigan, Churchill, Ena Lamont Stewart, Maugham, Arden, and Storey. These were shows where the happy harmony between play and architecture and audience set me thinking about those relationships and that history. My thanks to colleagues and collaborators from that time for illuminations discovered through chat and work. Similarly, the long Oscar Wilde season in the Vaudeville in 2017–18 provoked many insights and discussions. In the theatre, we are only ever as wise or informed as our village.

After my first book in 2000, I enjoyed a few years writing for the *Guardian*, the *New Statesman*, and the *Sunday Times* – essays here and there which became springboards for a handful of these chapters. General thanks to those editors, and particular thanks to my most regular employer then: Helen Hawkins at the Culture section of the *ST*, which was at that time a model of sass and erudition.

I continue to be blessed beyond deserts in my agent, Natasha Fairweather, who inherited this book and has smiled on it with grace and forbearance, and in the process become a friend. Further thanks are owed to an old and good friend, Nick Drake, for the title, and to a wit-smith sister, Jessica Dromgoole, for help with the captions.

I have been as lucky in my colleagues from Faber. The jacket design by Eliza Hart is a wonder, vibrant and appropriate. My copy-editor, Anna Swan, was shrewd, voluminous in her knowledge, and imaginative in her solutions. Anne Rieley, the proofreader, has been rigorous and gimlet-eyed. The whole project has been shepherded along with elegance and efficiency by Josephine Salverda.

Lily Levinson has proven a wise soundboard for various opinions throughout the editing, correcting some of the assumptions which have accreted to me over the decades, even though I may have clung on to a few. Faber is lucky to have her.

My prime editor, Dinah Wood, is something of a marvel of contemporary London. Always seemingly on a hectic bicycle dash from opening to salon to play-reading to tea, she manages to pause long enough at various stations to make a host of writers feel supported, befriended, and treasured beyond measure. We met to first discuss this book in Abney Cemetery (where by strange coincidence Tom Robertson is buried), and since then her support and enthusiasm and companionship have been a rich and rewarding delight. Her editing, with its adherence to grace and good sense, does not only make one a better writer, but a better person. The world of theatre has been lit up by her elan and éclat (to misquote Tom Stoppard) for several decades.

My father's presence is felt throughout this book, and his influence has been another source of good fortune. As a director of some of these plays, and a witness to the theatre of this era, it has always been a privilege to listen to the insight and gossip and acuity with which he has discussed it. For him, as for the authors of this age, the contrary human has always been the centre of fascination. A doctrine that was as true for my late mother, to whom my debt is as great.

Above all, in a strange reverse process, I have been taught lessons in manners and morals, in patience and kindness, in 'incalculable diffusiveness' and in the endless permeations of goodwill, by my three daughters, Siofra, Grainne, and Cara. Beyond.